BTOOOM!

JUNYA INOUE

01

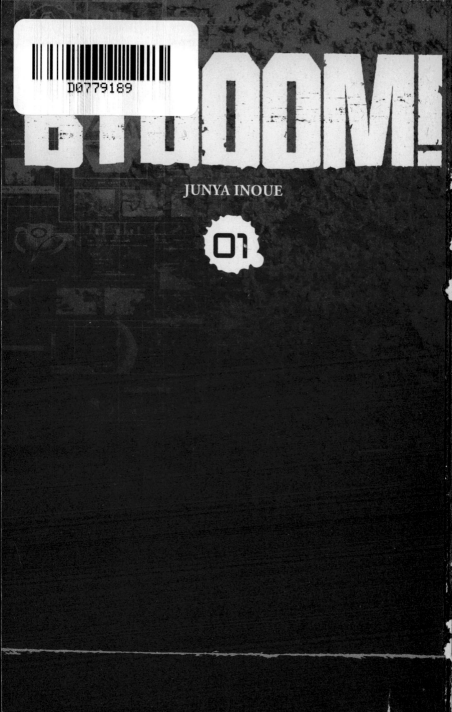

CONTENTS

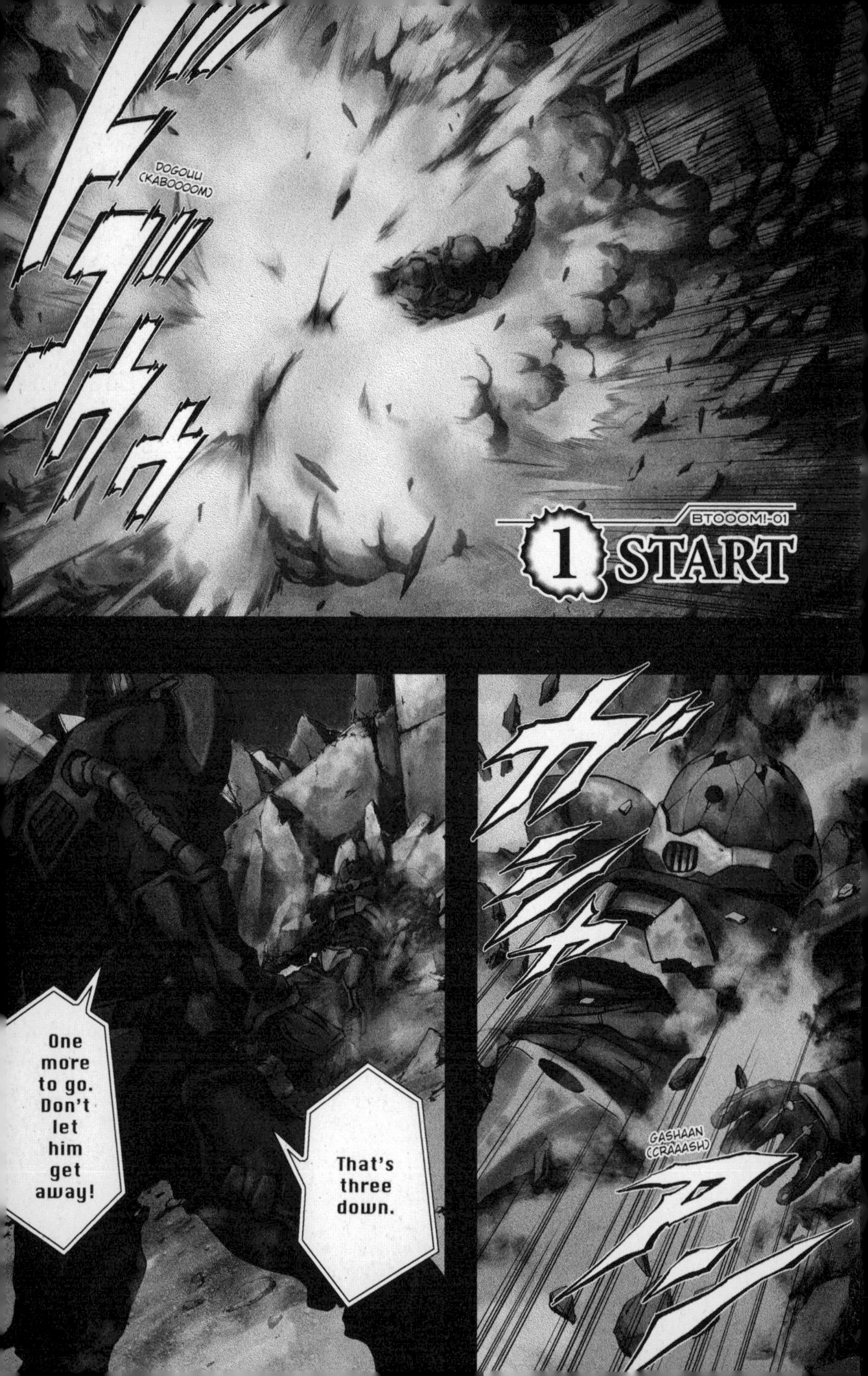
DOGOUU (KABOOOOM)
BTOOOM!-01
1 START
GASHAAN (CRAAASH)
That's three down.
One more to go. Don't let him get away!

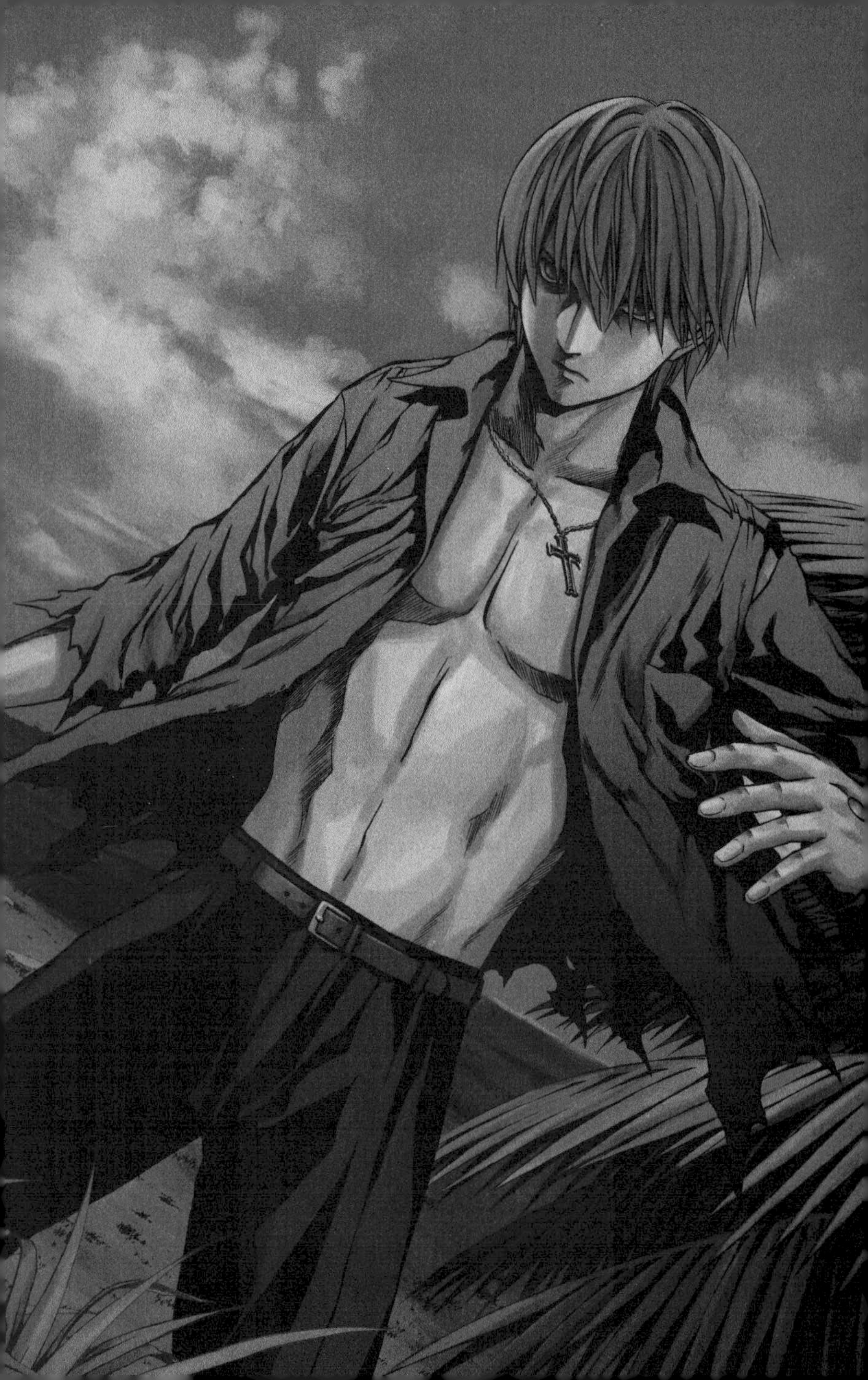

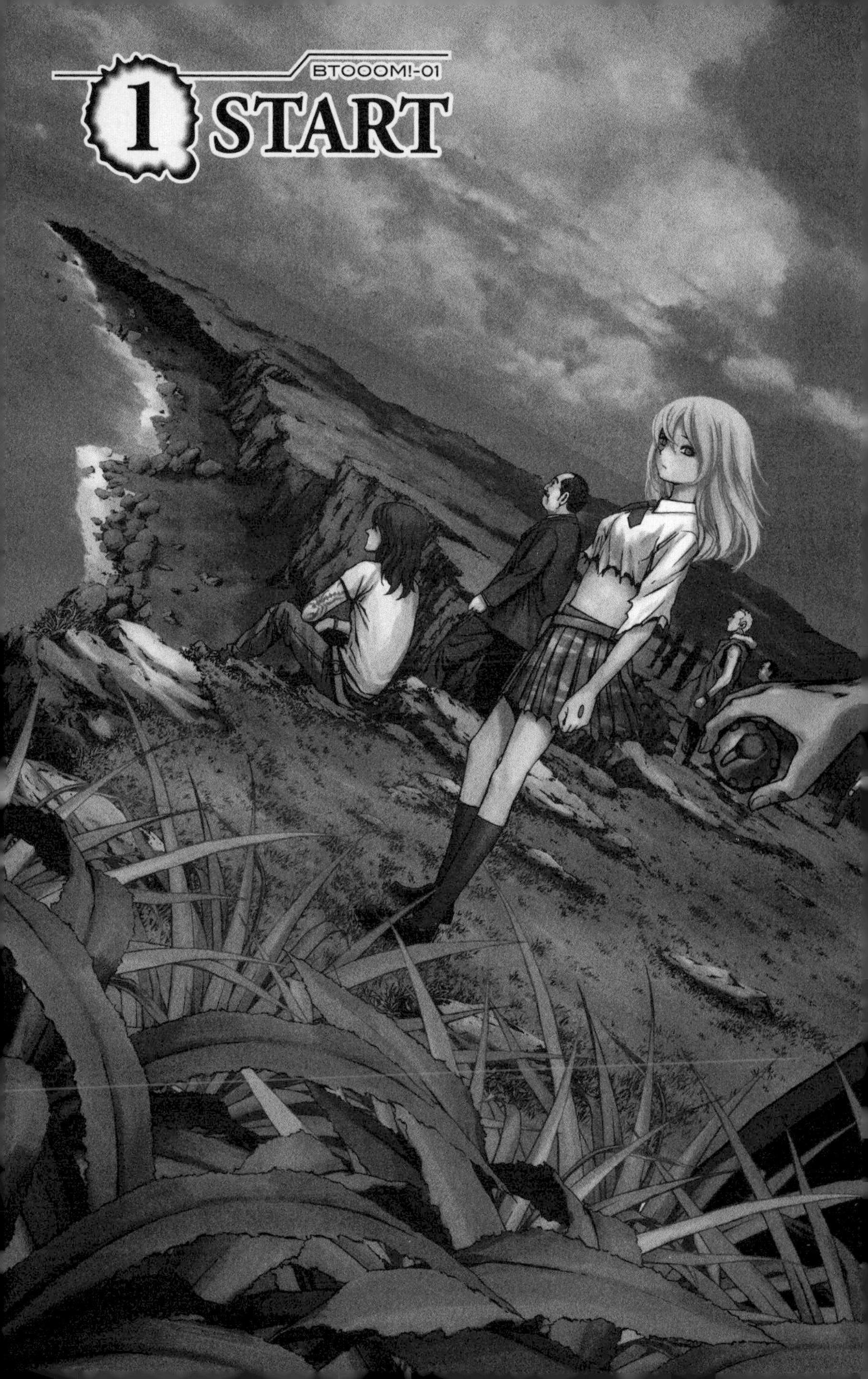
BTOOOM!-01
1 START

BTOOOM!
09
08
BTOOOM!
07
06
BTOOOM!
05
04
03
BTOOOM!
02
BTOOOM!
01

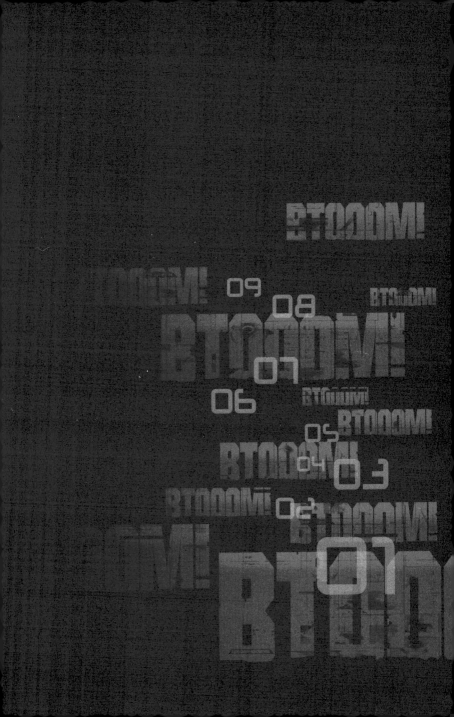

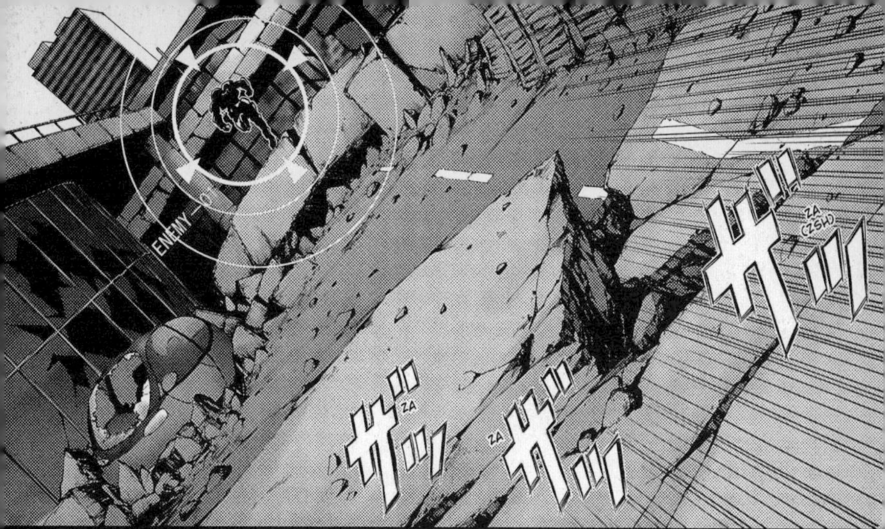
ZA (ZSH)
ENEMY
ZA
ZA

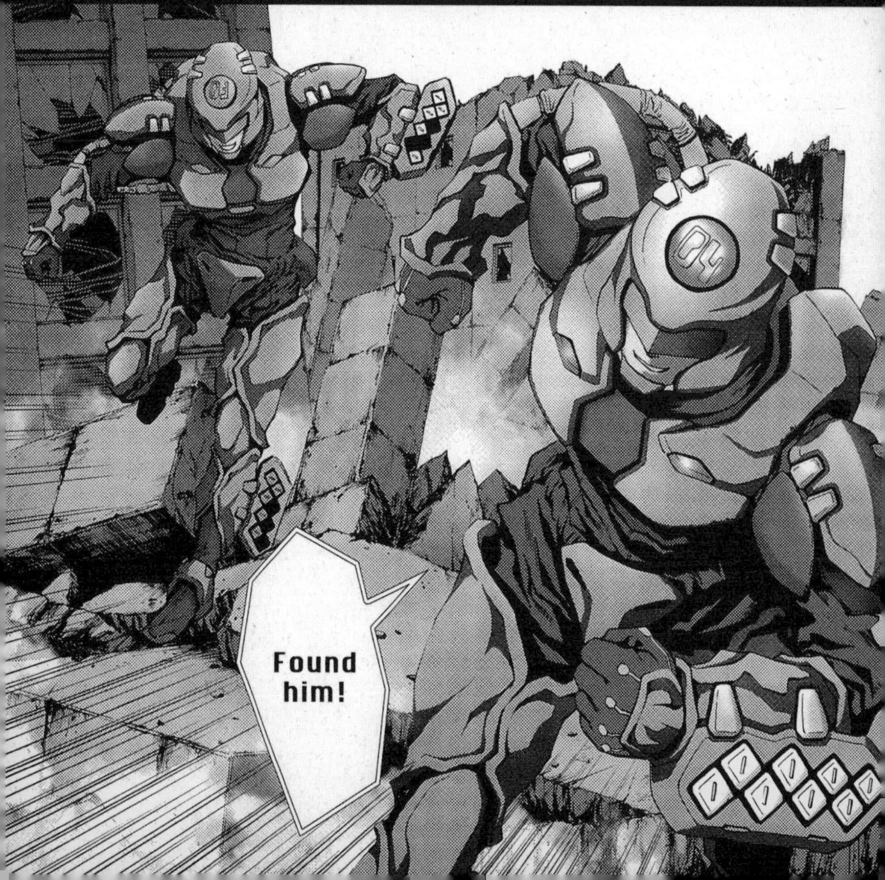
Found him!

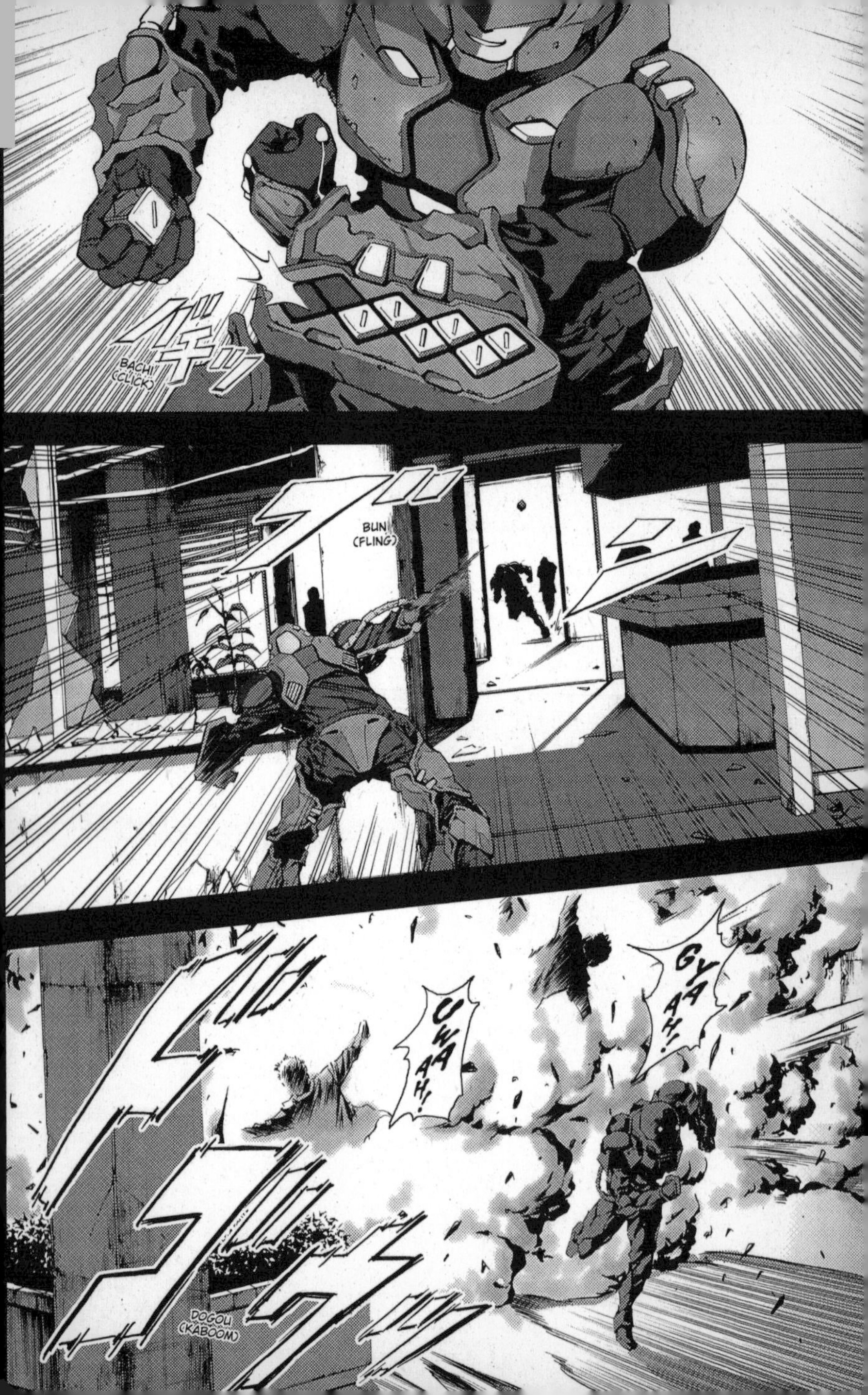
BACHI (CLICK)
BUN (FLING)
GYAAH!
UWAAH!
DOGOU (KABOOM)

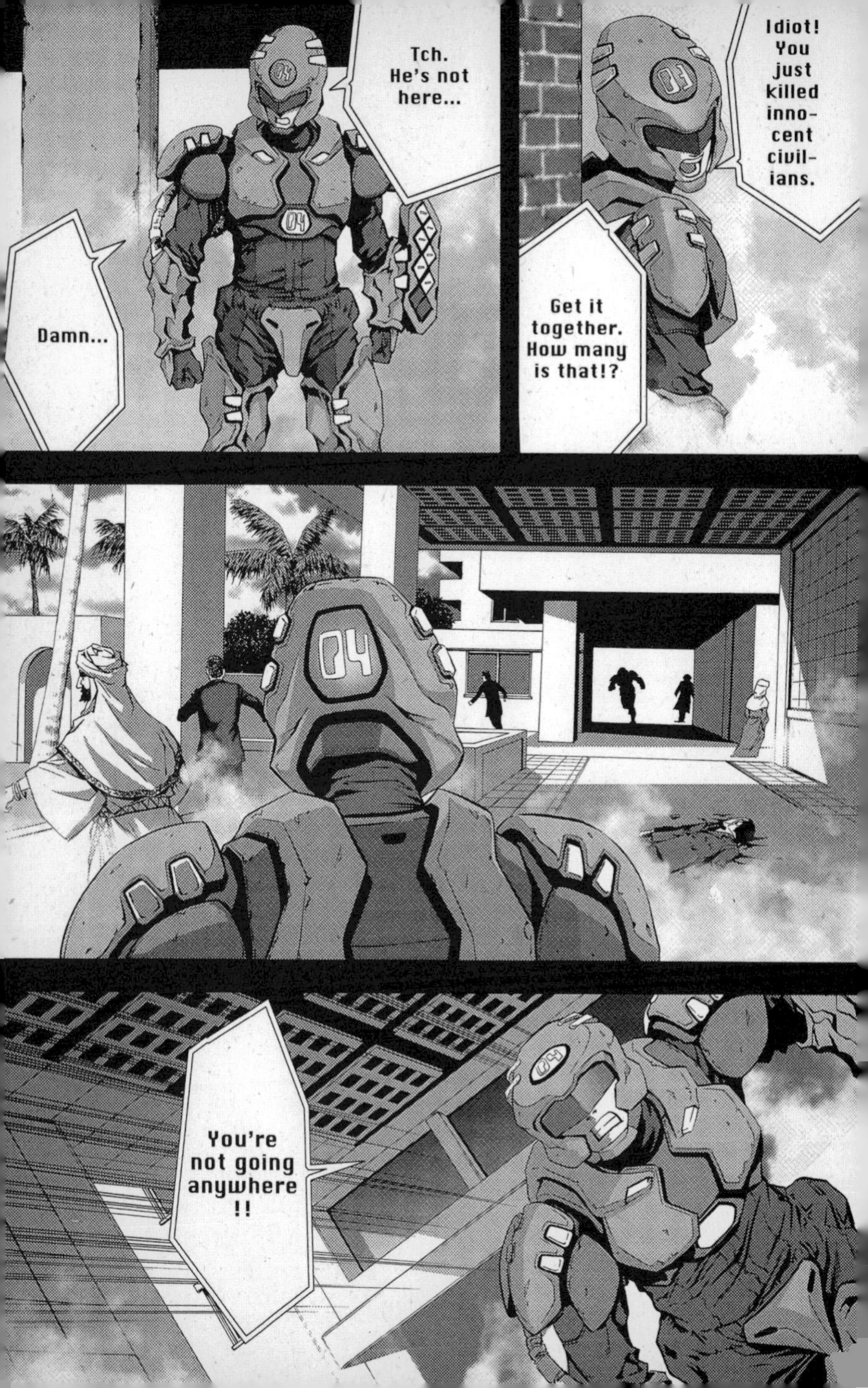
Idiot! You just killed inno-cent civil-ians.
Get it together. How many is that!?
Tch. He's not here...
Damn...
You're not going anywhere !!

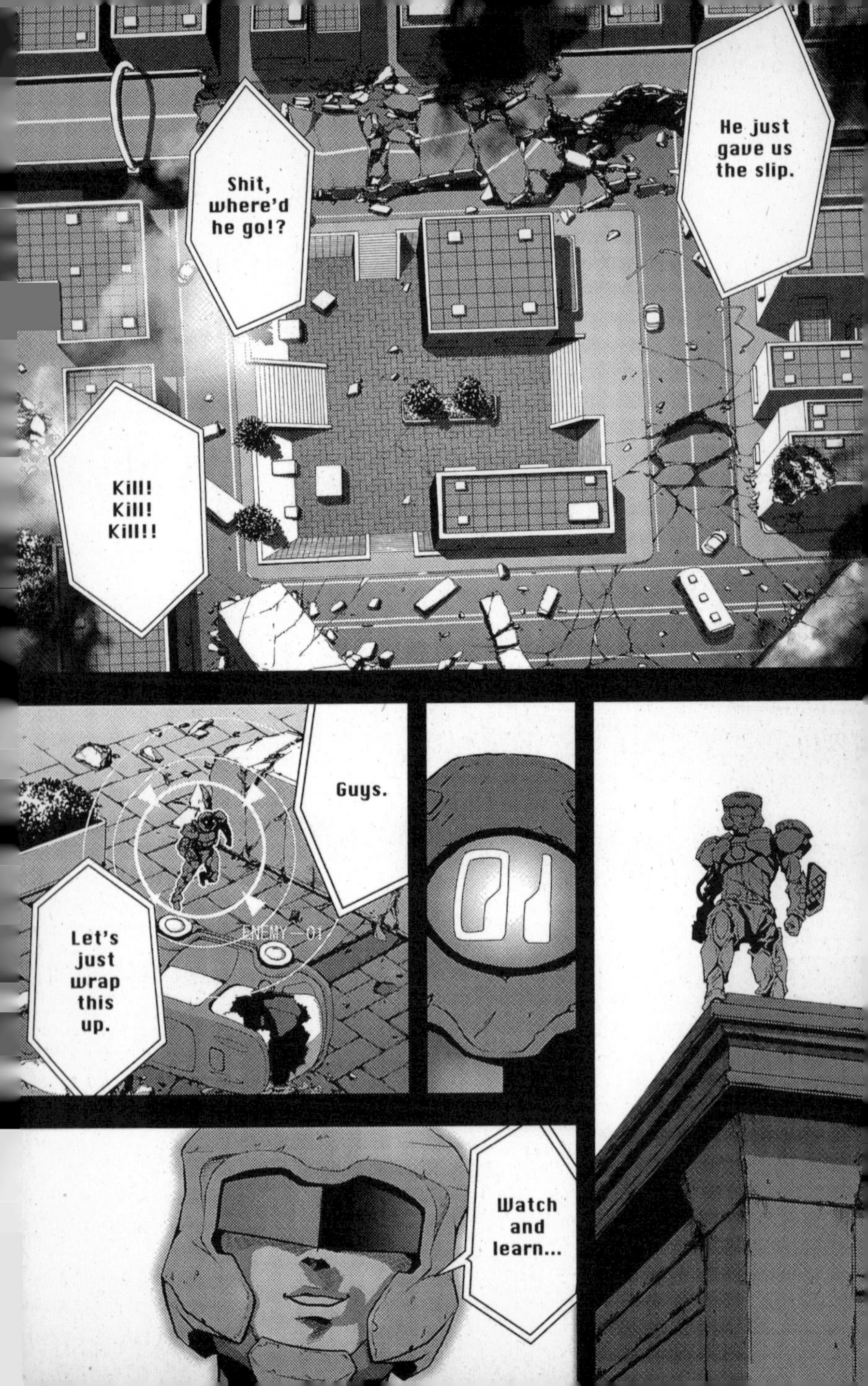
He just gave us the slip.
Shit, where'd he go!?
Kill! Kill! Kill!!
Guys.
Let's just wrap this up.
ENEMY—01
Watch and learn...

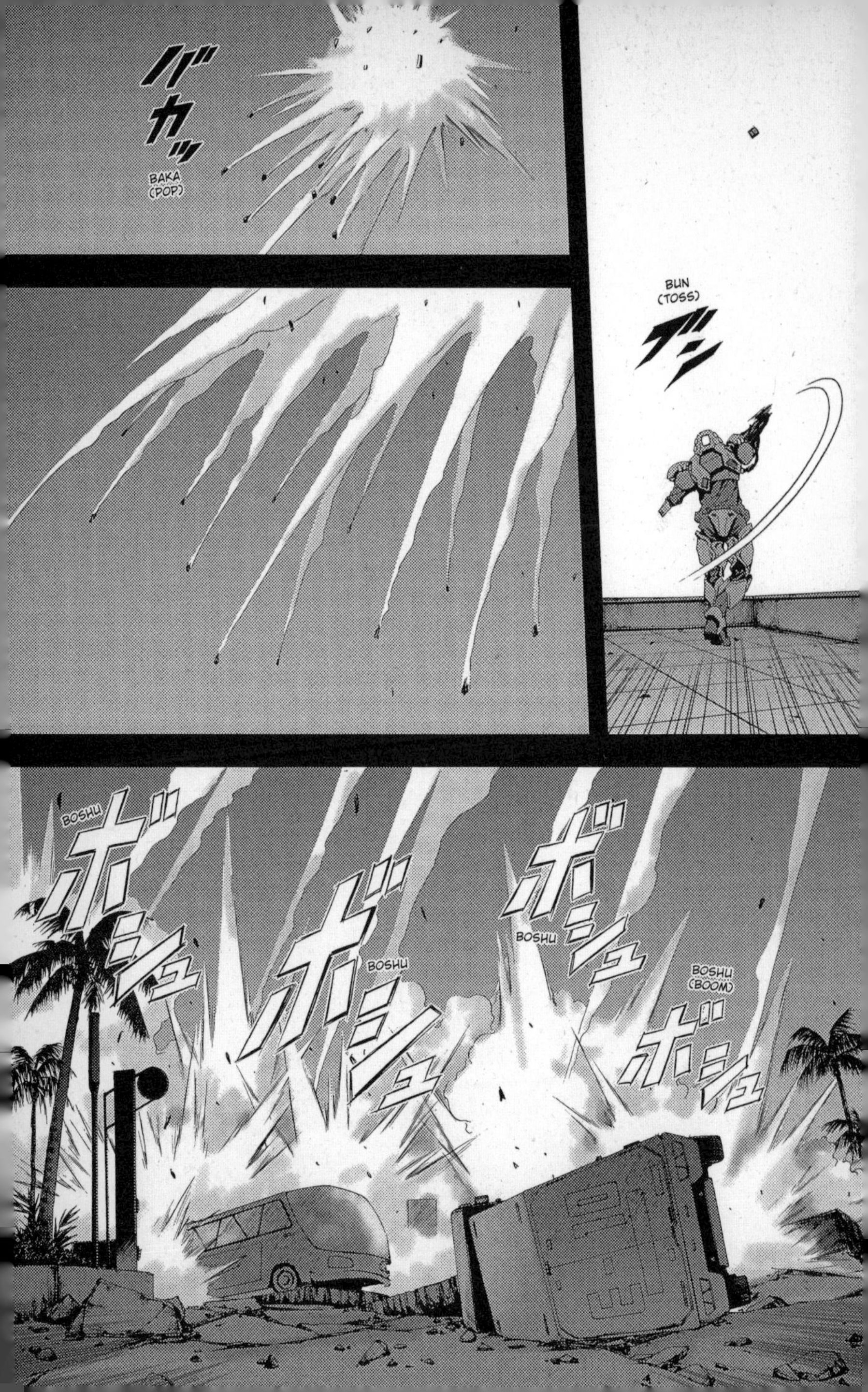
BUN (TOSS)
ブン
バカッ
BAKA (POP)
BOSHU (BOOM)
ボシュ
ボシュ
BOSHU
ボシュ
BOSHU
ボシュ
BOSHU

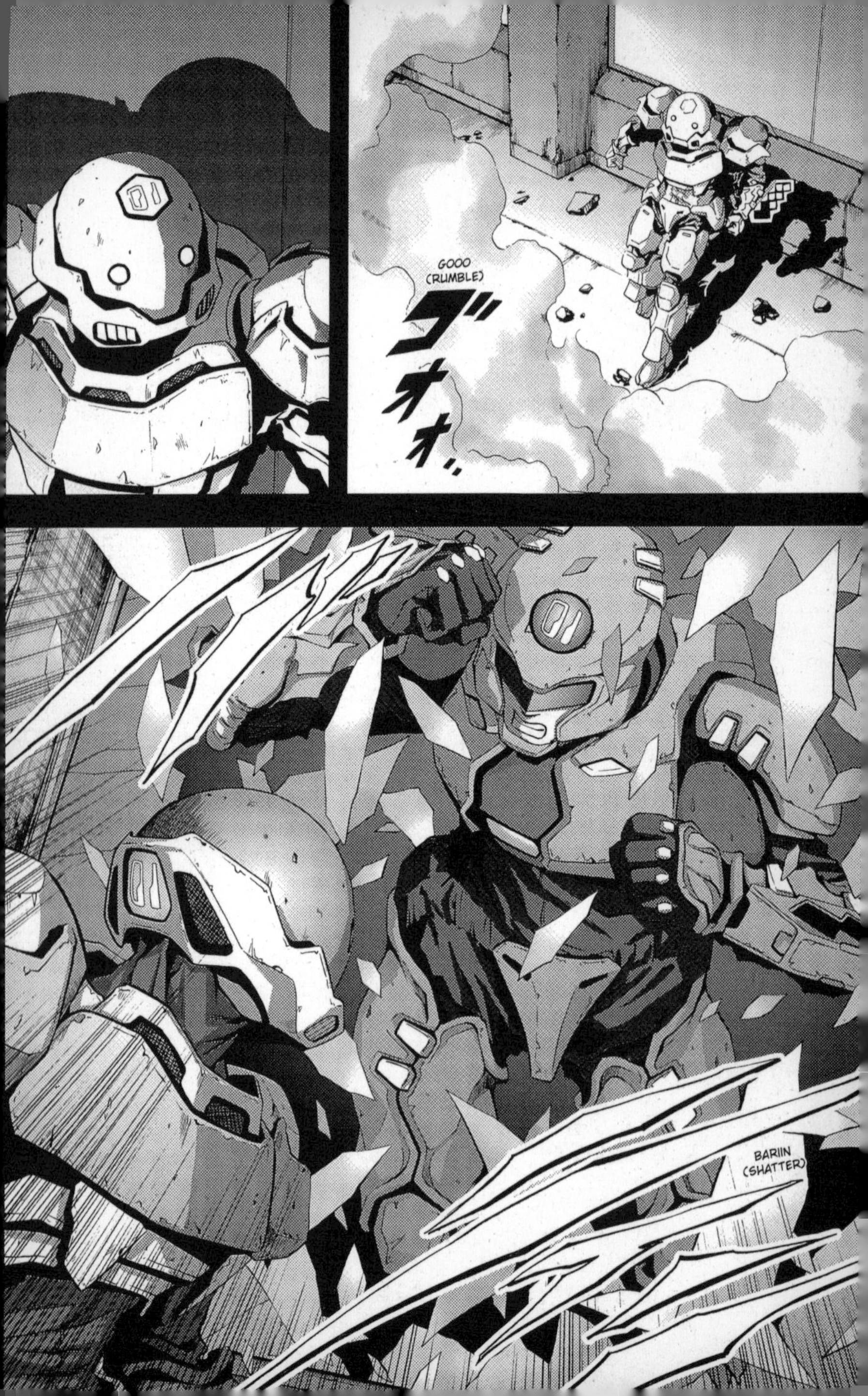
GOOO (RUMBLE)
ゴォォ…
BARIIN (SHATTER)

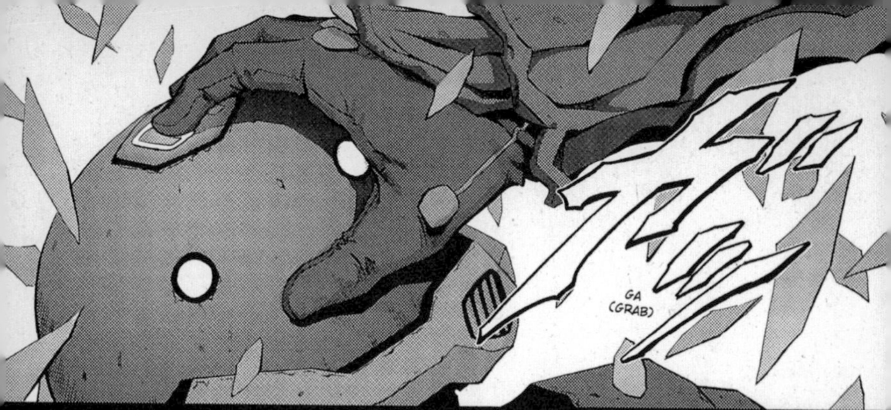
GA
(GRAB)
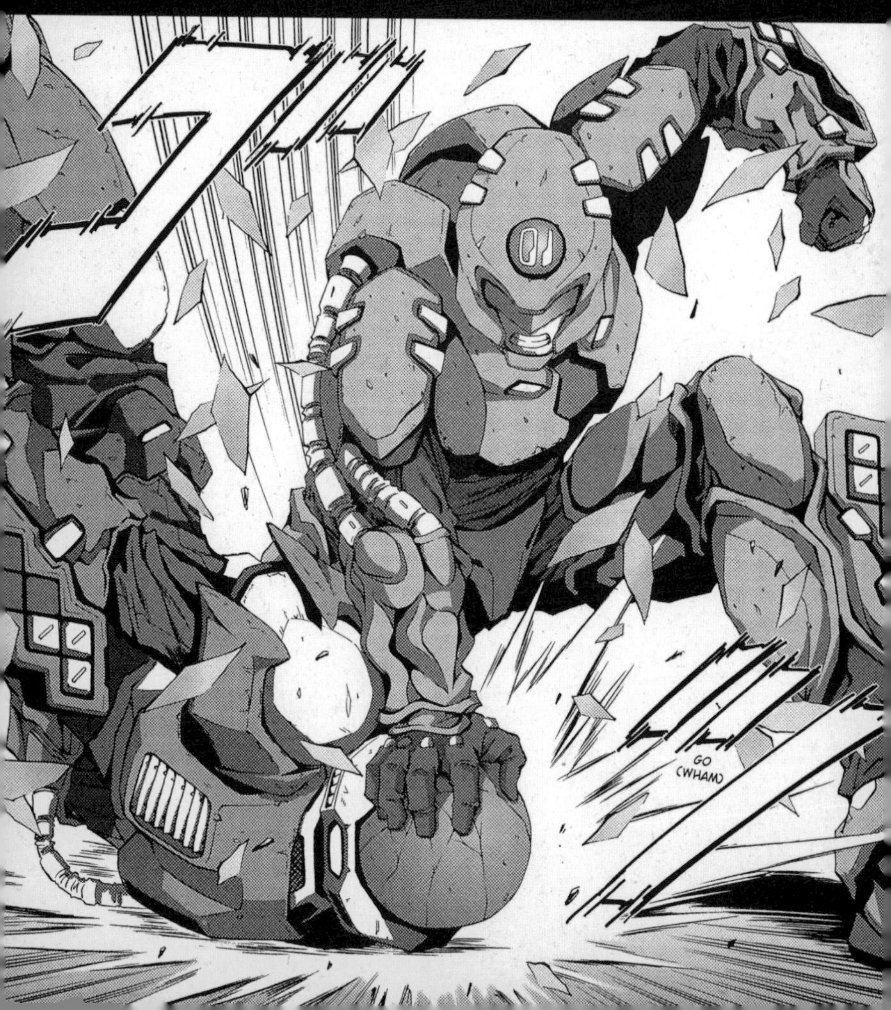
GO
(WHAM)

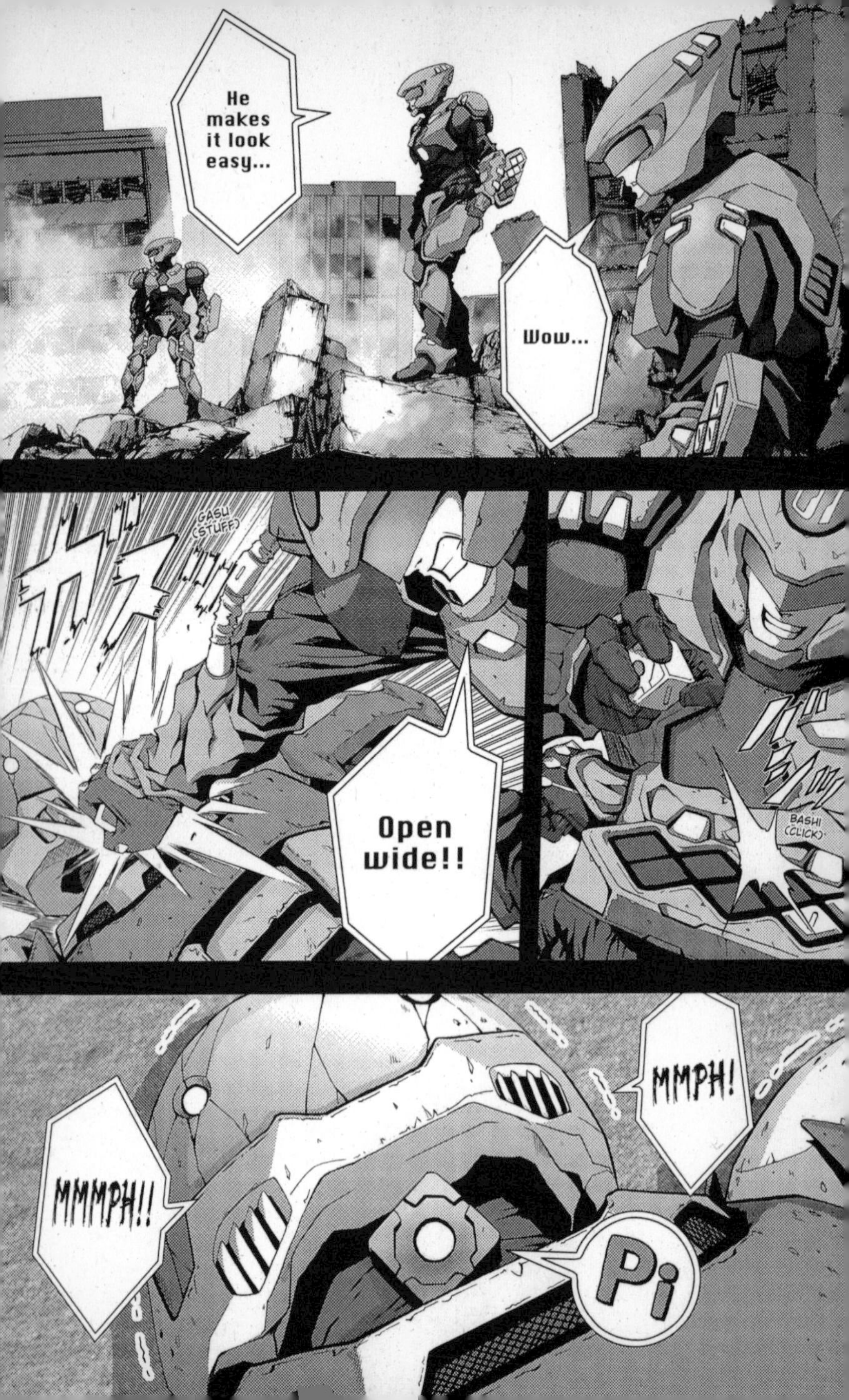
Wow...
He makes it look easy...
BASHI (CLICK)
GASU (STUFF)
Open wide!!
MMPH!
Pi
MMMPH!!

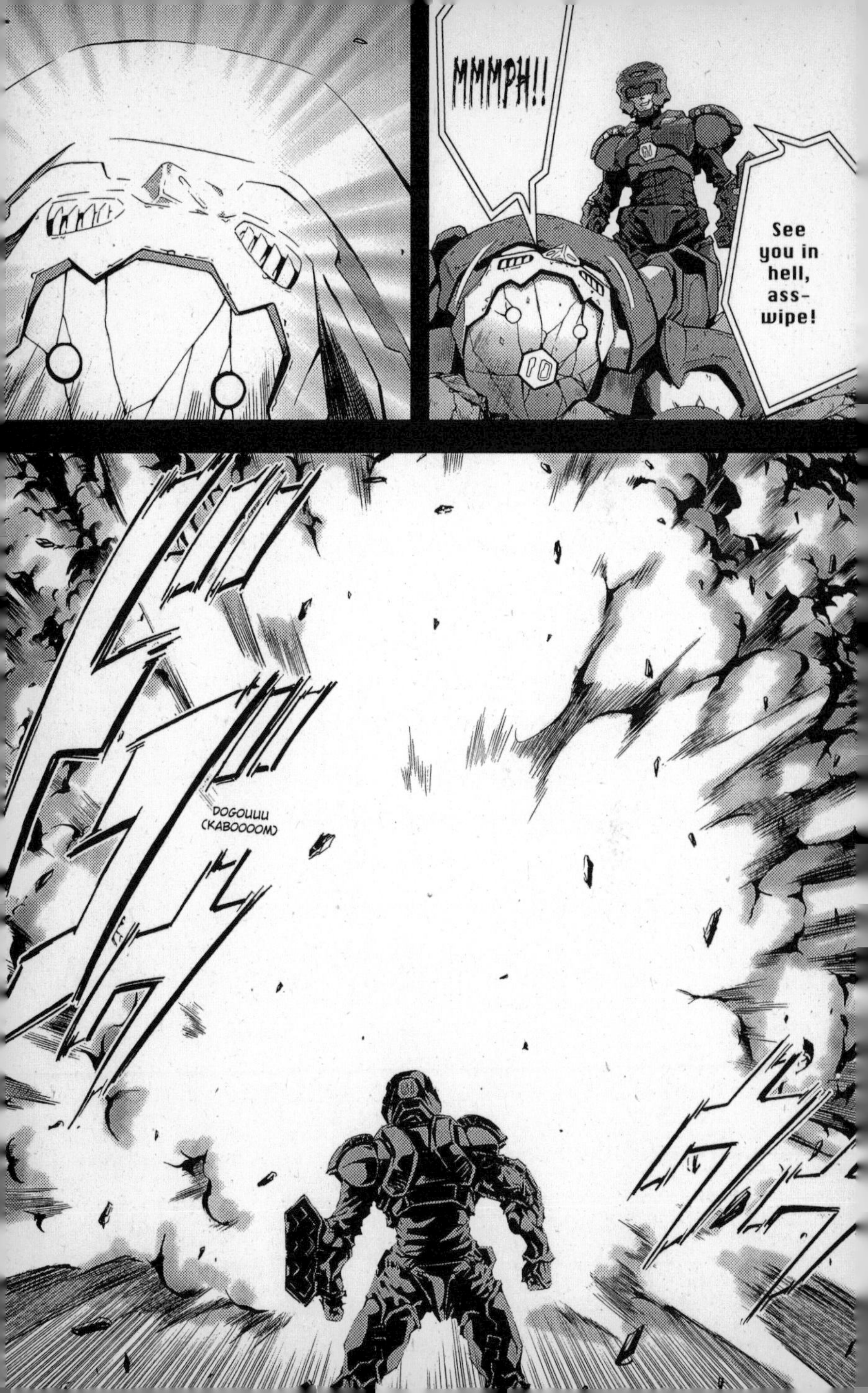
MMMPH!!
See you in hell, ass-wipe!
DOGOUUU (KABOOOM)

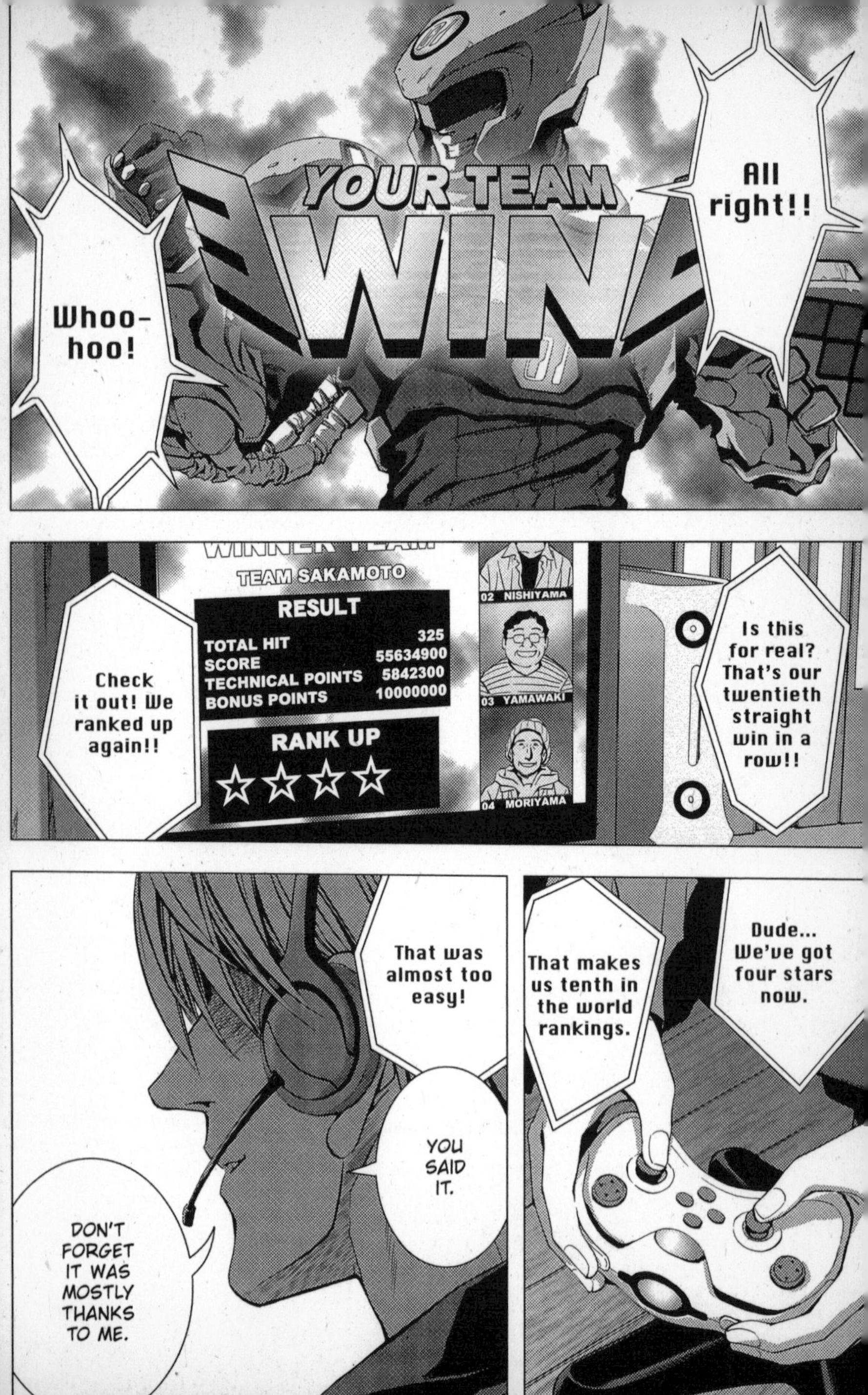
All right!!
YOUR TEAM
WIN
Whoo-hoo!
Is this for real? That's our twentieth straight win in a row!!
TEAM SAKAMOTO
RESULT
TOTAL HIT 325
SCORE 55634900
TECHNICAL POINTS 5842300
BONUS POINTS 10000000
RANK UP
02 NISHIYAMA
03 YAMAWAKI
04 MORIYAMA
Check it out! We ranked up again!!
Dude... We've got four stars now.
That makes us tenth in the world rankings.
That was almost too easy!
YOU SAID IT.
DON'T FORGET IT WAS MOSTLY THANKS TO ME.

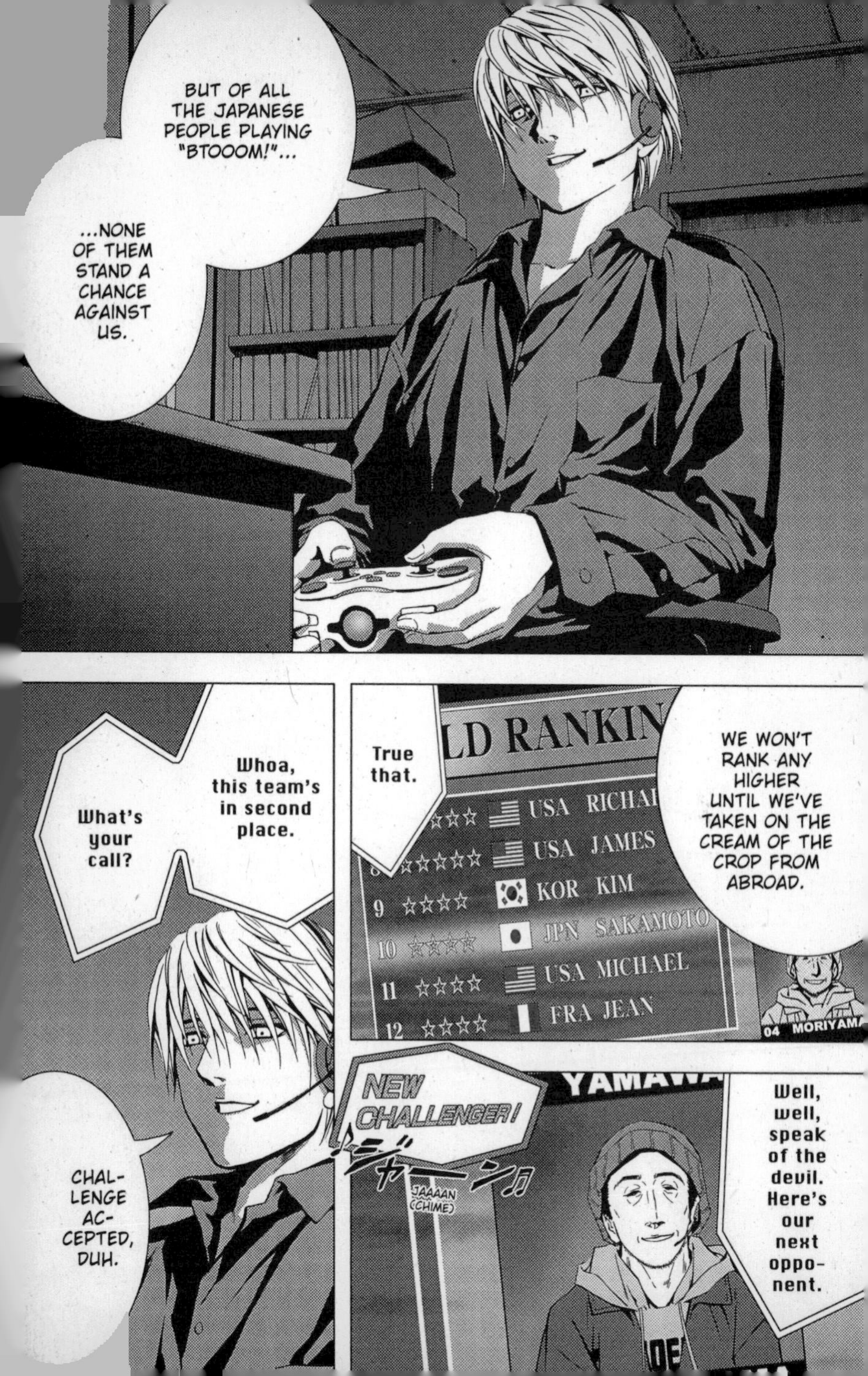
BUT OF ALL THE JAPANESE PEOPLE PLAYING "BTOOOM!"...
...NONE OF THEM STAND A CHANCE AGAINST US.
LD RANKIN
USA RICHAR
USA JAMES
9 KOR KIM
10 JPN SAKAMOTO
11 USA MICHAEL
12 FRA JEAN
04 MORIYAMA
WE WON'T RANK ANY HIGHER UNTIL WE'VE TAKEN ON THE CREAM OF THE CROP FROM ABROAD.
True that.
YAMAWA
NEW CHALLENGER!
♪ジャーン♫
JAAAAN (CHIME)
Well, well, speak of the devil. Here's our next opponent.
Whoa, this team's in second place.
What's your call?
CHAL-LENGE AC-CEPTED, DUH.

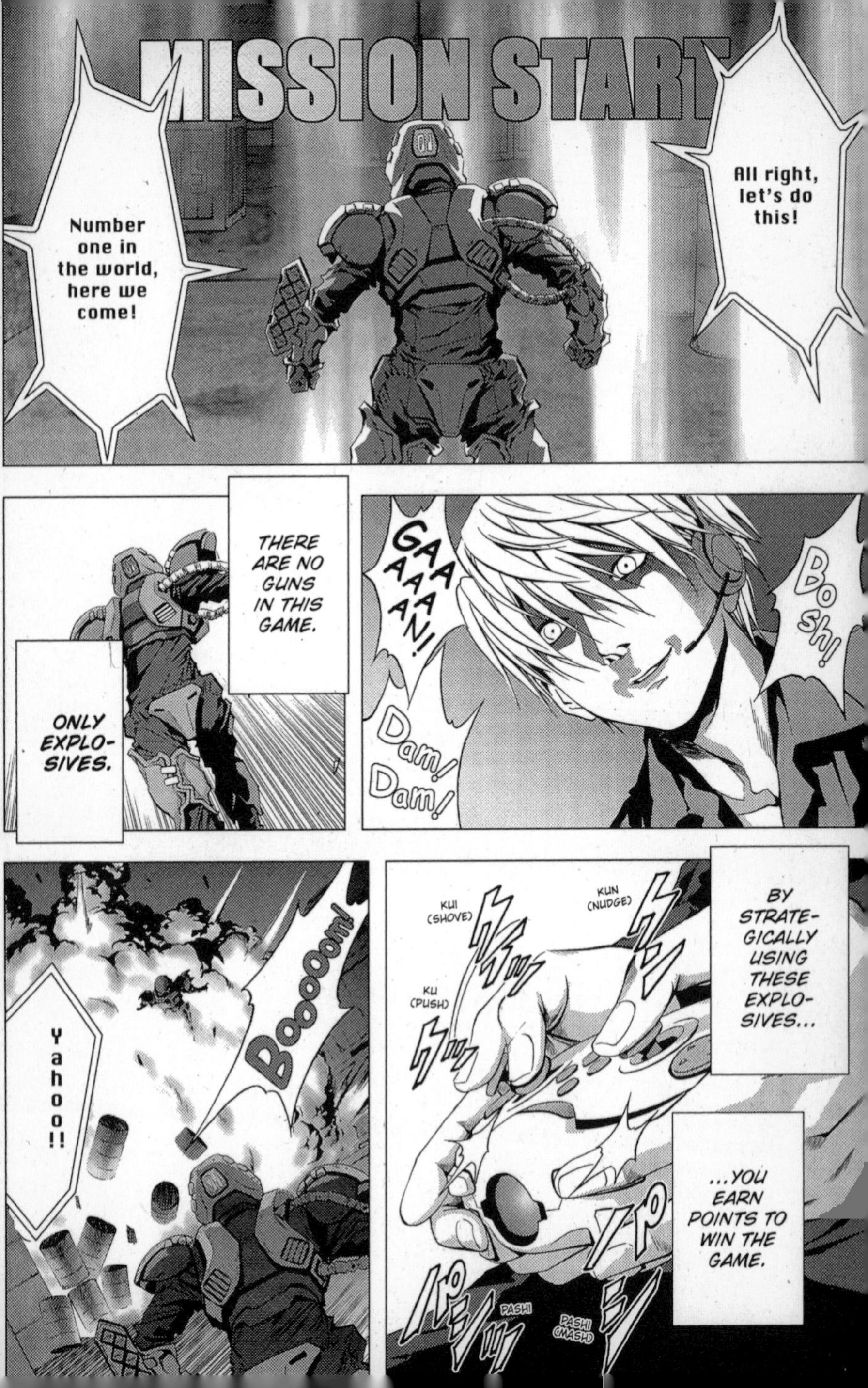
MISSION START
All right, let's do this!
Number one in the world, here we come!
Bosh!
GAAAAAN!
Dam! Dam!
THERE ARE NO GUNS IN THIS GAME.
ONLY EXPLOSIVES.
BY STRATEGICALLY USING THESE EXPLOSIVES...
KUN (NUDGE)
KUI (SHOVE)
KU (PUSH)
...YOU EARN POINTS TO WIN THE GAME.
PASHI
PASHI (MASH)
Boooooom!
Yahoooo!!

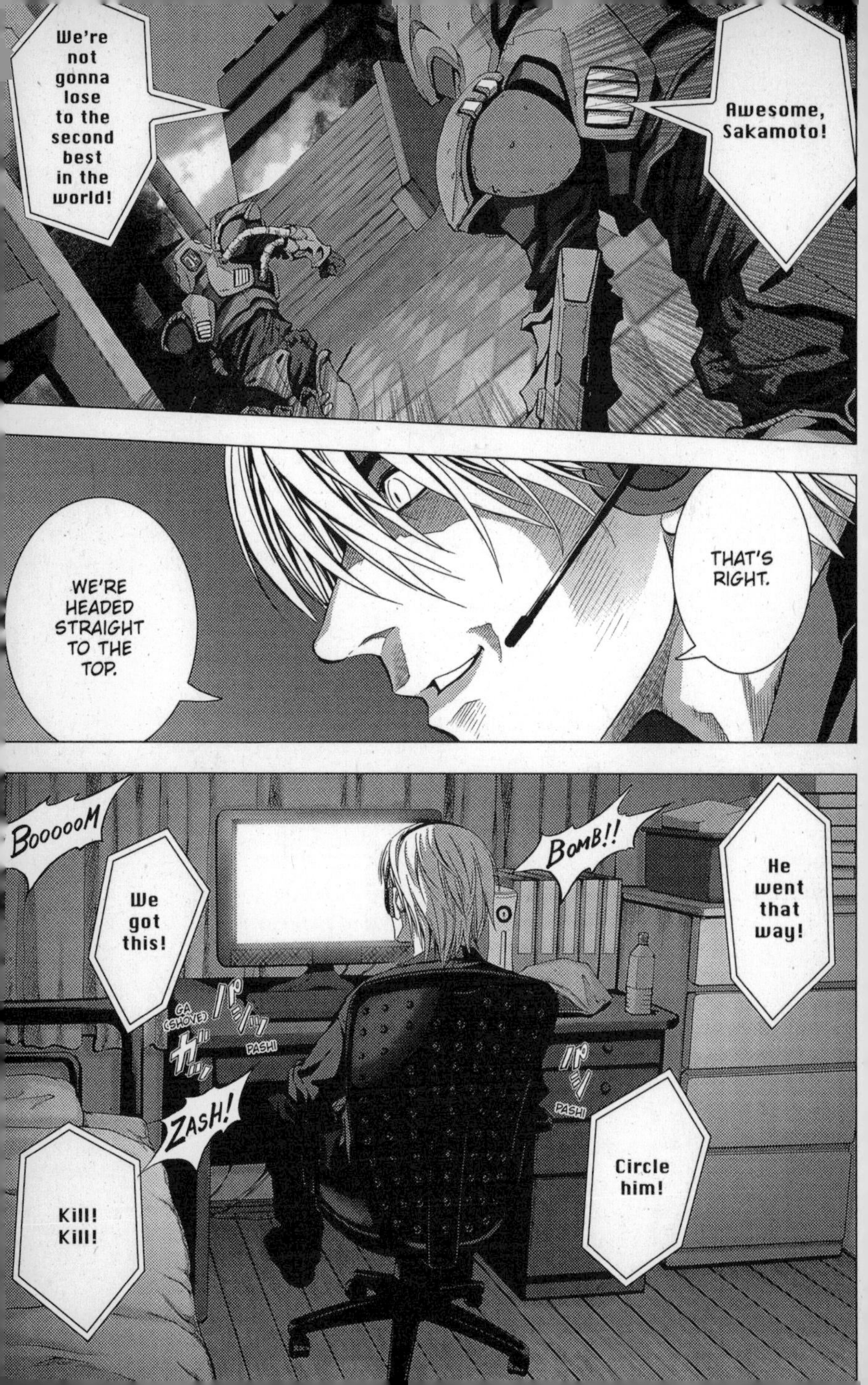
Awesome, Sakamoto!
We're not gonna lose to the second best in the world!
THAT'S RIGHT.
WE'RE HEADED STRAIGHT TO THE TOP.
He went that way!
BOMB!!
BoooooM
We got this!
PASHI
GA (SHOVE)
Circle him!
PASHI
ZASH!
Kill! Kill!

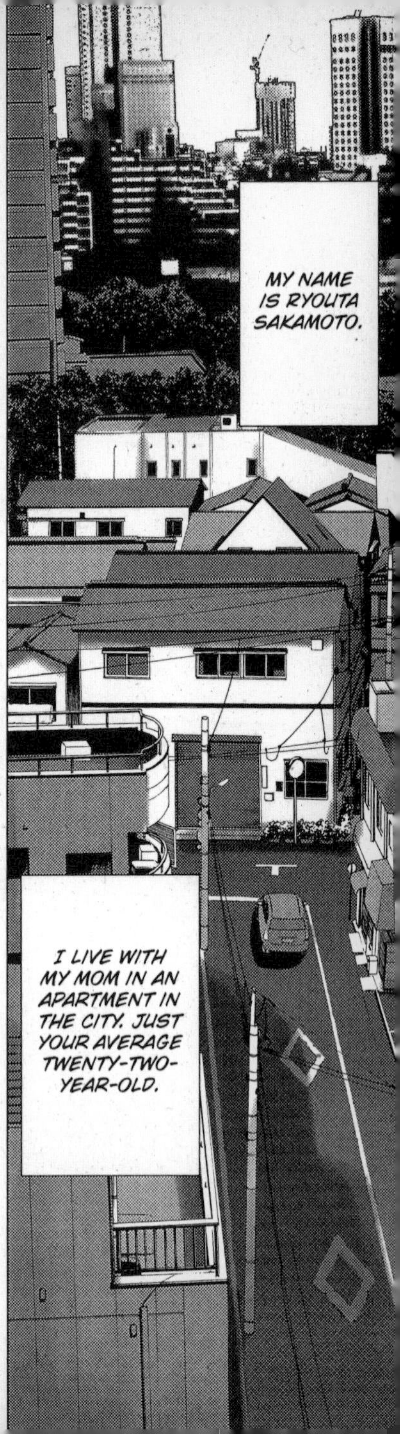
MY NAME IS RYOUTA SAKAMOTO.
I LIVE WITH MY MOM IN AN APARTMENT IN THE CITY. JUST YOUR AVERAGE TWENTY-TWO-YEAR-OLD.
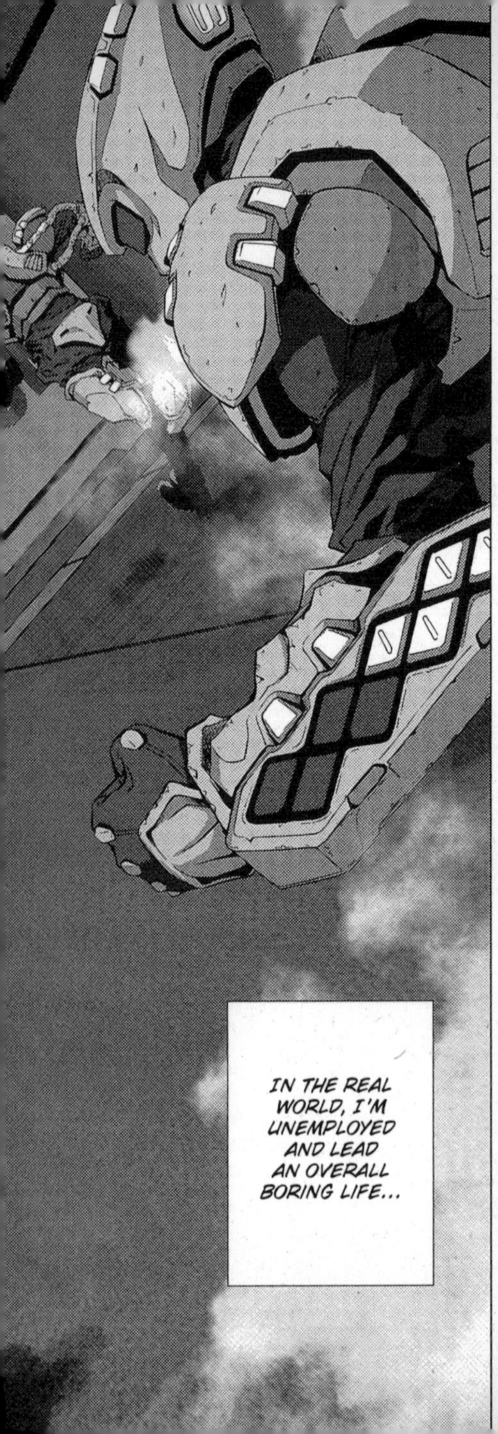
IN THE REAL WORLD, I'M UNEMPLOYED AND LEAD AN OVERALL BORING LIFE...

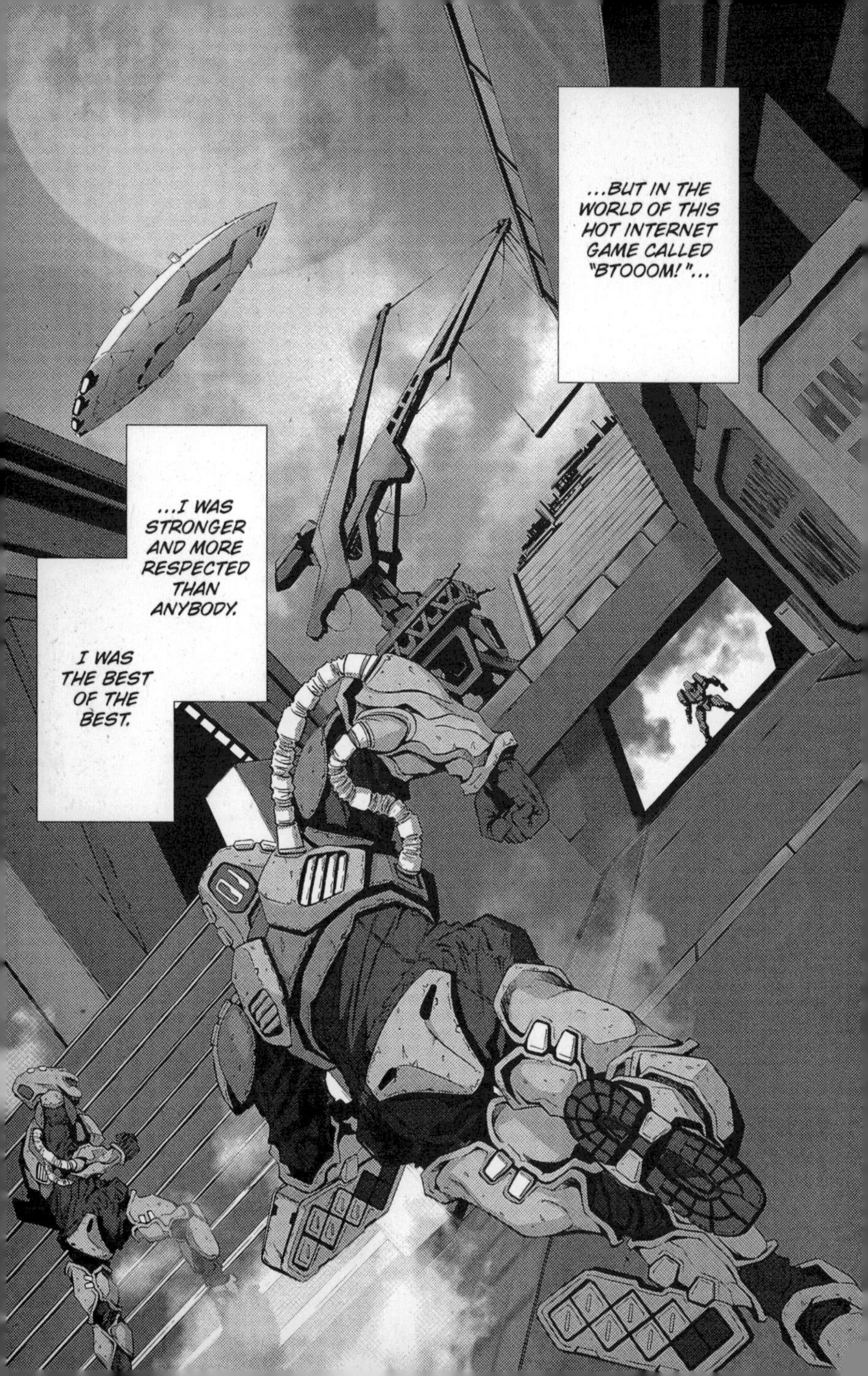
...BUT IN THE WORLD OF THIS HOT INTERNET GAME CALLED "BTOOOM!"...
...I WAS STRONGER AND MORE RESPECTED THAN ANYBODY.
I WAS THE BEST OF THE BEST.

MAYBE I WAS SEEKING
REFUGE IN THIS COZY
AND COMFORTABLE
ENVIRONMENT...

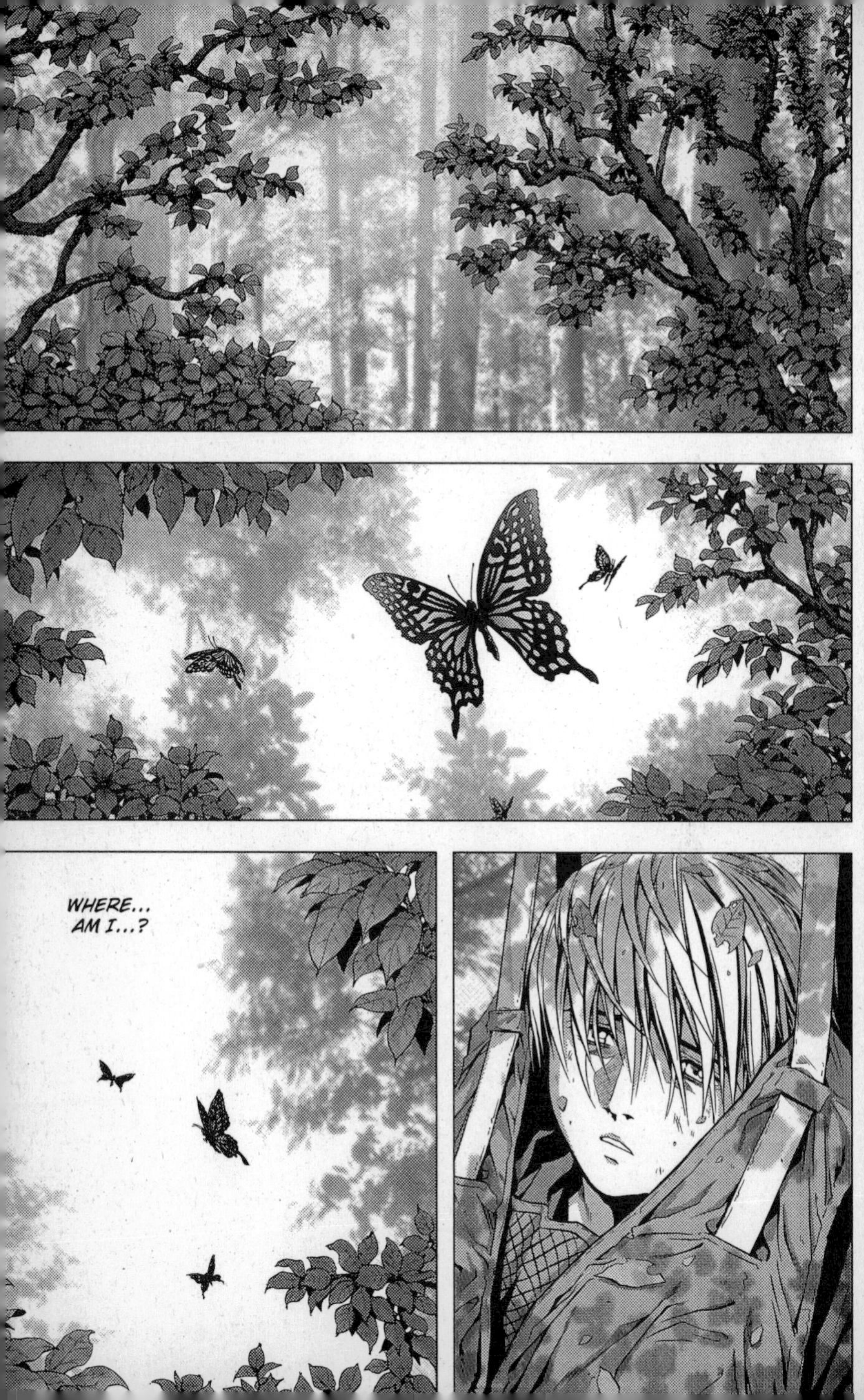
WHERE... AM I...?

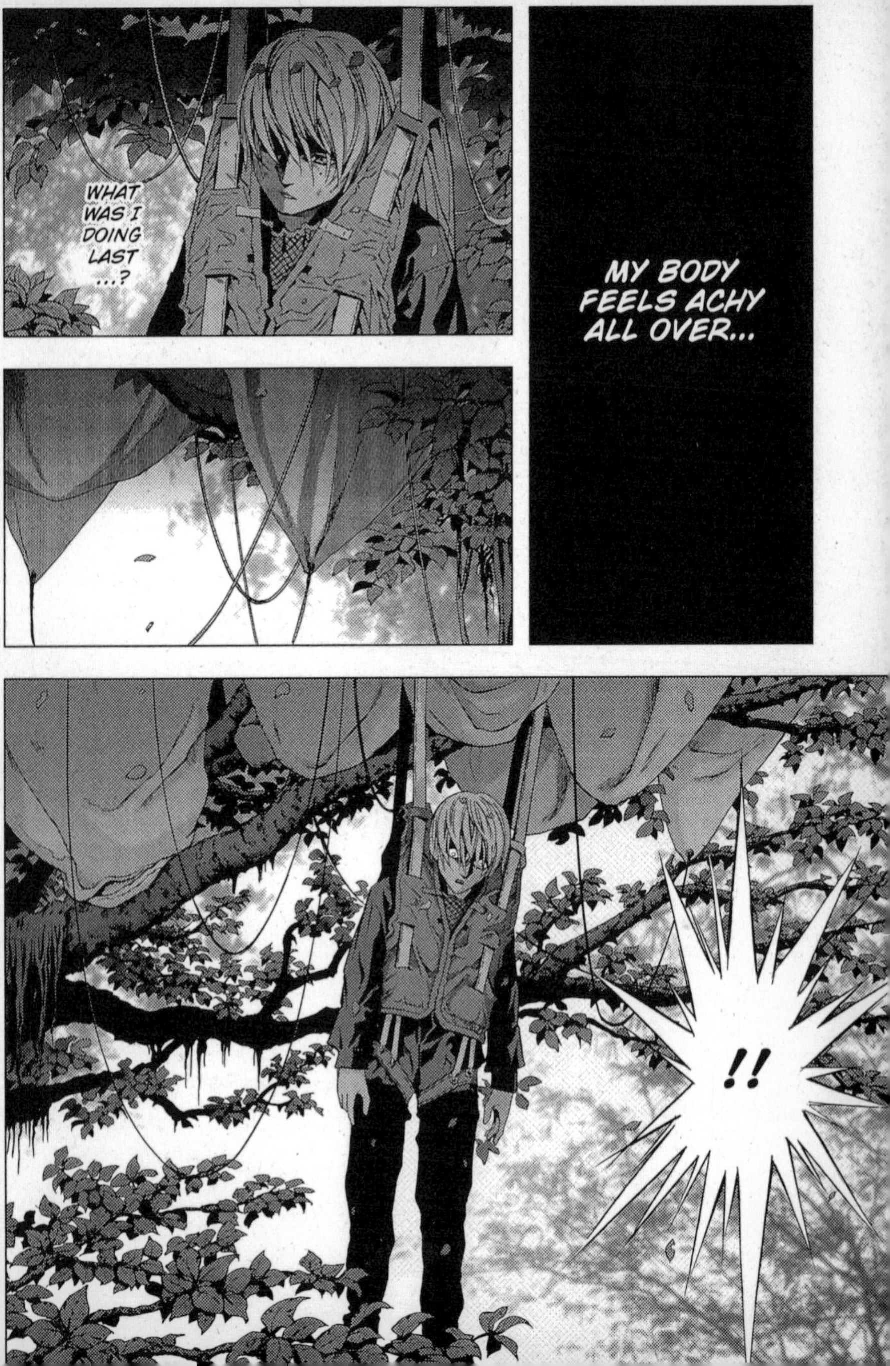
MY BODY FEELS ACHY ALL OVER...
WHAT WAS I DOING LAST ...?
!!

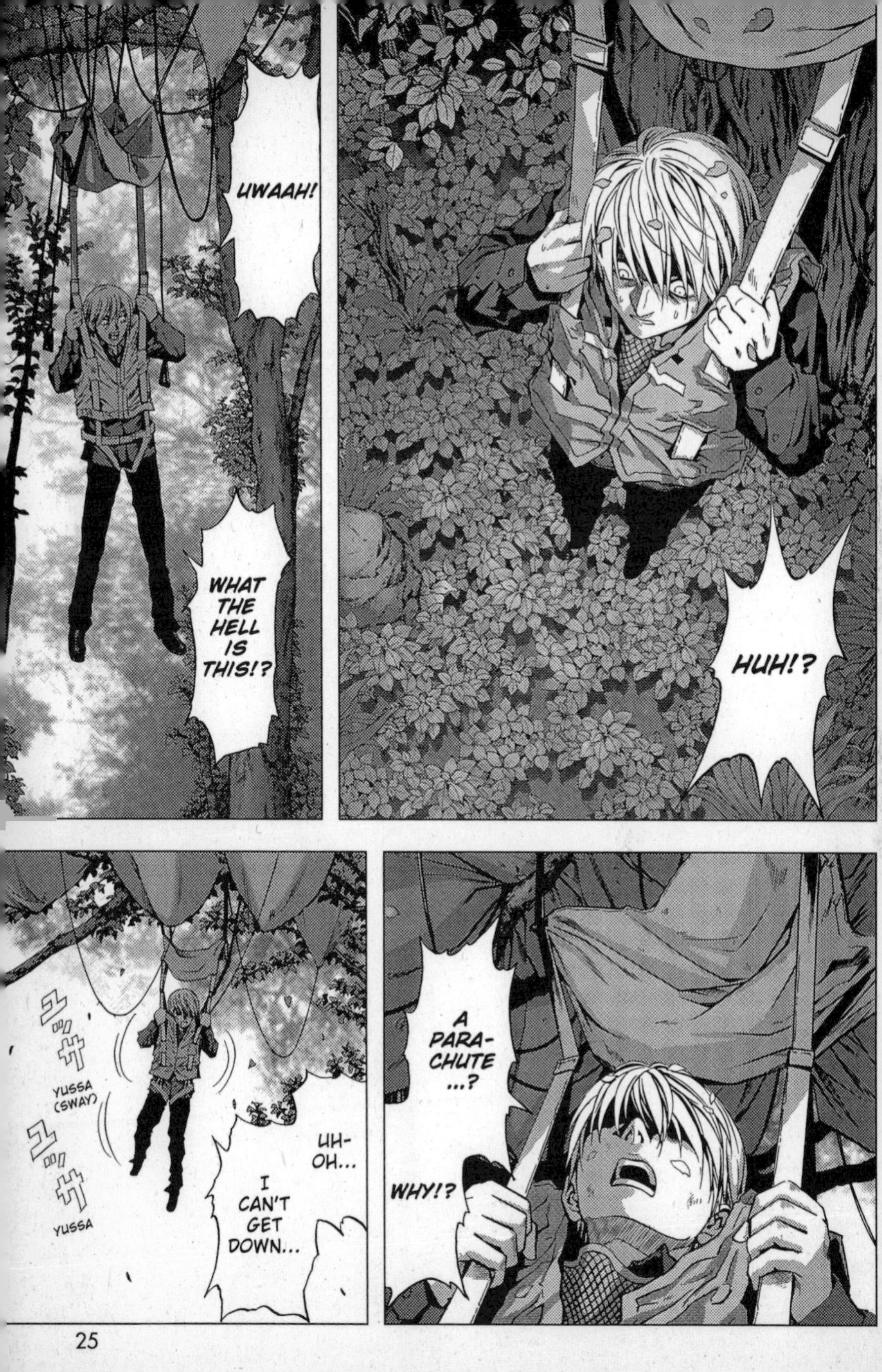
HUH!?
UWAAH!
WHAT THE HELL IS THIS!?
A PARA-CHUTE ...?
WHY!?
UH-OH...
I CAN'T GET DOWN...
ユッサ
YUSSA (SWAY)
ユッサ
YUSSA

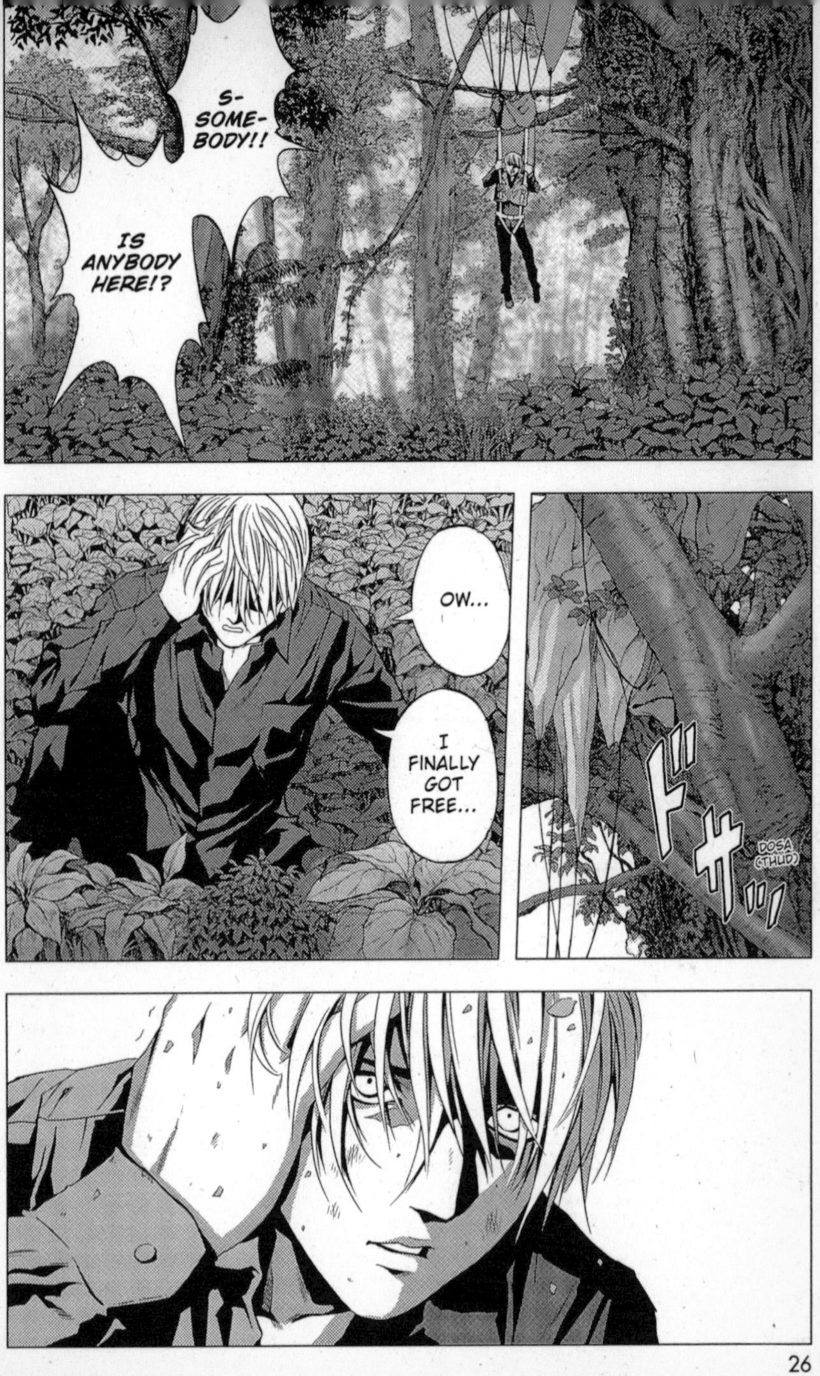
S-SOME-BODY!!
IS ANYBODY HERE!?
DOSA (THUD)
OW...
I FINALLY GOT FREE...

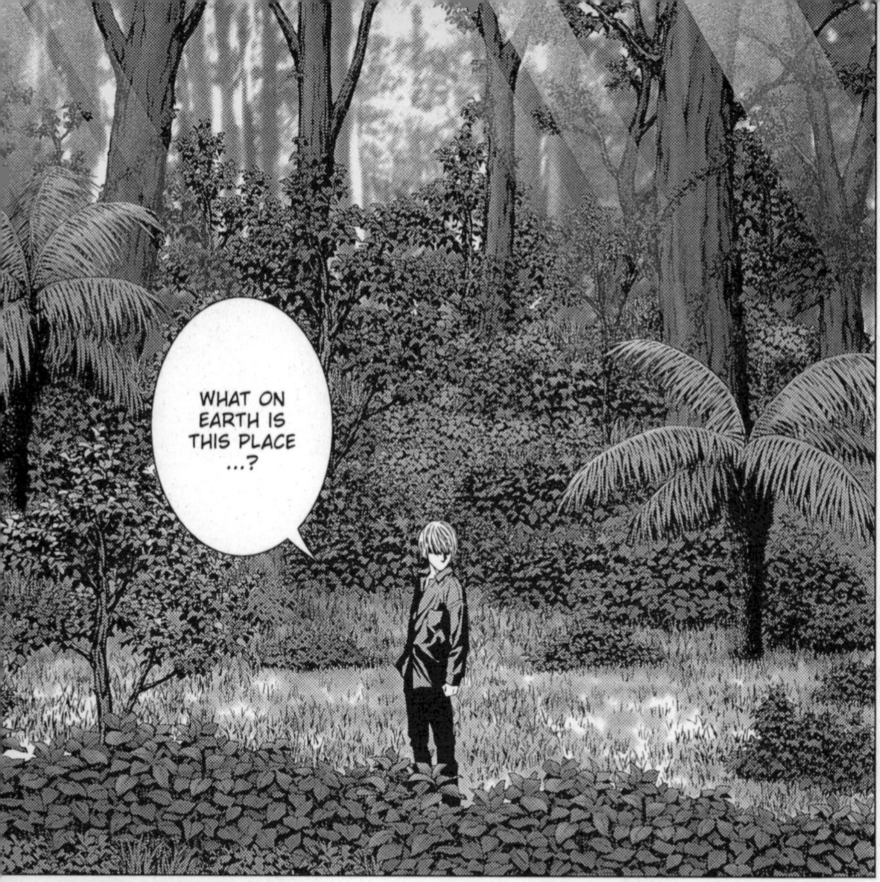
WHAT ON EARTH IS THIS PLACE ...?
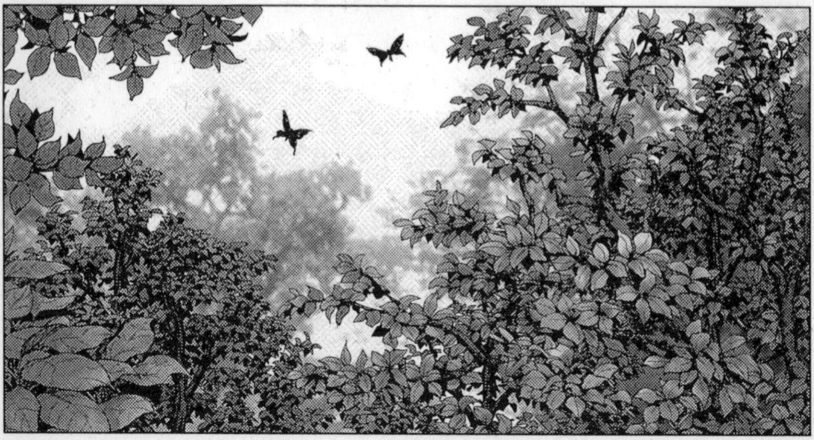

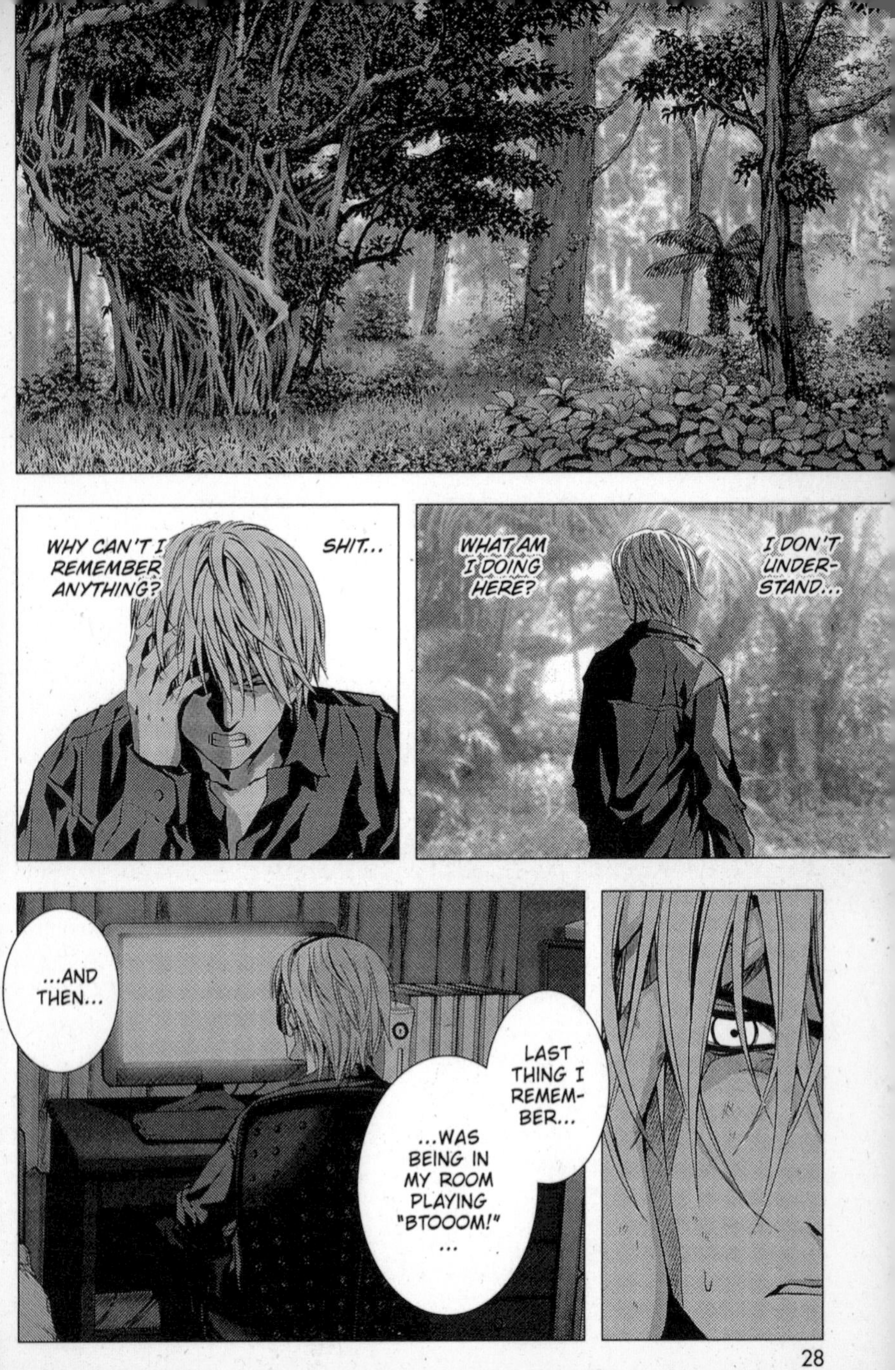
I DON'T UNDER-STAND...
WHAT AM I DOING HERE?
SHIT...
WHY CAN'T I REMEMBER ANYTHING?
LAST THING I REMEMBER...
...WAS BEING IN MY ROOM PLAYING "BTOOOM!" ...
...AND THEN...

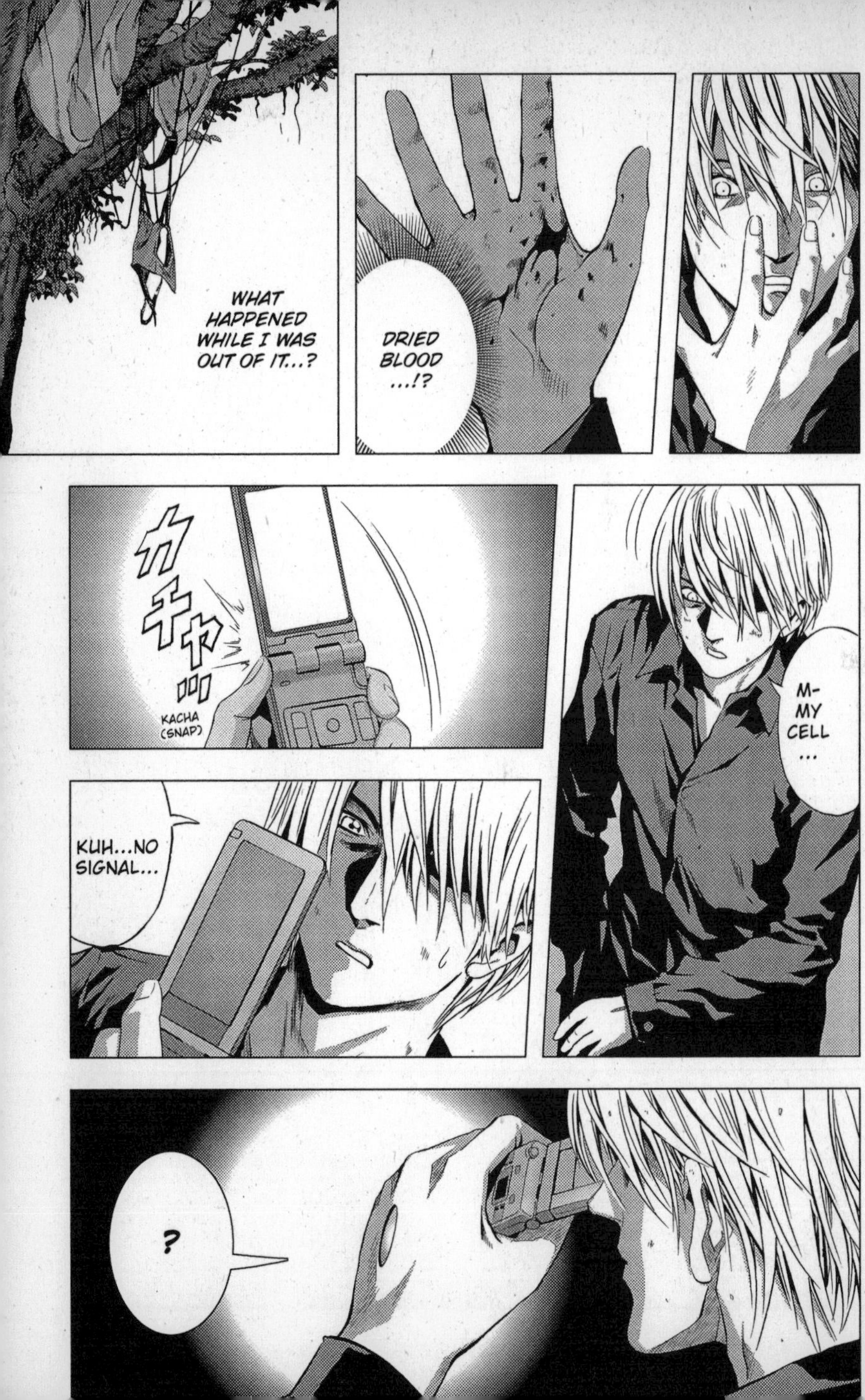
DRIED BLOOD ...!?
WHAT HAPPENED WHILE I WAS OUT OF IT...?
M-MY CELL ...
カチャッ
KACHA (SNAP)
KUH...NO SIGNAL...
?

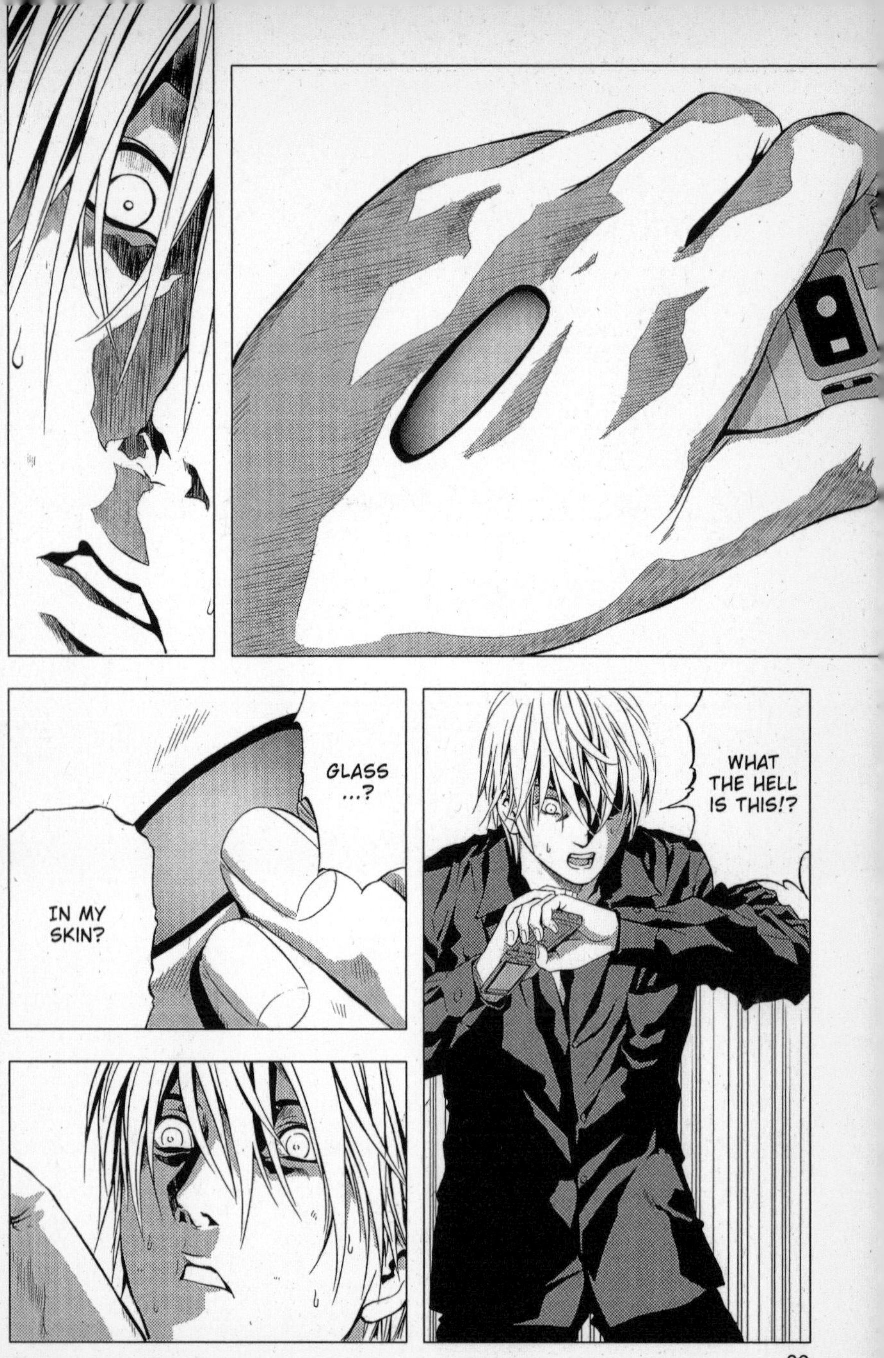
WHAT THE HELL IS THIS!?
GLASS ...?
IN MY SKIN?

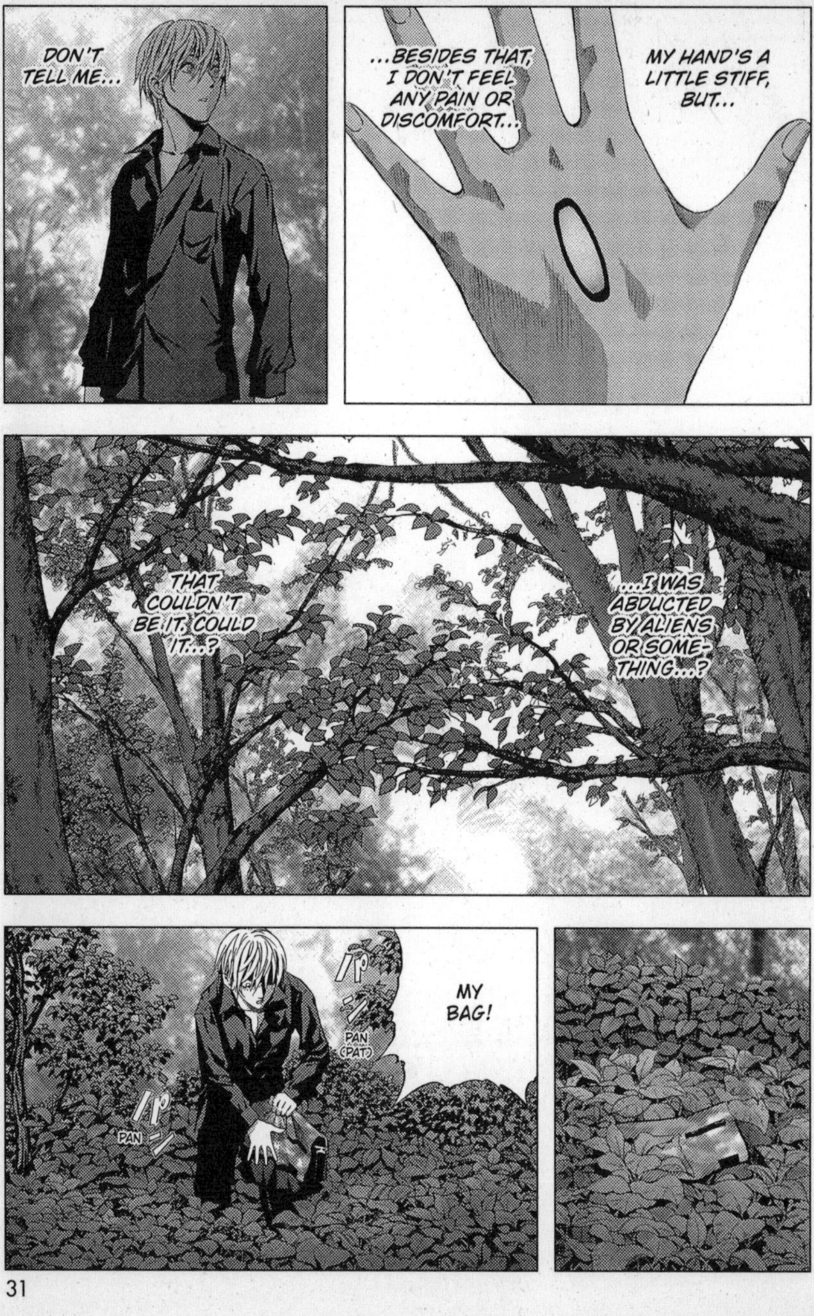
MY HAND'S A LITTLE STIFF, BUT...
...BESIDES THAT, I DON'T FEEL ANY PAIN OR DISCOMFORT...
DON'T TELL ME...
...I WAS ABDUCTED BY ALIENS OR SOME-THING...?
THAT COULDN'T BE IT, COULD IT...?
MY BAG!
PAN (PAT)
PAN

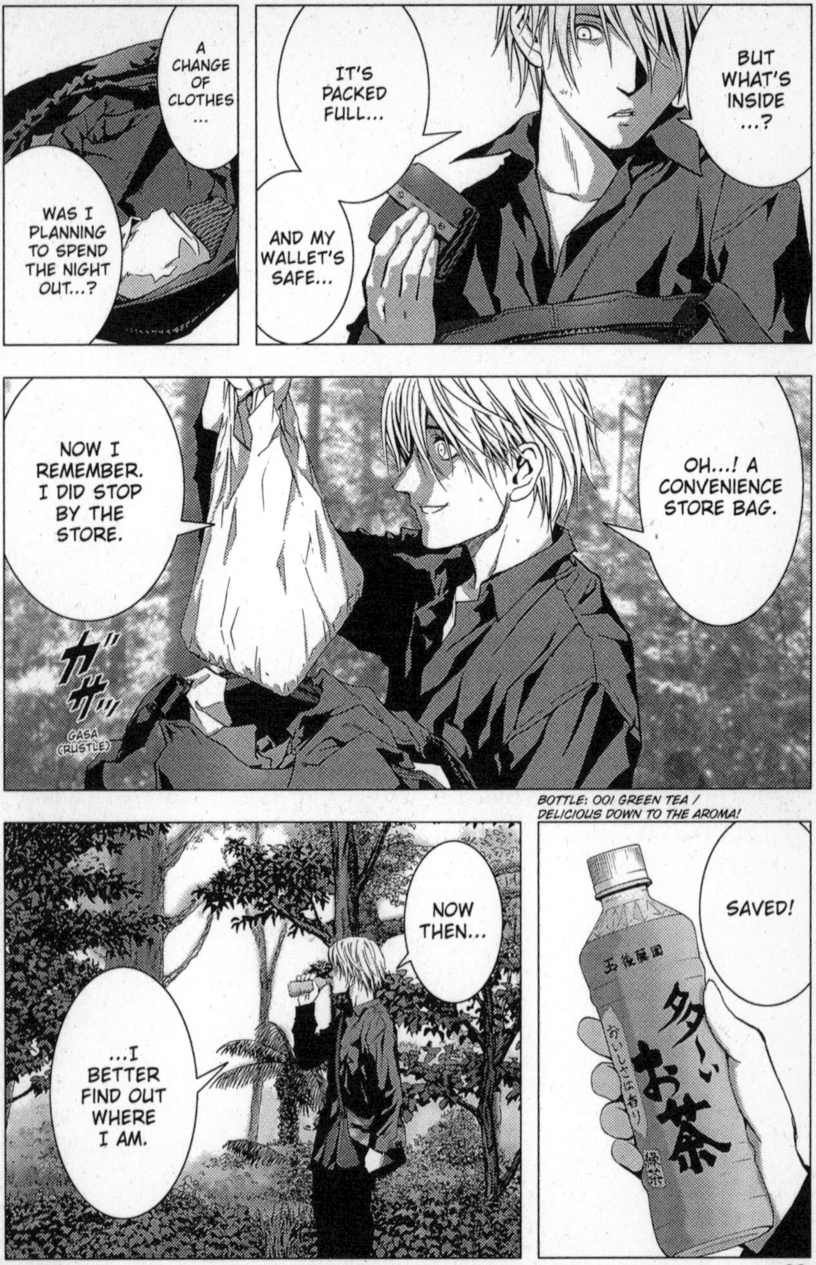
BUT WHAT'S INSIDE ...?
IT'S PACKED FULL...
AND MY WALLET'S SAFE...
A CHANGE OF CLOTHES ...
WAS I PLANNING TO SPEND THE NIGHT OUT...?
OH...! A CONVENIENCE STORE BAG.
NOW I REMEMBER. I DID STOP BY THE STORE.
GASA (RUSTLE)
BOTTLE: OOI GREEN TEA / DELICIOUS DOWN TO THE AROMA!
SAVED!
NOW THEN...
...I BETTER FIND OUT WHERE I AM.

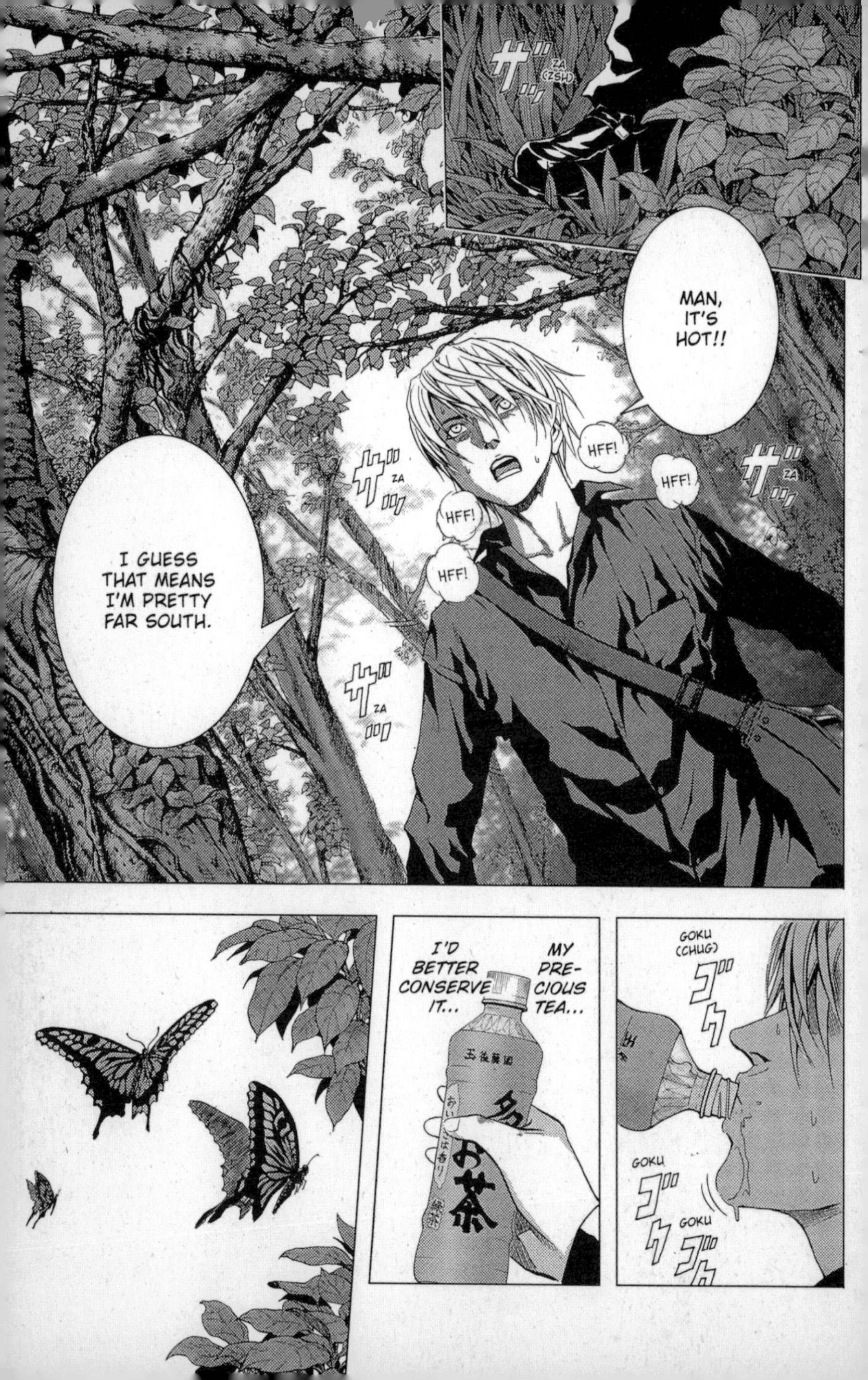

ZA (ZSH)
MAN, IT'S HOT!!
HFF!
HFF!
HFF!
HFF!
ZA
ZA
I GUESS THAT MEANS I'M PRETTY FAR SOUTH.
ZA
GOKU (CHUG)
GOKU
GOKU
MY PRECIOUS TEA...
I'D BETTER CONSERVE IT...
お茶
緑茶

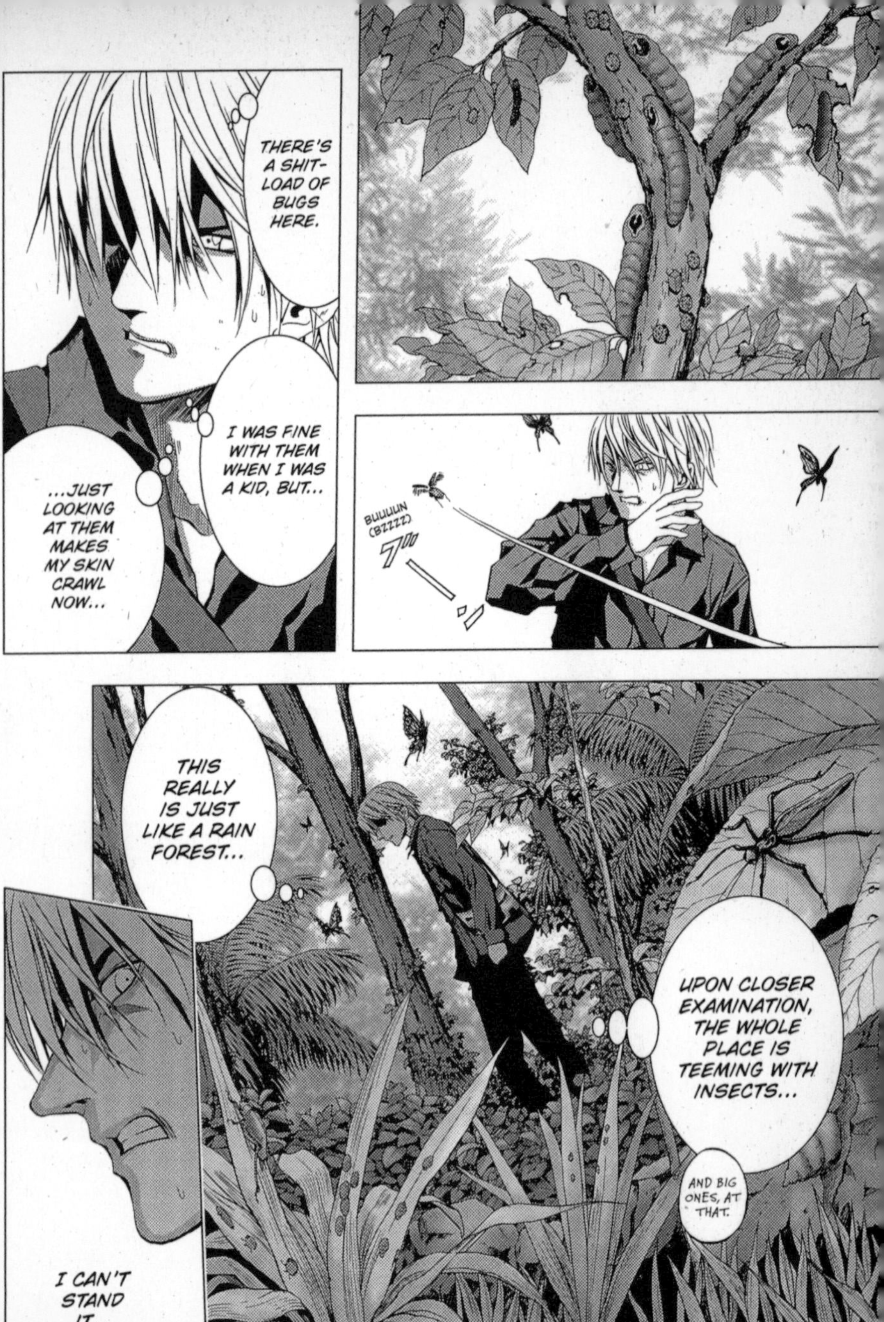
BUUUUN (BZZZZ)
THERE'S A SHIT-LOAD OF BUGS HERE.
I WAS FINE WITH THEM WHEN I WAS A KID, BUT...
...JUST LOOKING AT THEM MAKES MY SKIN CRAWL NOW...
THIS REALLY IS JUST LIKE A RAIN FOREST...
UPON CLOSER EXAMINATION, THE WHOLE PLACE IS TEEMING WITH INSECTS...
AND BIG ONES, AT THAT.
I CAN'T STAND IT...

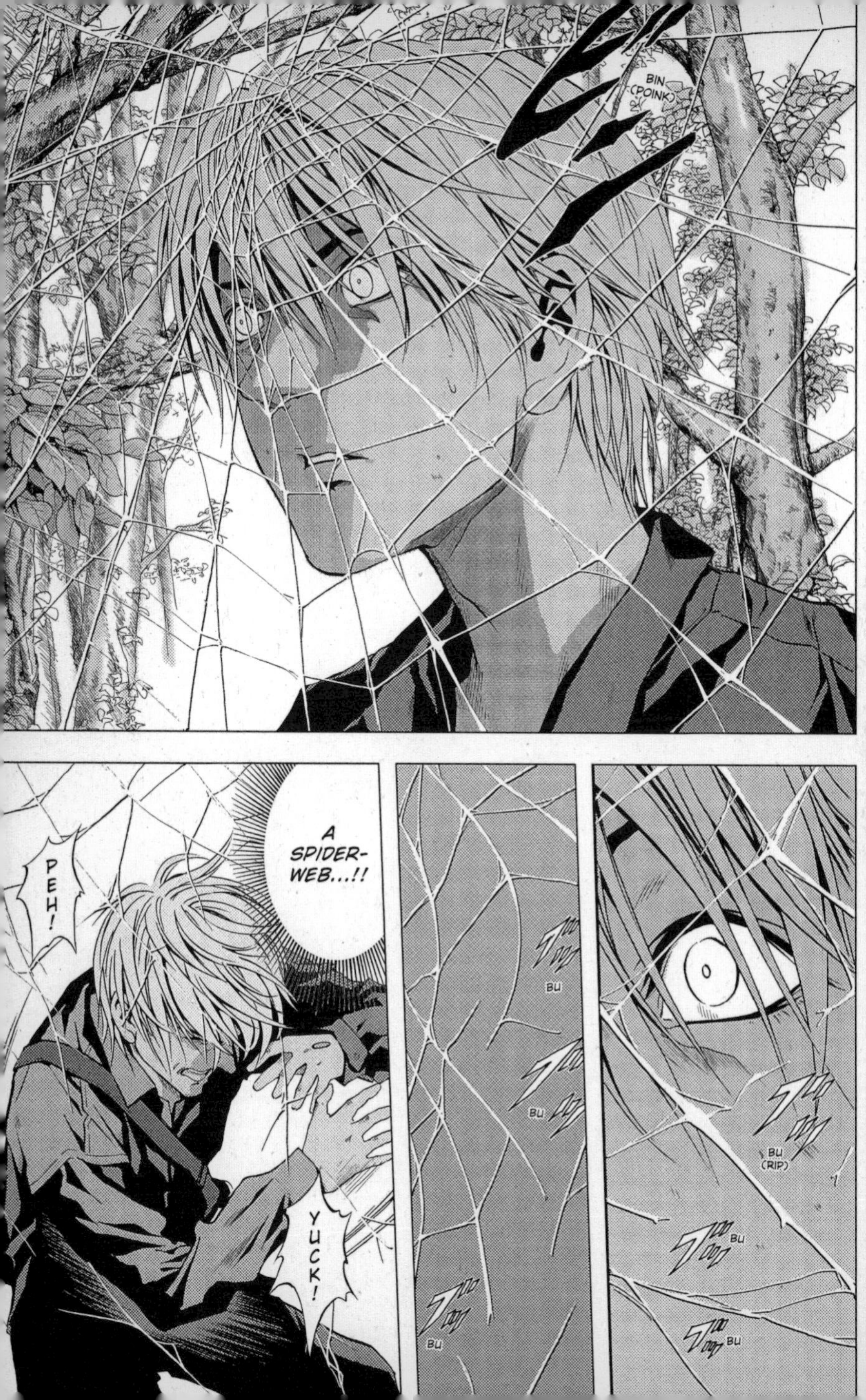
BIN
(POINK)
BU
(RIP)
BU
BU
BU
BU
BU
A SPIDER-WEB...!!
PEH!
YUCK!

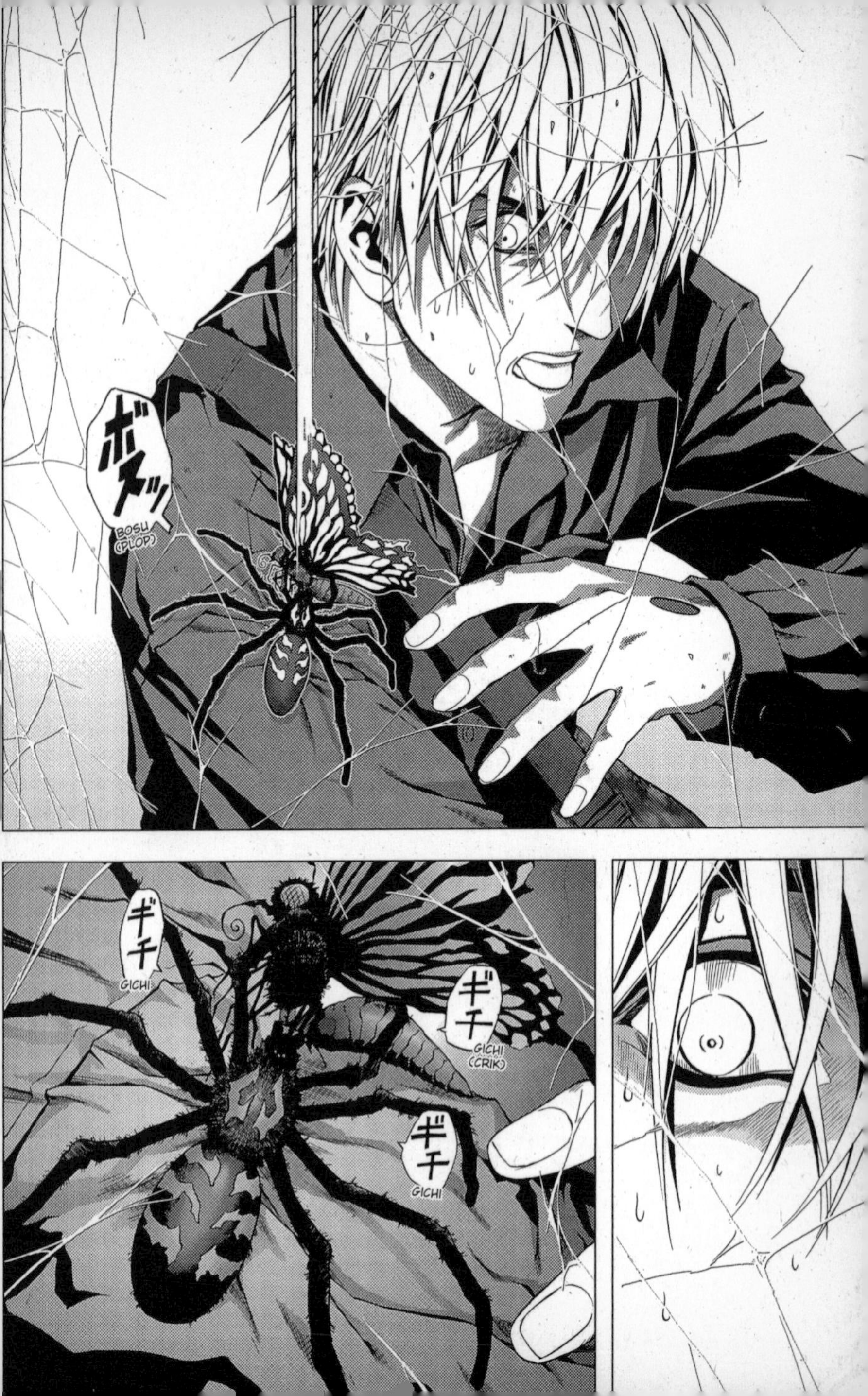
ボスッ
BOSU (PLOP)
ギチ
GICHI (CRIK)
ギチ
GICHI
ギチ
GICHI

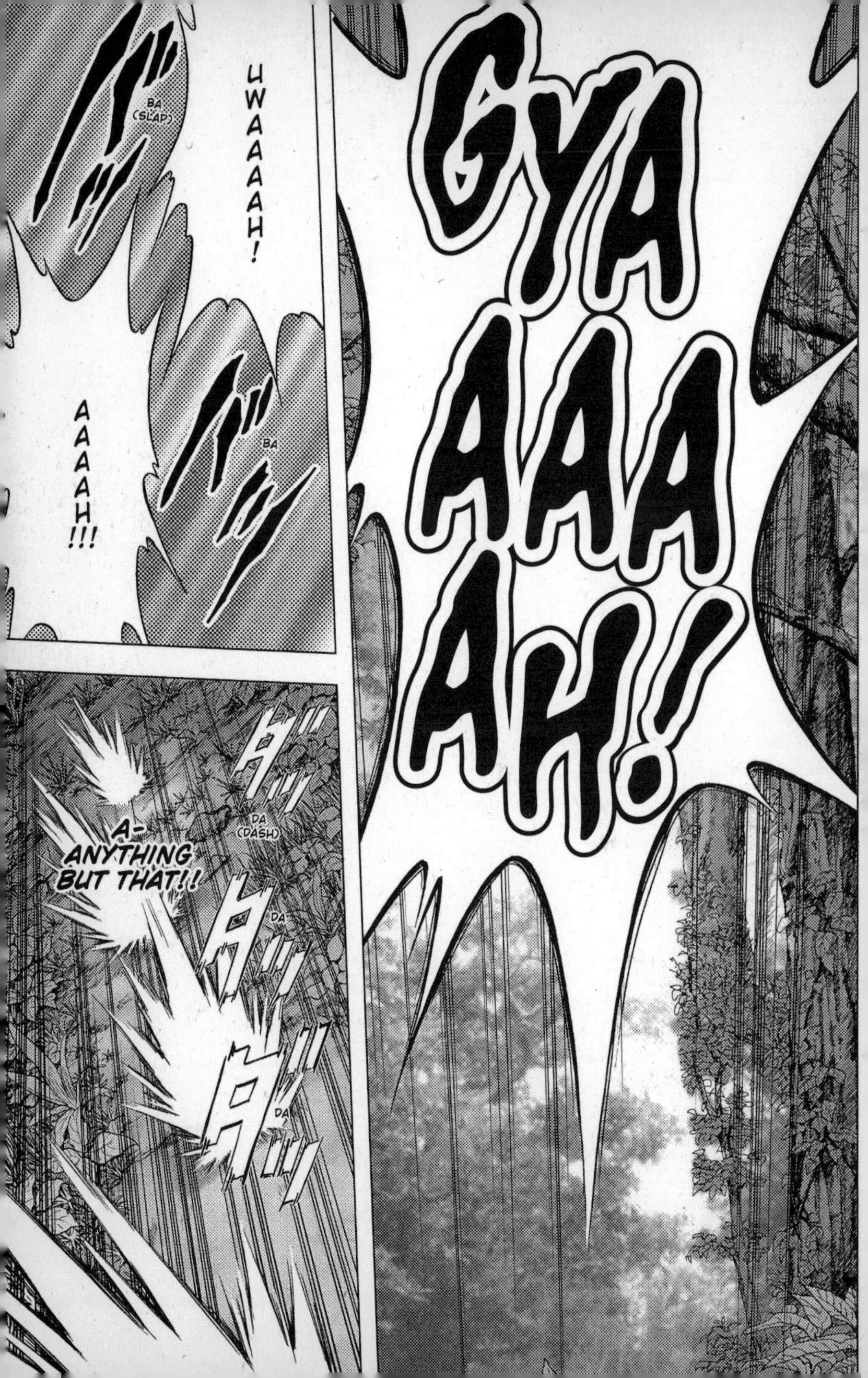
GYAAAAAAH!!
UWAAAAAH!
BA (SLAP)
BA
AAAAAH!!!
DA (DASH)
DA
DA
A- ANYTHING BUT THAT!!

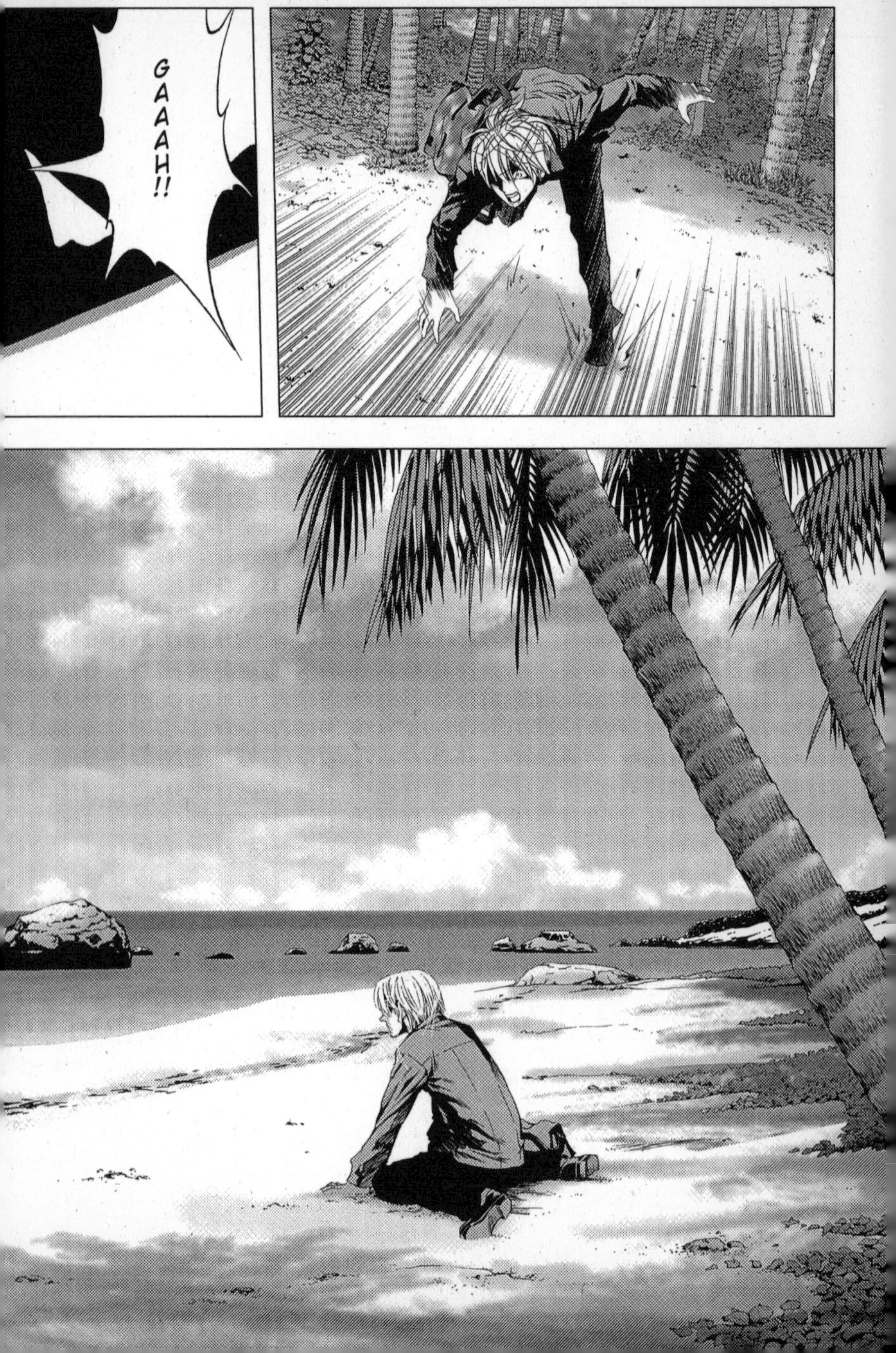
GAAAAH!!

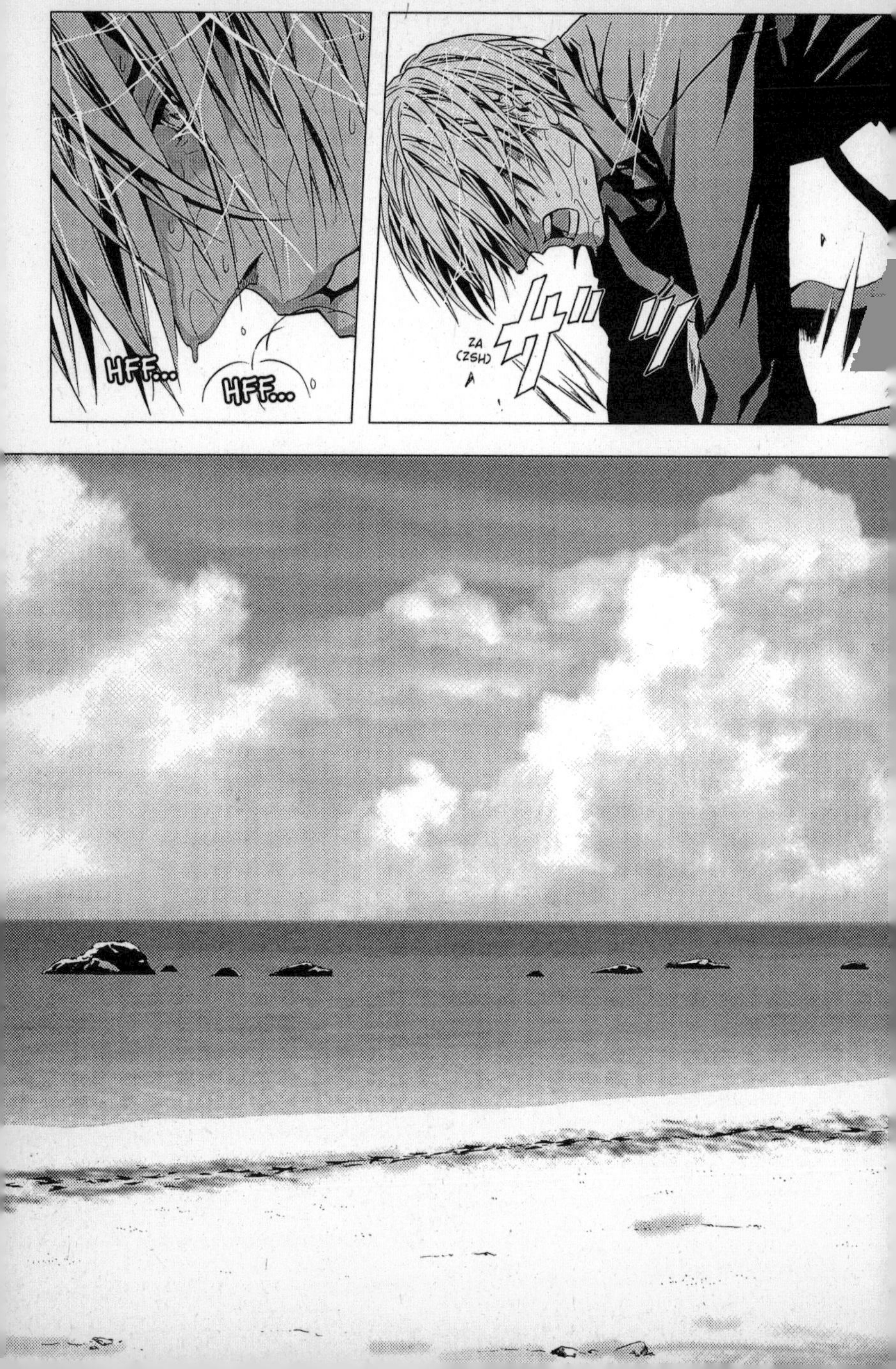
ザッ
ZA (ZSH)
HFF...
HFF...

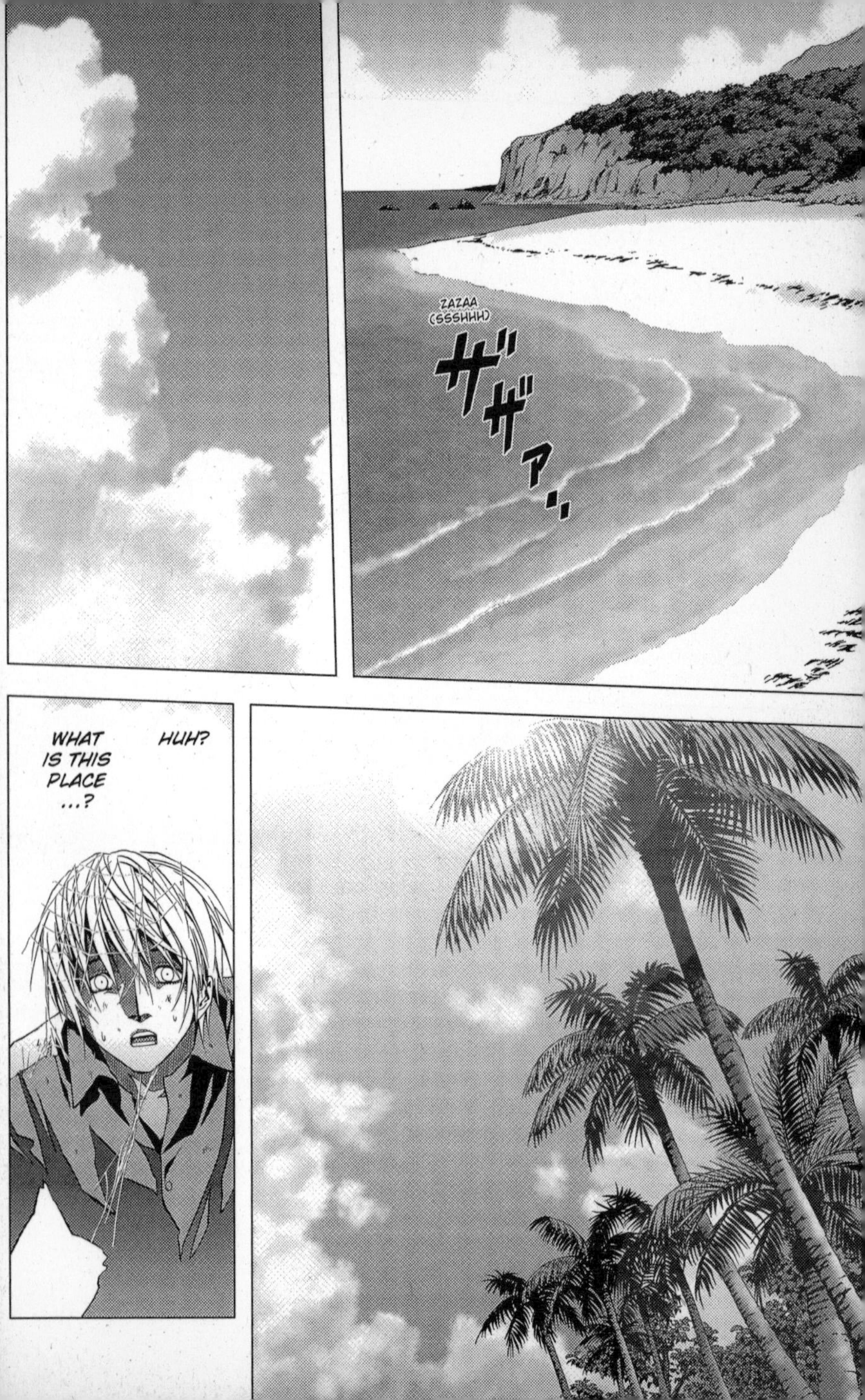
ZAZAA (SSSHHH)
ザザァ
HUH?
WHAT IS THIS PLACE ...?

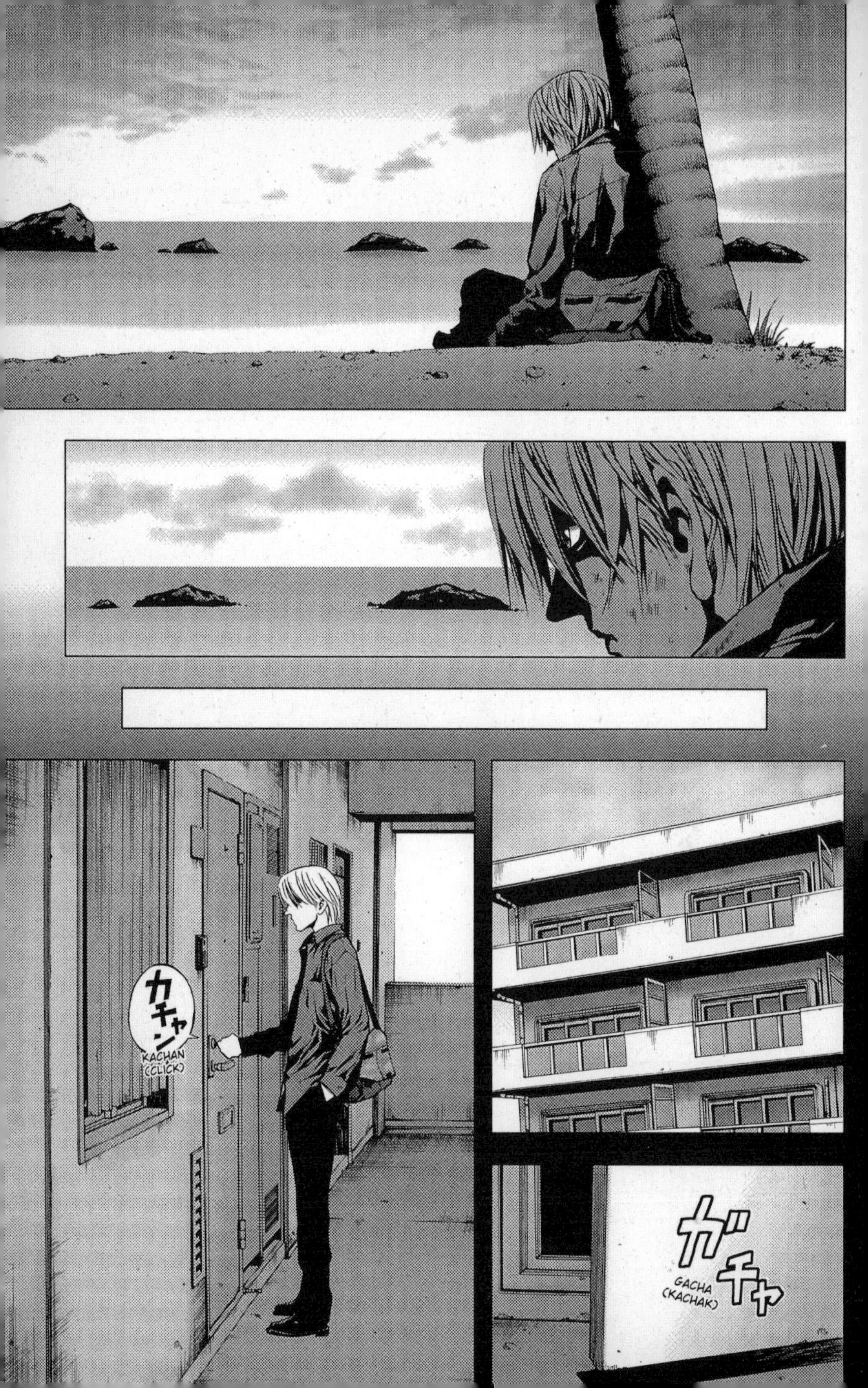
ガチャ
GACHA (KACHAK)
カチャン
KACHAN (CLICK)

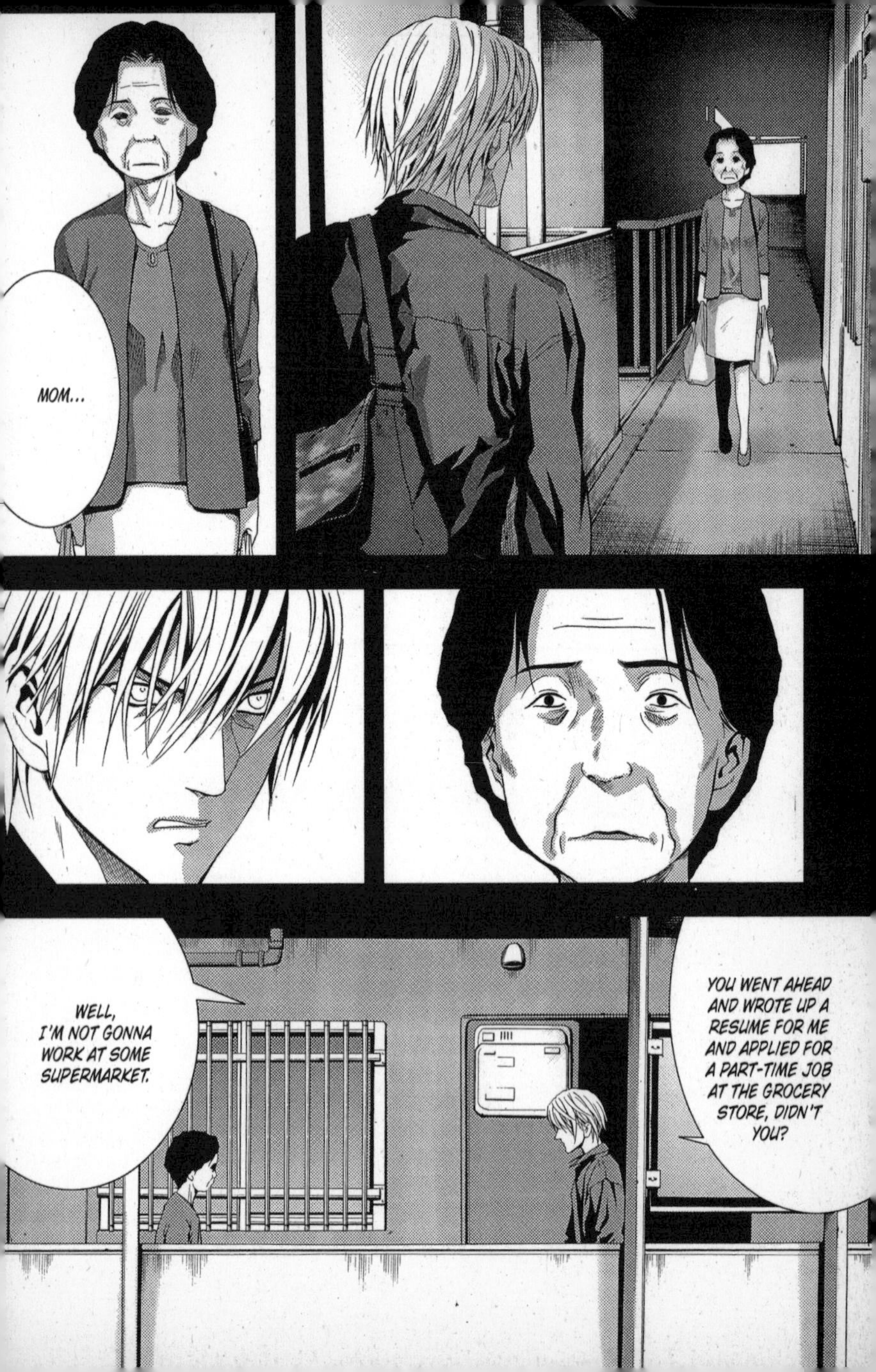
MOM...
YOU WENT AHEAD AND WROTE UP A RESUME FOR ME AND APPLIED FOR A PART-TIME JOB AT THE GROCERY STORE, DIDN'T YOU?
WELL, I'M NOT GONNA WORK AT SOME SUPERMARKET.

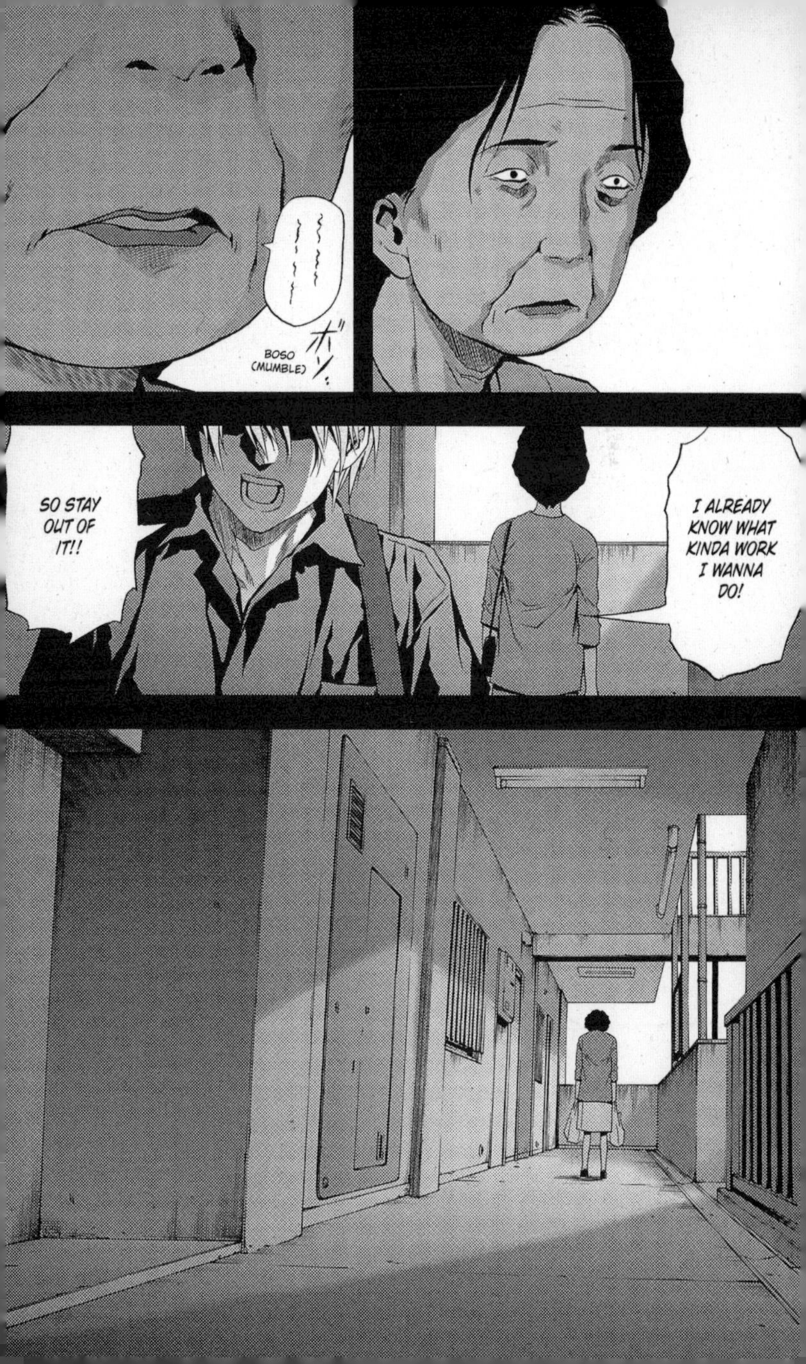
ボソ
BOSO (MUMBLE)
I ALREADY KNOW WHAT KINDA WORK I WANNA DO!
SO STAY OUT OF IT!!

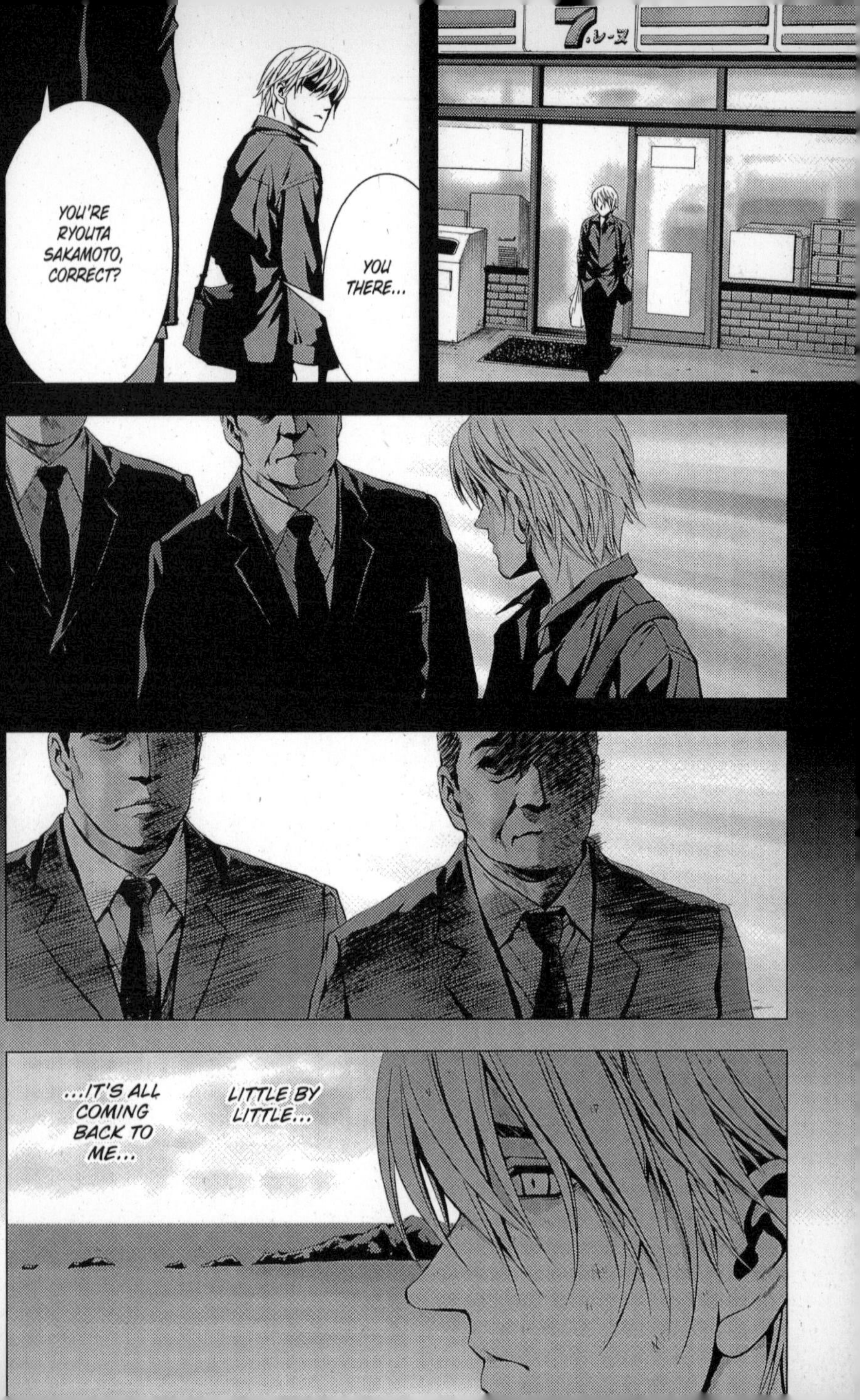
YOU THERE...
YOU'RE RYOUTA SAKAMOTO, CORRECT?
LITTLE BY LITTLE...
...IT'S ALL COMING BACK TO ME...

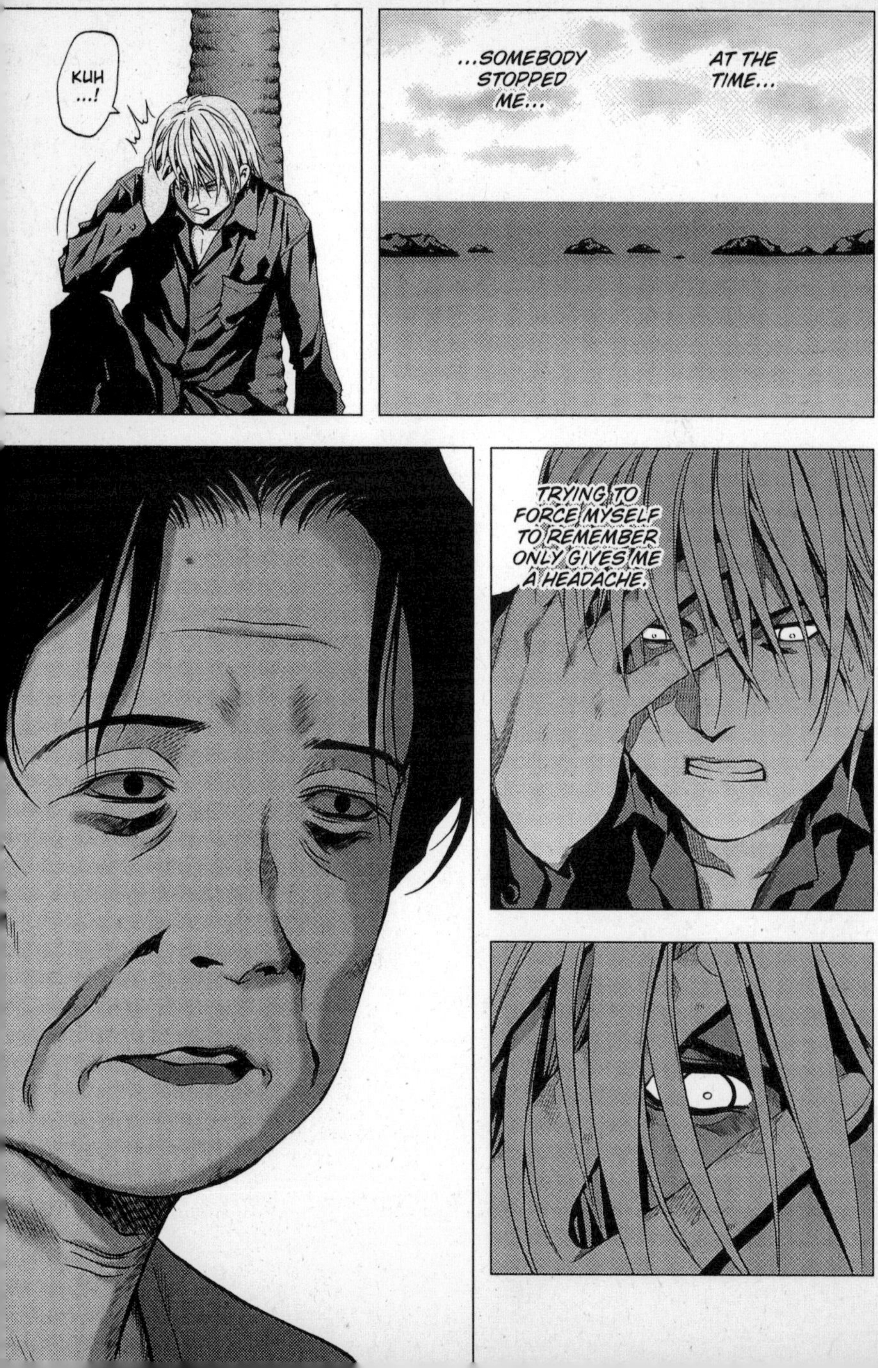
AT THE TIME...
...SOMEBODY STOPPED ME...
KUH ...!
TRYING TO FORCE MYSELF TO REMEMBER ONLY GIVES ME A HEADACHE.

TCH!

ZAZAA (SSSHHH)
ザザァ

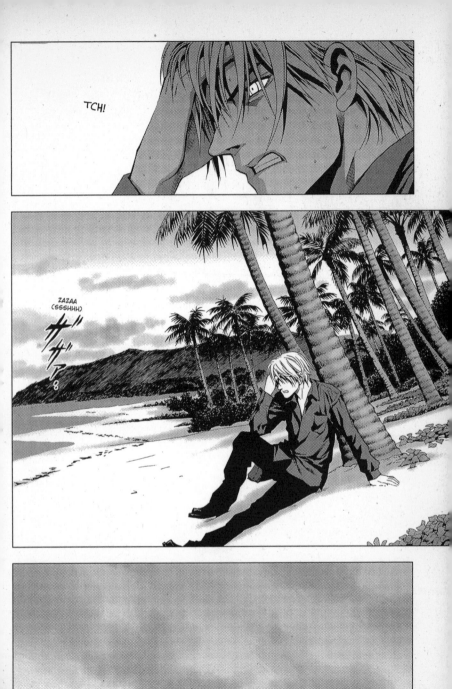

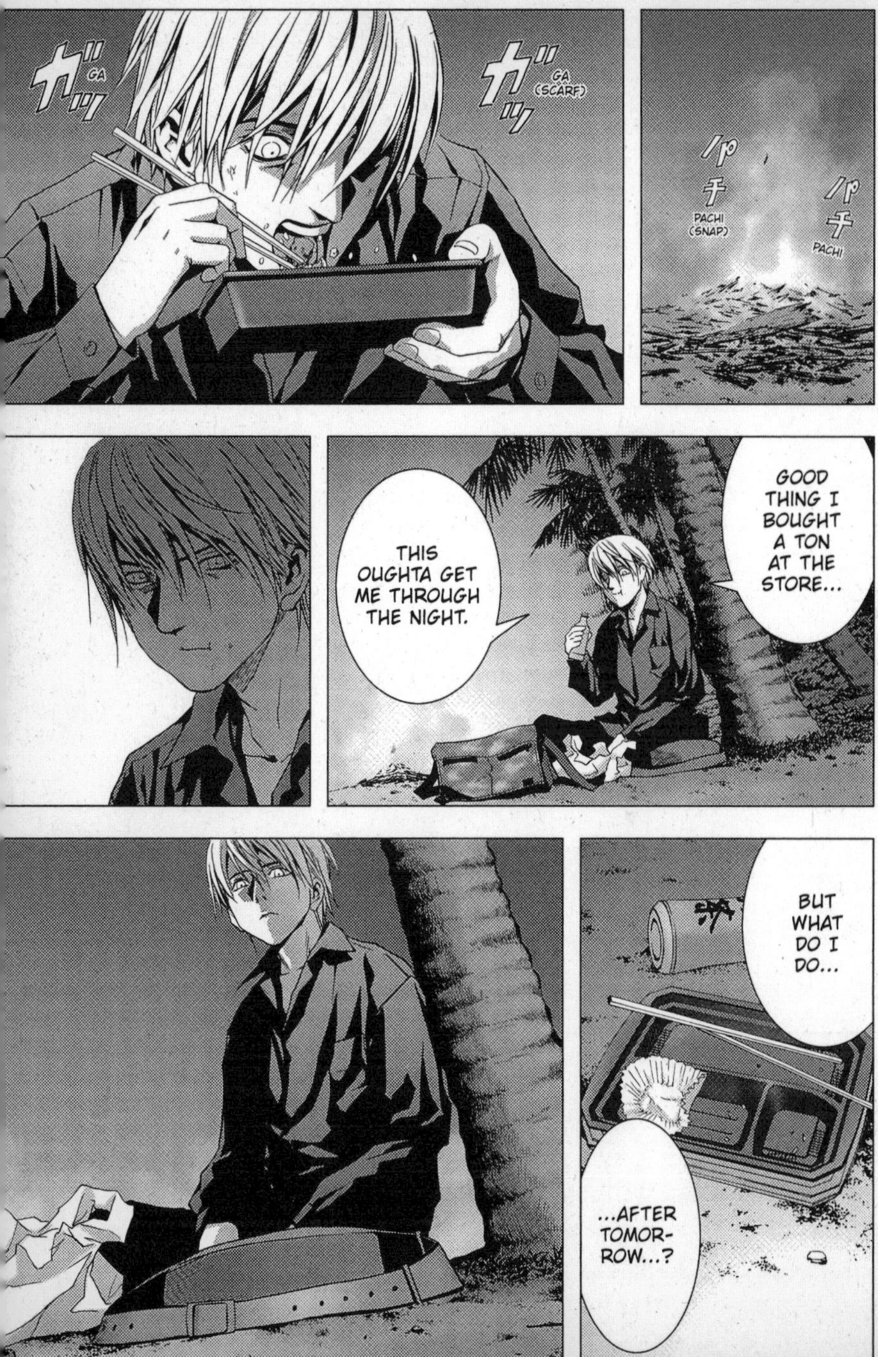
パチ
PACHI
パチ
PACHI (SNAP)
ガッ
GA (SCARF)
ガッ
GA
GOOD THING I BOUGHT A TON AT THE STORE...
THIS OUGHTA GET ME THROUGH THE NIGHT.
BUT WHAT DO I DO...
...AFTER TOMORROW...?

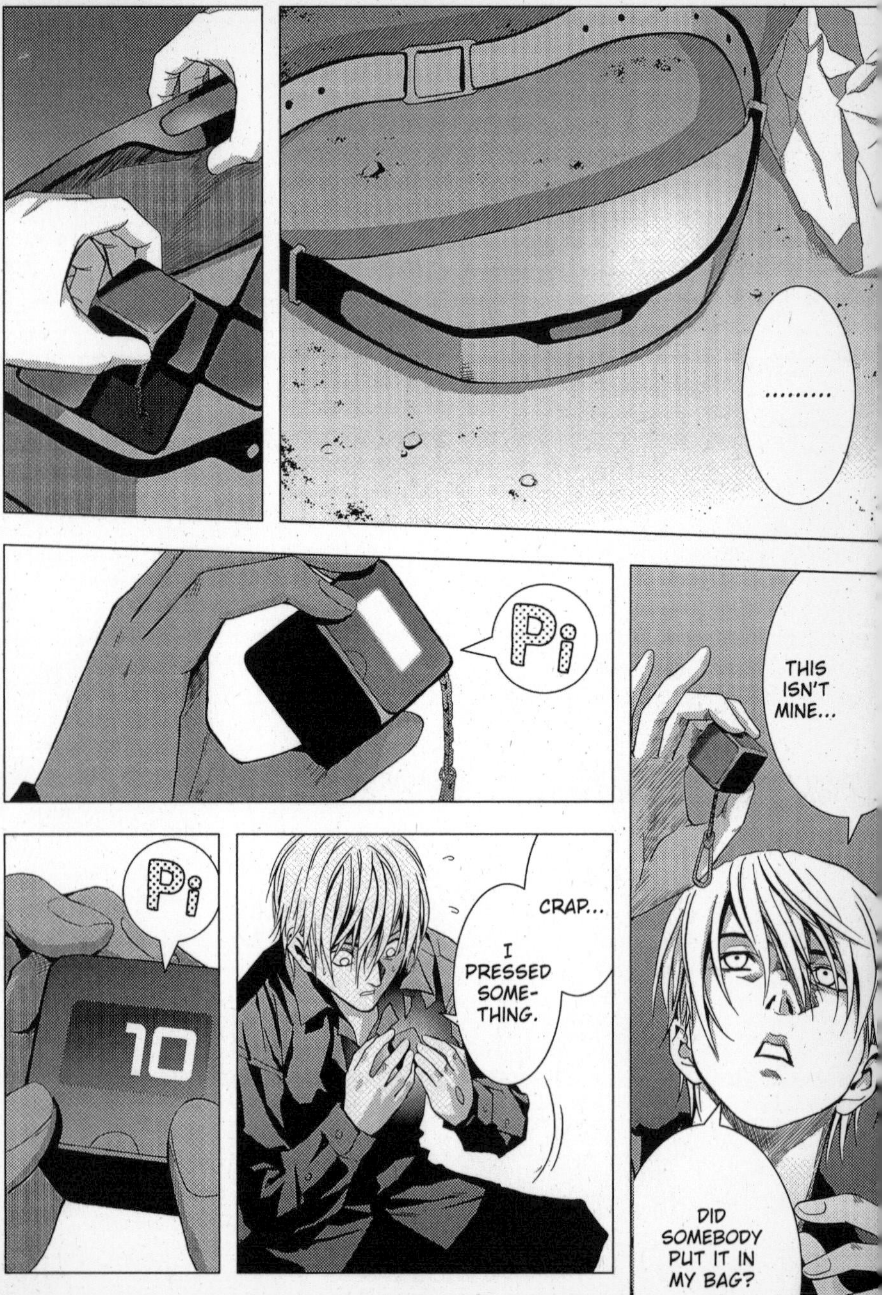
....
THIS ISN'T MINE...
DID SOMEBODY PUT IT IN MY BAG?
Pi
CRAP...
I PRESSED SOMETHING.
Pi
10

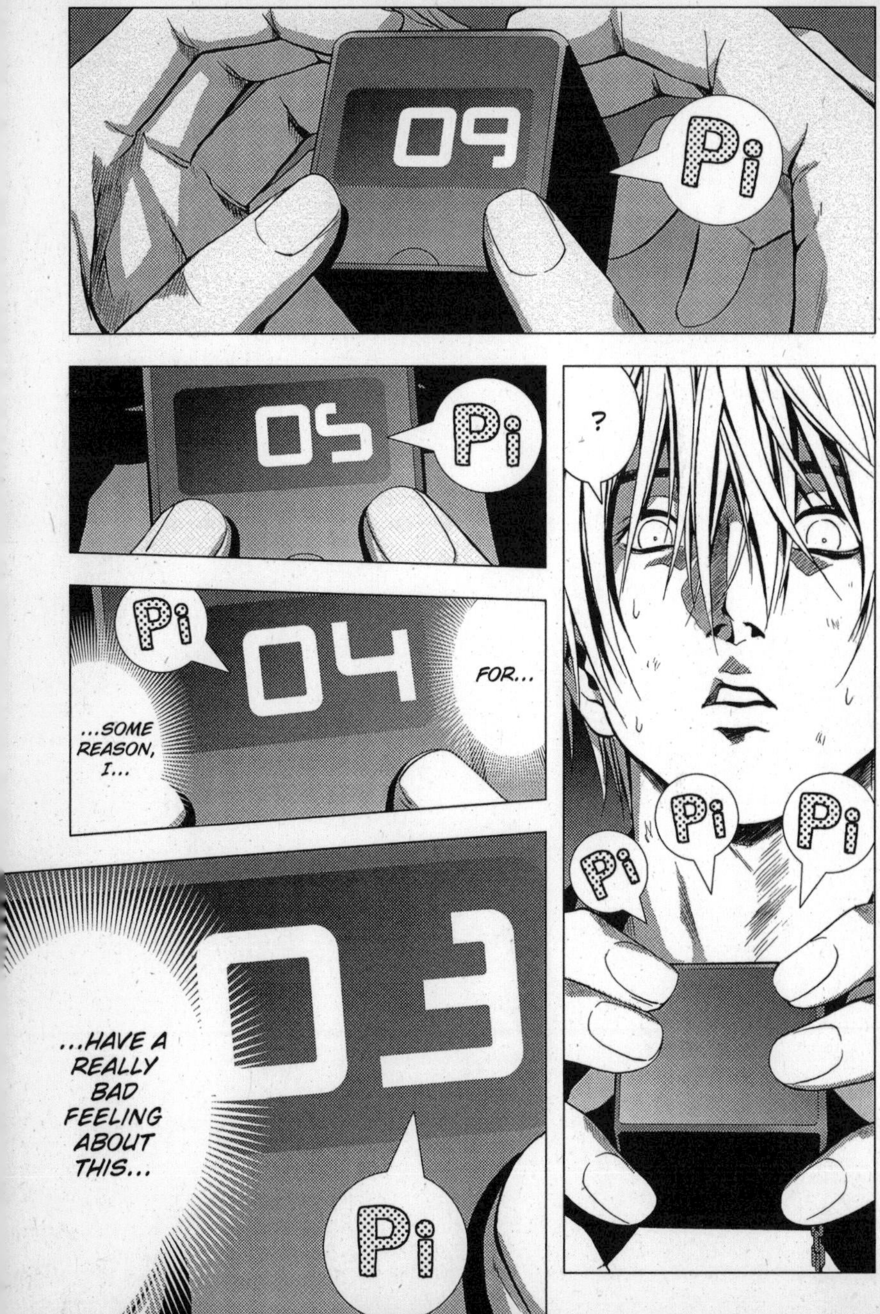

09
Pi
?
Pi
Pi
Pi
05
Pi
FOR...
Pi
04
...SOME REASON, I...
03
...HAVE A REALLY BAD FEELING ABOUT THIS...
Pi

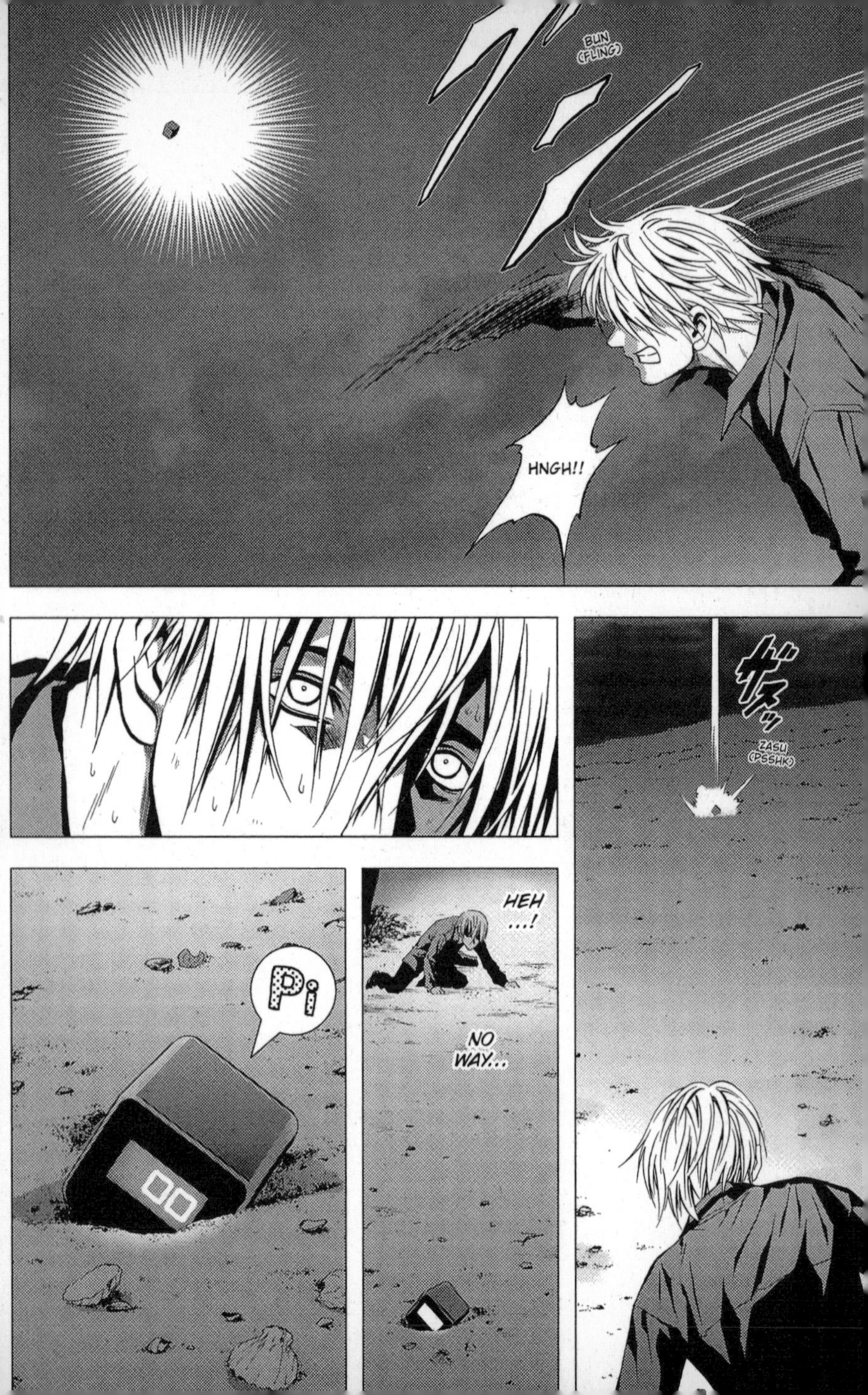
BUN (FLING)
HNGH!!
ZASU (PSSHK)
...
HEH ...!
NO WAY...
Pi

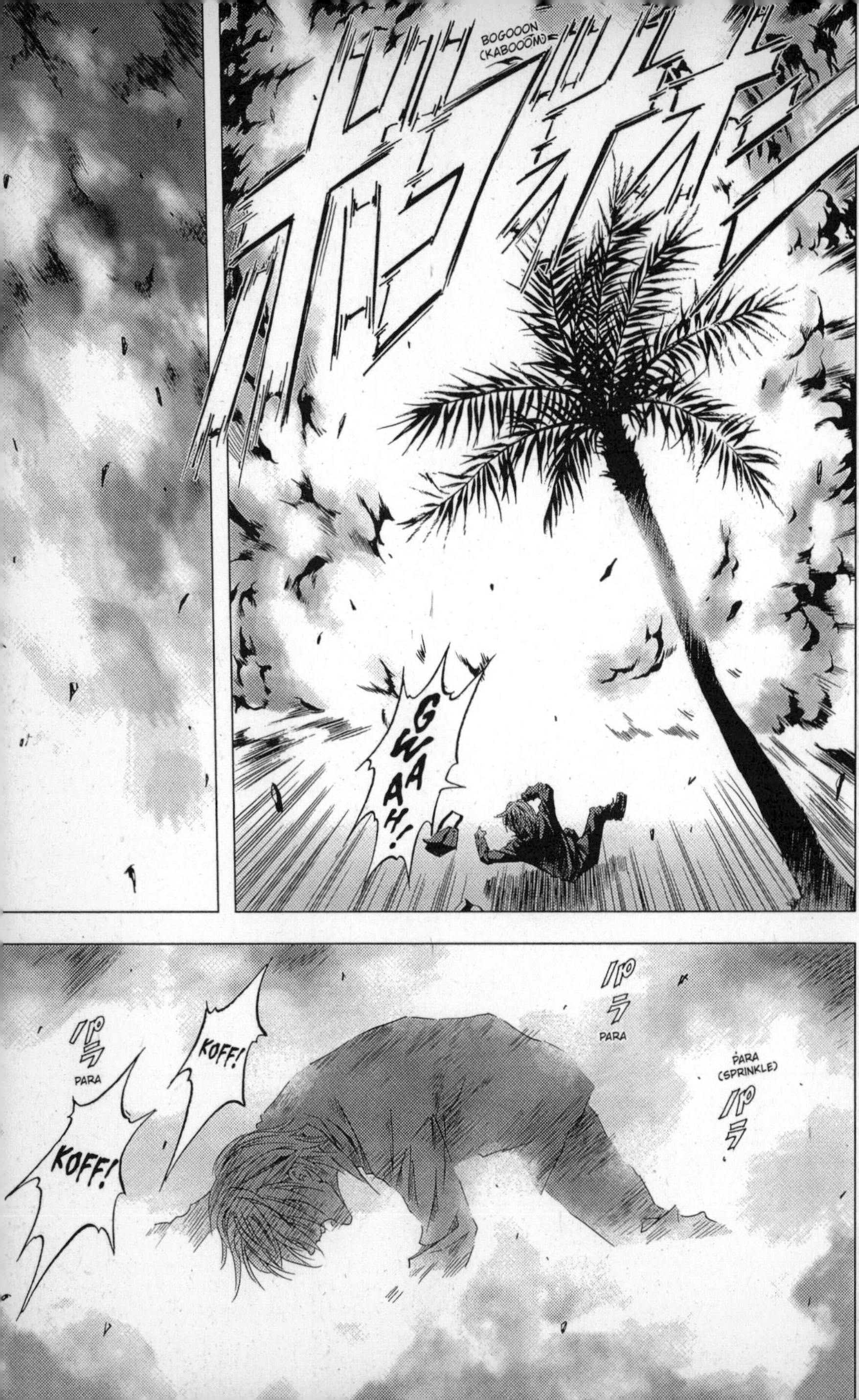
BOGOOON (KABOOOM)
GWAAH!
パラ
PARA (SPRINKLE)
パラ
PARA
KOFF!
パラ
PARA
KOFF!

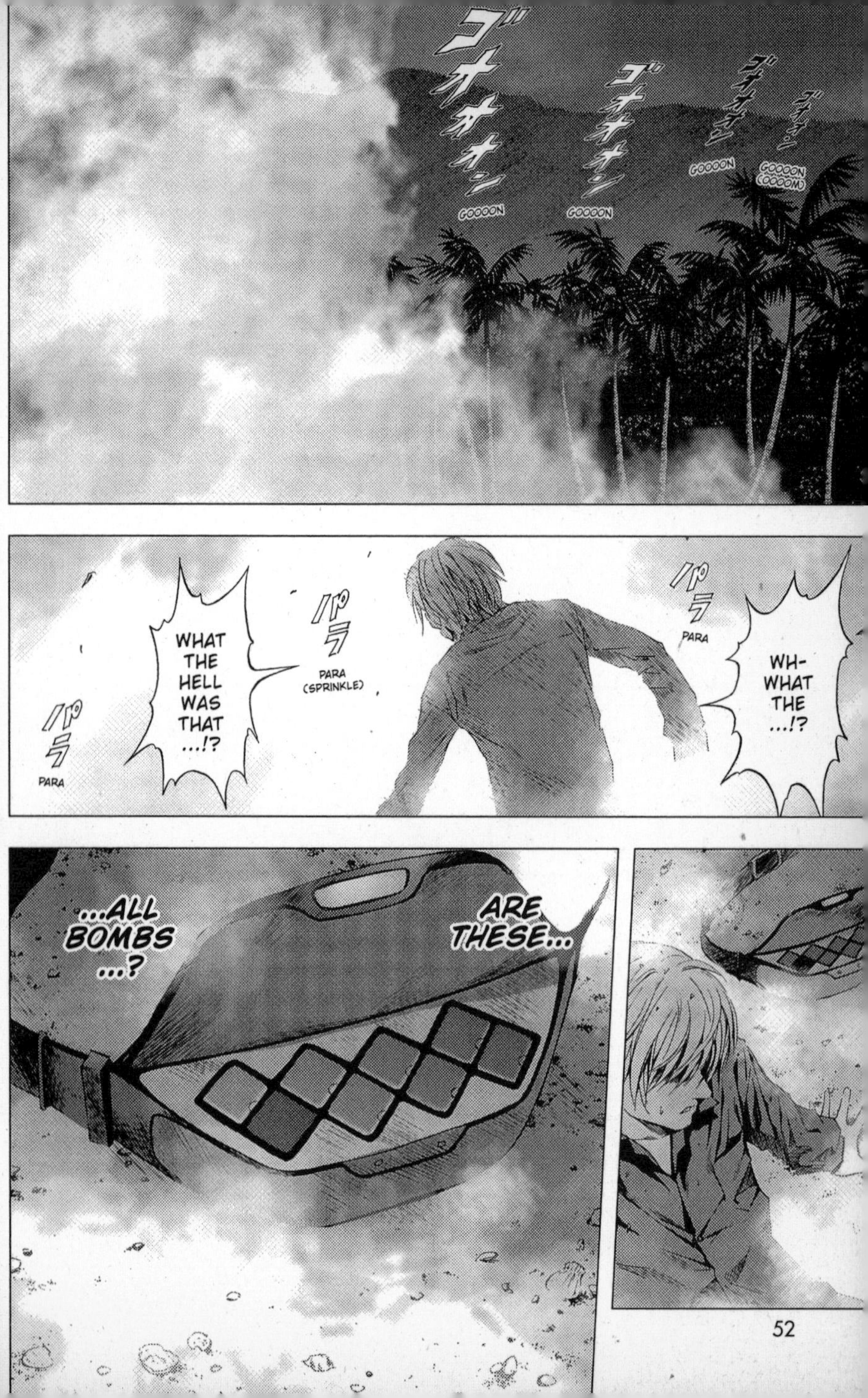

ゴオオン
GOOOON (GOOOM)
ゴオオオン
GOOOON
ゴオオオン
GOOOON
ゴオオオン
GOOOON
パラ
PARA
WH- WHAT THE ...!?
パラ
PARA (SPRINKLE)
WHAT THE HELL WAS THAT ...!?
パラ
PARA
ARE THESE...
...ALL BOMBS ...?

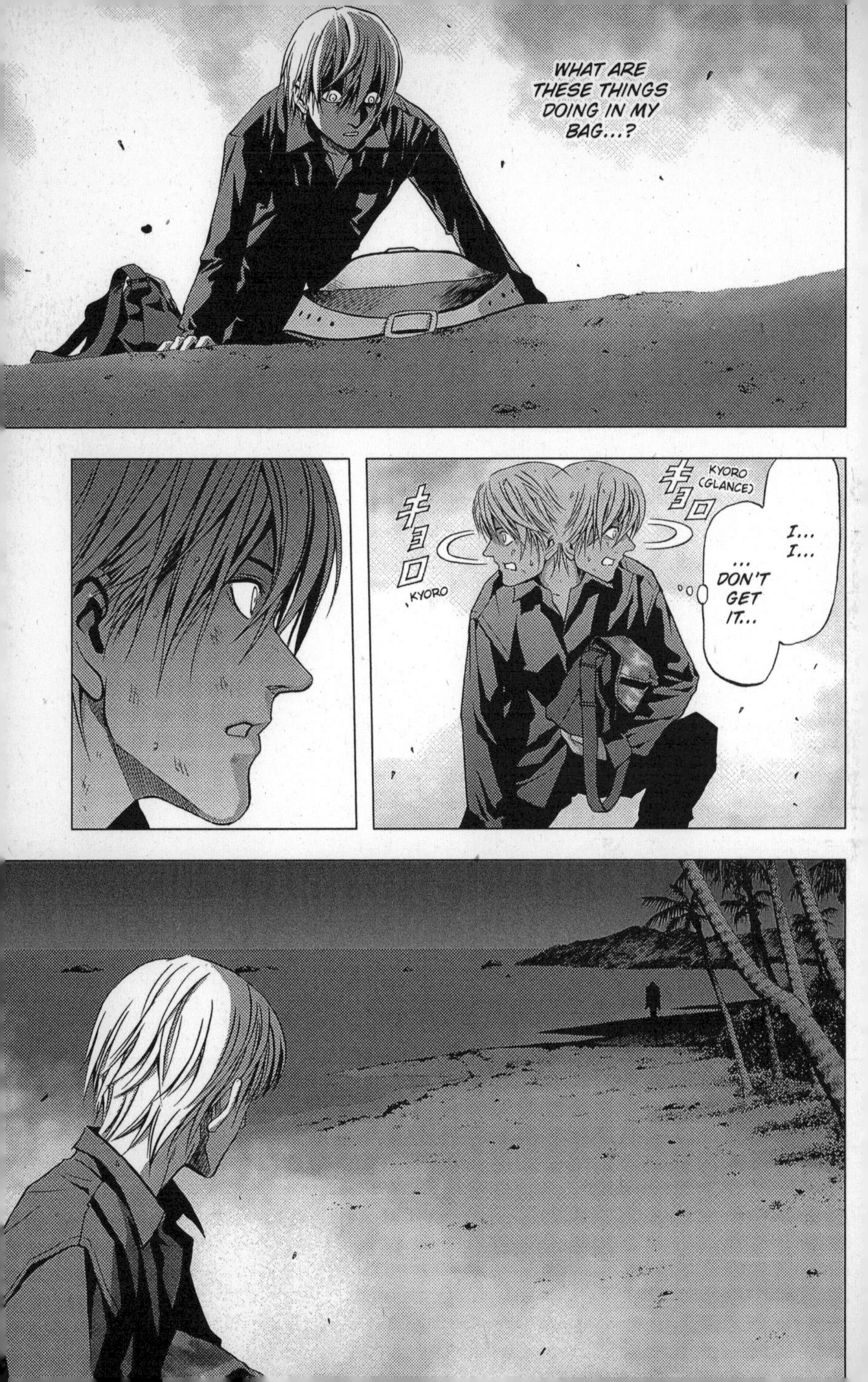
WHAT ARE THESE THINGS DOING IN MY BAG...?
I... I... ...DON'T GET IT...
キョロ KYORO (GLANCE)
キョロ KYORO

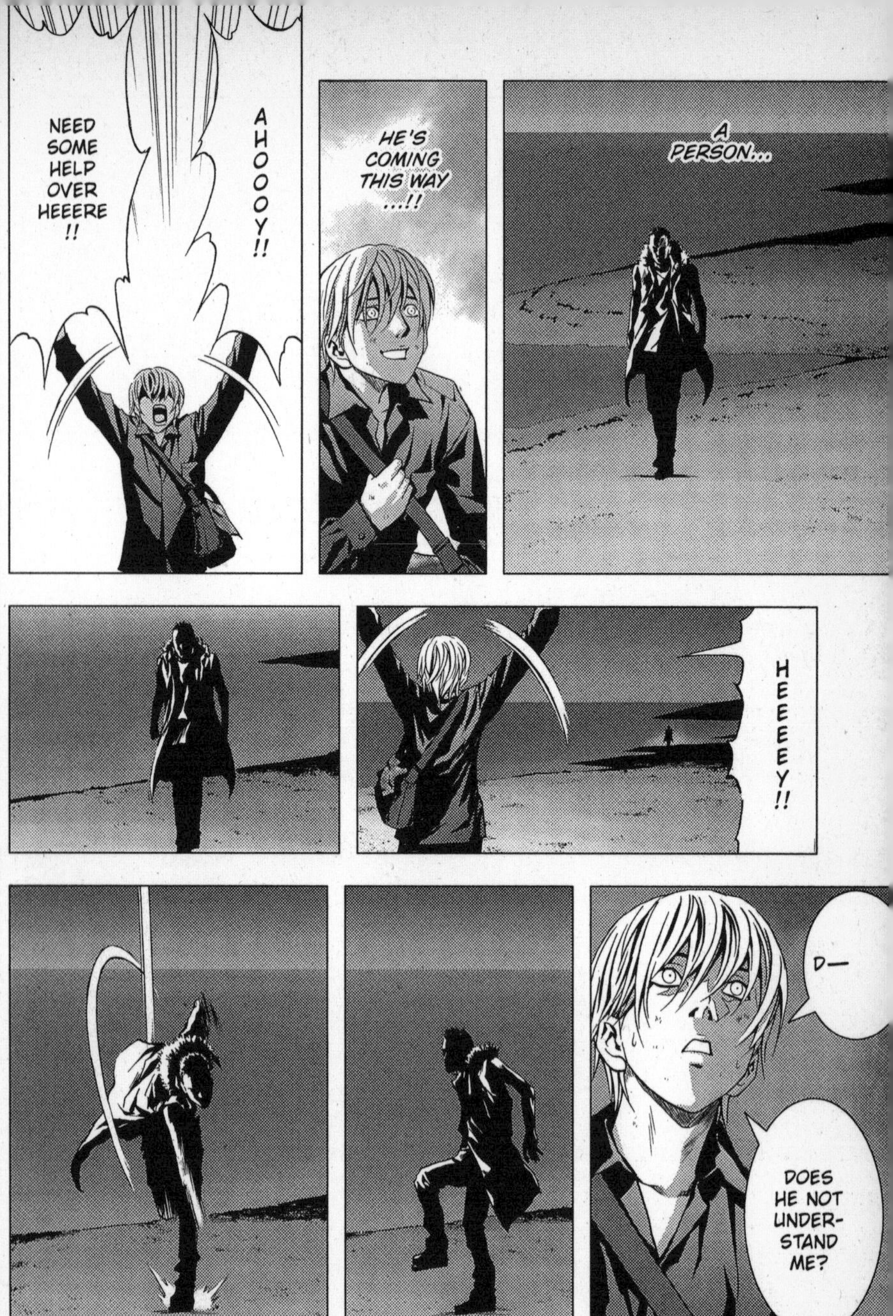
A PERSON...
HE'S COMING THIS WAY ...!!
AHOOOOY!!
NEED SOME HELP OVER HEEERE !!
HEEEEEY!!
D—
DOES HE NOT UNDER-STAND ME?

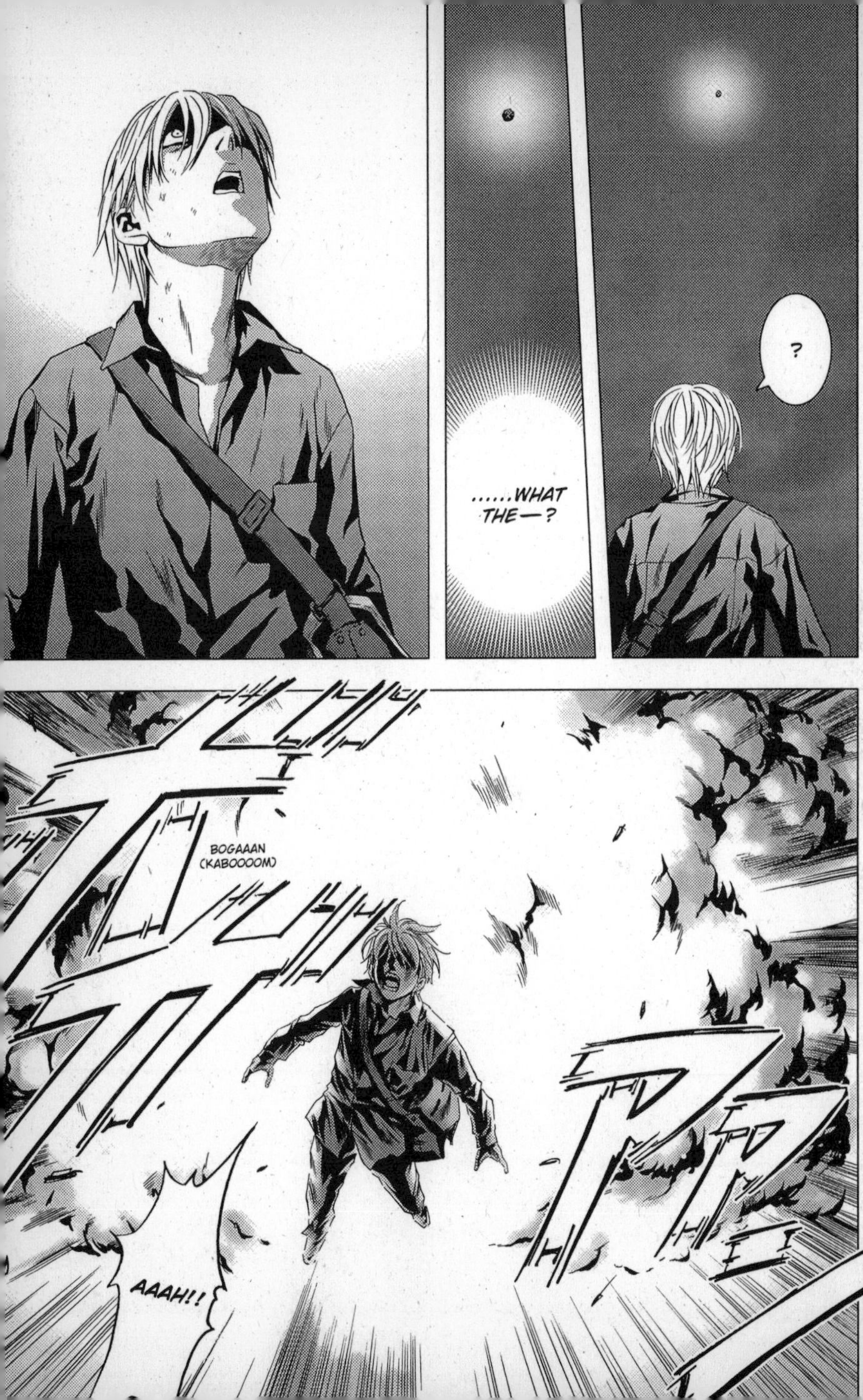
?
......WHAT THE—?
BOGAAAN (KABOOOOM)
AAAH!!

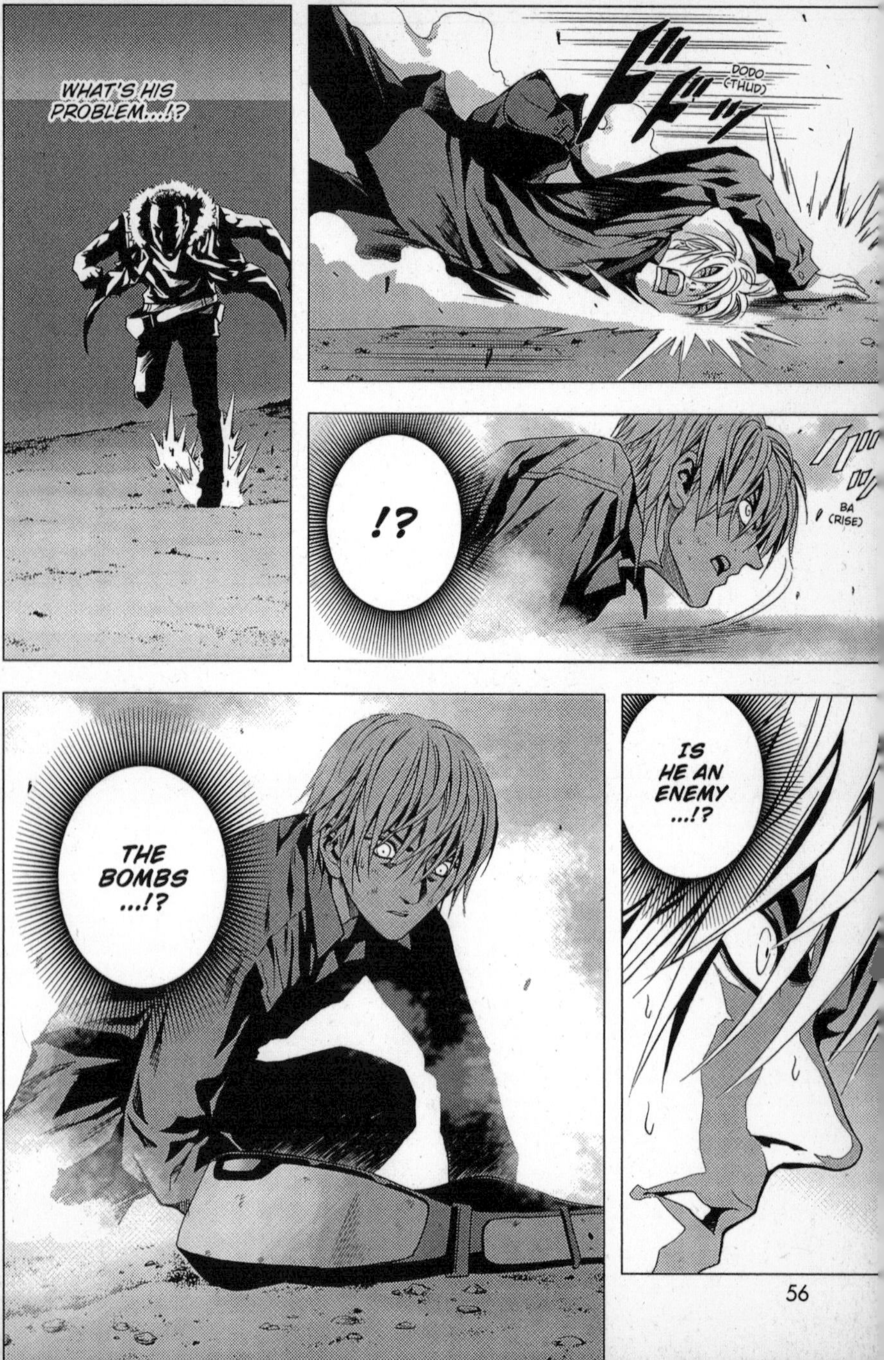
DODO
(THUD)
!?
BA
(RISE)
WHAT'S HIS PROBLEM...!?
IS HE AN ENEMY ...!?
THE BOMBS ...!?

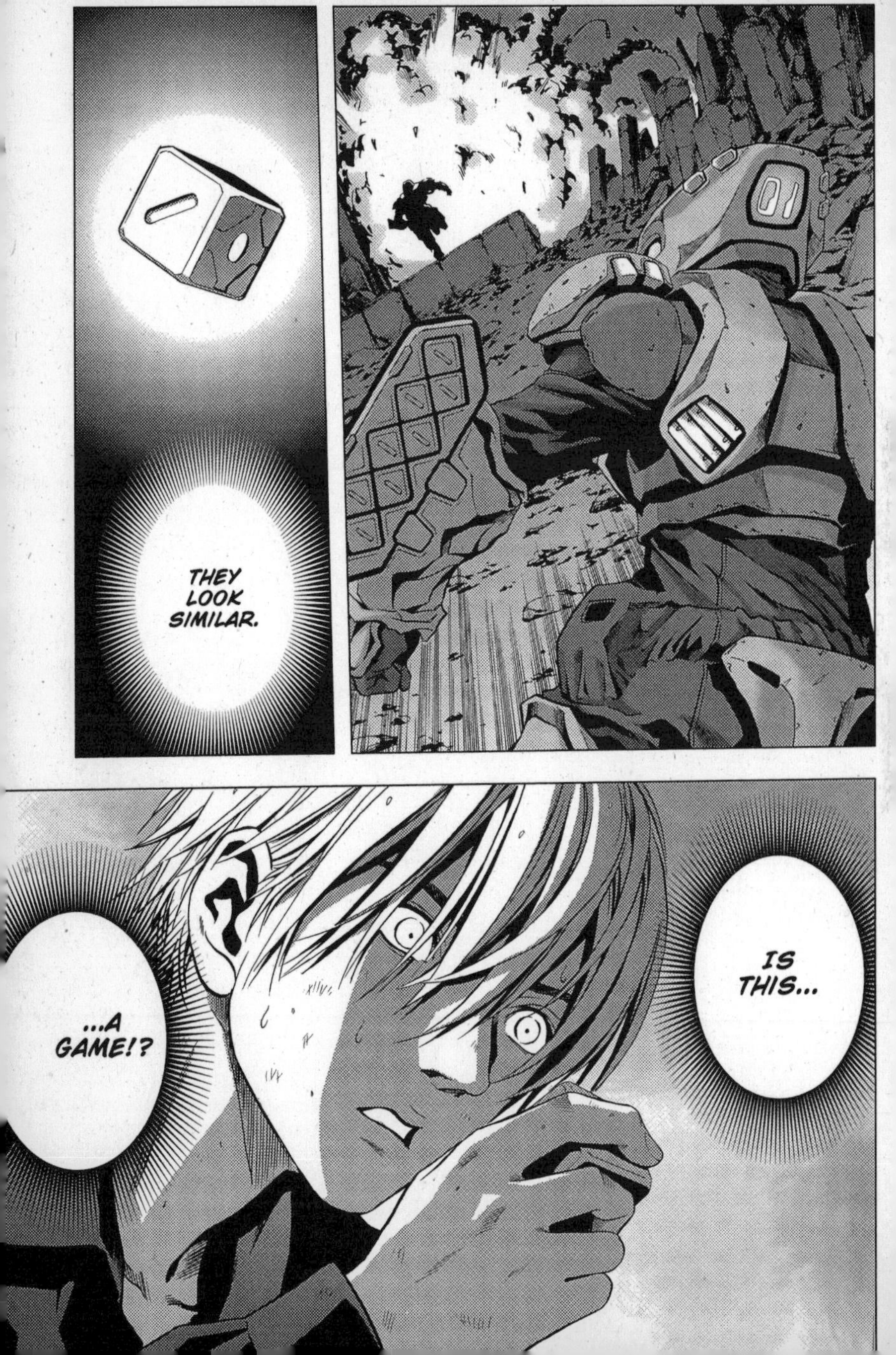
THEY LOOK SIMILAR.
IS THIS...
...A GAME!?

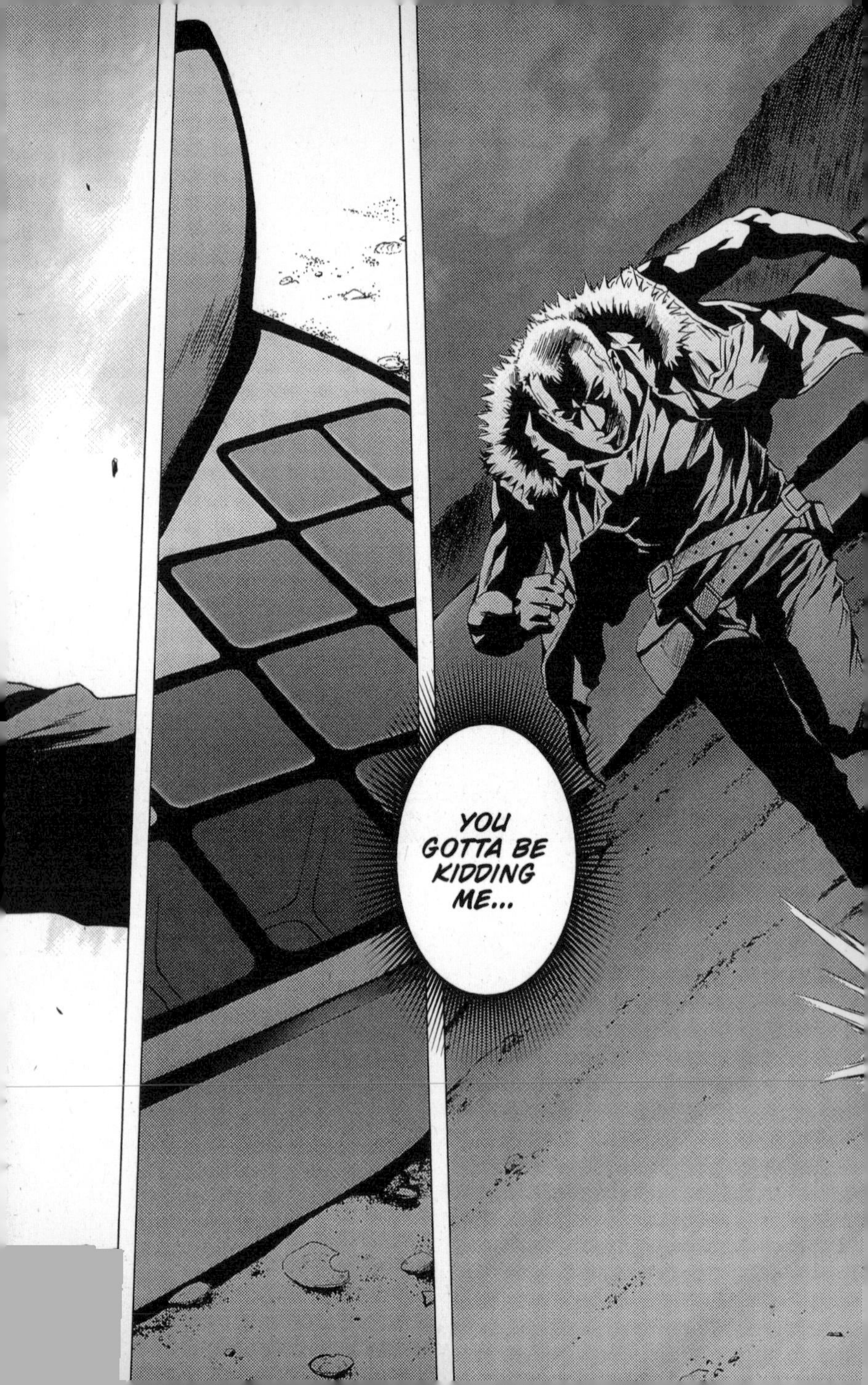
YOU GOTTA BE KIDDING ME...

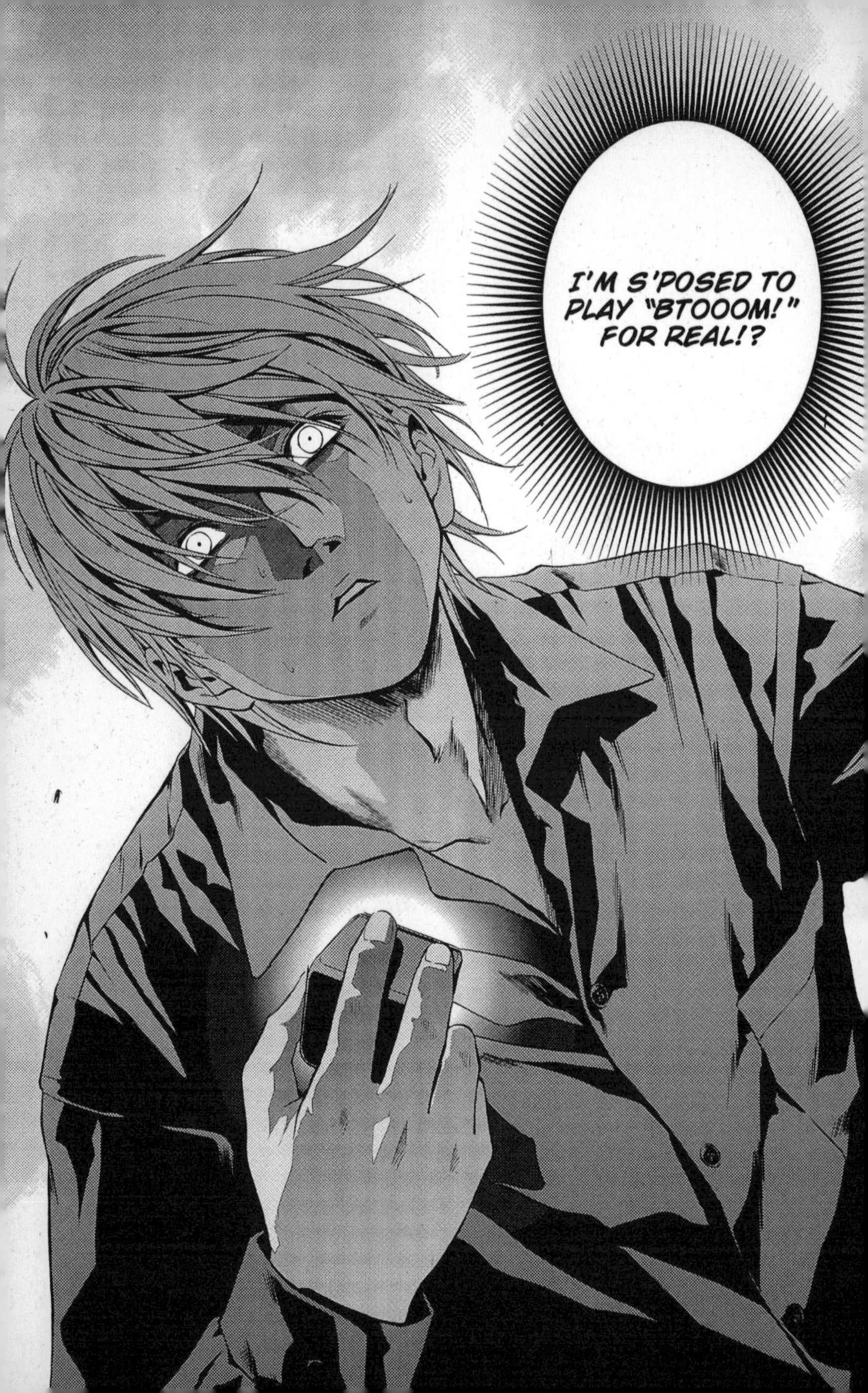
I'M S'POSED TO PLAY "BTOOOM!" FOR REAL!?

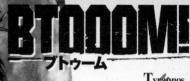

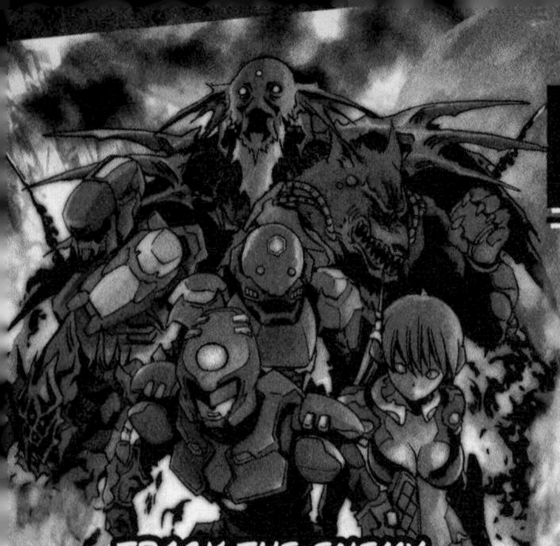

BTOOOM!

ブトゥーム

Tyrannos JAPAN

SUPPLIER: TYRANNOS JAPAN	
DEVELOPER: TYRANNOS JAPAN	
GENRE: 3RD-PERSON SHOOTER	
MSRP: ¥7,329 (TAX INCLUDED)	
AGE RATING: 18+	
ONLINE PLAY: ONE PLAYER	
SYSTEM LINK: 2~32 PEOPLE	
OTHER: LIVE VISION LINKUP	

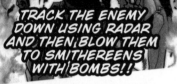

TRACK THE ENEMY DOWN USING RADAR AND THEN BLOW THEM TO SMITHEREENS WITH BOMBS!!

USE A VARIETY OF EXPLOSIVES, CALLED BIMS, TO FIGHT IN THIS *BATTLE ROYALE*-STYLE ACTION GAME. IT'S IMPORTANT TO KNOW EACH EXPLOSIVE'S SIGNATURE CAPABILITY TO USE THEM MOST EFFECTIVELY, BUT LET'S JUST SAY IT'S YOUR ENEMY-LOCATOR RADAR THAT IS STRATEGICALLY INDISPENSABLE.

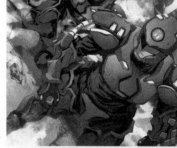

MASTER A VARIETY OF BIMS!!

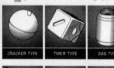

CRACKER TYPE
TIMER TYPE
GAS TYPE
HOMING TYPE
IMPLOSION TYPE
REMOTE TYPE

THE BIMS YOU START WITH ARE DECIDED AT RANDOM, AND IT'S ESSENTIAL THAT YOU MASTER HOW TO WIELD THEM AND THEIR MYRIAD ABILITIES. AFTER DEFEATING AN ENEMY, YOU CAN GAIN DIFFERENT TYPES OF BIMS!

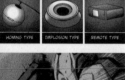

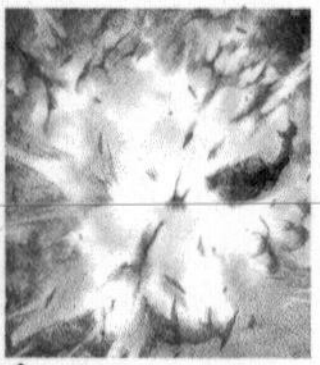

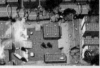

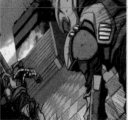

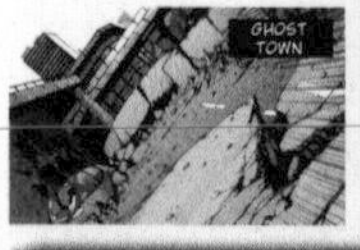

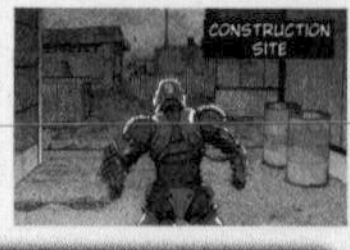

↑A TIMER TYPE DETONATES WITH FLAIR!

←WORK WITH YOUR TEAMMATES TO FORCE THE ENEMY INTO A TRAP!

FORM TEAMS OF UP TO FOUR WHILE PARTICIPATING WITH UP TO EIGHT TEAMS!

THE CONVOLUTED MAP IS NOTHING SHORT OF A MAZE!

WITH PLENTY OF OBSTRUCTIONS BLOCKING YOUR SIGHT, THE FIELD IS ALMOST LIKE A LABYRINTH. HIDE YOURSELF FROM ENEMY VIEW AND USE YOUR RADAR TO STRIKE BACK!!

GHOST TOWN

CONSTRUCTION SITE

GET READY FOR ITS WORLDWIDE RELEASE!!

BATTLE AGAINST INTERNATIONAL OPPONENTS AND EARN POINTS TO MOVE UP IN THE WORLD RANKINGS. BY FIGHTING STRONG TEAMS, YOU CAN INCREASE YOUR STATUS. YOU TOO CAN MAKE IT TO THE TOP!!

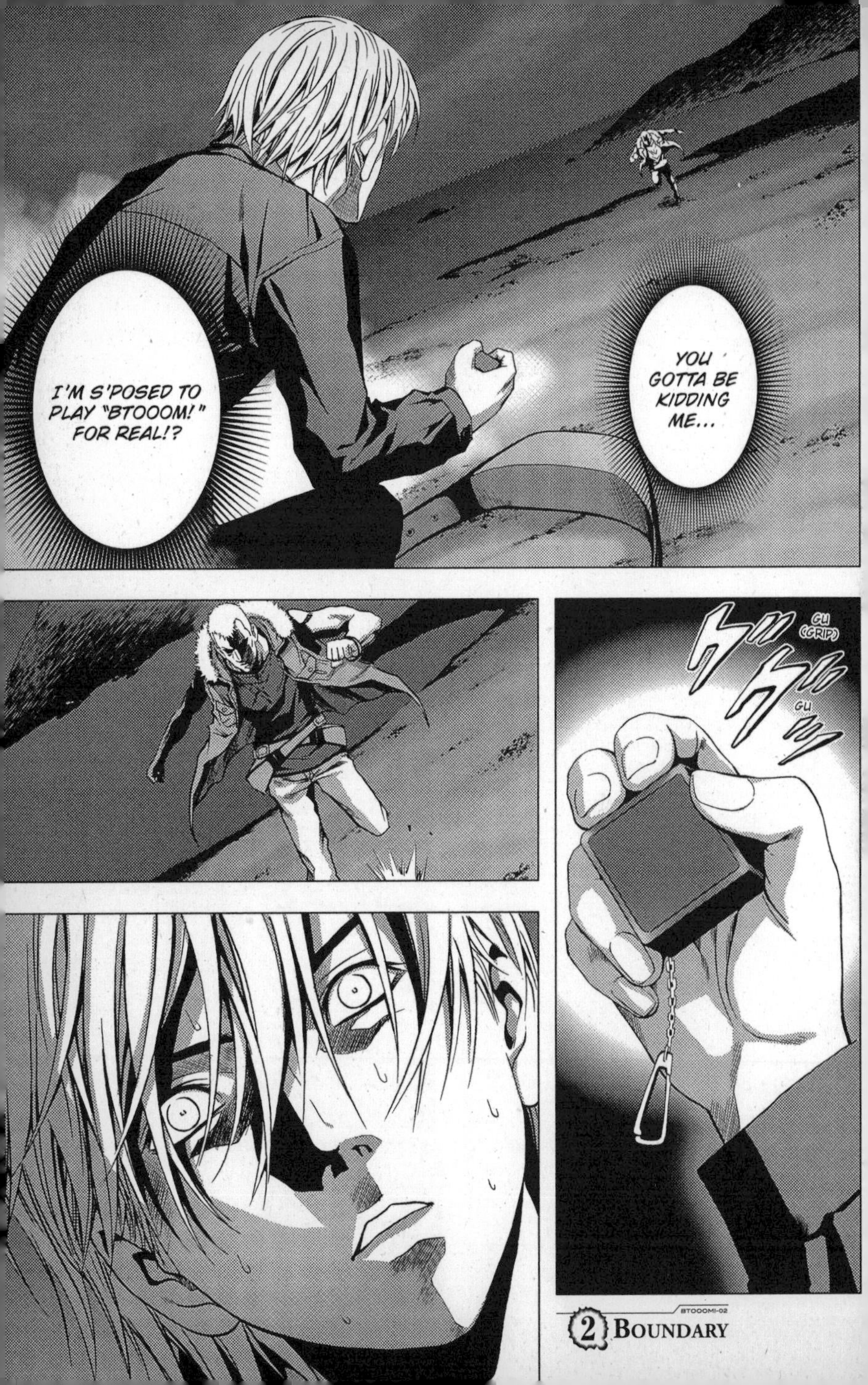
YOU GOTTA BE KIDDING ME...
I'M S'POSED TO PLAY "BTOOOM!" FOR REAL!?
GU (GRIP)
GU
BTOOOMI-02
2 BOUNDARY

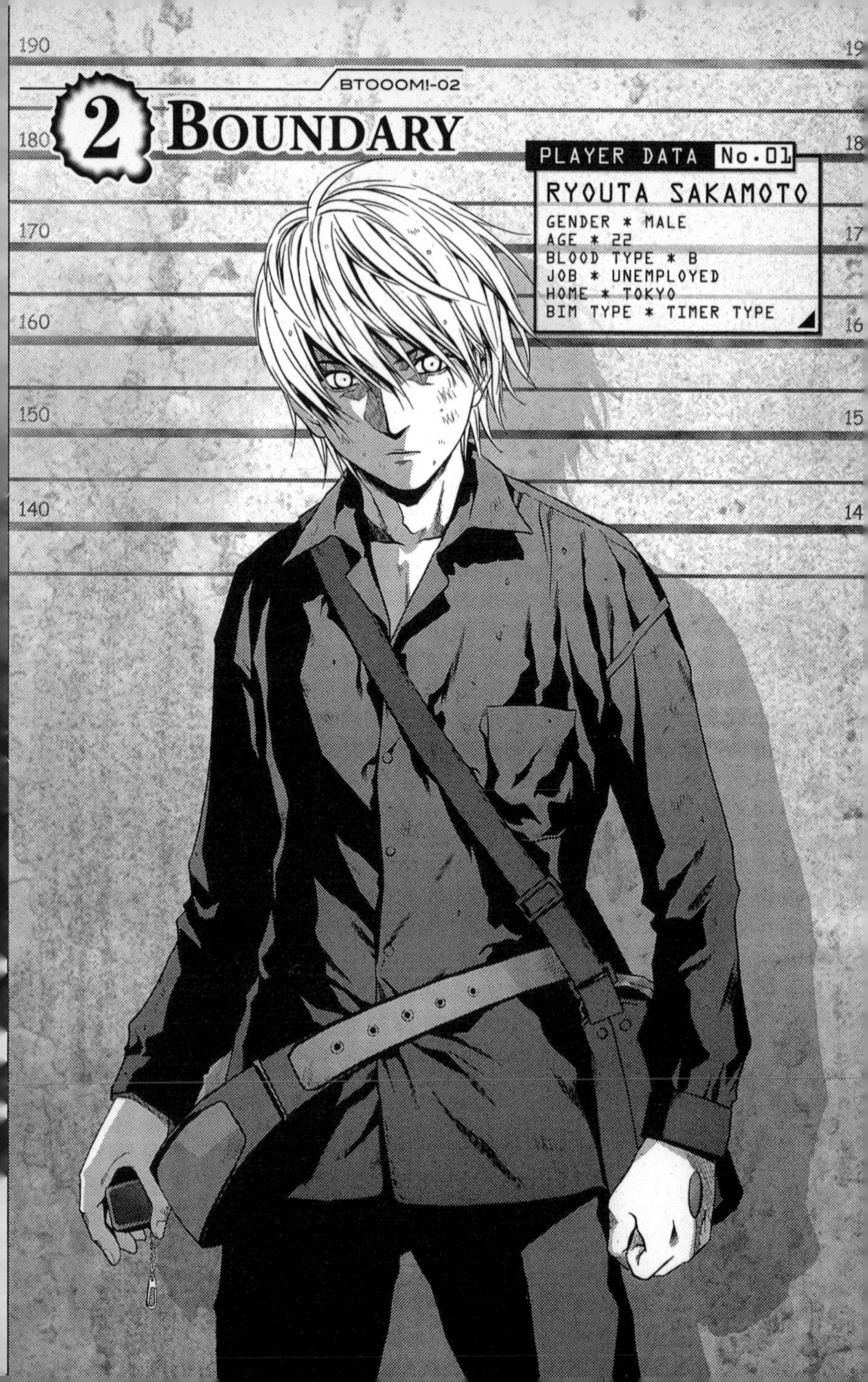
190
180
170
160
150
140
BTOOOM!-02
2 BOUNDARY
PLAYER DATA No.01
RYOUTA SAKAMOTO
GENDER * MALE
AGE * 22
BLOOD TYPE * B
JOB * UNEMPLOYED
HOME * TOKYO
BIM TYPE * TIMER TYPE

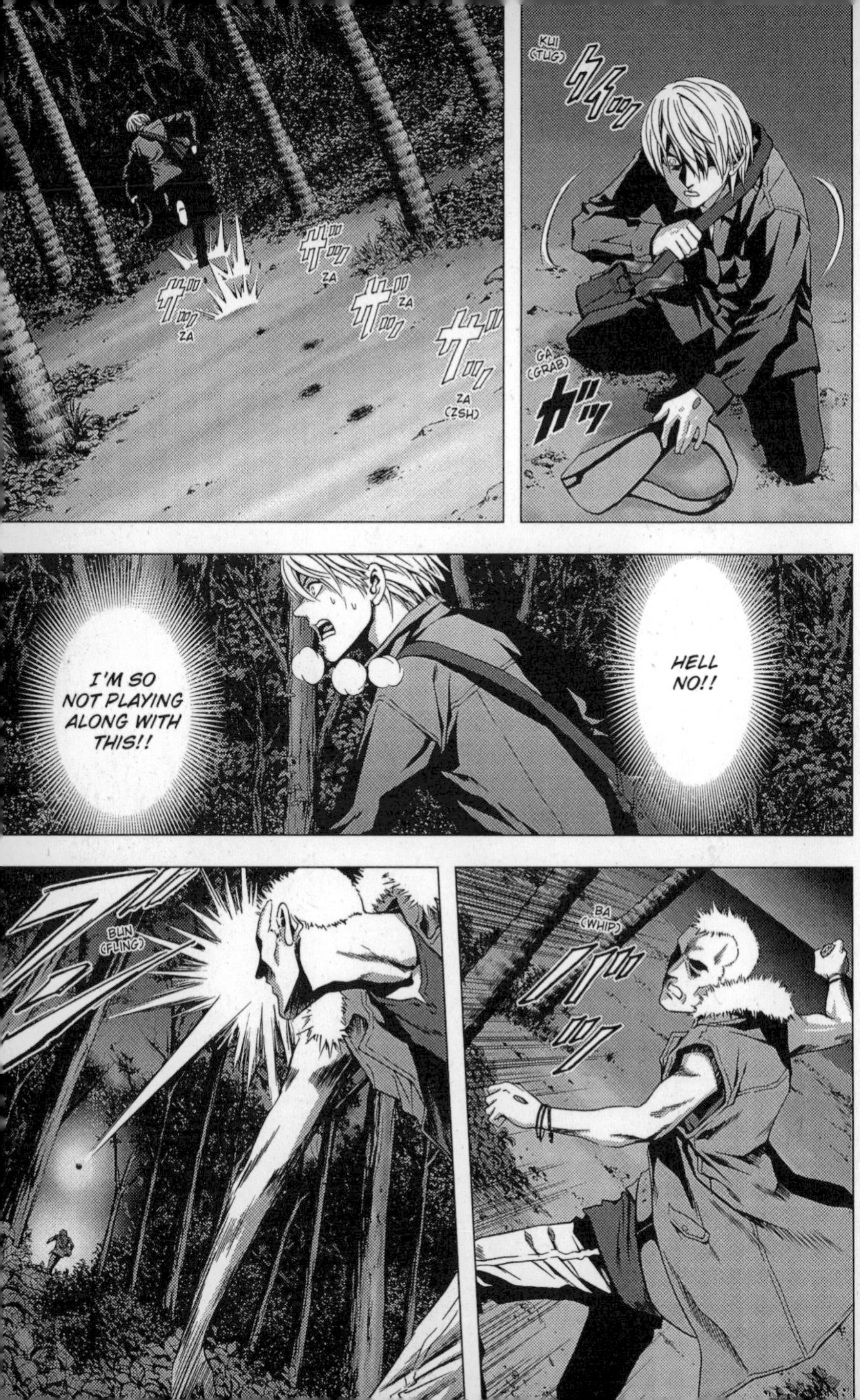
KUI
(TUG)
GA
(GRAB)
ZA
(ZSH)
ZA
ZA
ZA
HELL NO!!
I'M SO NOT PLAYING ALONG WITH THIS!!
BA
(WHIP)
BUN
(FLING)

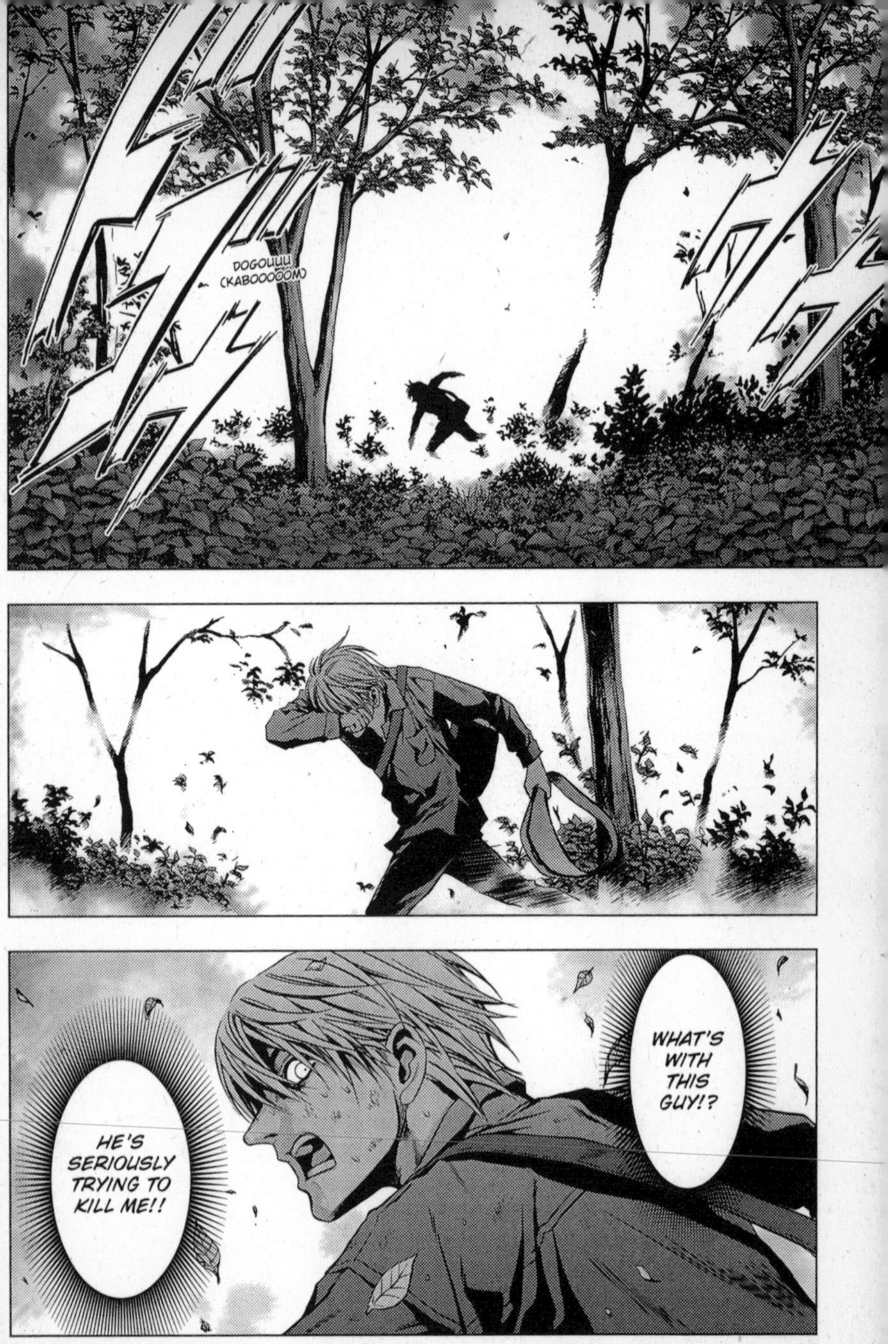
DOGOUUU (KABOOOOOM)
WHAT'S WITH THIS GUY!?
HE'S SERIOUSLY TRYING TO KILL ME!!

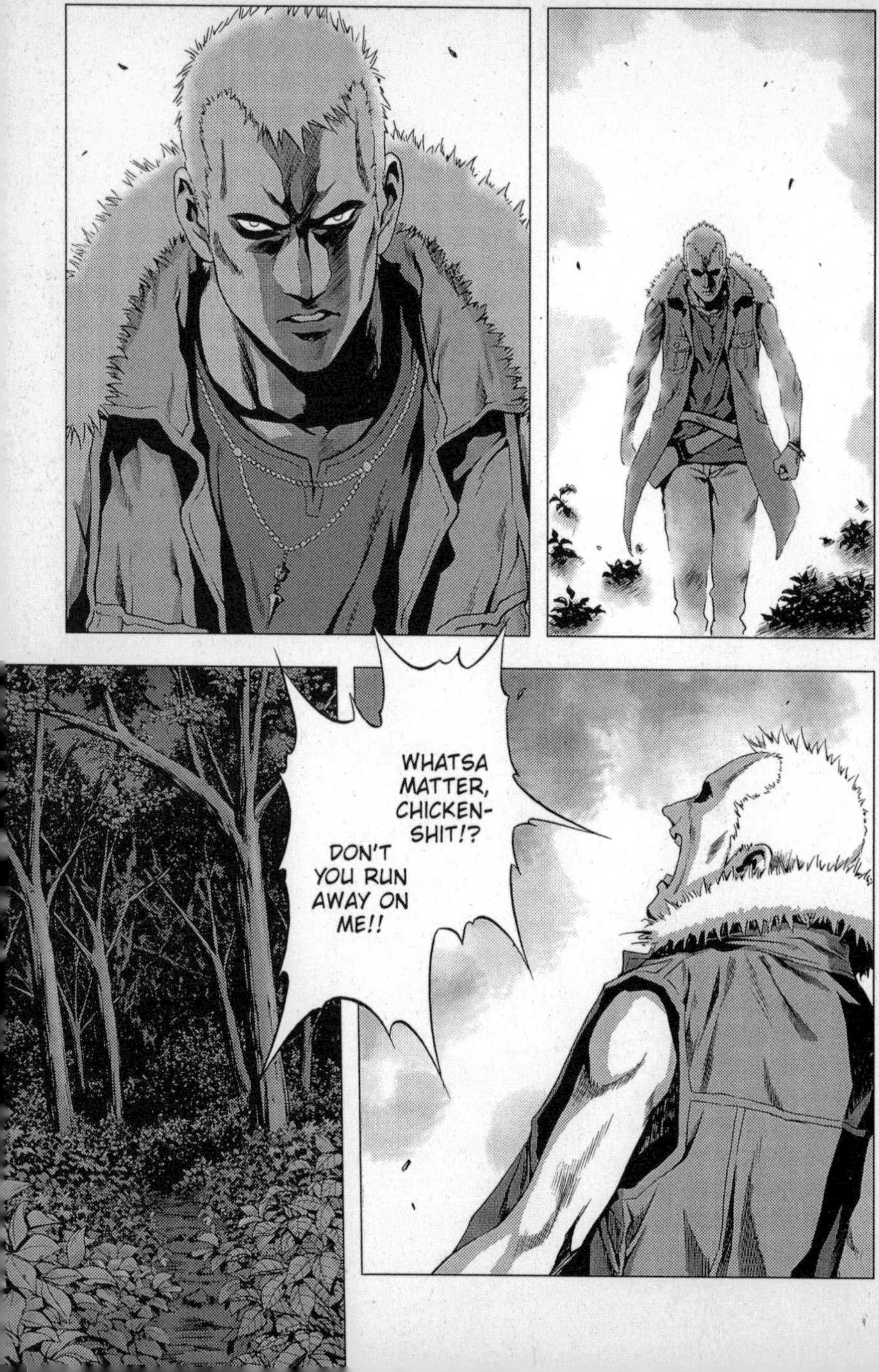
WHATSA MATTER, CHICKEN-SHIT!?
DON'T YOU RUN AWAY ON ME!!

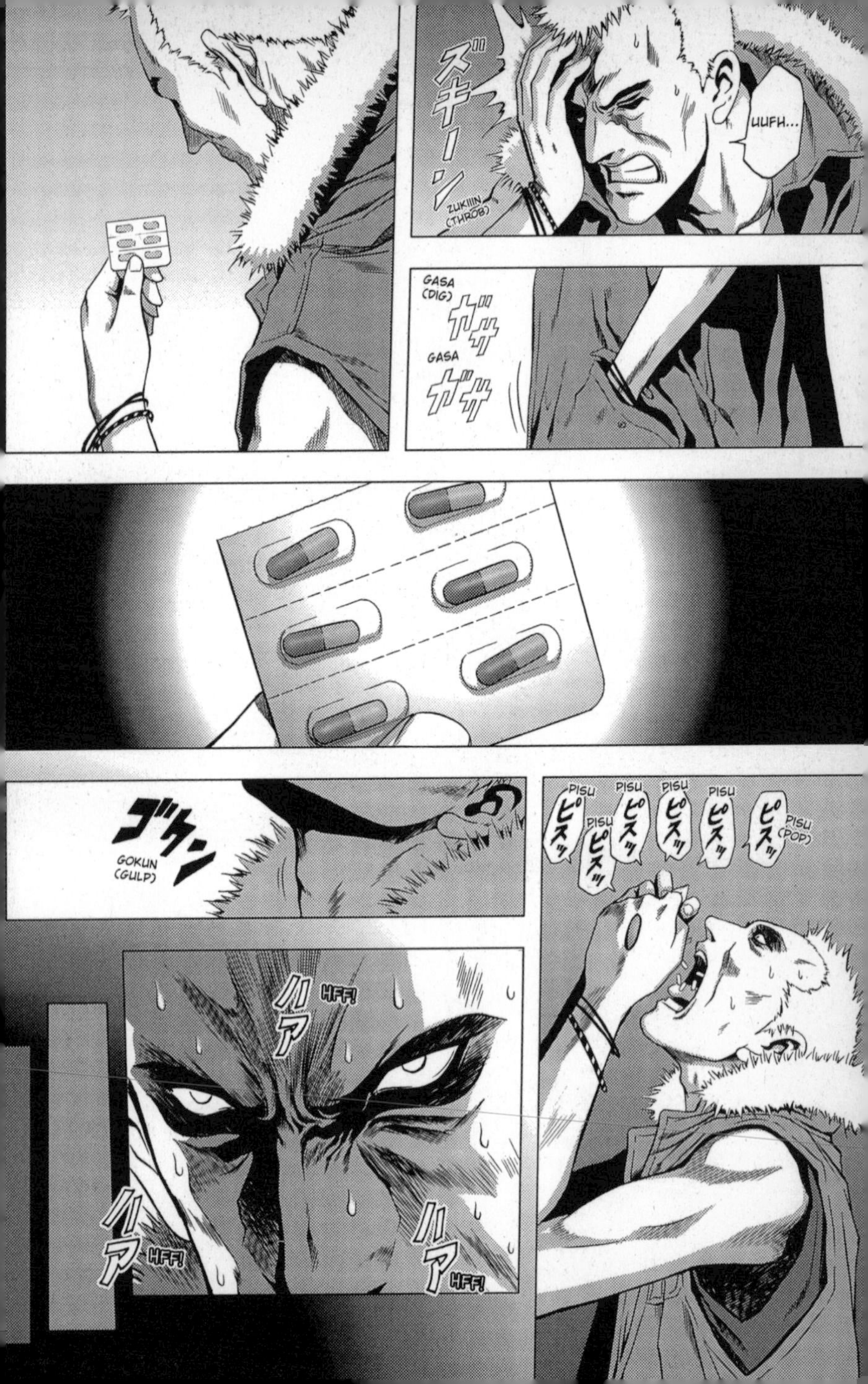
ズキーン
ZUKIIIN (THROB)
UUFH...
GASA (DIG)
ガサ
GASA
ガサ
ピスッ
PISU (POP)
ピスッ
PISU
ピスッ
PISU
ピスッ
PISU
ピスッ
PISU
ピスッ
PISU
ゴクン
GOKUN (GULP)
ハァ
HFF!
ハァ
HFF!
ハァ
HFF!

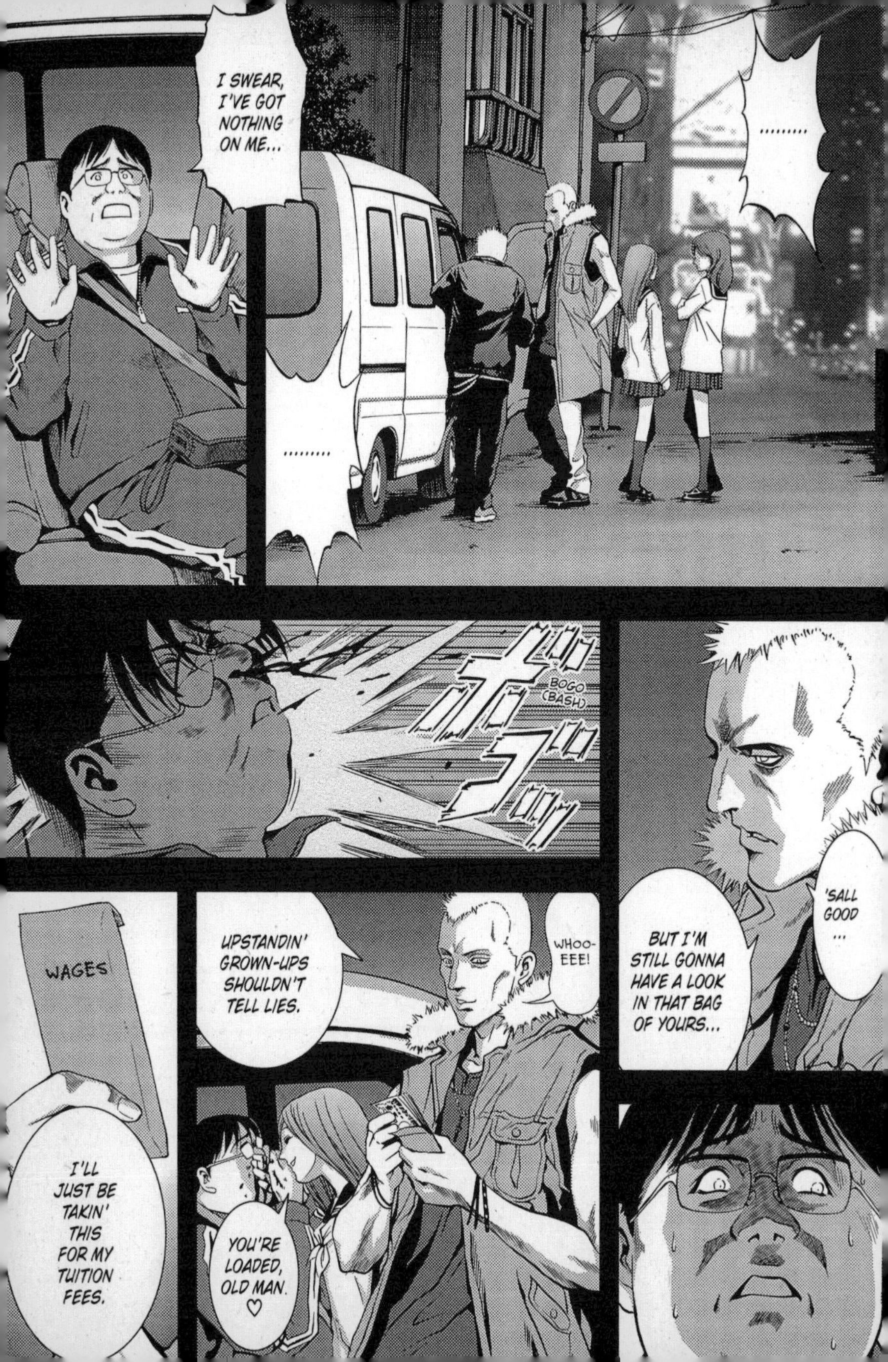
....
....
I SWEAR, I'VE GOT NOTHING ON ME...
'SALL GOOD ...
BUT I'M STILL GONNA HAVE A LOOK IN THAT BAG OF YOURS...
BOGO (BASH)
WHOOO-EEE!
UPSTANDIN' GROWN-UPS SHOULDN'T TELL LIES.
YOU'RE LOADED, OLD MAN. ♡
WAGES
I'LL JUST BE TAKIN' THIS FOR MY TUITION FEES.

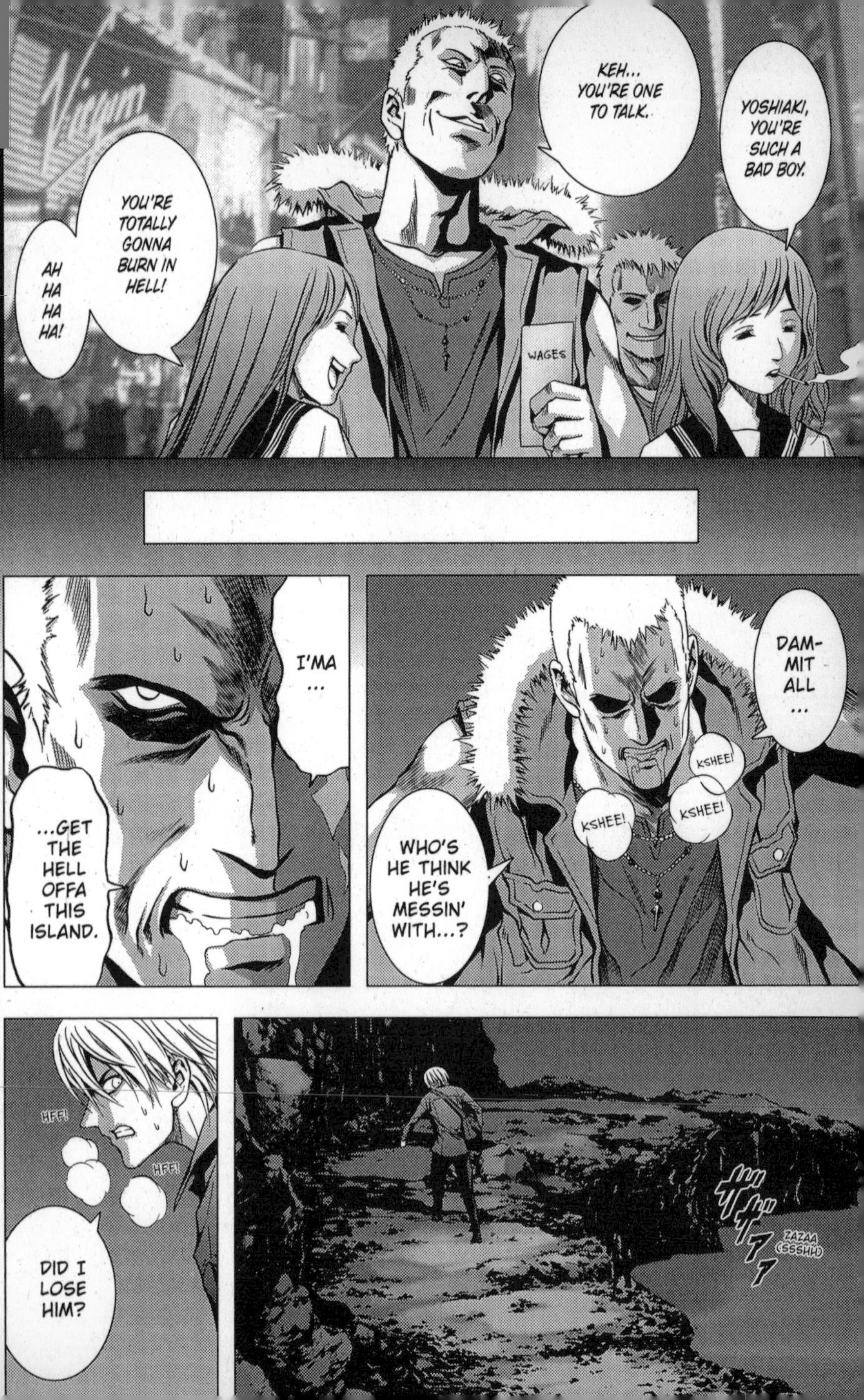

YOSHIAKI, YOU'RE SUCH A BAD BOY.
KEH... YOU'RE ONE TO TALK.
WAGES
YOU'RE TOTALLY GONNA BURN IN HELL!
AH HA HA HA!
DAM-MIT ALL...
KSHEE!
KSHEE!
KSHEE!
WHO'S HE THINK HE'S MESSIN' WITH...?
I'MA...
...GET THE HELL OFFA THIS ISLAND.
ZAZAA (SSSHH)
HFF!
HFF!
DID I LOSE HIM?

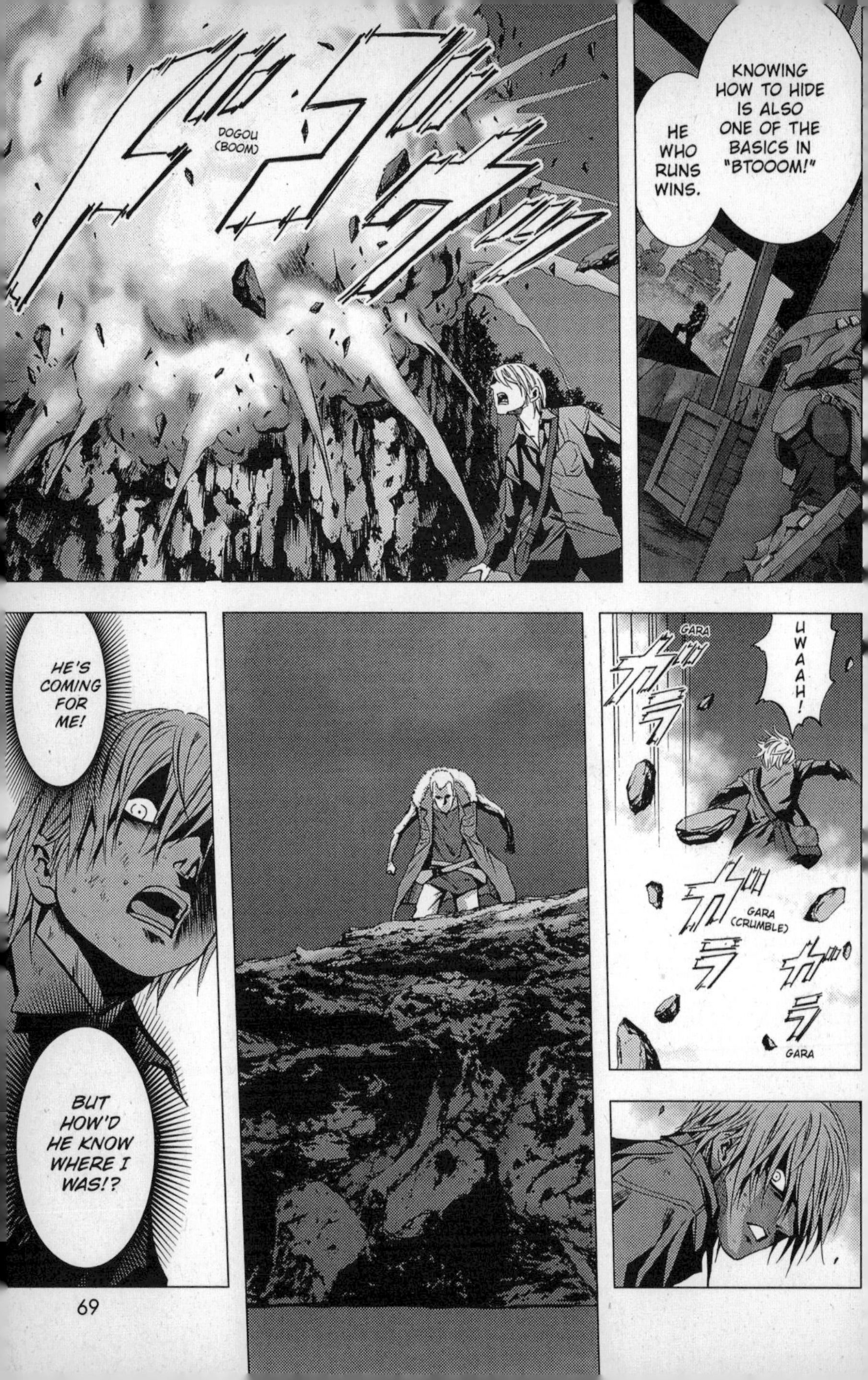
KNOWING HOW TO HIDE IS ALSO ONE OF THE BASICS IN "BTOOOM!"
HE WHO RUNS WINS.
DOGOU (BOOM)
UWAAH!
GARA
GARA (CRUMBLE)
GARA
HE'S COMING FOR ME!
BUT HOW'D HE KNOW WHERE I WAS!?

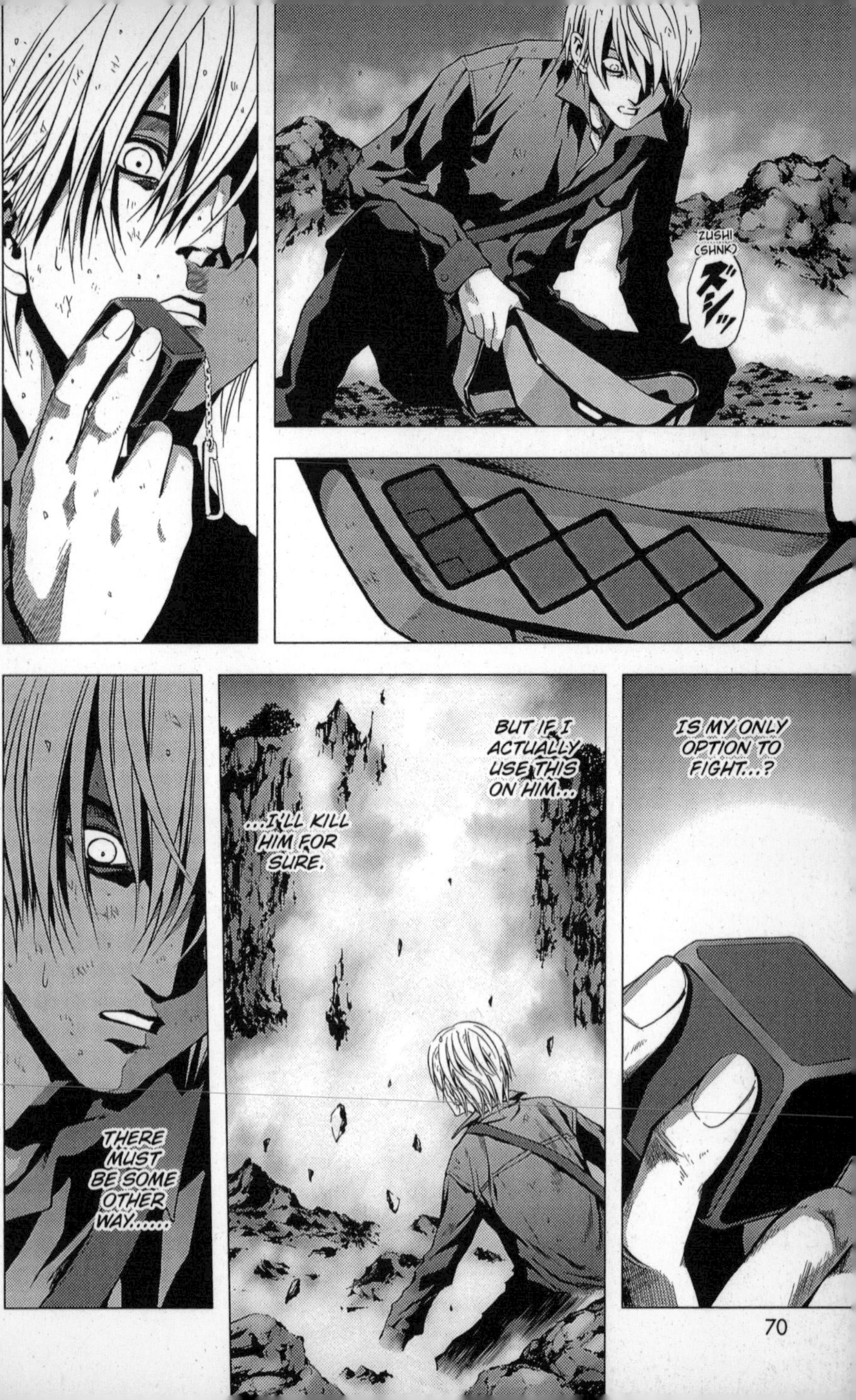
ZUSHI (SHNK)
ズシッ
IS MY ONLY OPTION TO FIGHT...?
BUT IF I ACTUALLY USE THIS ON HIM...
...I'LL KILL HIM FOR SURE.
THERE MUST BE SOME OTHER WAY......

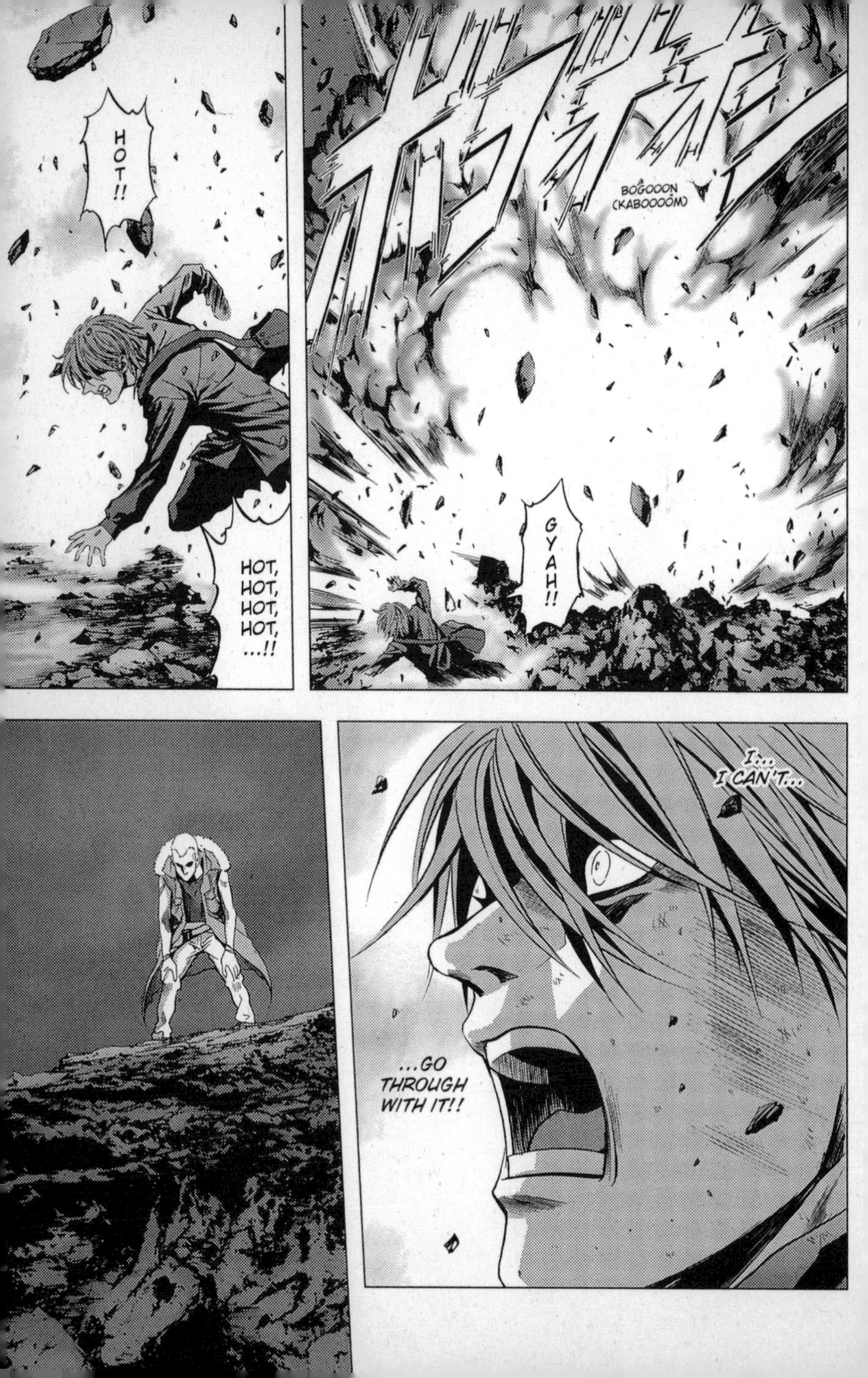
BOGOOON (KABOOOOM)
GYAH!!
HOT!!
HOT, HOT, HOT, HOT, ...!!
I... I CAN'T...
...GO THROUGH WITH IT!!

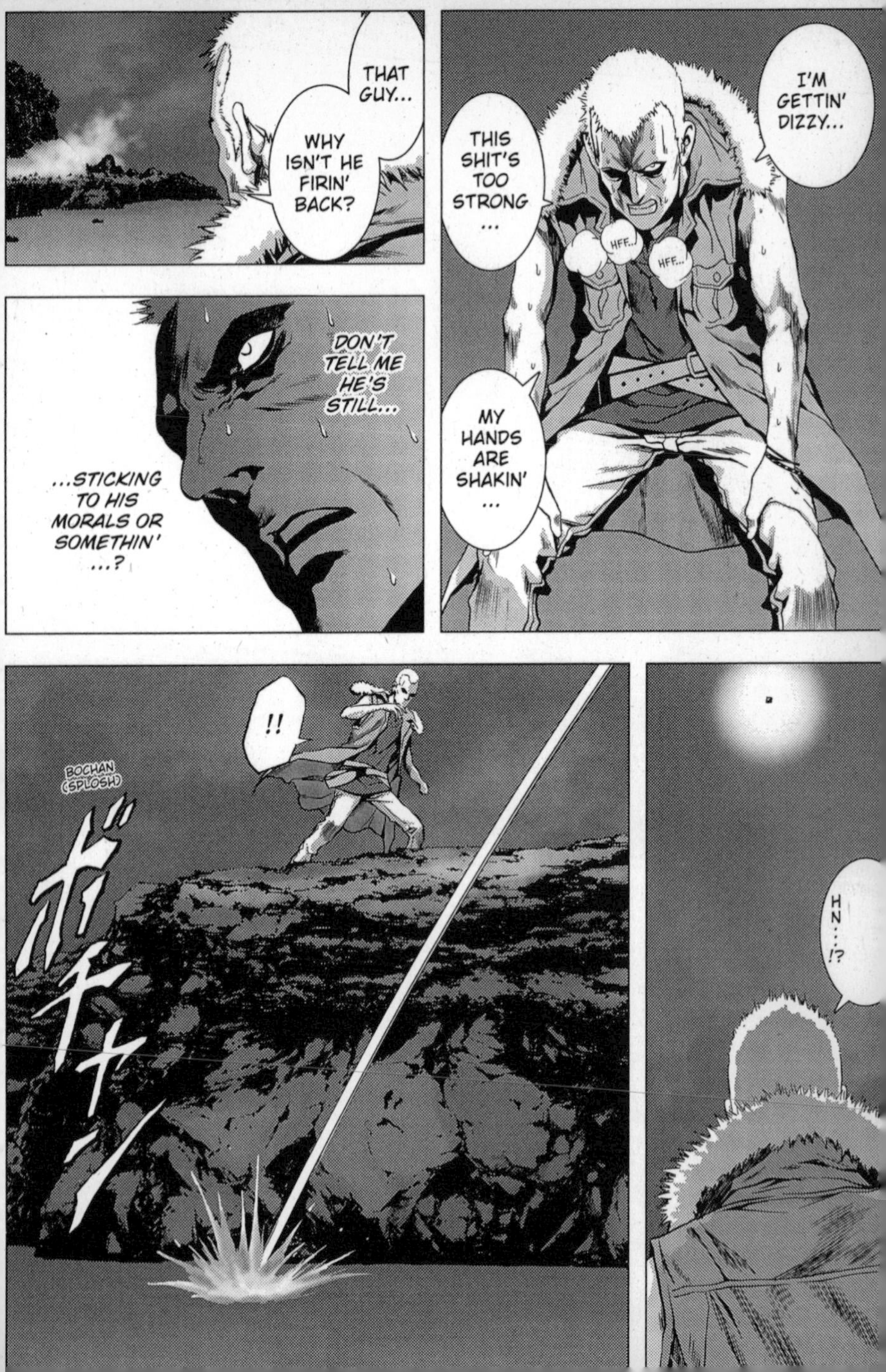
I'M GETTIN' DIZZY...
THIS SHIT'S TOO STRONG...
HFF...
HFF...
MY HANDS ARE SHAKIN'...
THAT GUY...
WHY ISN'T HE FIRIN' BACK?
DON'T TELL ME HE'S STILL...
...STICKING TO HIS MORALS OR SOMETHIN'...?
HN...!?
!!
BOCHAN (SPLOSH)
ボチャン

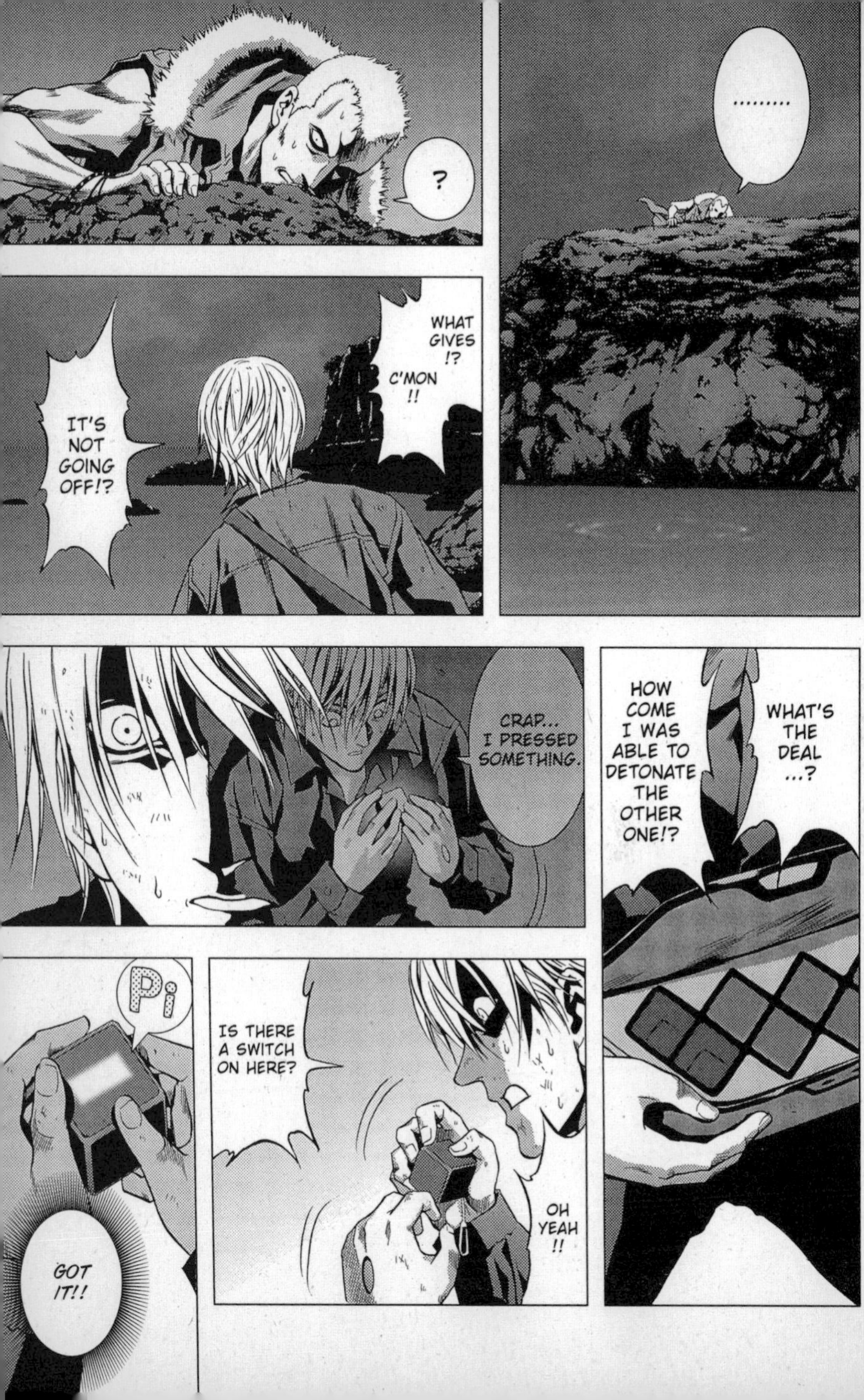
....
?
WHAT GIVES!?
C'MON!!
IT'S NOT GOING OFF!?
WHAT'S THE DEAL...?
HOW COME I WAS ABLE TO DETONATE THE OTHER ONE!?
CRAP... I PRESSED SOMETHING.
IS THERE A SWITCH ON HERE?
OH YEAH!!
Pi
GOT IT!!

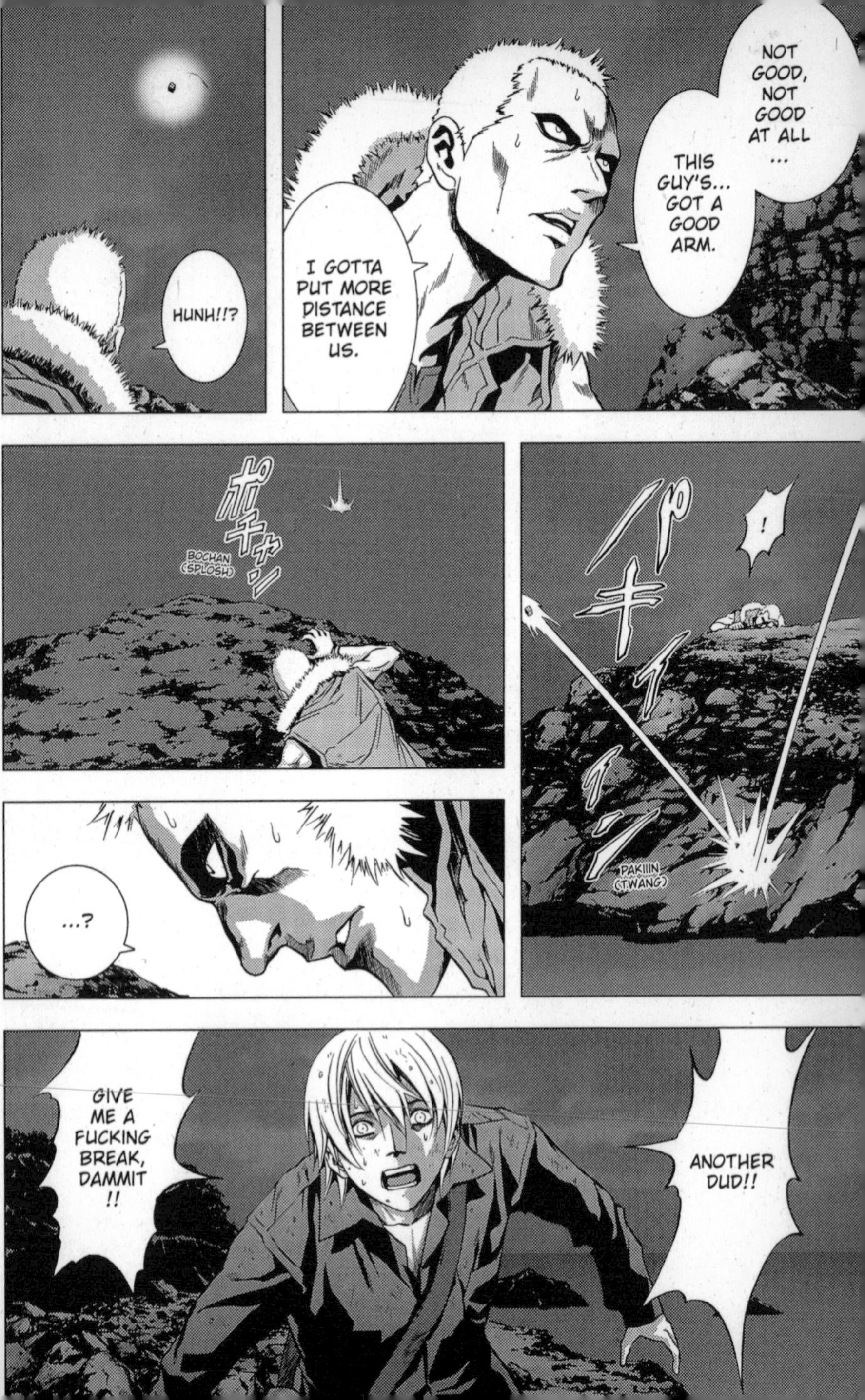
NOT GOOD, NOT GOOD AT ALL ...
THIS GUY'S... GOT A GOOD ARM.
I GOTTA PUT MORE DISTANCE BETWEEN US.
HUNH!!?
!
PAKIIIN (T'WANG)
BOCHAN (SPLOSH)
...?
ANOTHER DUD!!
GIVE ME A FUCKING BREAK, DAMMIT !!

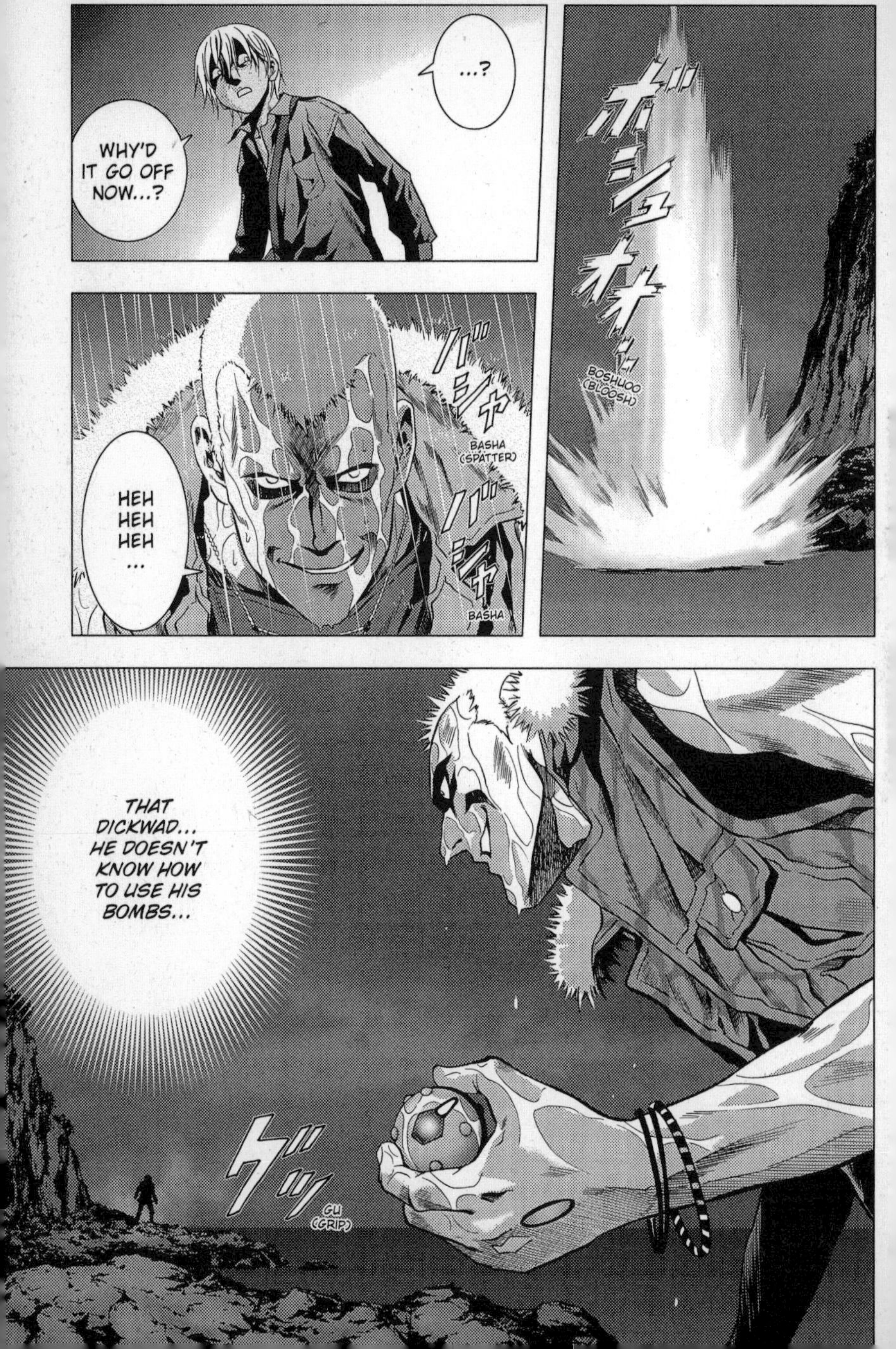
BOSHUOO
(BLOOSH)
...?
WHY'D IT GO OFF NOW...?
BASHA
(SPATTER)
BASHA
HEH HEH HEH ...
THAT DICKWAD... HE DOESN'T KNOW HOW TO USE HIS BOMBS...
GU
(GRIP)

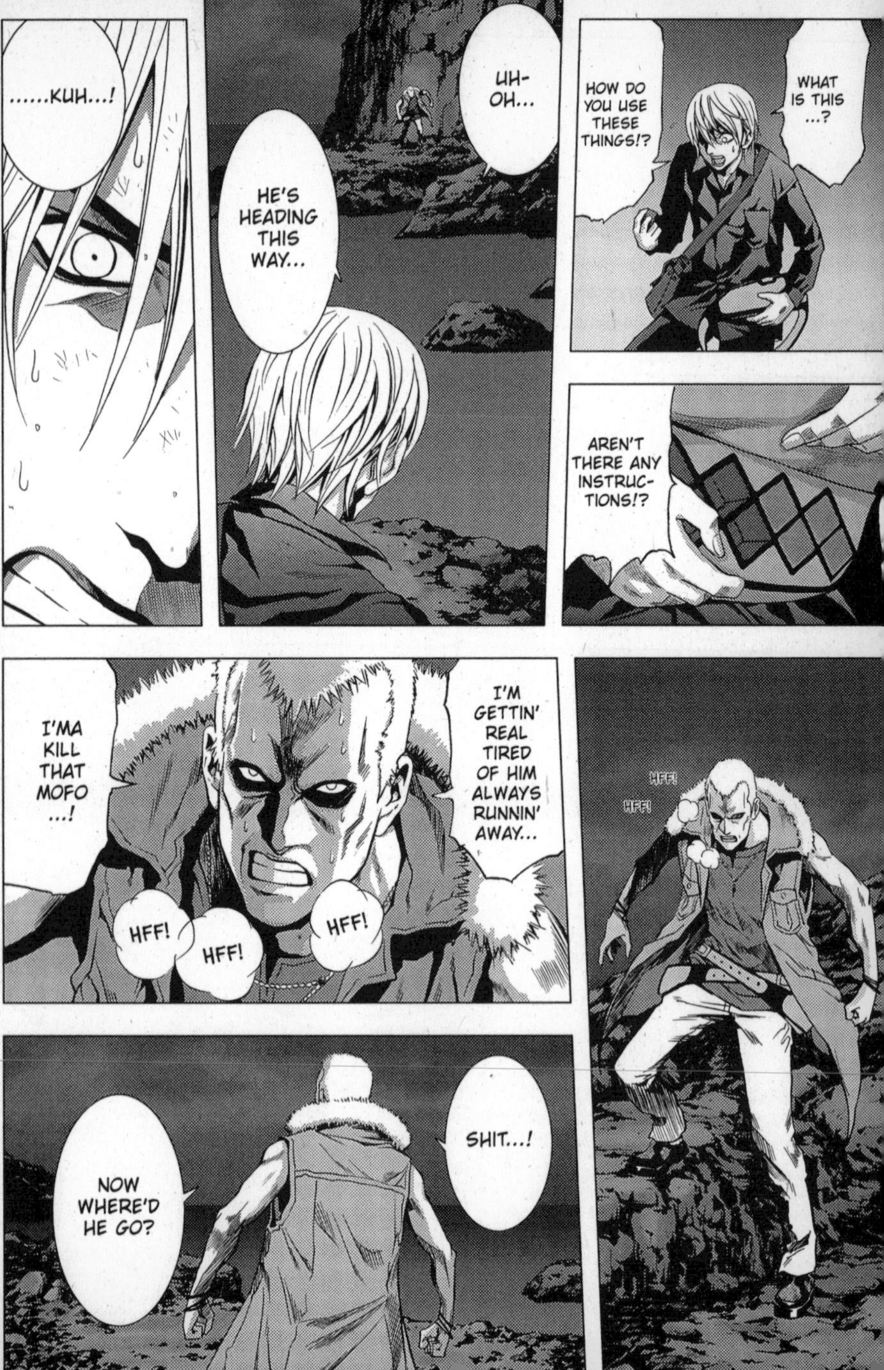
WHAT IS THIS ...?
HOW DO YOU USE THESE THINGS!?
AREN'T THERE ANY INSTRUC-TIONS!?
UH-OH...
HE'S HEADING THIS WAY...
......KUH...!
HFF!
HFF!
I'M GETTIN' REAL TIRED OF HIM ALWAYS RUNNIN' AWAY...
I'MA KILL THAT MOFO ...!
HFF!
HFF!
HFF!
SHIT...!
NOW WHERE'D HE GO?

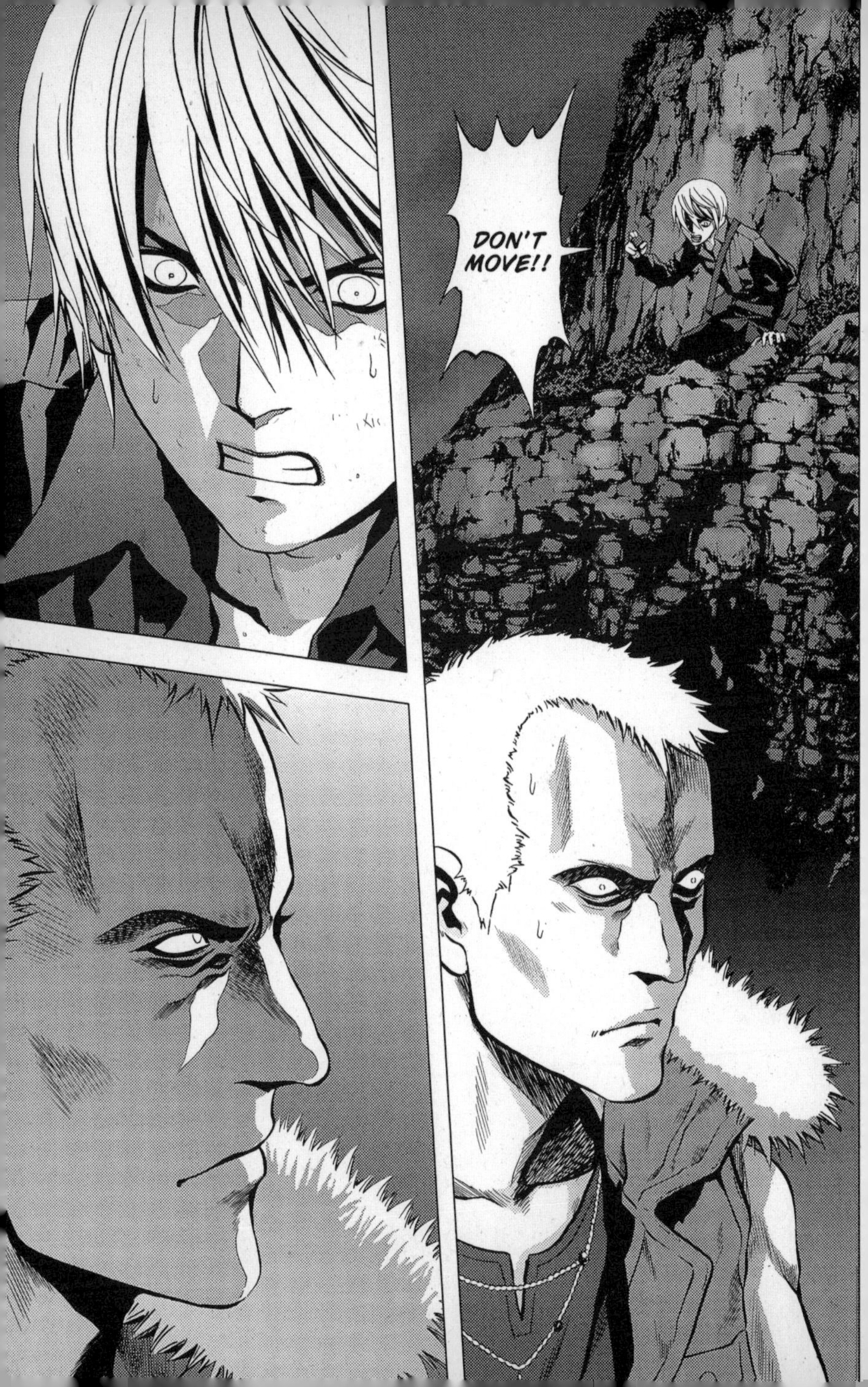
DON'T MOVE!!

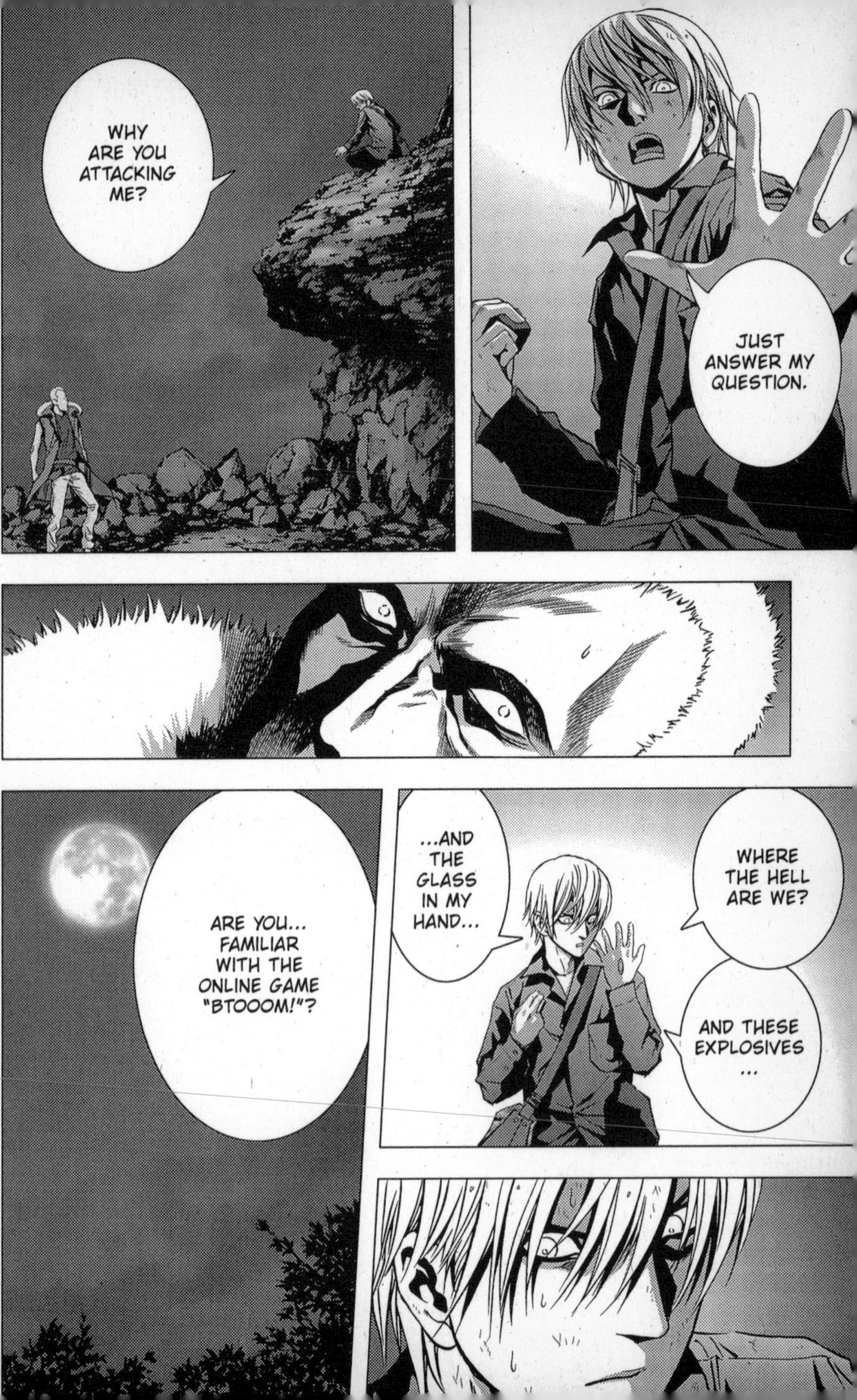
JUST ANSWER MY QUESTION.
WHY ARE YOU ATTACKING ME?
WHERE THE HELL ARE WE?
AND THESE EXPLOSIVES ...
...AND THE GLASS IN MY HAND...
ARE YOU... FAMILIAR WITH THE ONLINE GAME "BTOOOM!"?

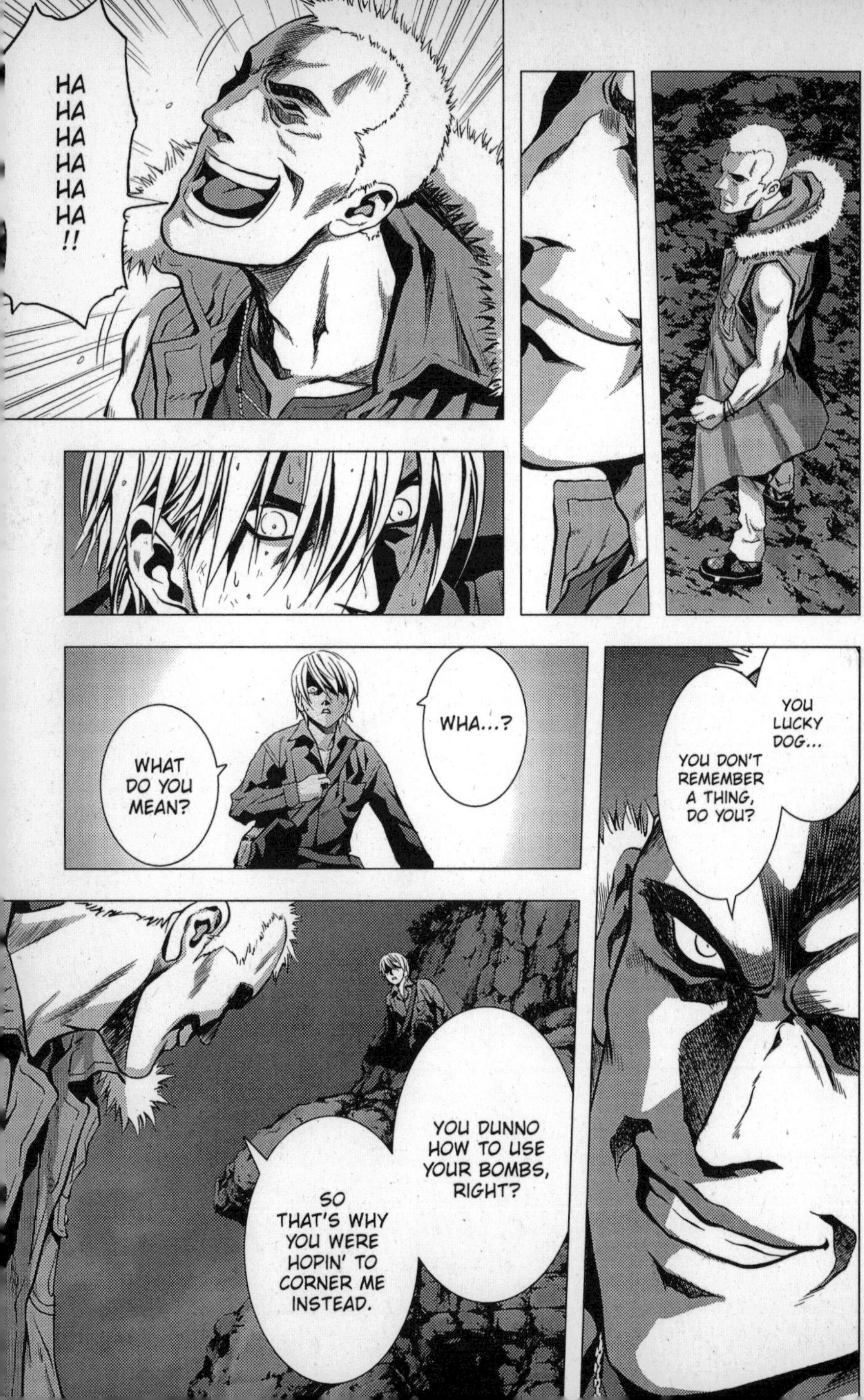
HA HA HA HA HA HA!!
YOU LUCKY DOG...
YOU DON'T REMEMBER A THING, DO YOU?
WHA...?
WHAT DO YOU MEAN?
YOU DUNNO HOW TO USE YOUR BOMBS, RIGHT?
SO THAT'S WHY YOU WERE HOPIN' TO CORNER ME INSTEAD.

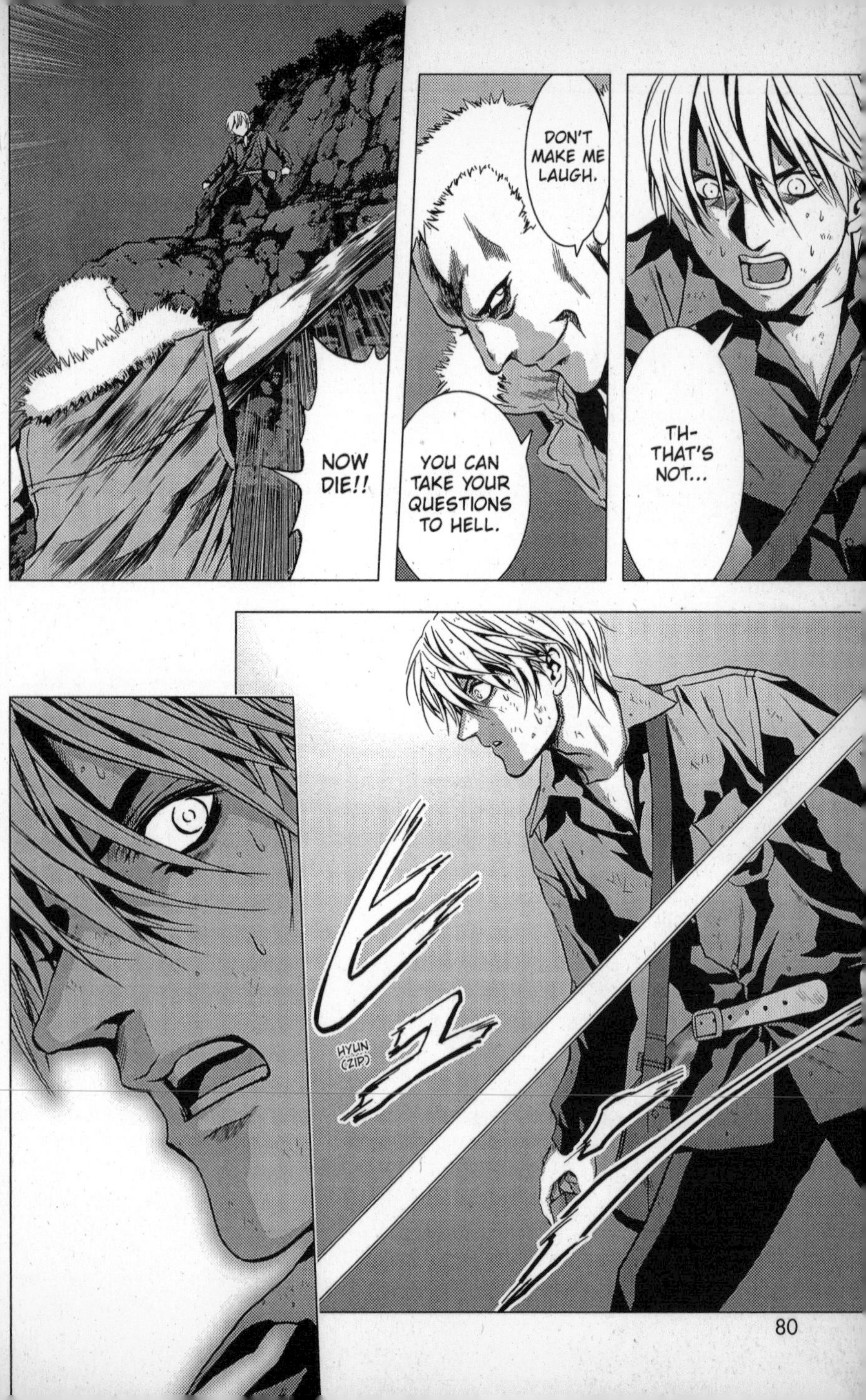
TH- THAT'S NOT...
DON'T MAKE ME LAUGH.
YOU CAN TAKE YOUR QUESTIONS TO HELL.
NOW DIE!!
HYUN (ZIP)

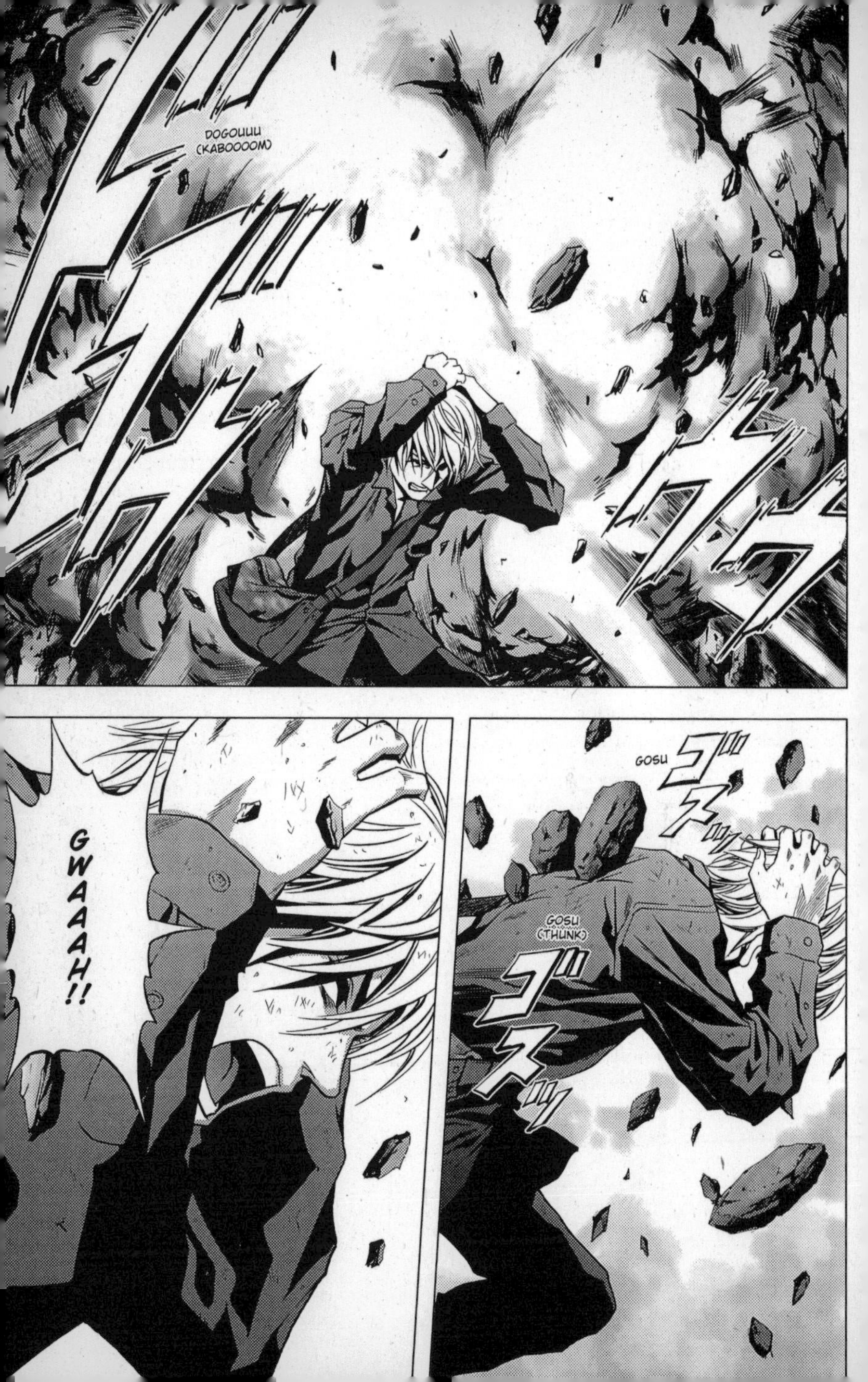
DOGOUUU
(KABOOOOM)
GOSU
GOSU
(THUNK)
GWAAAAH!!

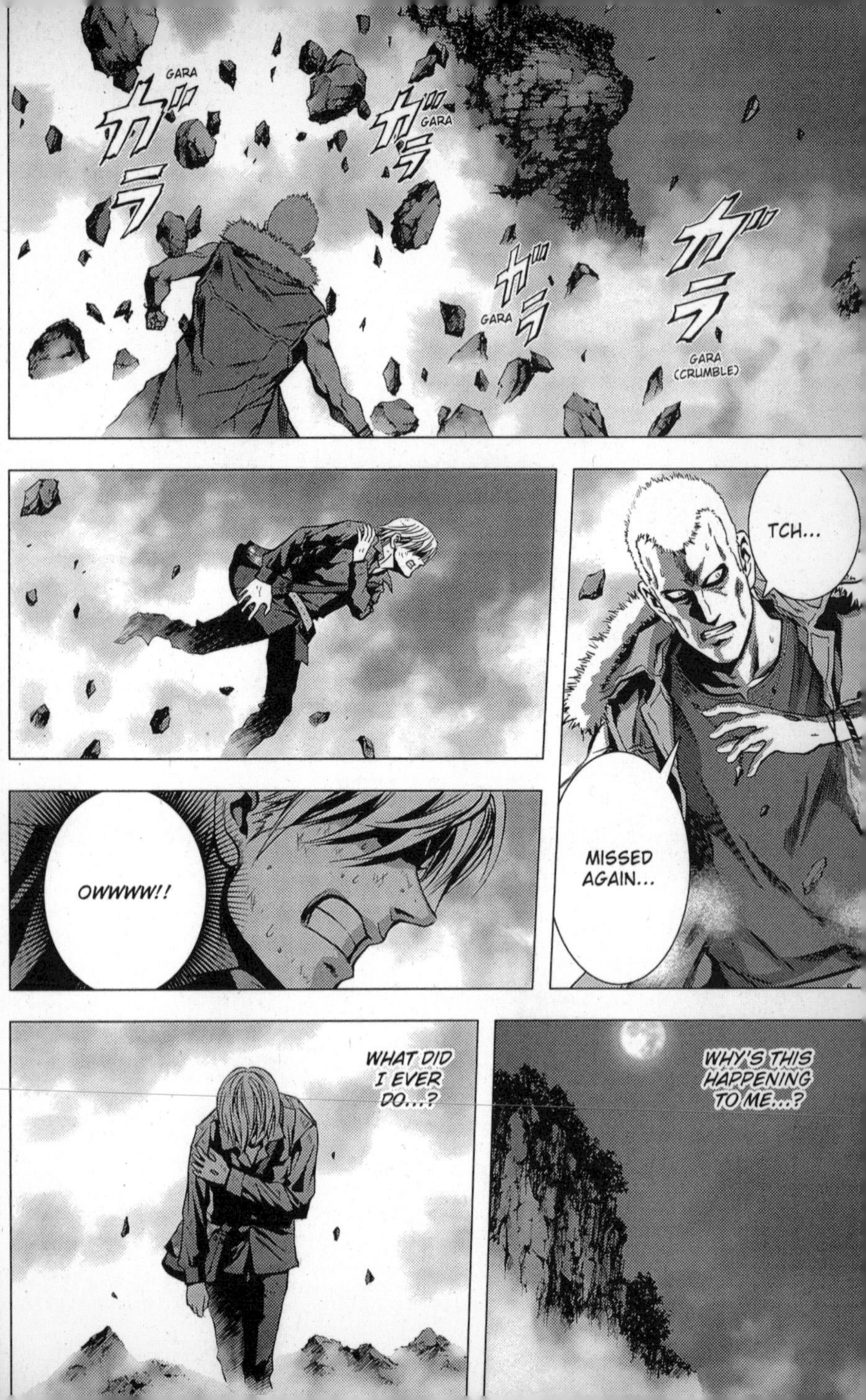
ガラ
GARA
(CRUMBLE)
ガラ
GARA
ガラ
GARA
ガラ
GARA
TCH...
MISSED AGAIN...
OWWWW!!
WHY'S THIS HAPPENING TO ME...?
WHAT DID I EVER DO...?

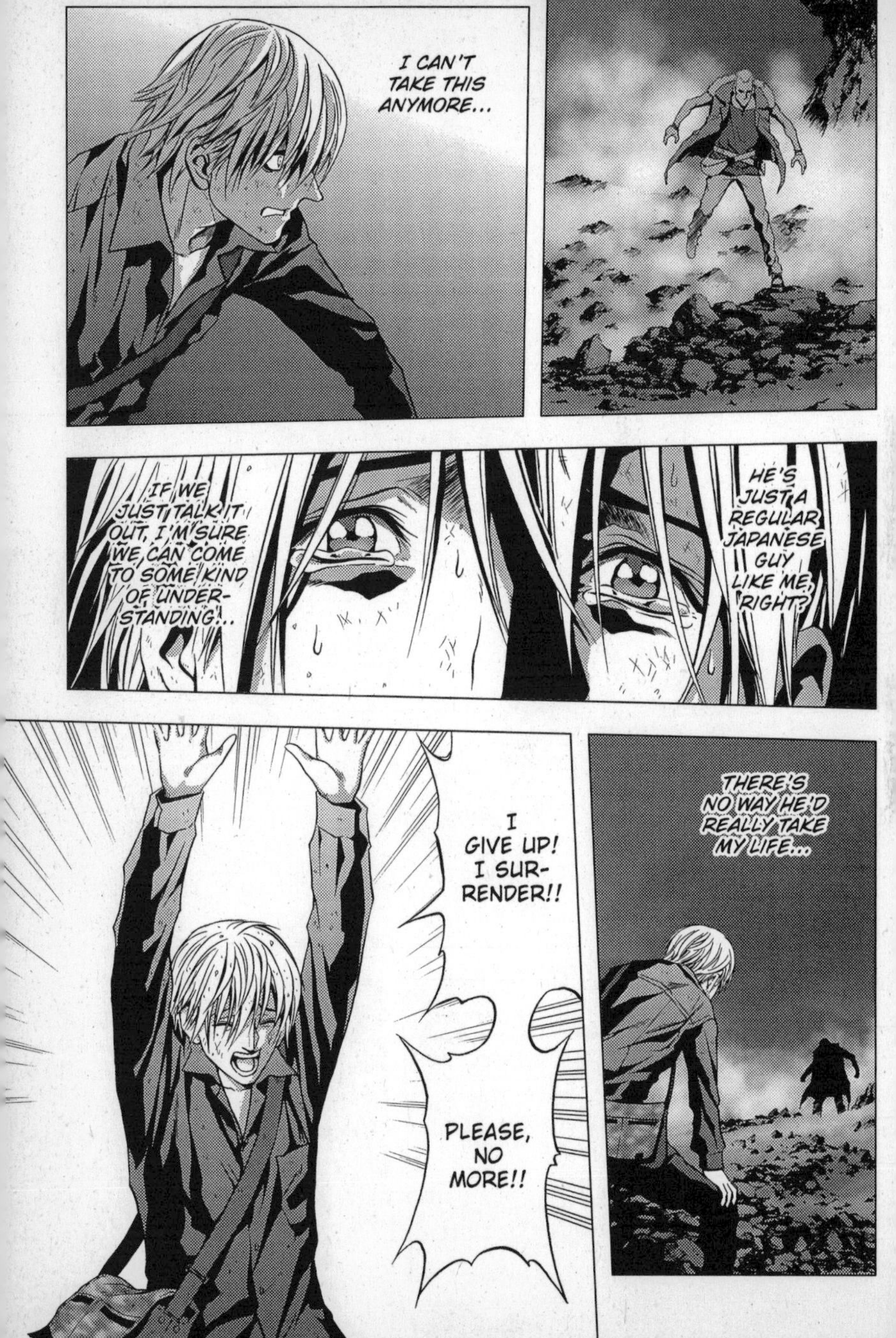

I CAN'T TAKE THIS ANYMORE...
HE'S JUST A REGULAR JAPANESE GUY LIKE ME, RIGHT?
IF WE JUST TALK IT OUT, I'M SURE WE CAN COME TO SOME KIND OF UNDER-STANDING...
THERE'S NO WAY HE'D REALLY TAKE MY LIFE...
I GIVE UP! I SUR-RENDER!!
PLEASE, NO MORE!!

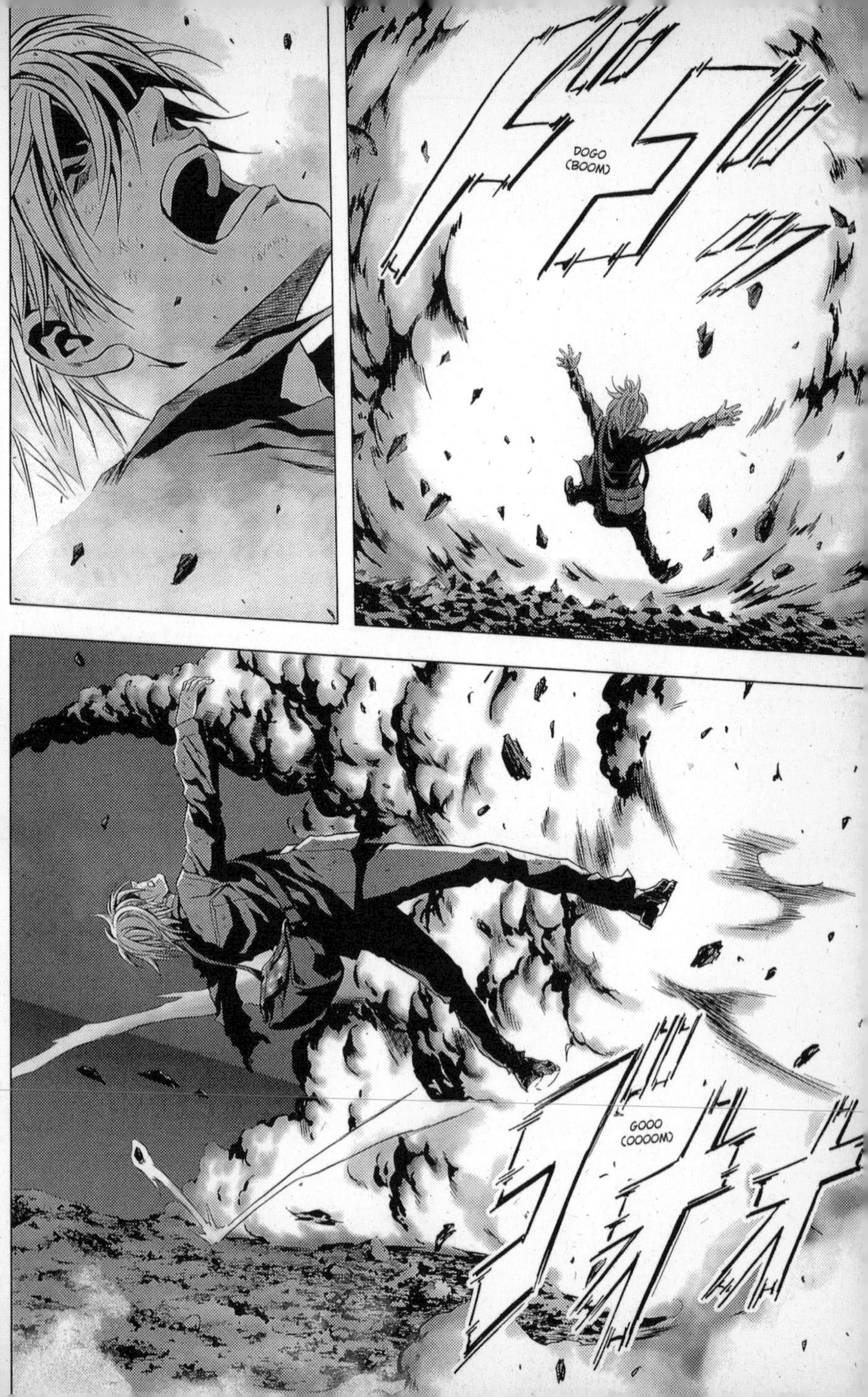
DOGO (BOOM)
GOOO (OOOOM)

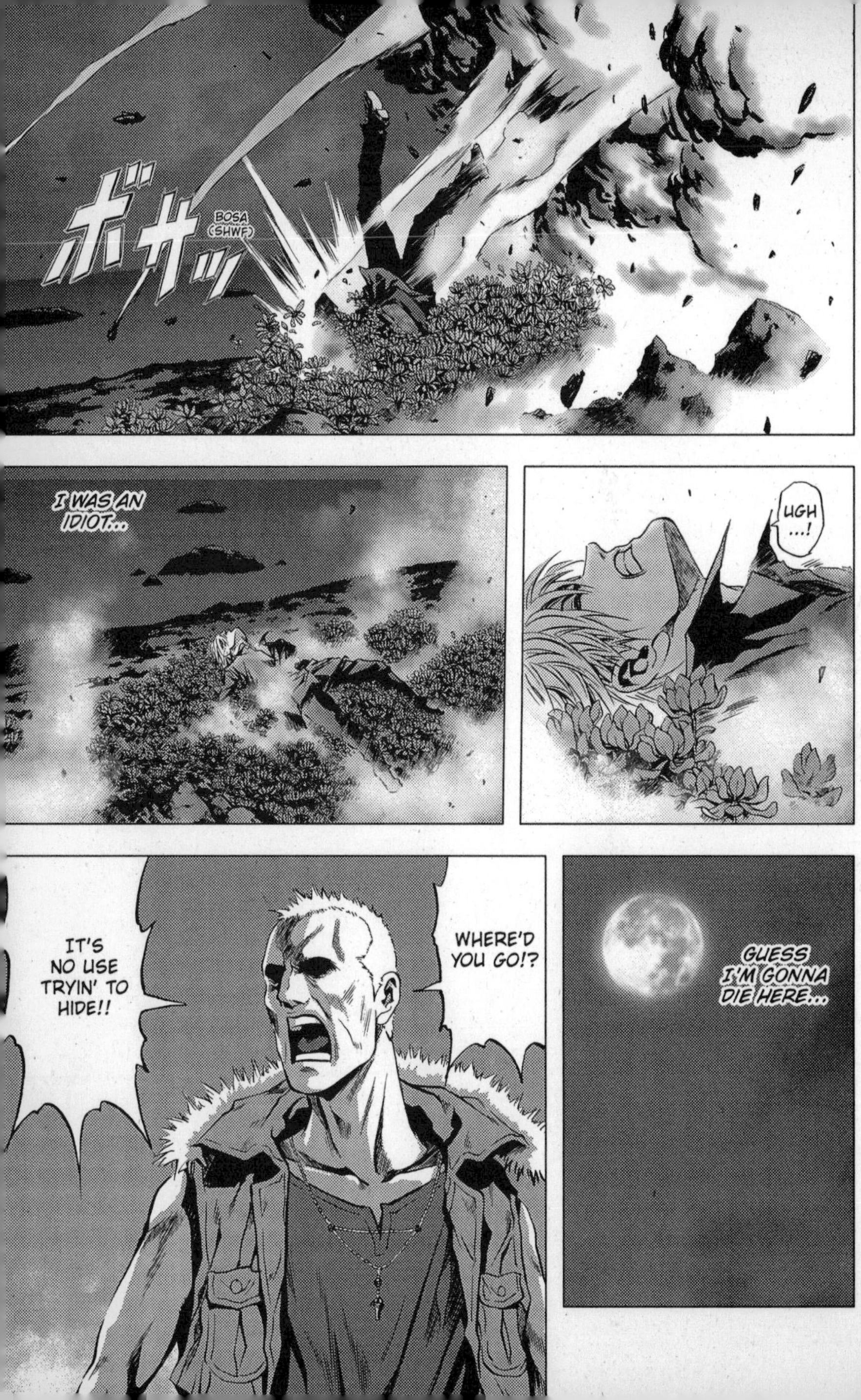
ボサッ
BOSA (SHWF)
UGH ...!
I WAS AN IDIOT...
GUESS I'M GONNA DIE HERE...
WHERE'D YOU GO!?
IT'S NO USE TRYIN' TO HIDE!!

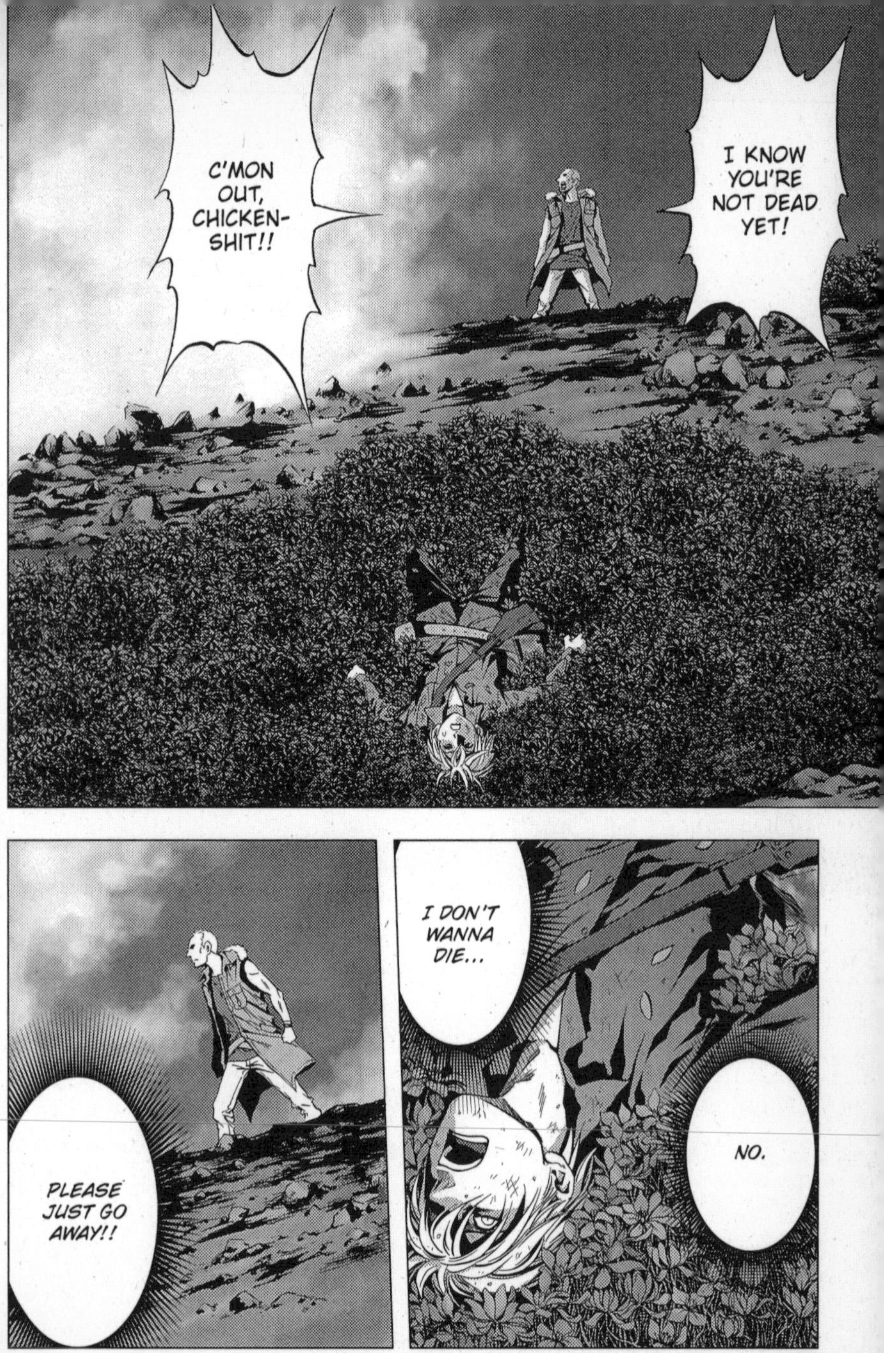
I KNOW YOU'RE NOT DEAD YET!
C'MON OUT, CHICKEN-SHIT!!
I DON'T WANNA DIE...
NO.
PLEASE JUST GO AWAY!!

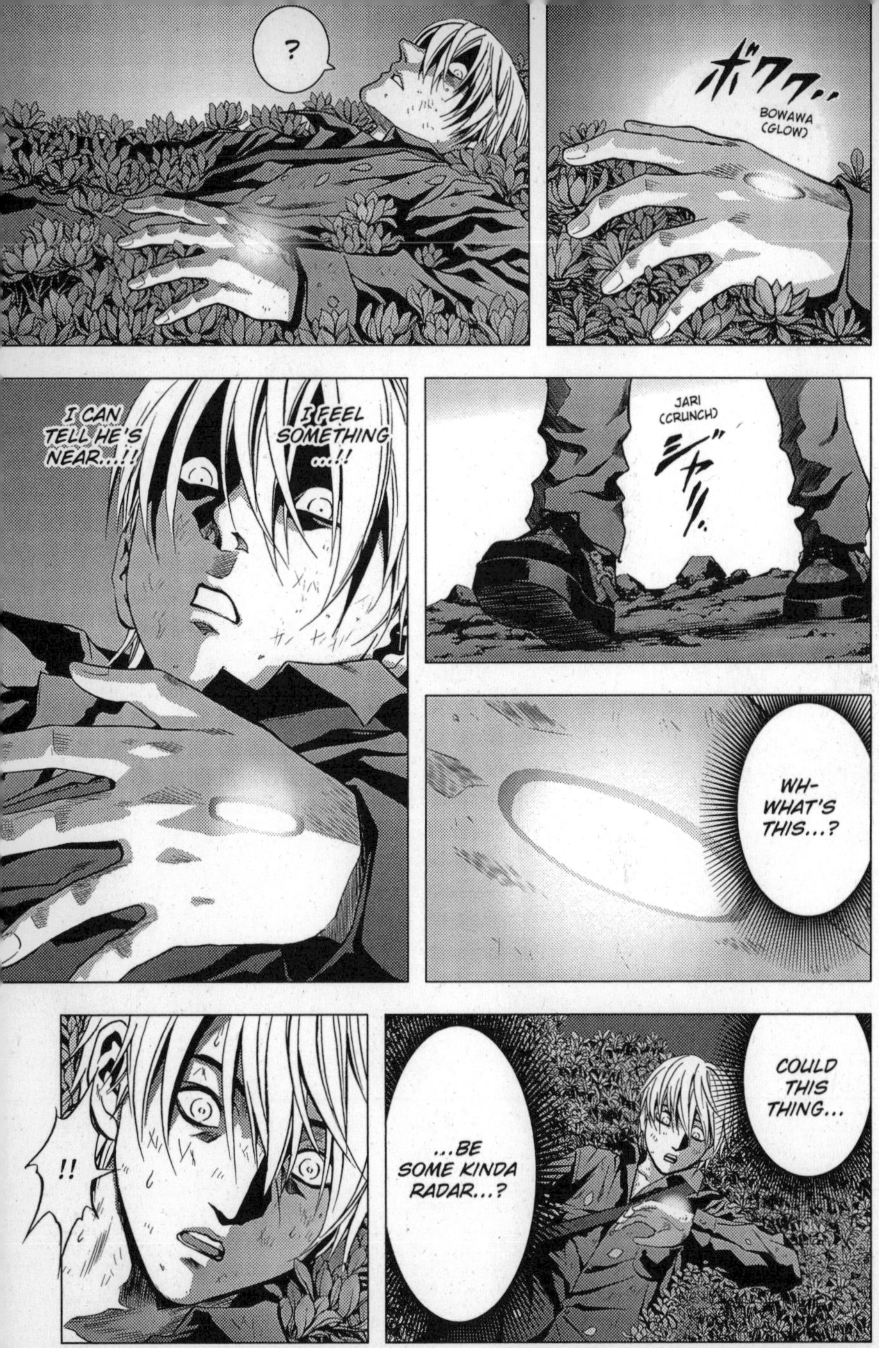

ボワワ‥
BOWAWA (GLOW)
?
JARI (CRUNCH)
ジャリ‥
WH-WHAT'S THIS...?
I FEEL SOMETHING...!!
I CAN TELL HE'S NEAR...!!
COULD THIS THING...
...BE SOME KINDA RADAR...?
!!

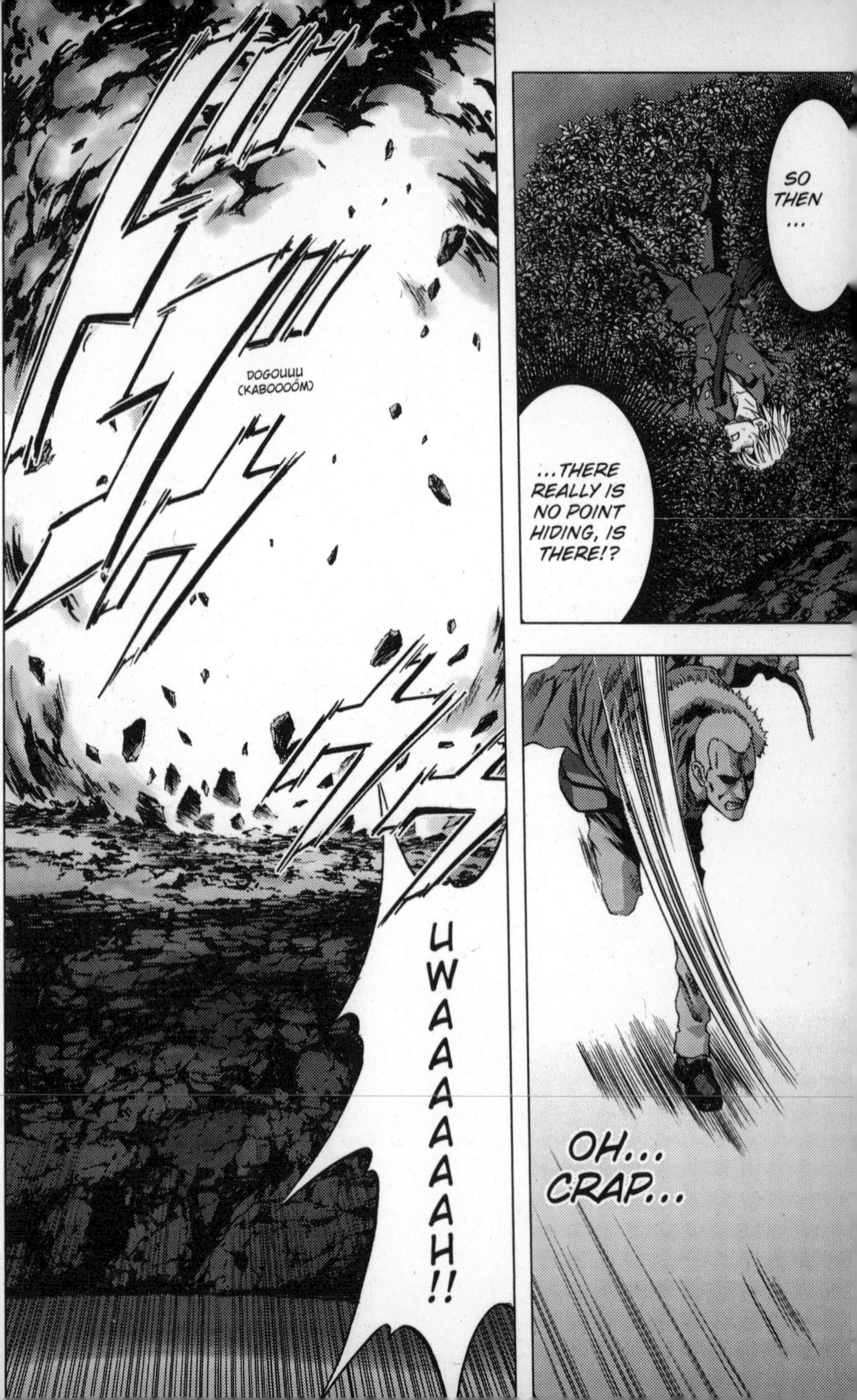
SO THEN ...
...THERE REALLY IS NO POINT HIDING, IS THERE!?
OH... CRAP...
DOGOUUU (KABOOOOM)
UWAAAAAAAAH!!

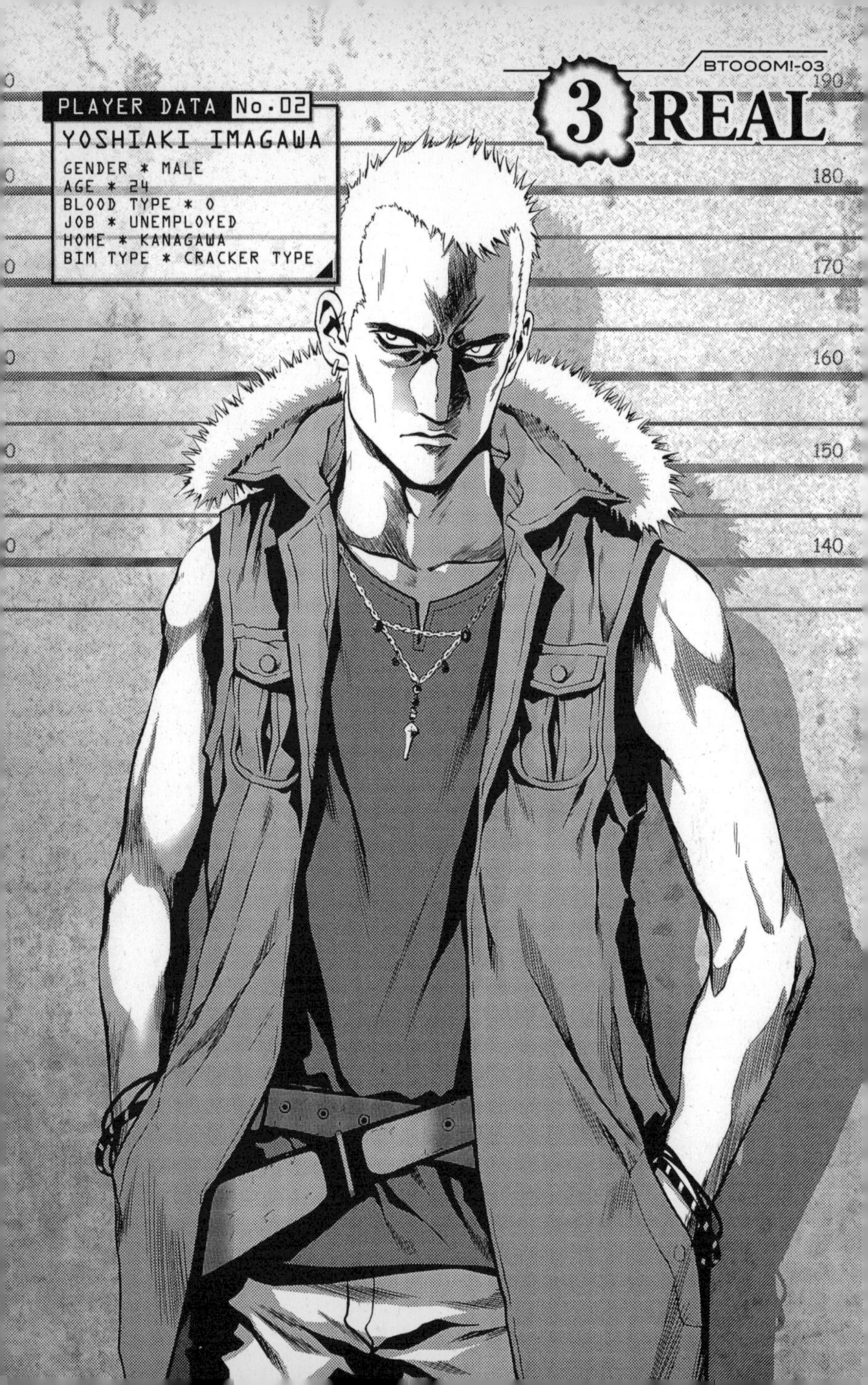
BTOOOM!-03
3 REAL
PLAYER DATA No.02
YOSHIAKI IMAGAWA
GENDER * MALE
AGE * 24
BLOOD TYPE * O
JOB * UNEMPLOYED
HOME * KANAGAWA
BIM TYPE * CRACKER TYPE
190
180
170
160
150
140

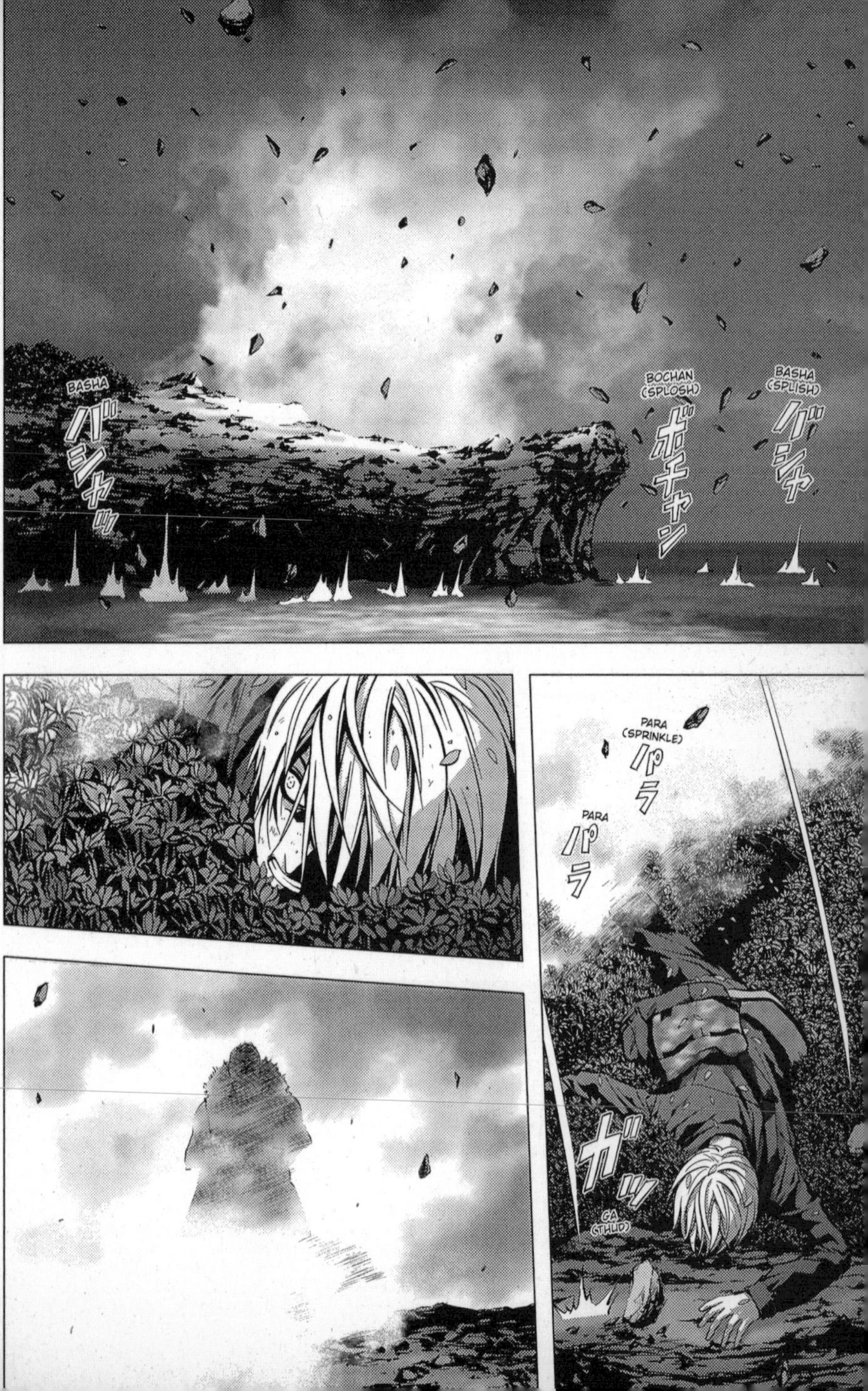
BASHA (SPLISH)
バシャ
BOCHAN (SPLOSH)
ボチャン
BASHA
バシャッ
PARA (SPRINKLE)
パラ
PARA
パラ
GA (THUD)
ガッ

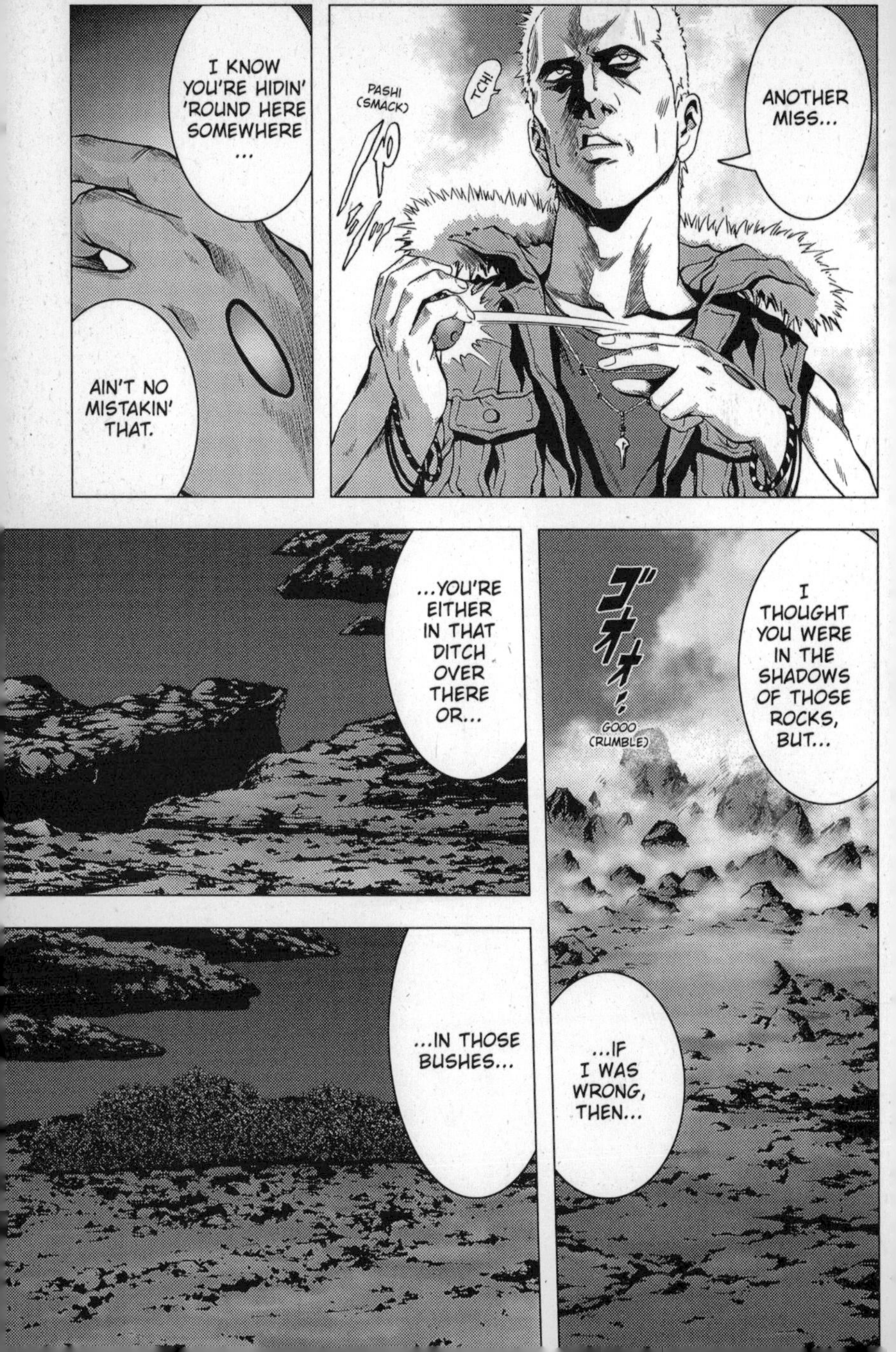
ANOTHER MISS...
TCH!
PASHI (SMACK)
I KNOW YOU'RE HIDIN' 'ROUND HERE SOMEWHERE ...
AIN'T NO MISTAKIN' THAT.
I THOUGHT YOU WERE IN THE SHADOWS OF THOSE ROCKS, BUT...
ゴオォ!
GOOO (RUMBLE)
...IF I WAS WRONG, THEN...
...YOU'RE EITHER IN THAT DITCH OVER THERE OR...
...IN THOSE BUSHES...

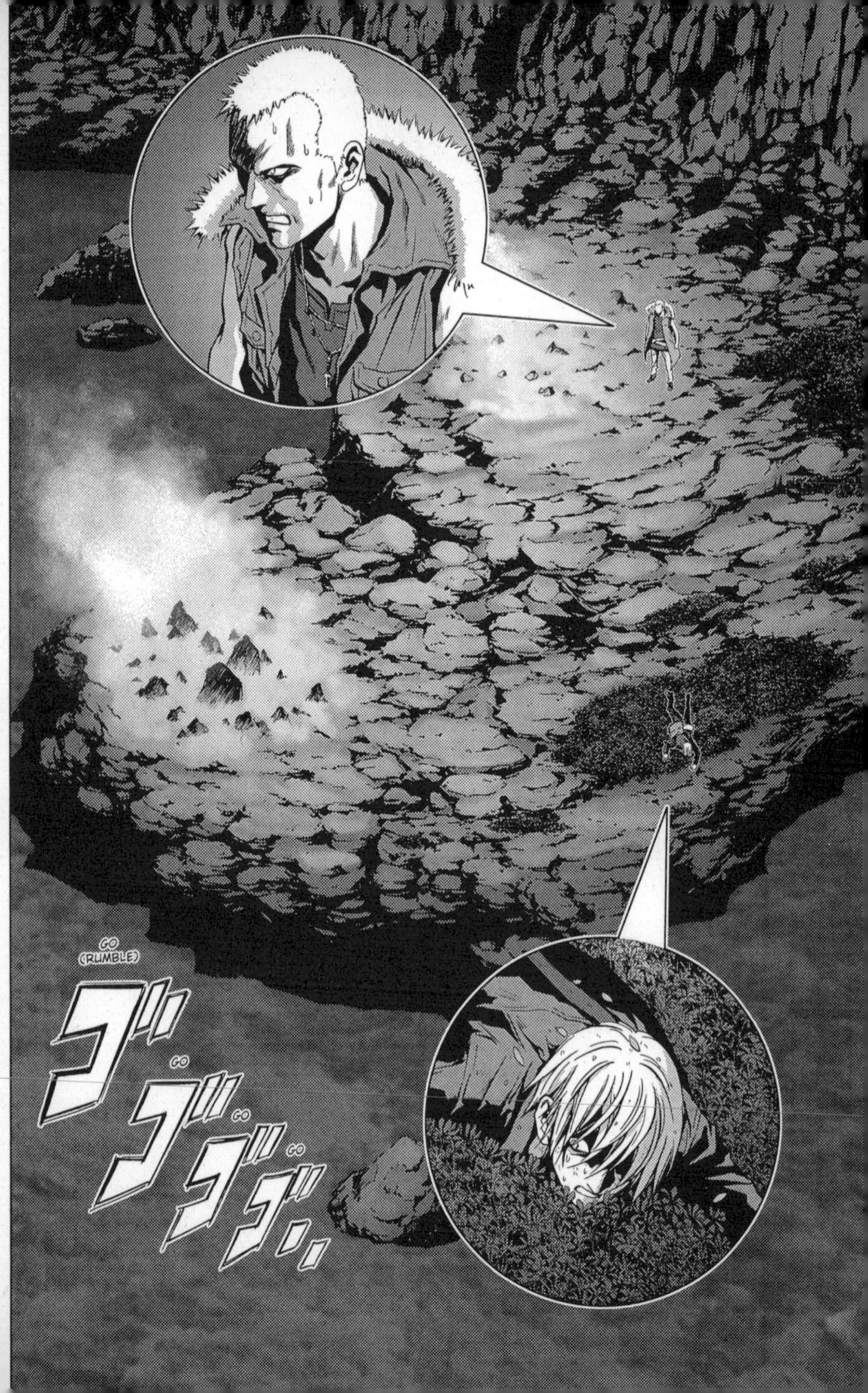
GO (RUMBLE)
ゴ
GO
ゴ
GO
ゴ
GO
ゴ

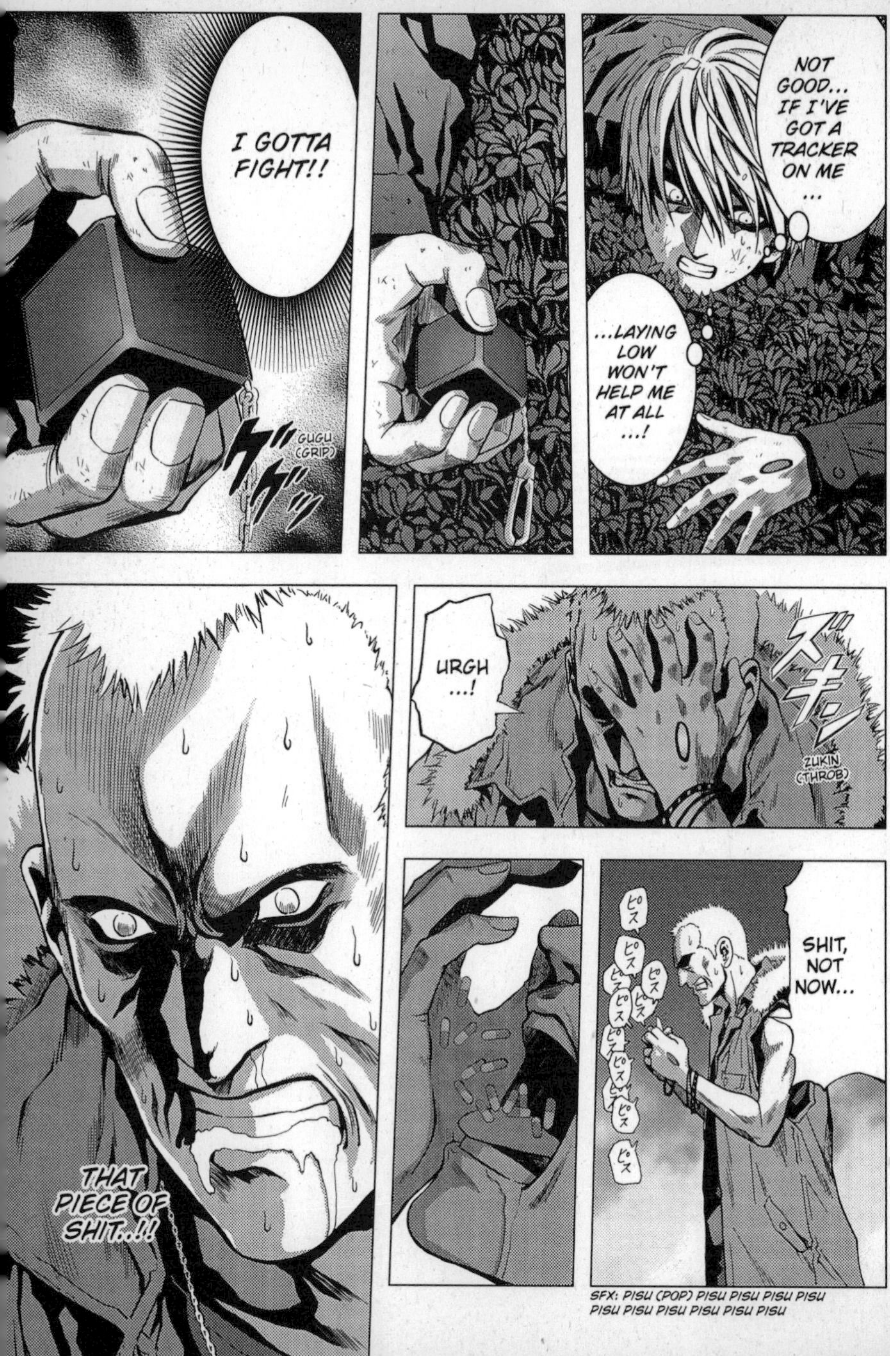
NOT GOOD... IF I'VE GOT A TRACKER ON ME ...
...LAYING LOW WON'T HELP ME AT ALL ...!
I GOTTA FIGHT!!
GUGU (GRIP)
URGH ...!
ZUKIN (THROB)
SHIT, NOT NOW...
THAT PIECE OF SHIT..!!
SFX: PISU (POP) PISU PISU PISU PISU PISU PISU PISU PISU PISU

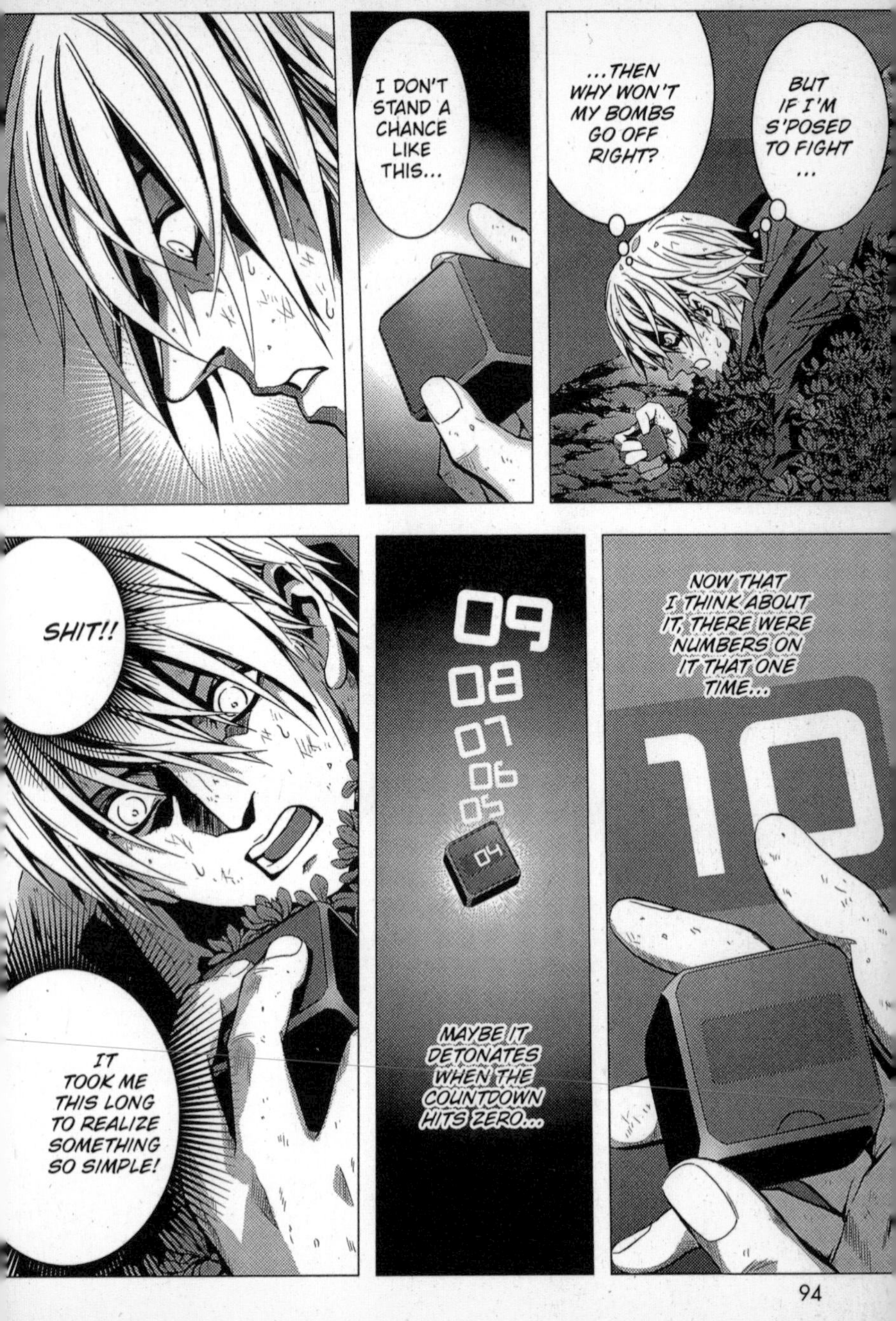
BUT IF I'M S'POSED TO FIGHT ...
...THEN WHY WON'T MY BOMBS GO OFF RIGHT?
I DON'T STAND A CHANCE LIKE THIS...
NOW THAT I THINK ABOUT IT, THERE WERE NUMBERS ON IT THAT ONE TIME...
10
09
08
07
06
05
04
MAYBE IT DETONATES WHEN THE COUNTDOWN HITS ZERO...
SHIT!!
IT TOOK ME THIS LONG TO REALIZE SOMETHING SO SIMPLE!

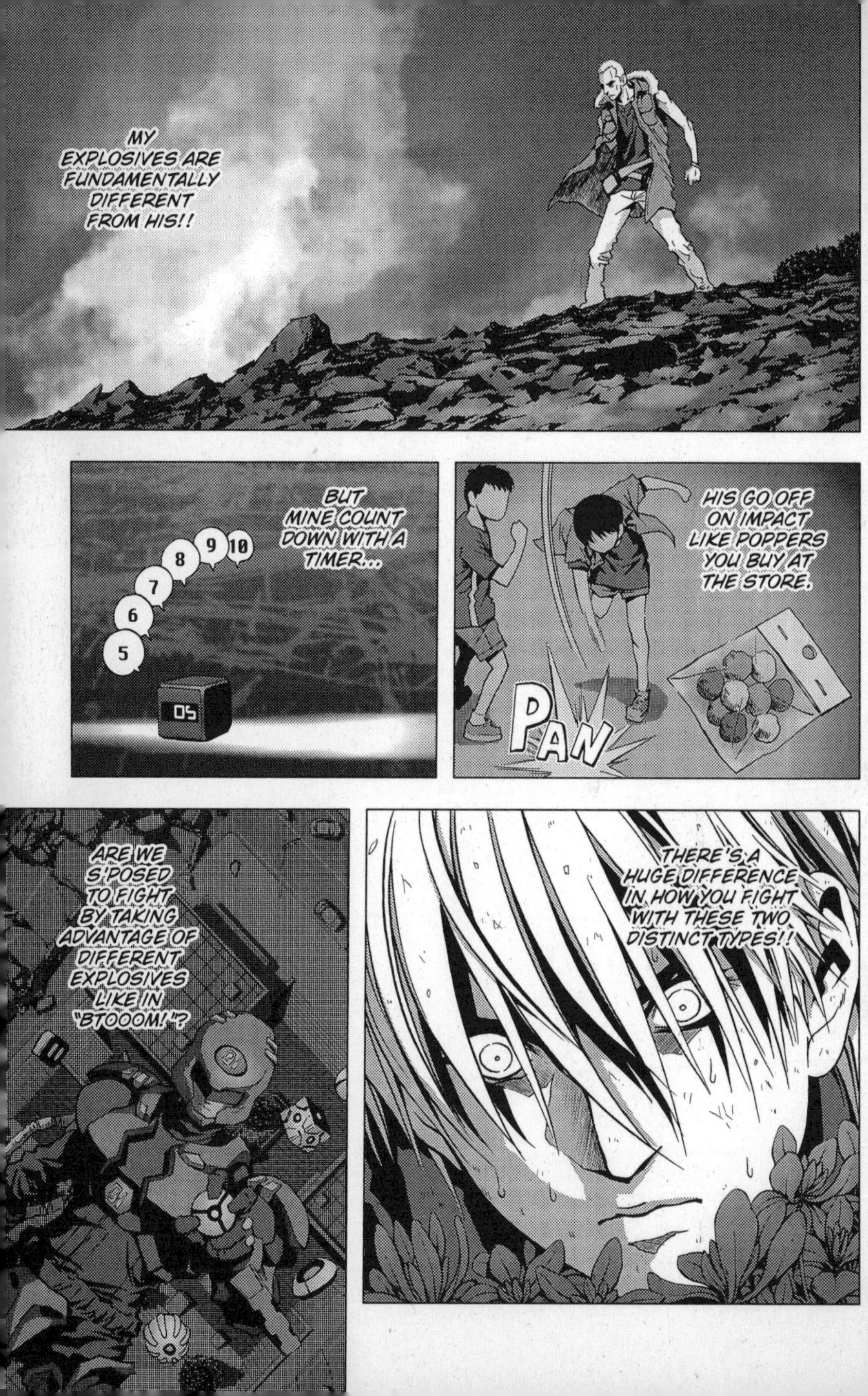
MY EXPLOSIVES ARE FUNDAMENTALLY DIFFERENT FROM HIS!!
HIS GO OFF ON IMPACT LIKE POPPERS YOU BUY AT THE STORE.
PAN
BUT MINE COUNT DOWN WITH A TIMER...
10
9
8
7
6
5
05
THERE'S A HUGE DIFFERENCE IN HOW YOU FIGHT WITH THESE TWO DISTINCT TYPES!!
ARE WE S'POSED TO FIGHT BY TAKING ADVANTAGE OF DIFFERENT EXPLOSIVES LIKE IN "BTOOOM!"?

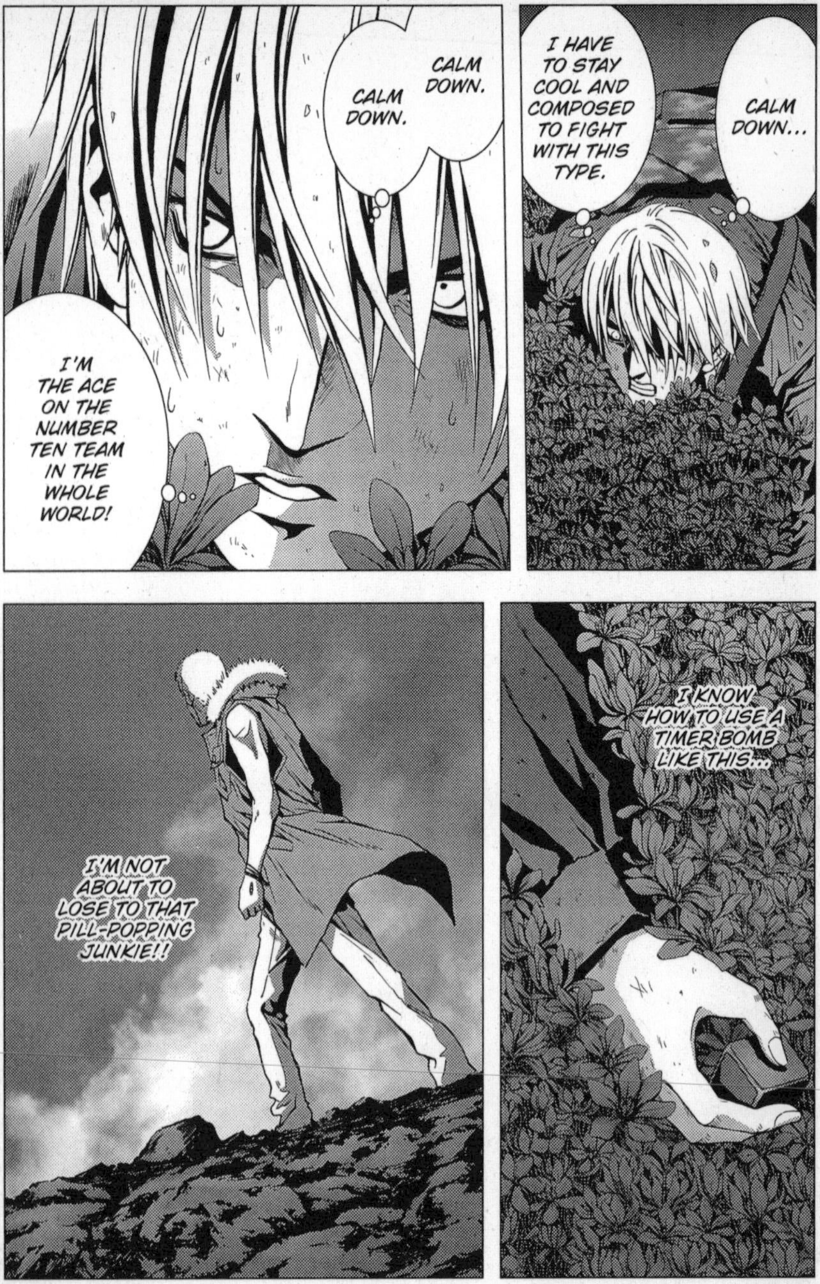
CALM DOWN...
I HAVE TO STAY COOL AND COMPOSED TO FIGHT WITH THIS TYPE.
CALM DOWN.
CALM DOWN.
I'M THE ACE ON THE NUMBER TEN TEAM IN THE WHOLE WORLD!
I KNOW HOW TO USE A TIMER BOMB LIKE THIS...
I'M NOT ABOUT TO LOSE TO THAT PILL-POPPING JUNKIE!!

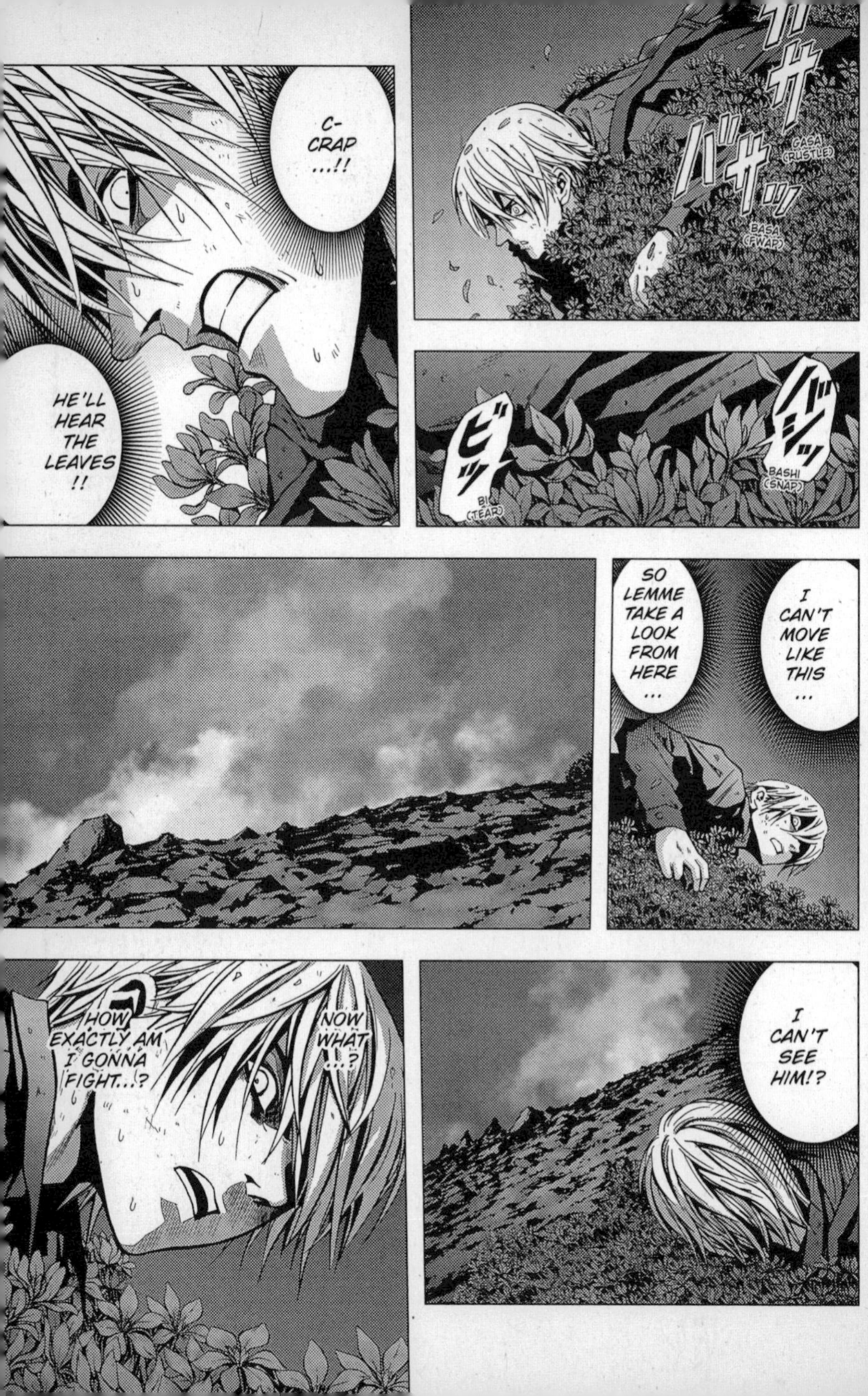
GASA (RUSTLE)
BASA (FWAP)
BASHI (SNAP)
BI (TEAR)
C-CRAP ...!!
HE'LL HEAR THE LEAVES !!
I CAN'T MOVE LIKE THIS ...
SO LEMME TAKE A LOOK FROM HERE ...
I CAN'T SEE HIM!?
NOW WHAT ...?
HOW EXACTLY AM I GONNA FIGHT...?

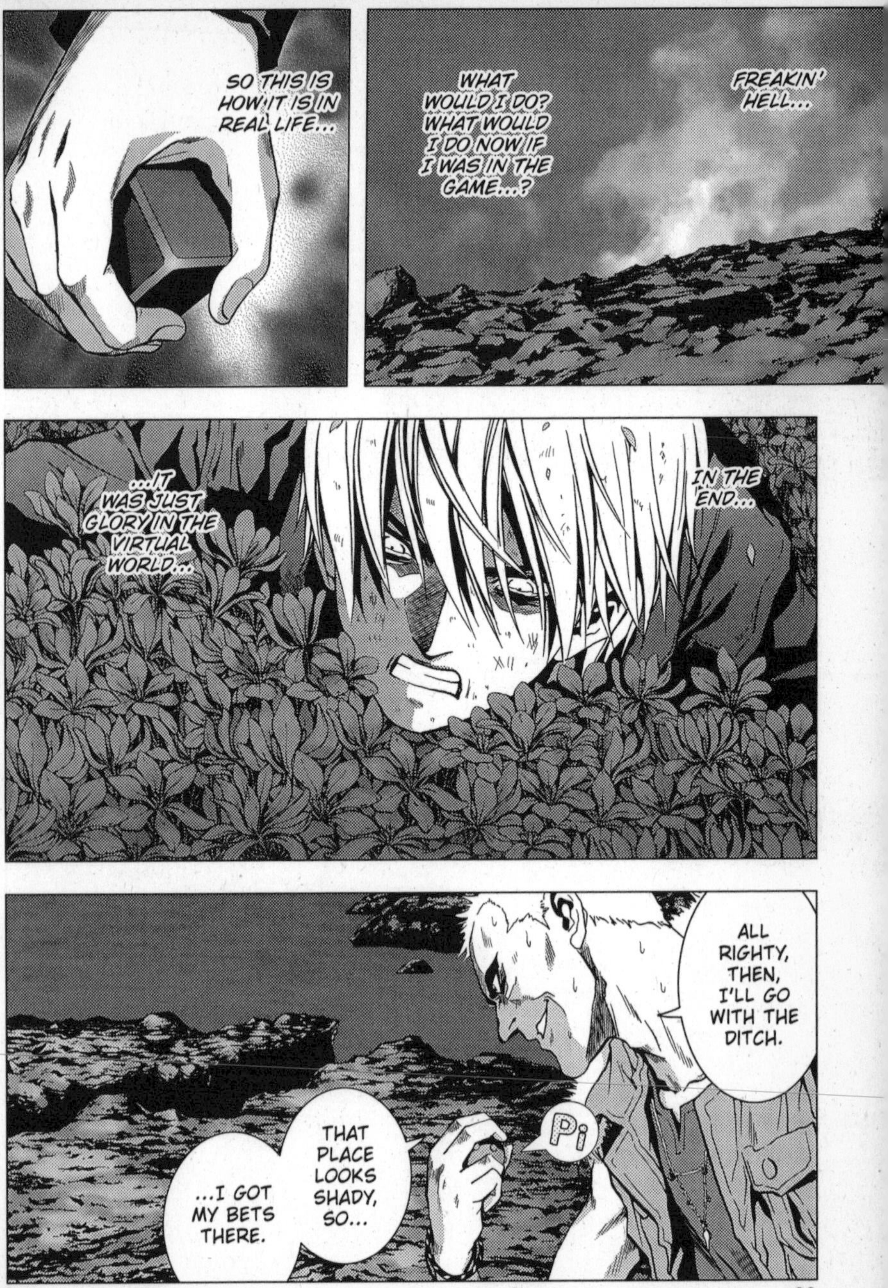
FREAKIN' HELL...
WHAT WOULD I DO? WHAT WOULD I DO NOW IF I WAS IN THE GAME...?
SO THIS IS HOW IT IS IN REAL LIFE...
IN THE END...
...IT WAS JUST GLORY IN THE VIRTUAL WORLD...
ALL RIGHTY, THEN, I'LL GO WITH THE DITCH.
Pi
THAT PLACE LOOKS SHADY, SO...
...I GOT MY BETS THERE.

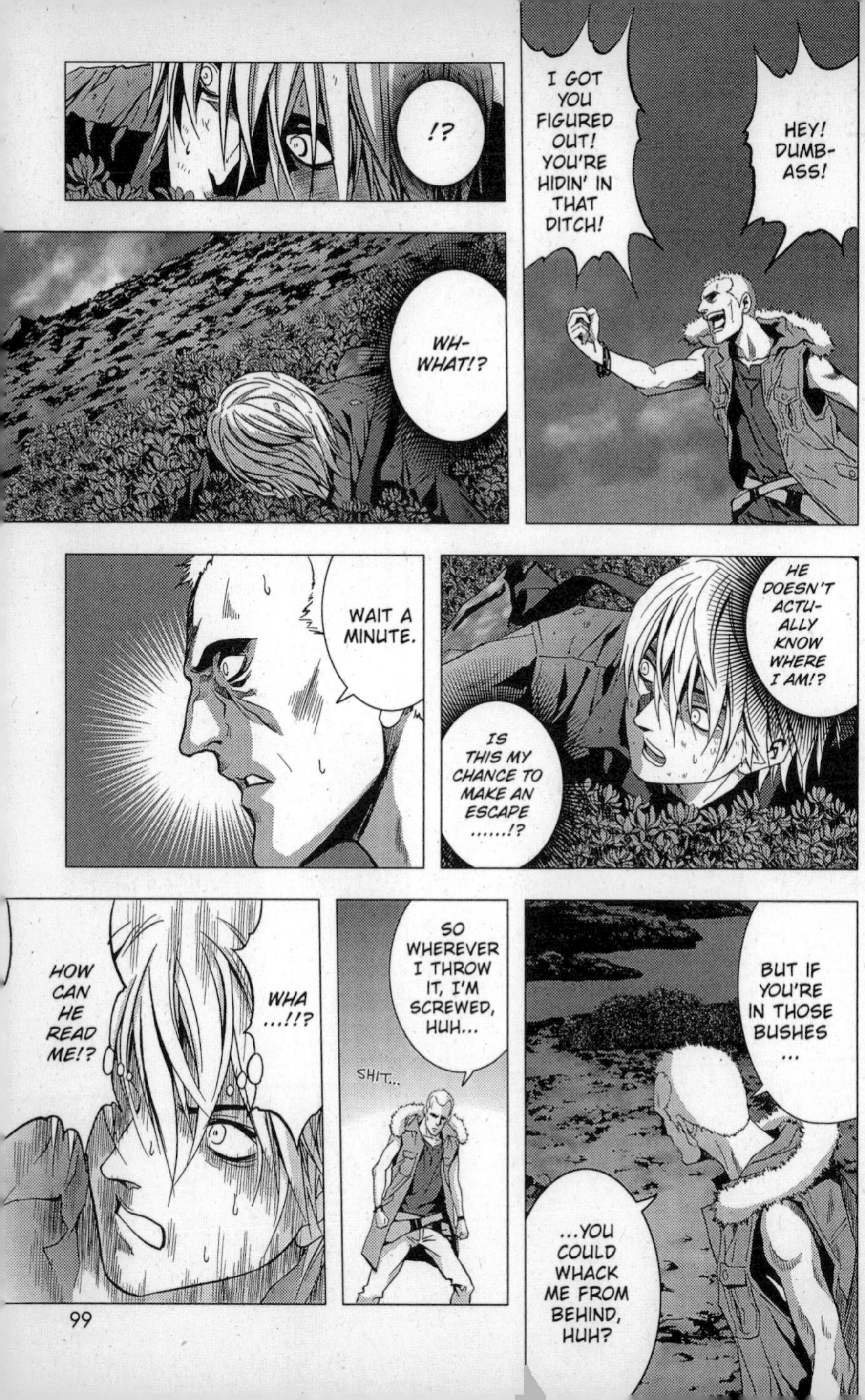
HEY! DUMB-ASS!
I GOT YOU FIGURED OUT! YOU'RE HIDIN' IN THAT DITCH!
!?
WH-WHAT!?
HE DOESN'T ACTU-ALLY KNOW WHERE I AM!?
IS THIS MY CHANCE TO MAKE AN ESCAPE ......!?
WAIT A MINUTE.
BUT IF YOU'RE IN THOSE BUSHES ...
...YOU COULD WHACK ME FROM BEHIND, HUH?
SO WHEREVER I THROW IT, I'M SCREWED, HUH...
SHIT...
WHA ...!!?
HOW CAN HE READ ME!?

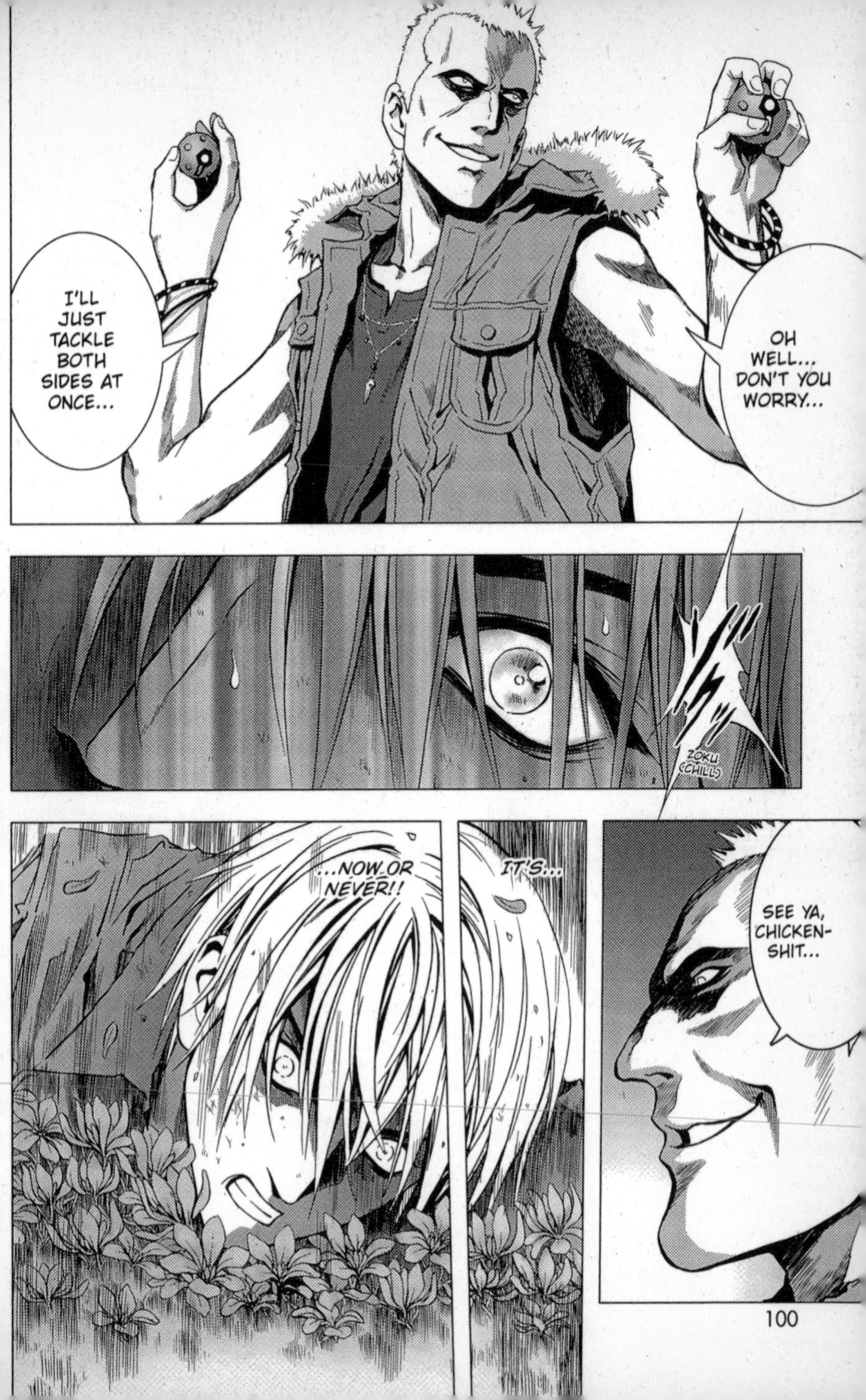
OH WELL... DON'T YOU WORRY...
I'LL JUST TACKLE BOTH SIDES AT ONCE...
ZOKU (CHILL)
SEE YA, CHICKEN-SHIT...
IT'S...
...NOW OR NEVER!!

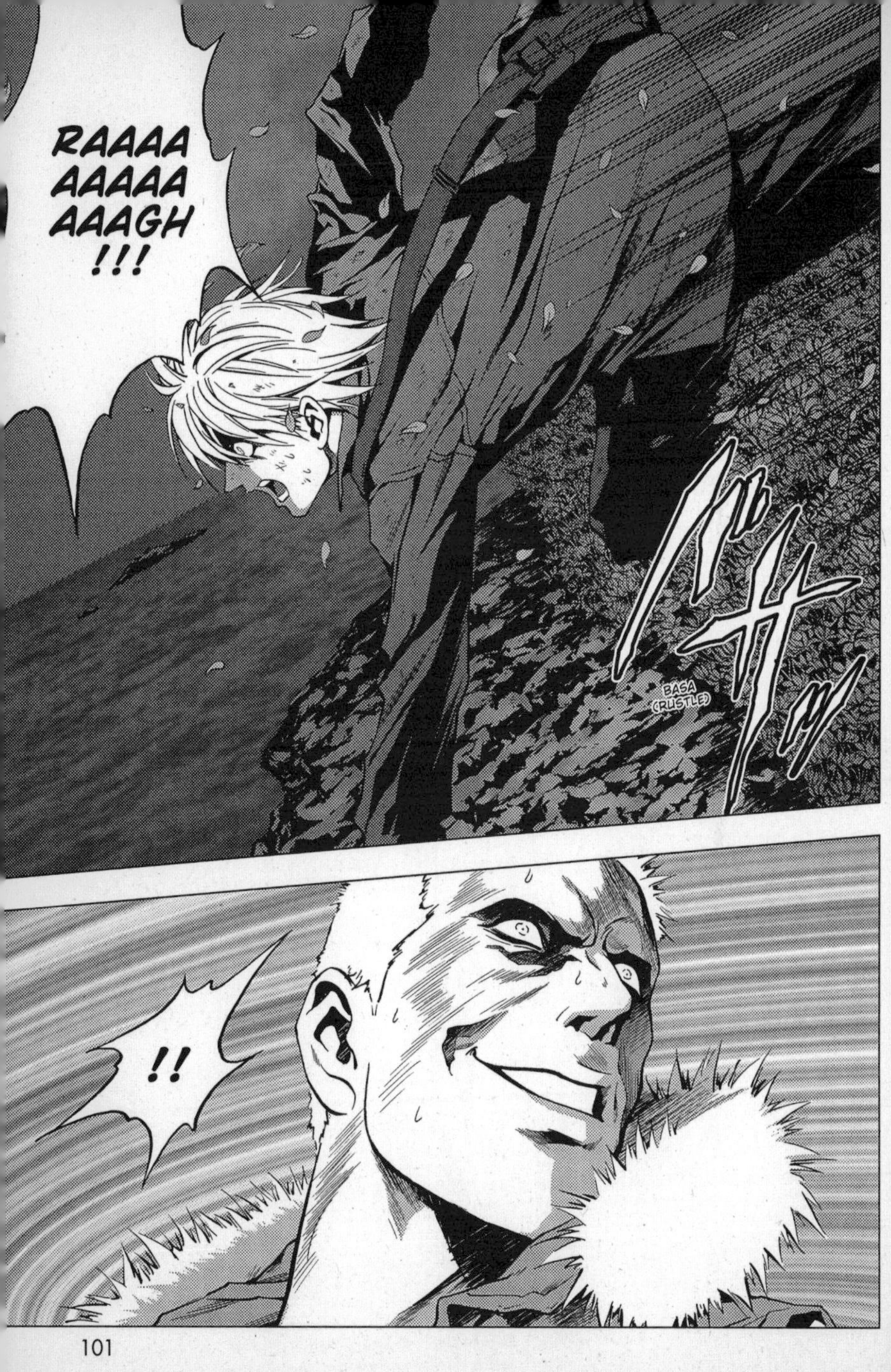
RAAAA AAAAA AAAGH !!!
BASA (RUSTLE)
!!

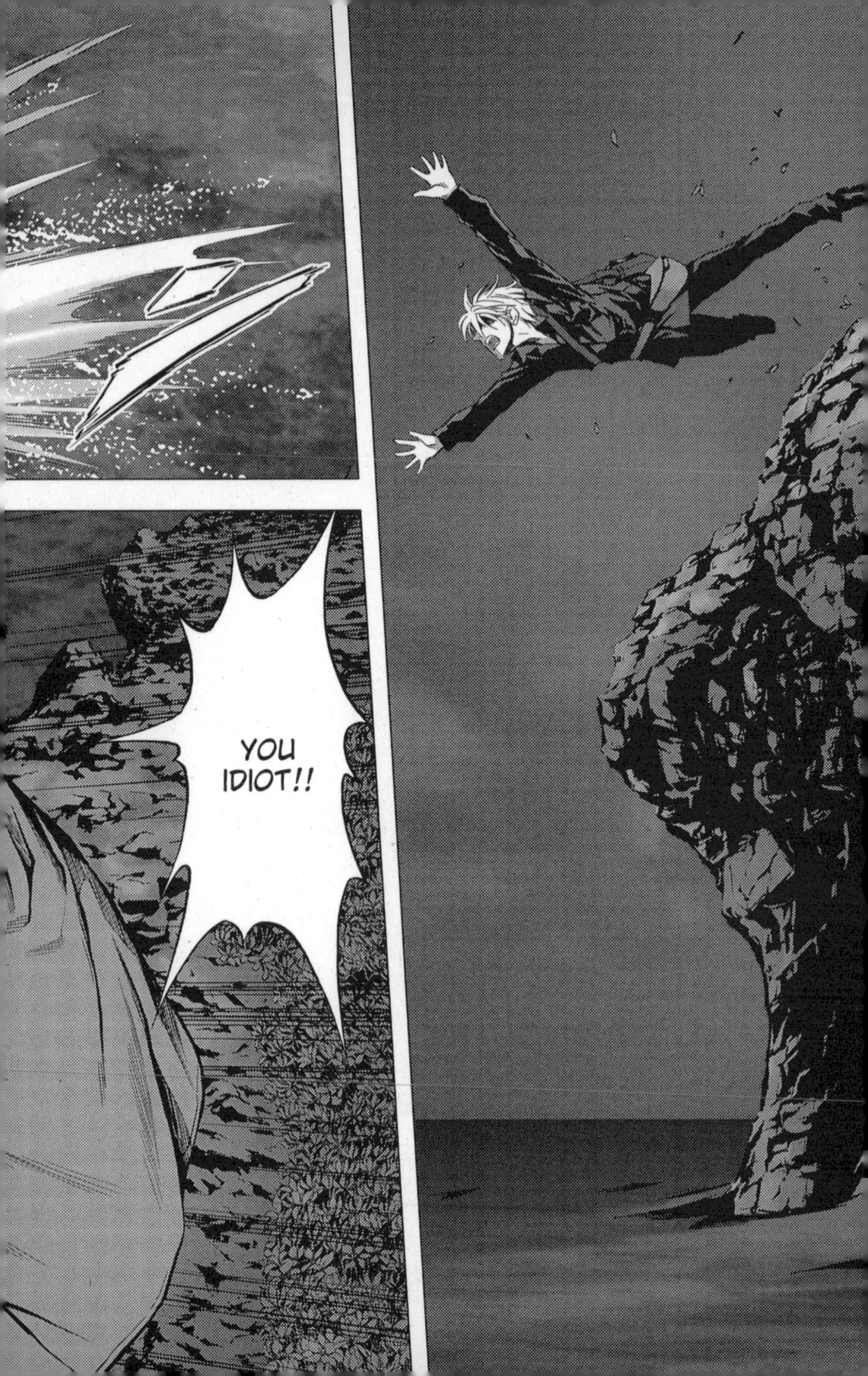
YOU IDIOT!!

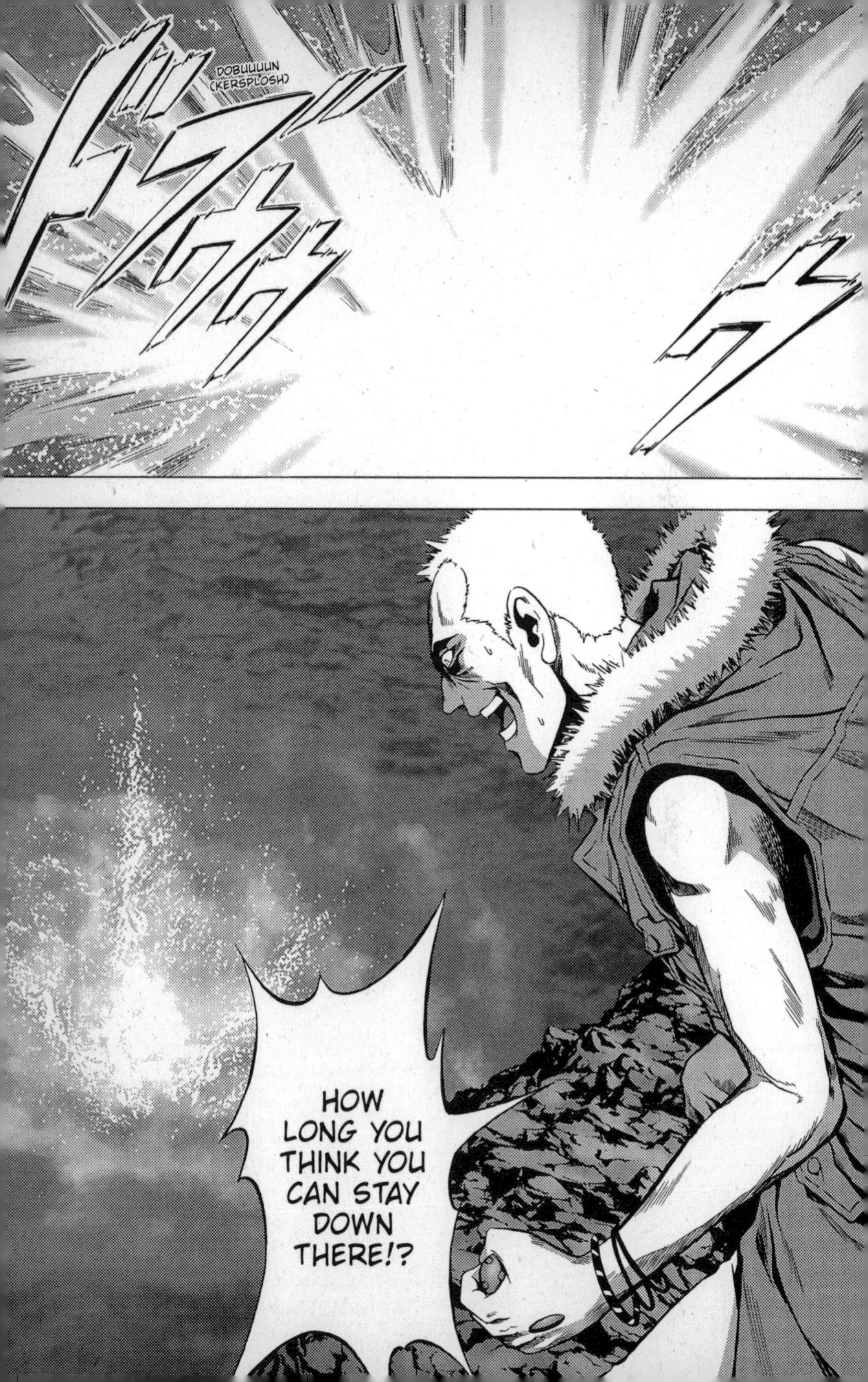
DOBUUUUN (KERSPLOSH)
HOW LONG YOU THINK YOU CAN STAY DOWN THERE!?

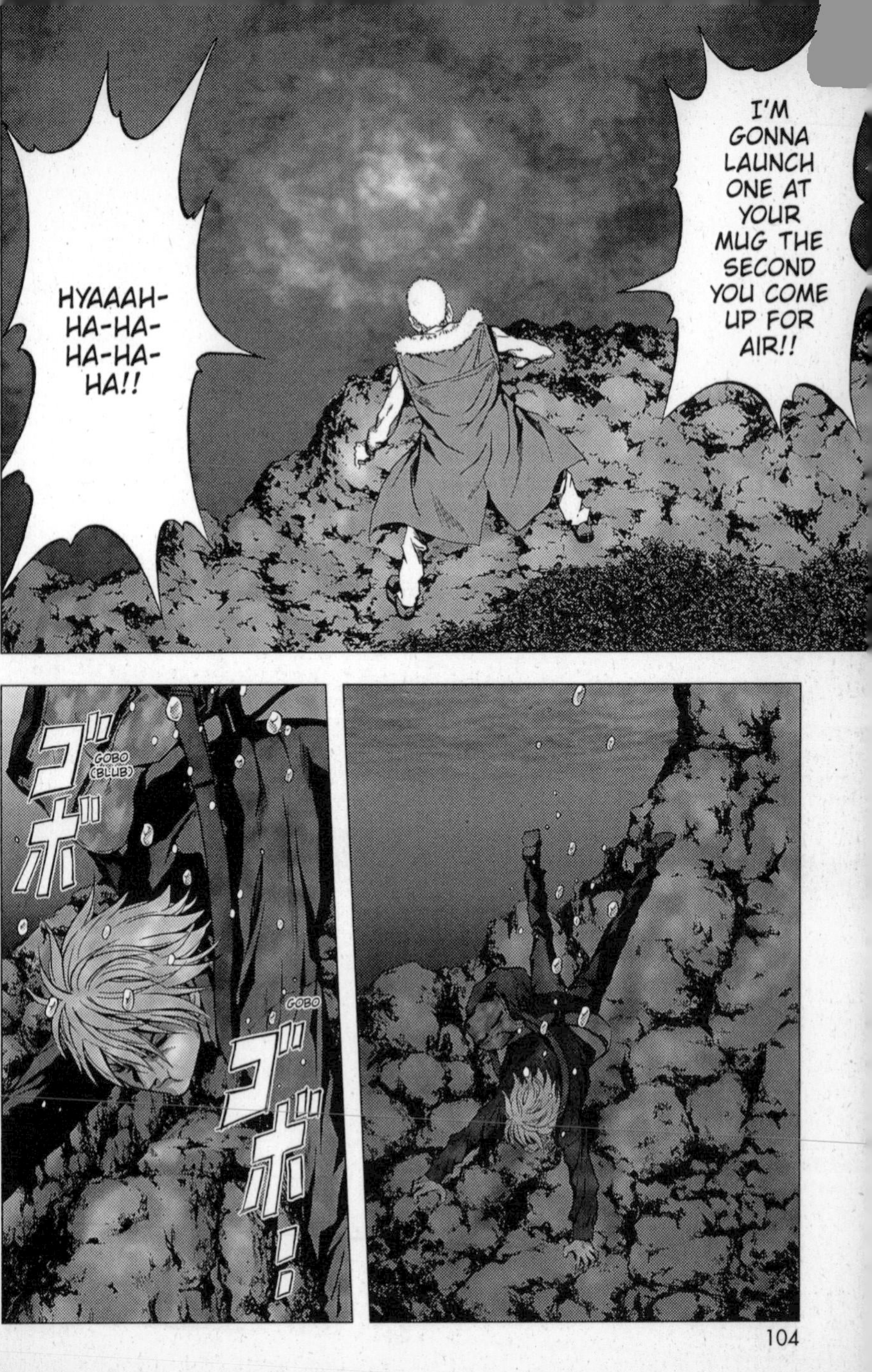
I'M GONNA LAUNCH ONE AT YOUR MUG THE SECOND YOU COME UP FOR AIR!!
HYAAAH-HA-HA-HA-HA-HA!!
ゴボ
GOBO (BLUB)
ゴボ…
GOBO

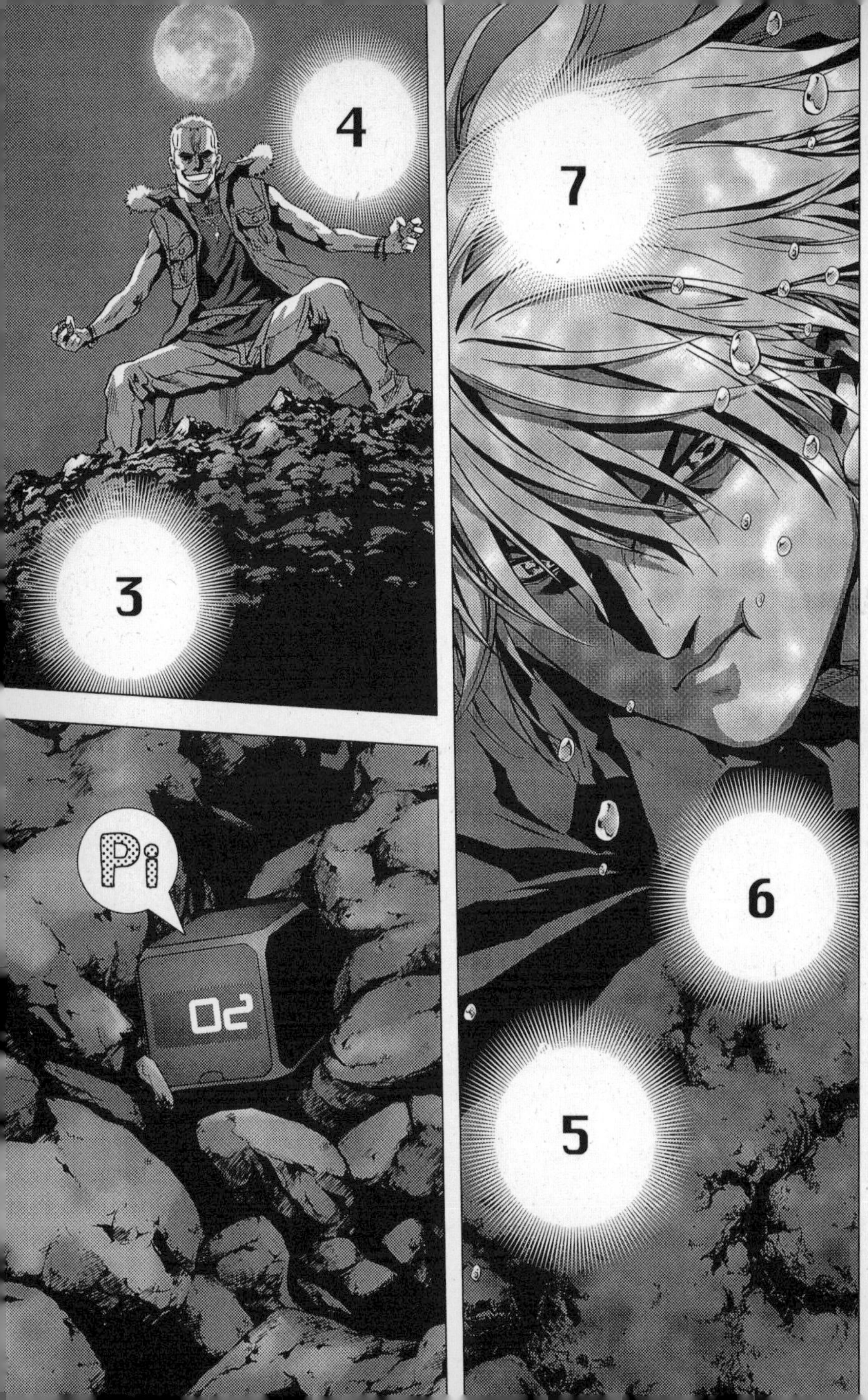

7
6
5
4
3
Pi
02

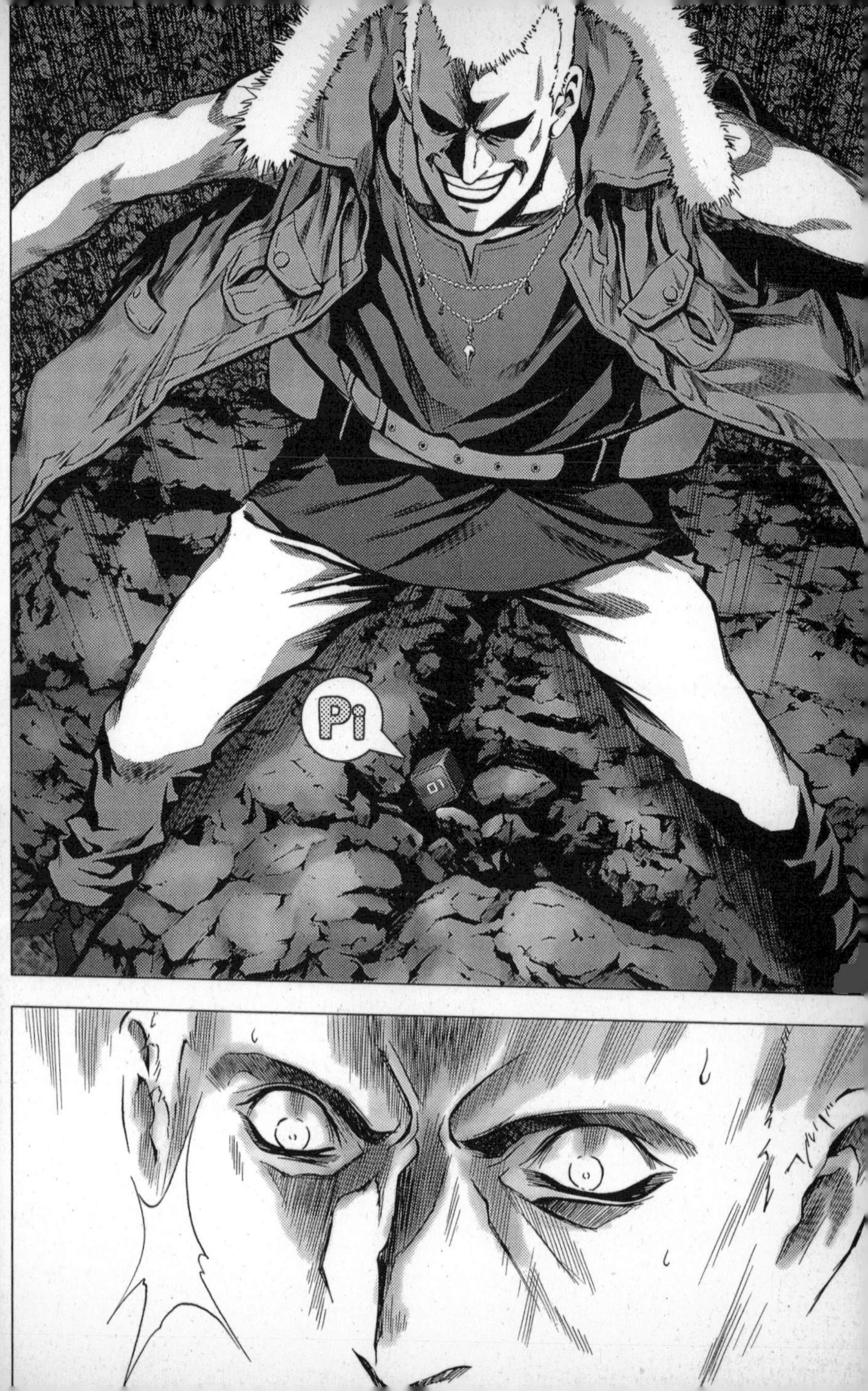
Pi
01

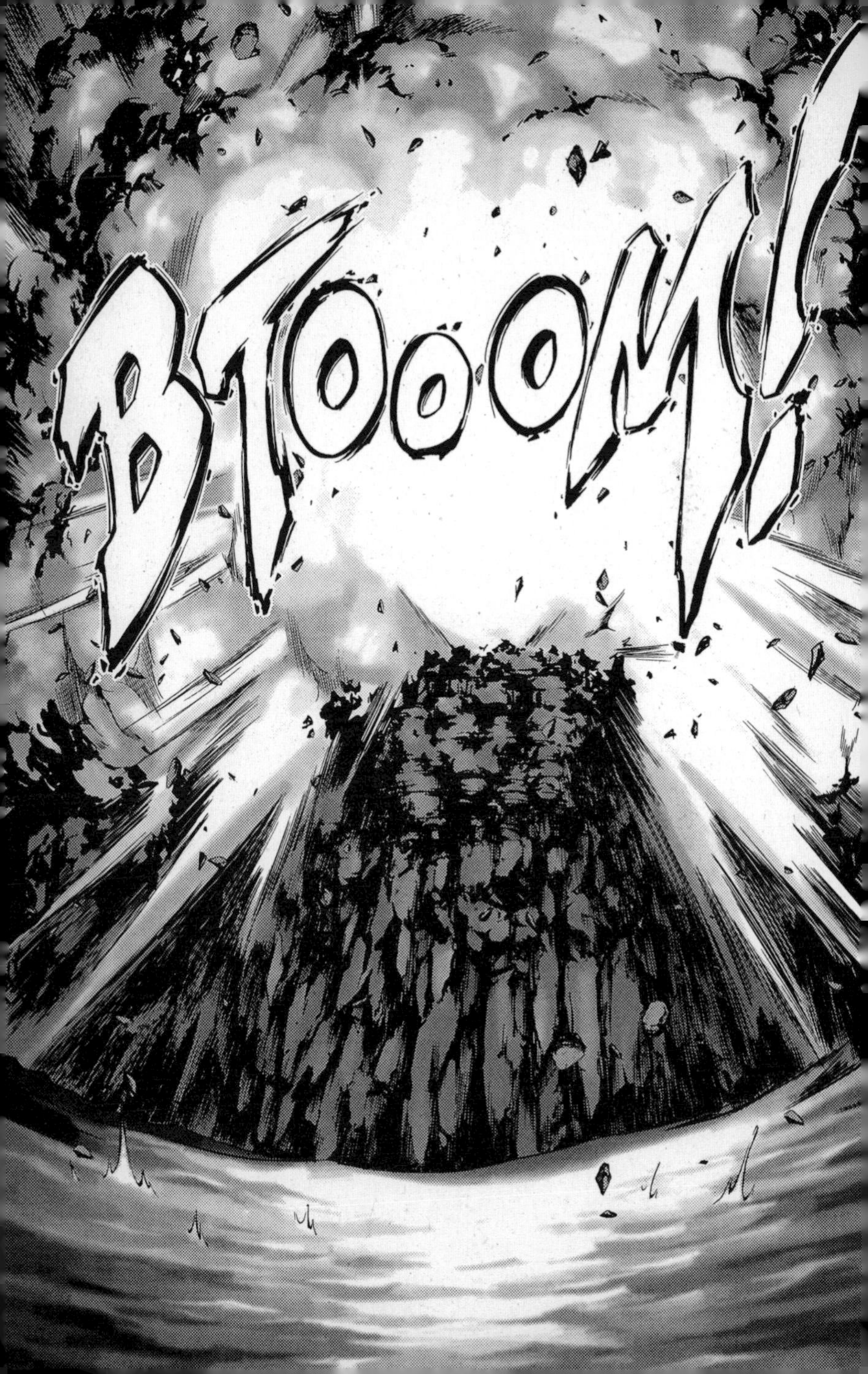
BTOOOM!!

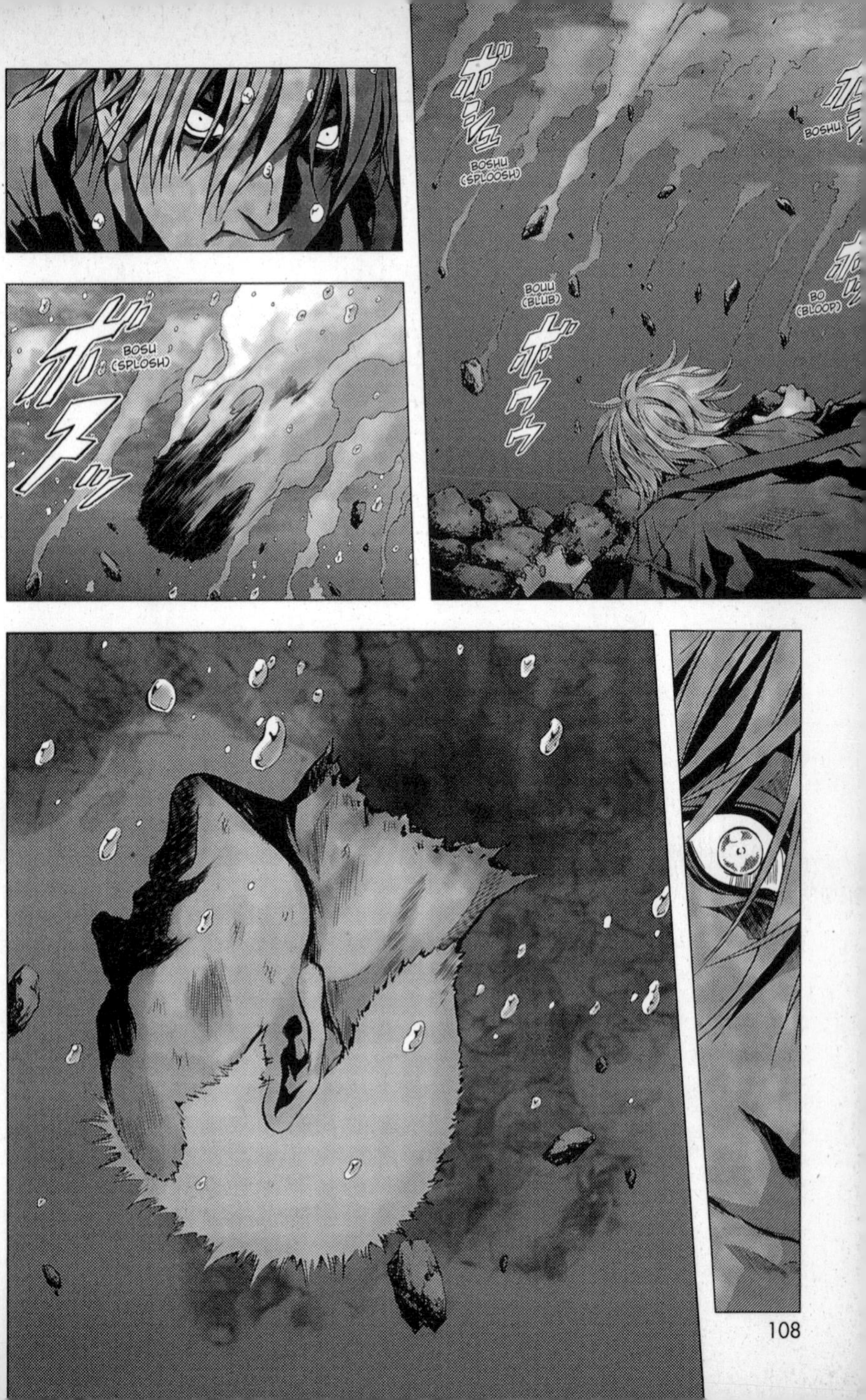
BOSHU
BOSHU (SPLOOSH)
BO (BLOOP)
BOUU (BLUB)
BOSU (SPLOSH)

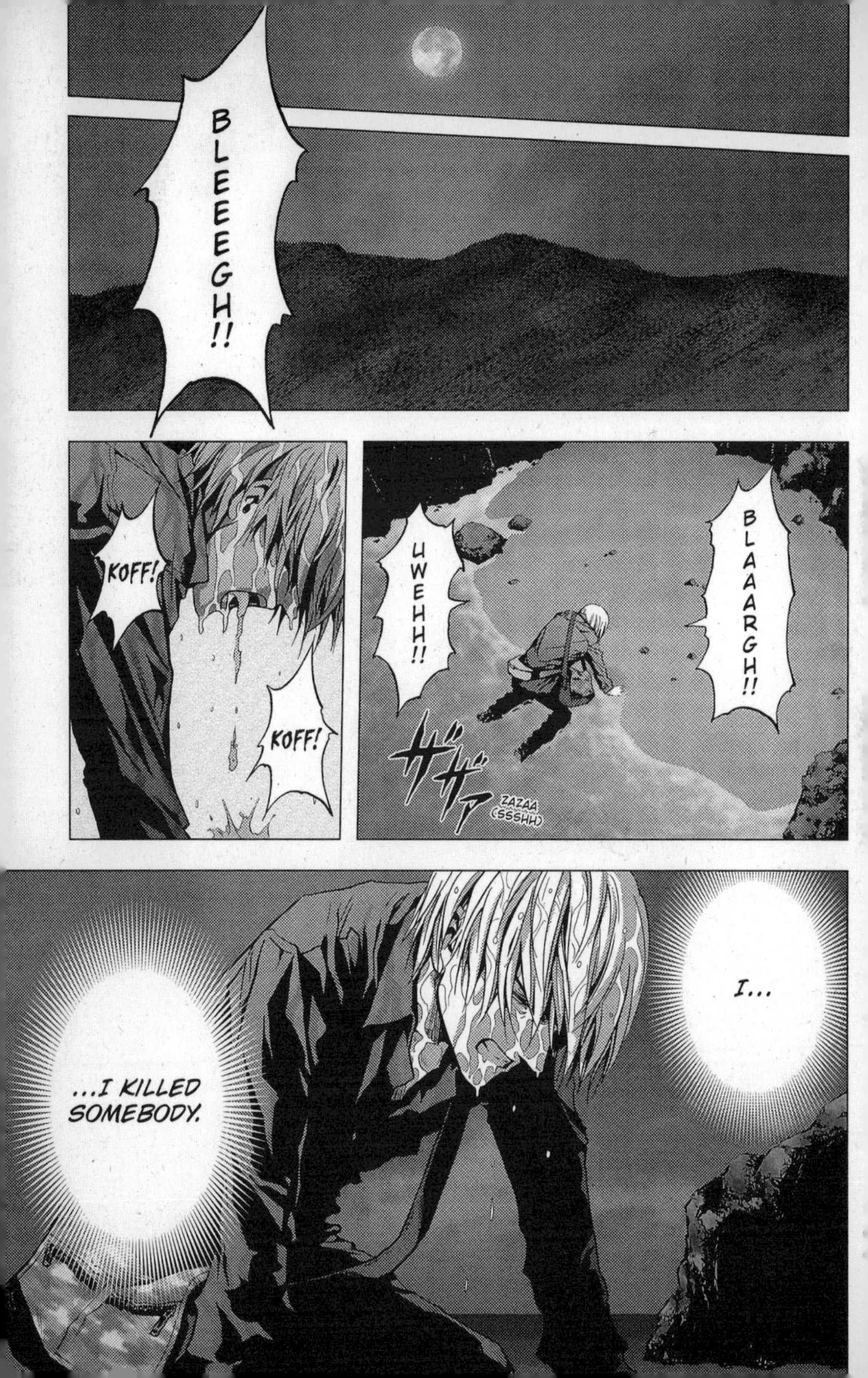
BLEEEEGH!!
BLAAARGH!!
UWEHH!!
ザザァ
ZAZAA (SSSHH)
KOFF!
KOFF!
I...
...I KILLED SOMEBODY.

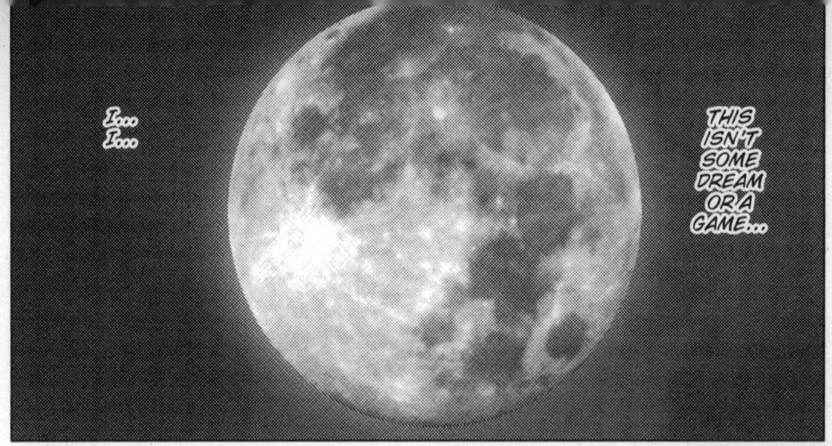
THIS ISN'T SOME DREAM OR A GAME...
I... I...
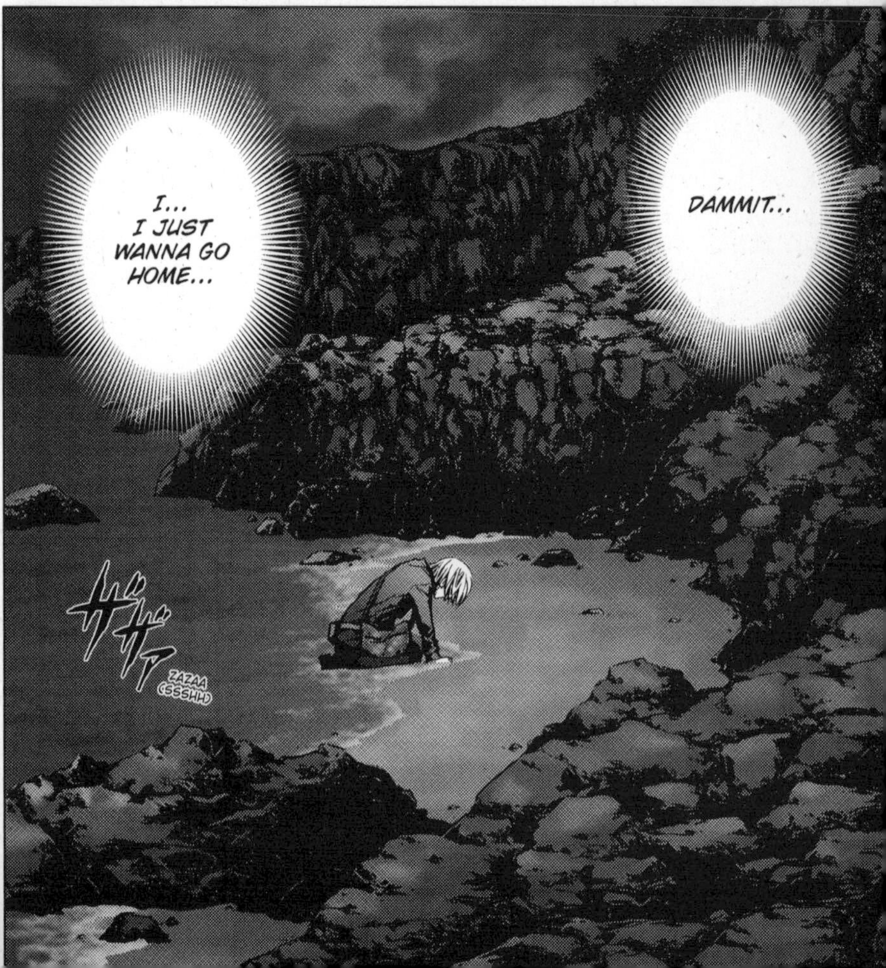
DAMMIT...
I... I JUST WANNA GO HOME...
ザザァ
ZAZAA (SSSHH)

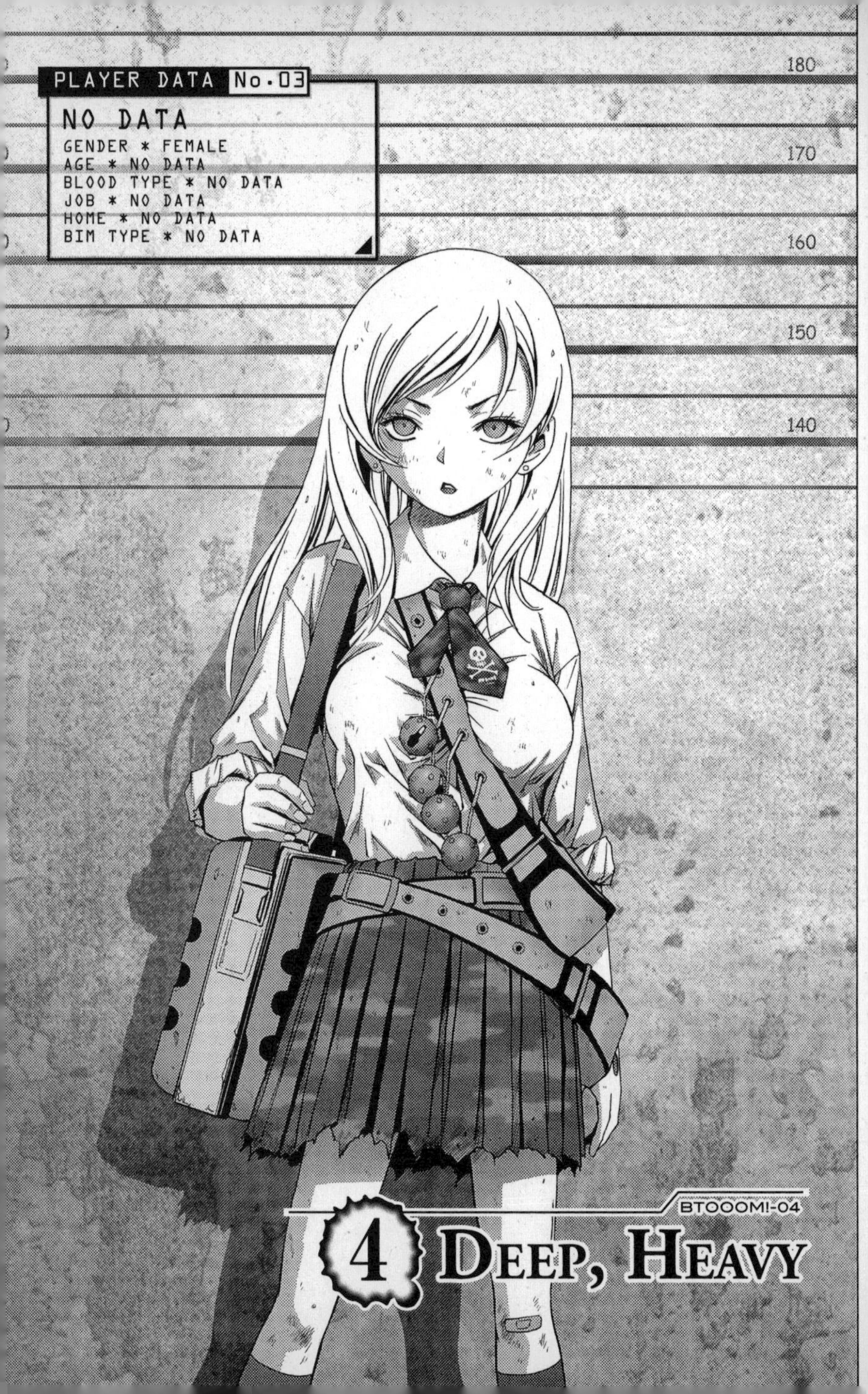
PLAYER DATA No.03
NO DATA
GENDER * FEMALE
AGE * NO DATA
BLOOD TYPE * NO DATA
JOB * NO DATA
HOME * NO DATA
BIM TYPE * NO DATA
180
170
160
150
140
BTOOOM!-04
4 DEEP, HEAVY

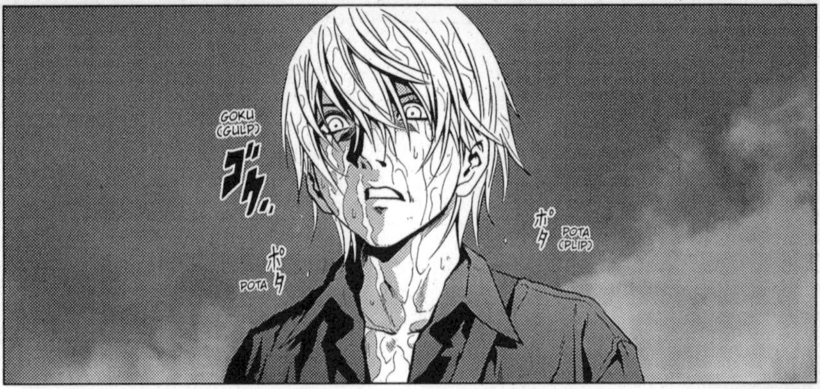
GOKU (GULP)
ゴクッ
ポタ
POTA (PLIP)
ポタ
POTA

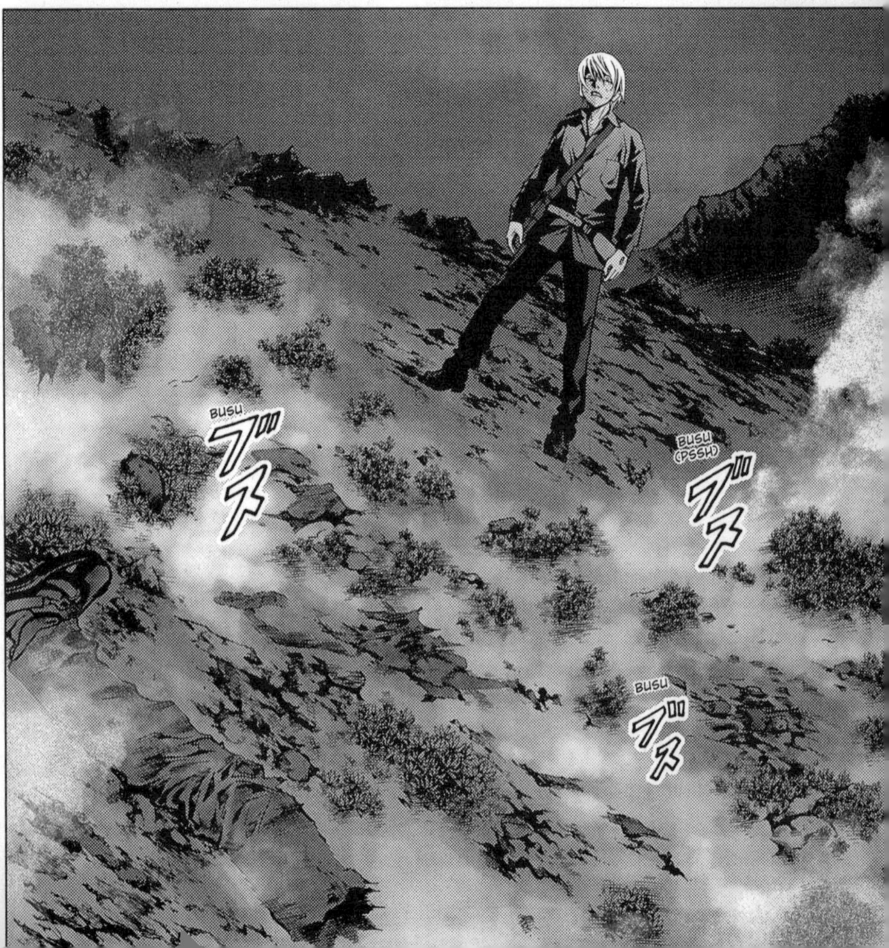
BUSU
ブスッ
BUSU (PSSH)
ブスッ
BUSU
ブスッ

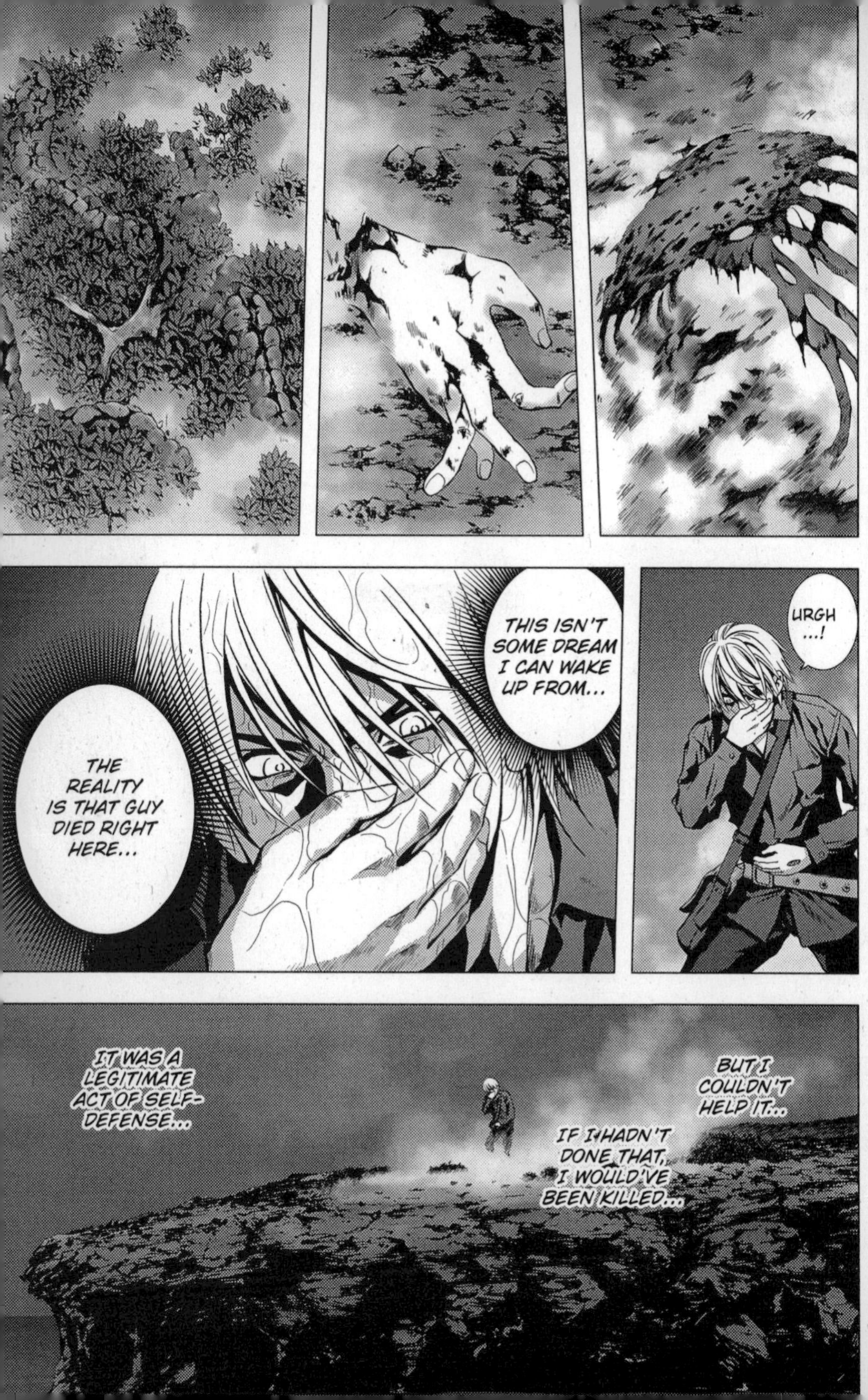
URGH ...!
THIS ISN'T SOME DREAM I CAN WAKE UP FROM...
THE REALITY IS THAT GUY DIED RIGHT HERE...
BUT I COULDN'T HELP IT...
IF I HADN'T DONE THAT, I WOULD'VE BEEN KILLED...
IT WAS A LEGITIMATE ACT OF SELF-DEFENSE...

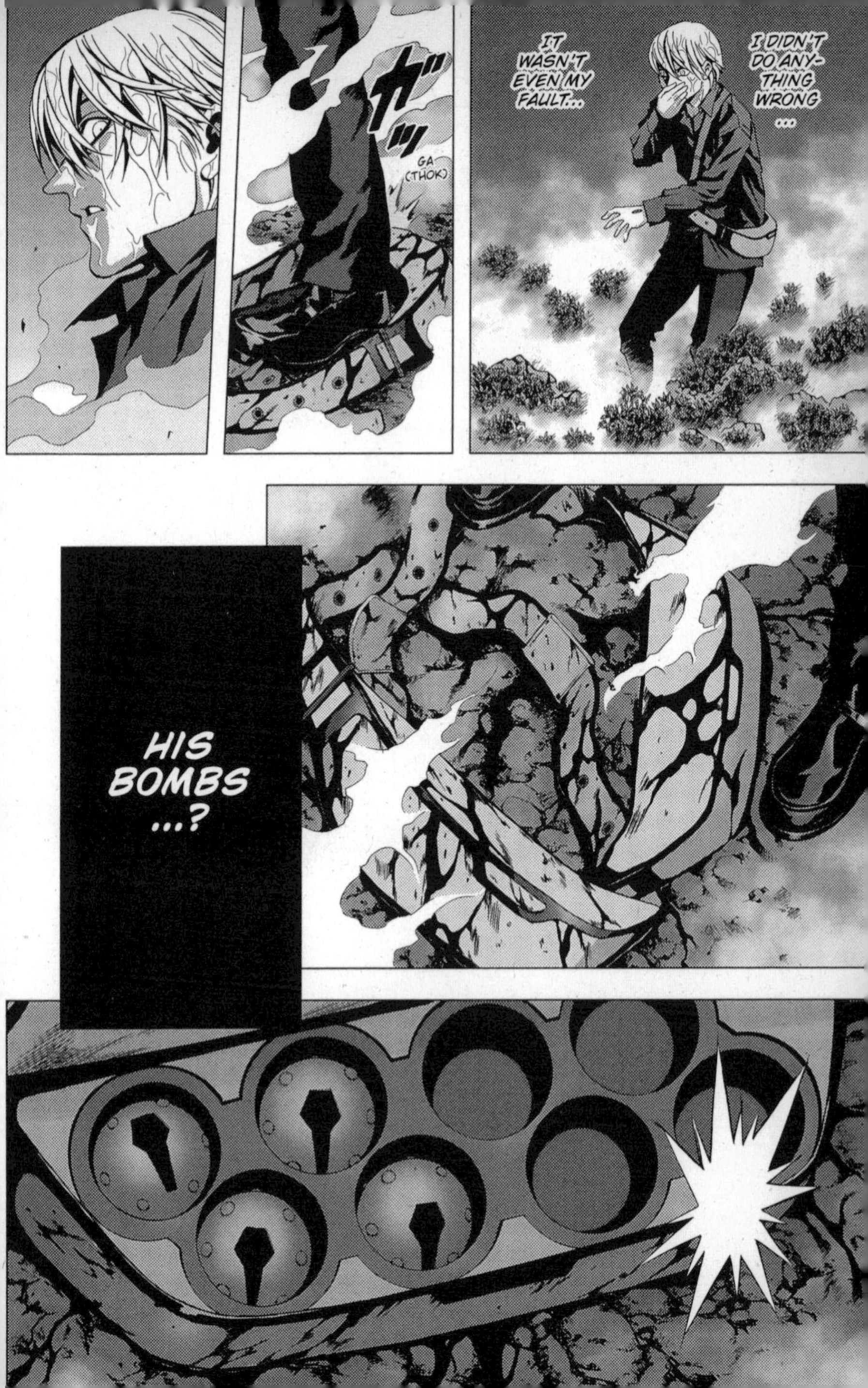
I DIDN'T DO ANY-THING WRONG ...
IT WASN'T EVEN MY FAULT...
GA (THOK)
HIS BOMBS ...?

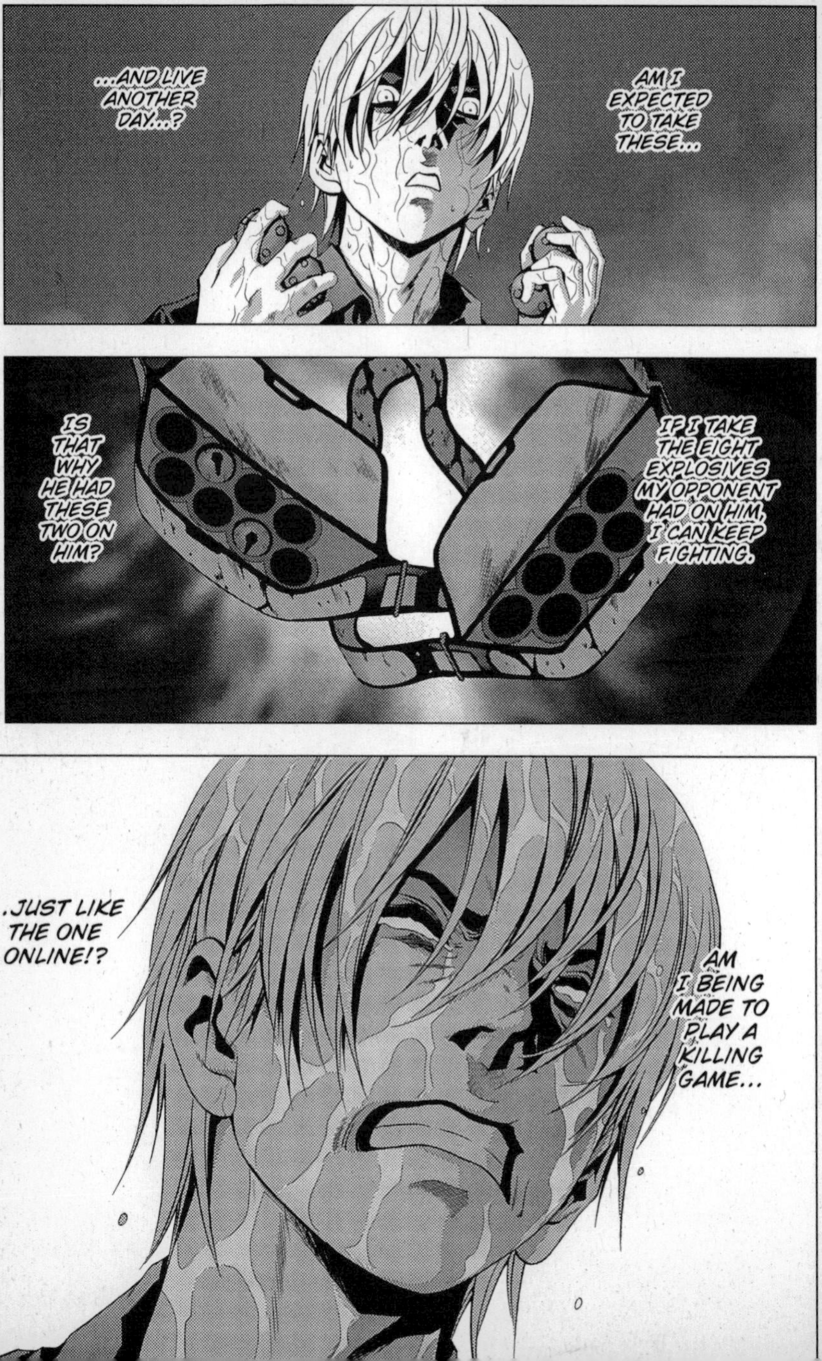
AM I EXPECTED TO TAKE THESE...
...AND LIVE ANOTHER DAY...?
IF I TAKE THE EIGHT EXPLOSIVES MY OPPONENT HAD ON HIM, I CAN KEEP FIGHTING.
IS THAT WHY HE HAD THESE TWO ON HIM?
AM I BEING MADE TO PLAY A KILLING GAME...
...JUST LIKE THE ONE ONLINE!?

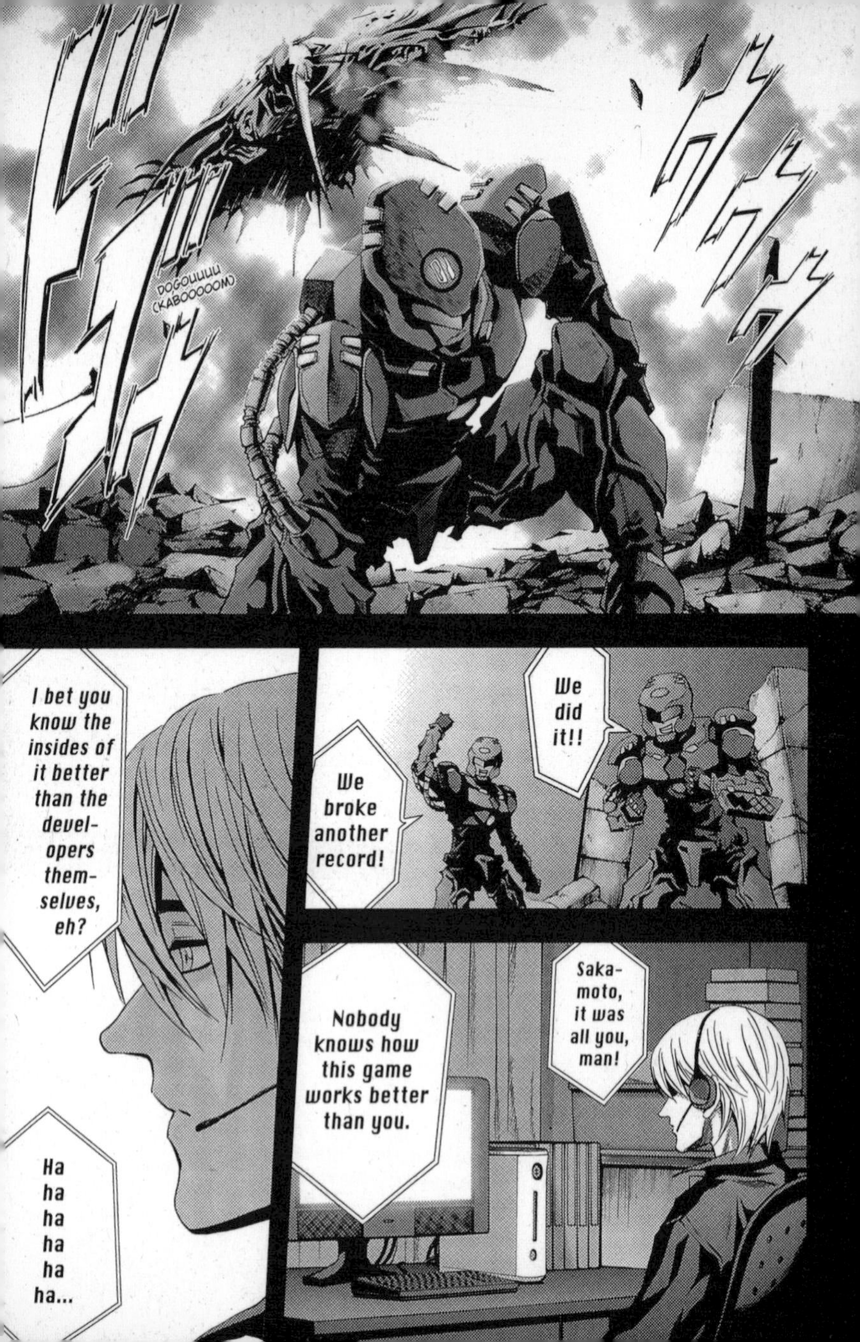
DOGOUUUU
(KABOOOOOM)
We did it!!
We broke another record!
Sakamoto, it was all you, man!
Nobody knows how this game works better than you.
I bet you know the insides of it better than the developers themselves, eh?
Ha ha ha ha ha ha...

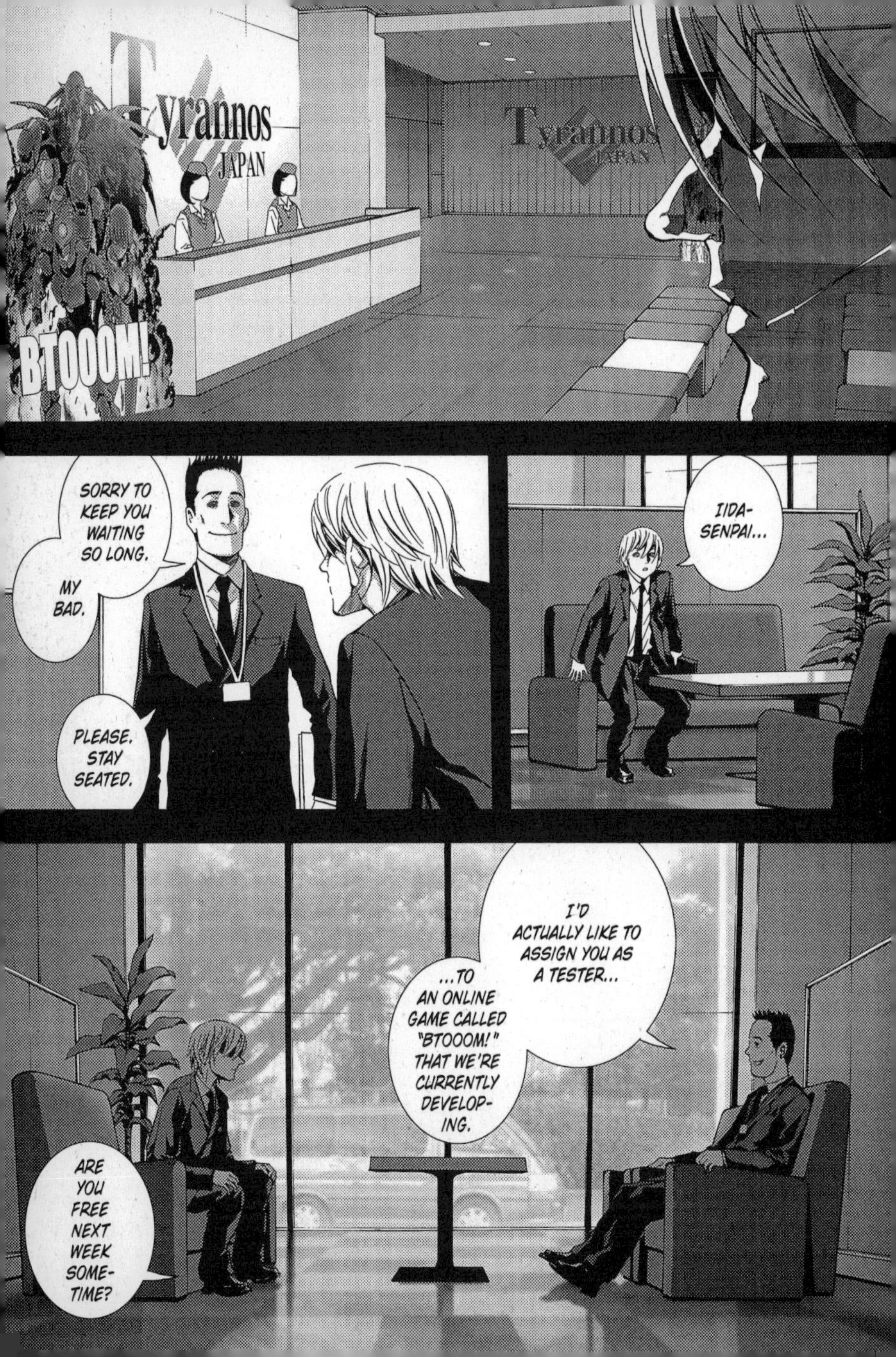
Tyrannos JAPAN
Tyrannos JAPAN
BTOOOM!
IIDA-SENPAI...
SORRY TO KEEP YOU WAITING SO LONG.
MY BAD.
PLEASE. STAY SEATED.
I'D ACTUALLY LIKE TO ASSIGN YOU AS A TESTER...
...TO AN ONLINE GAME CALLED "BTOOOM!" THAT WE'RE CURRENTLY DEVELOP-ING.
ARE YOU FREE NEXT WEEK SOME-TIME?

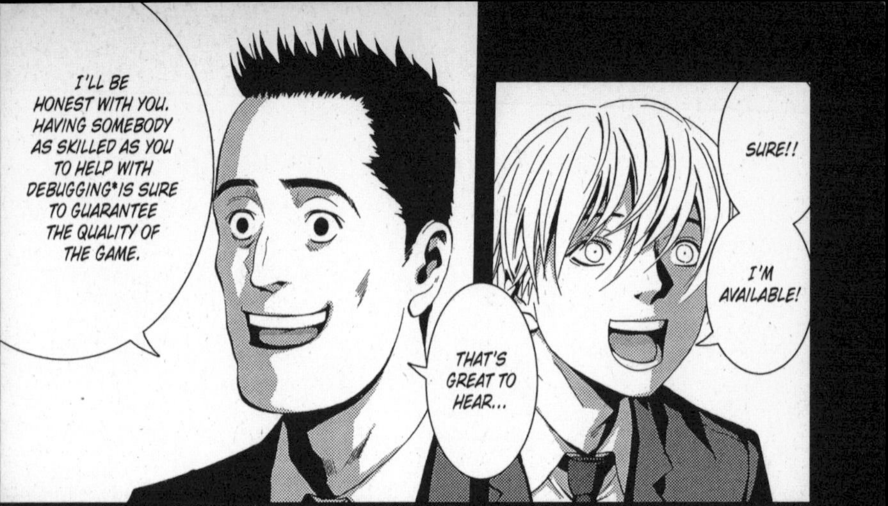
SURE!!
I'M AVAILABLE!
I'LL BE HONEST WITH YOU. HAVING SOMEBODY AS SKILLED AS YOU TO HELP WITH DEBUGGING* IS SURE TO GUARANTEE THE QUALITY OF THE GAME.
THAT'S GREAT TO HEAR...

*THE JOB OF FINDING AND CORRECTING BUGS AND FLAWS IN COMPUTER PROGRAMS AND THE LIKE.

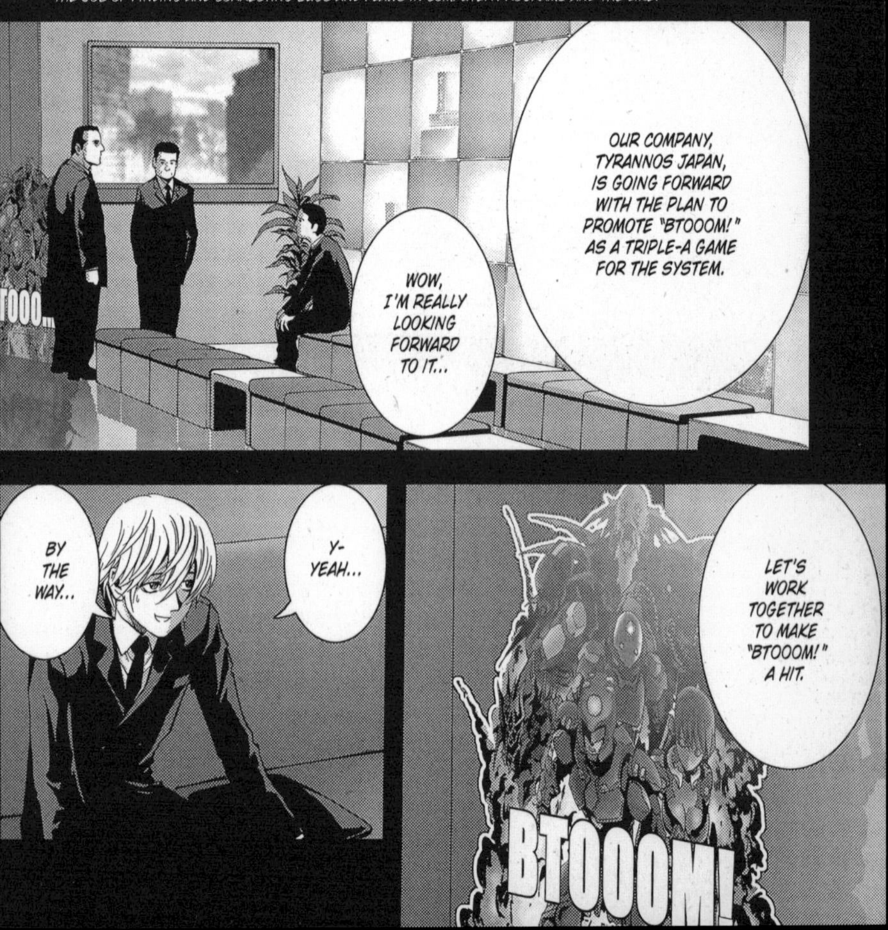
OUR COMPANY, TYRANNOS JAPAN, IS GOING FORWARD WITH THE PLAN TO PROMOTE "BTOOOM!" AS A TRIPLE-A GAME FOR THE SYSTEM.
WOW, I'M REALLY LOOKING FORWARD TO IT...
TOOO...
LET'S WORK TOGETHER TO MAKE "BTOOOM!" A HIT.
BTOOOM!
Y-YEAH...
BY THE WAY...

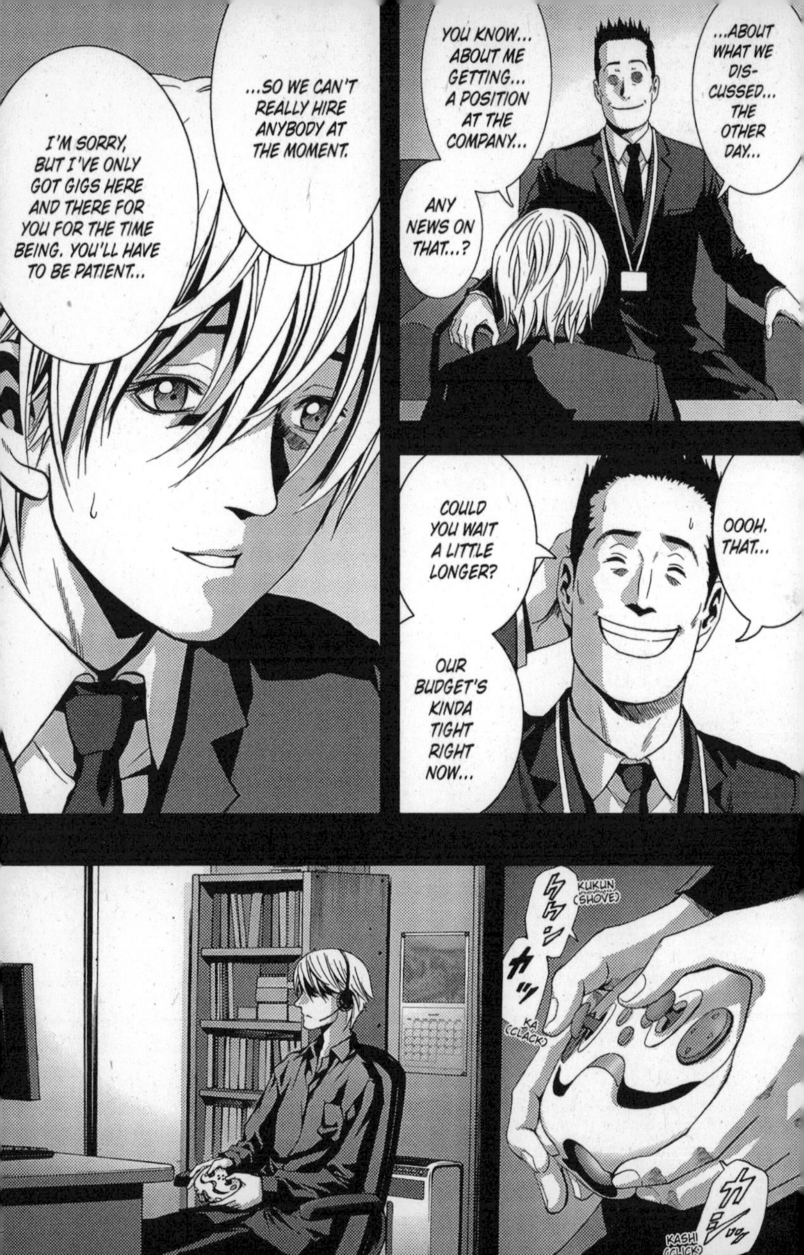
...ABOUT WHAT WE DIS-CUSSED... THE OTHER DAY...
YOU KNOW... ABOUT ME GETTING... A POSITION AT THE COMPANY...
ANY NEWS ON THAT...?
OOOH. THAT...
COULD YOU WAIT A LITTLE LONGER?
OUR BUDGET'S KINDA TIGHT RIGHT NOW...
...SO WE CAN'T REALLY HIRE ANYBODY AT THE MOMENT.
I'M SORRY, BUT I'VE ONLY GOT GIGS HERE AND THERE FOR YOU FOR THE TIME BEING. YOU'LL HAVE TO BE PATIENT...
KUKUN (SHOVE)
KA (CLACK)
KASHI (CLICK)

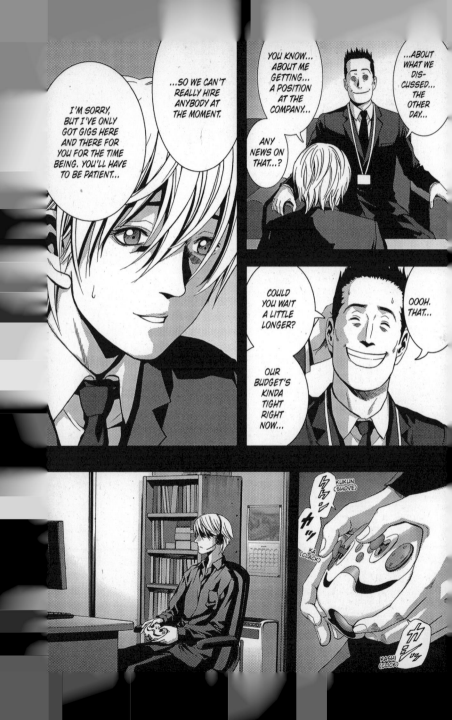

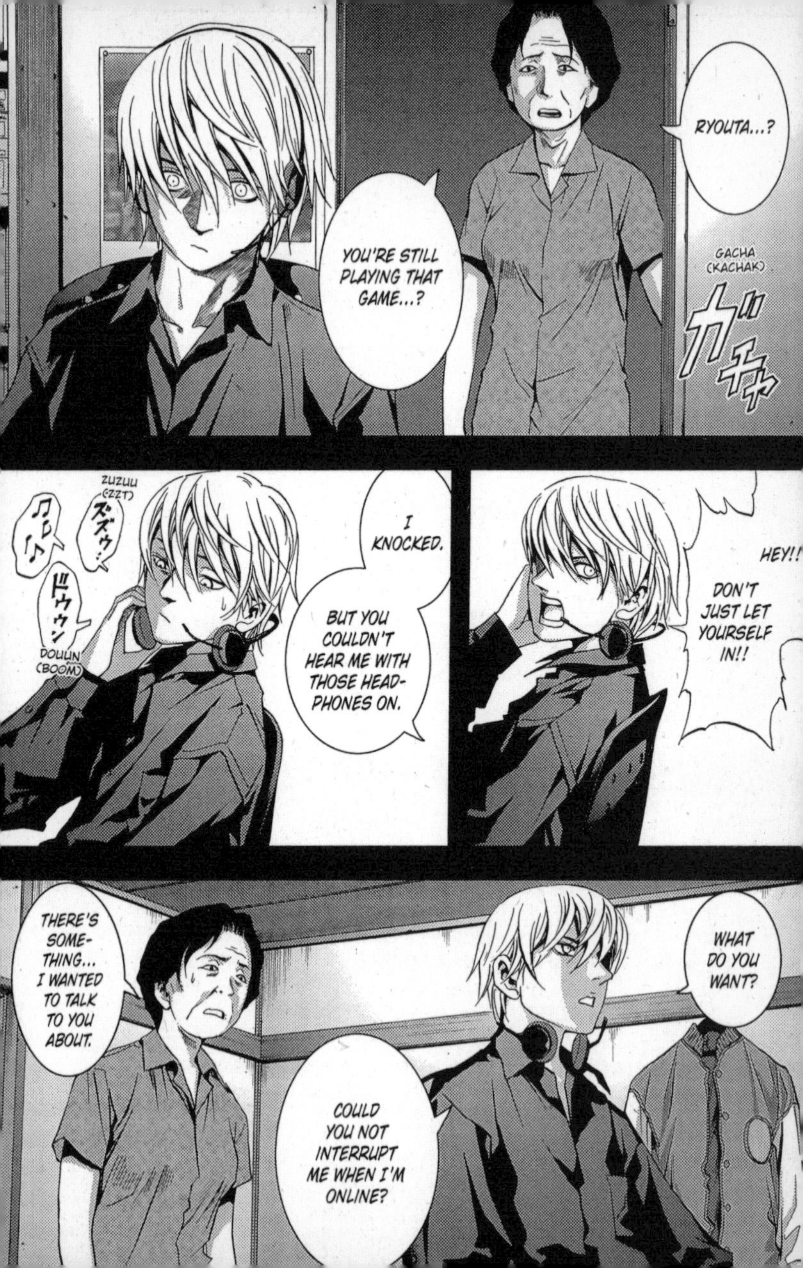
RYOUTA...?
GACHA (KACHAK)
ガチャ
YOU'RE STILL PLAYING THAT GAME...?
HEY!!
DON'T JUST LET YOURSELF IN!!
I KNOCKED.
BUT YOU COULDN'T HEAR ME WITH THOSE HEAD-PHONES ON.
ZUZUU (ZZT)
ズズゥ…
ドゥゥン
DOUUN (BOOM)
WHAT DO YOU WANT?
COULD YOU NOT INTERRUPT ME WHEN I'M ONLINE?
THERE'S SOME-THING... I WANTED TO TALK TO YOU ABOUT.

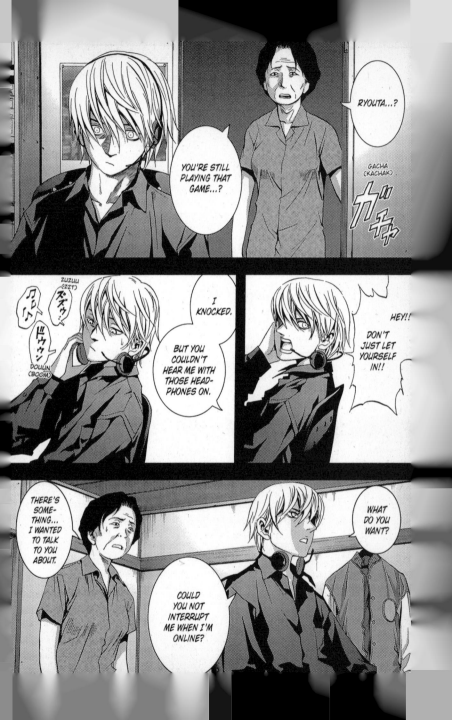

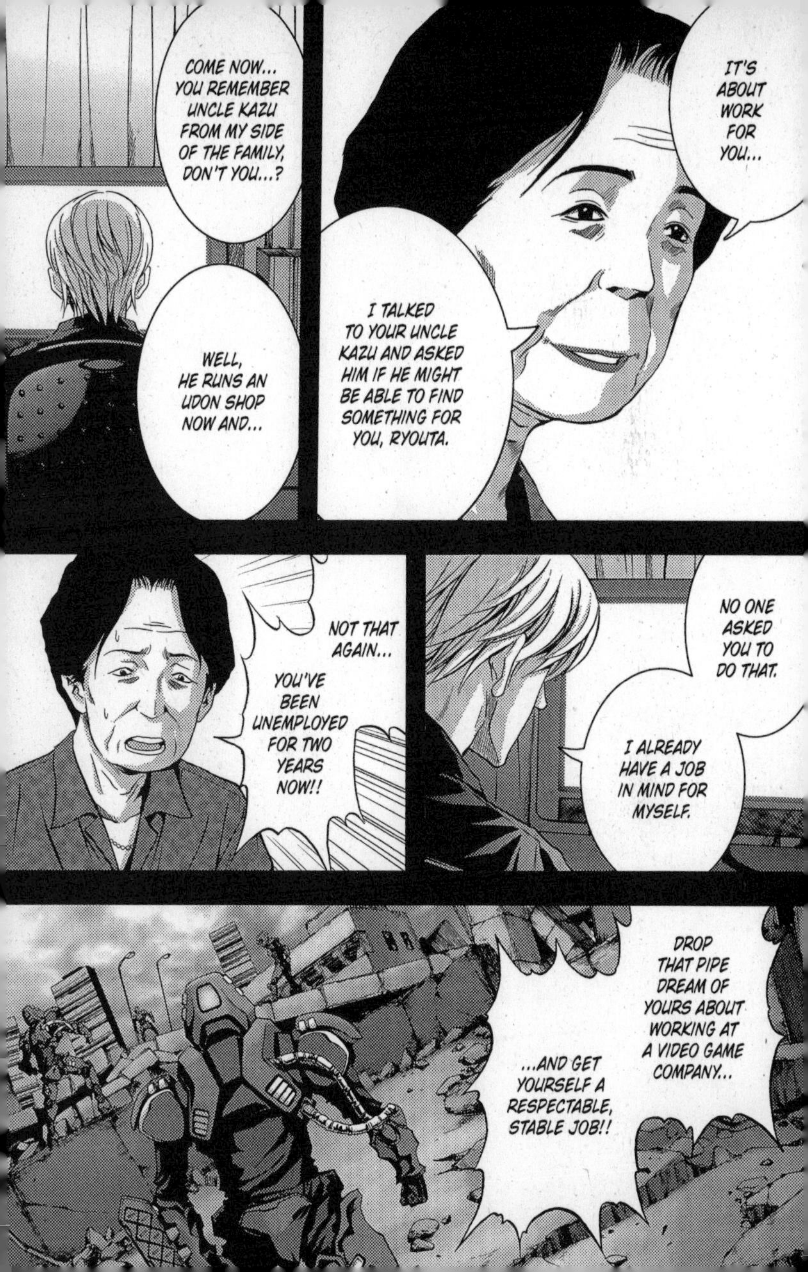
IT'S ABOUT WORK FOR YOU...
I TALKED TO YOUR UNCLE KAZU AND ASKED HIM IF HE MIGHT BE ABLE TO FIND SOMETHING FOR YOU, RYOUTA.
COME NOW... YOU REMEMBER UNCLE KAZU FROM MY SIDE OF THE FAMILY, DON'T YOU...?
WELL, HE RUNS AN UDON SHOP NOW AND...
NO ONE ASKED YOU TO DO THAT.
I ALREADY HAVE A JOB IN MIND FOR MYSELF.
NOT THAT AGAIN...
YOU'VE BEEN UNEMPLOYED FOR TWO YEARS NOW!!
DROP THAT PIPE DREAM OF YOURS ABOUT WORKING AT A VIDEO GAME COMPANY...
...AND GET YOURSELF A RESPECTABLE, STABLE JOB!!

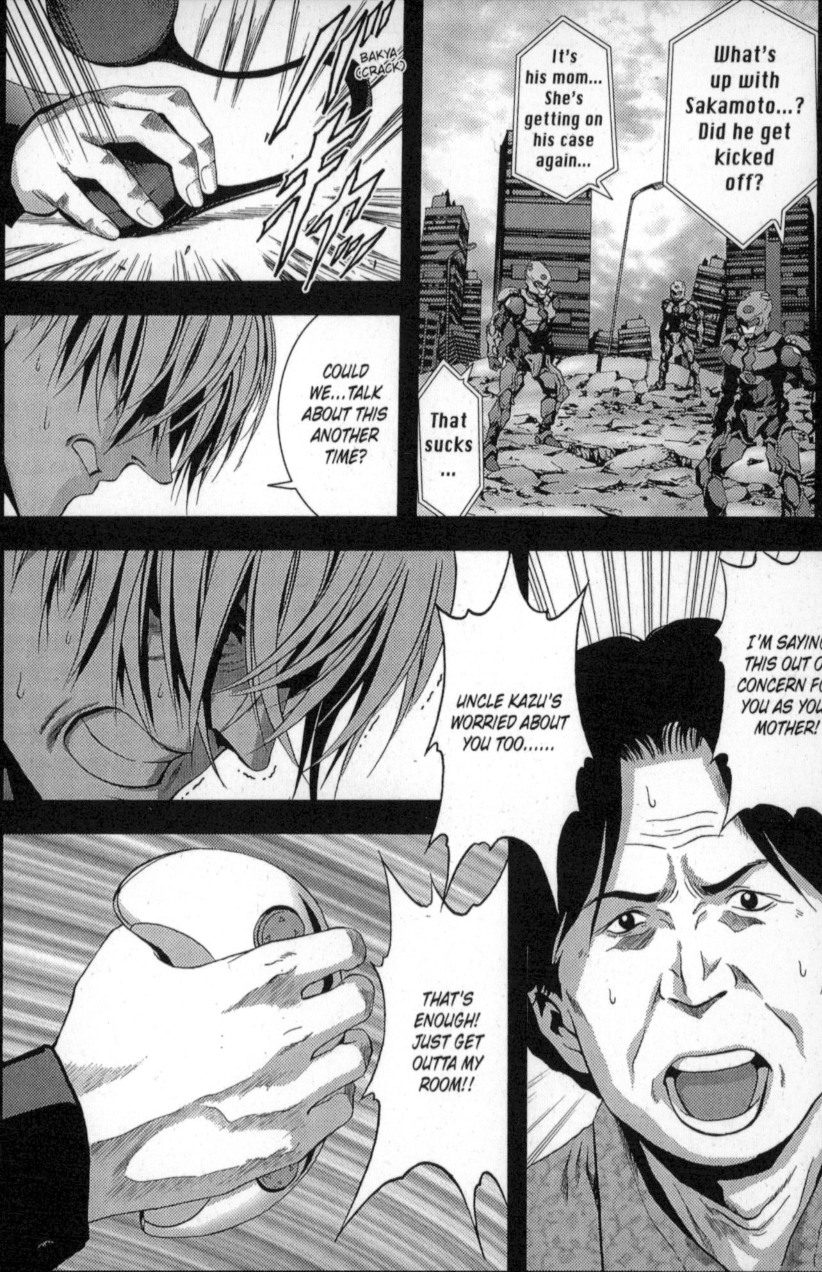
What's up with Sakamoto...? Did he get kicked off?
It's his mom... She's getting on his case again...
That sucks ...
BAKYA (CRACK)
COULD WE...TALK ABOUT THIS ANOTHER TIME?
I'M SAYING THIS OUT OF CONCERN FOR YOU AS YOUR MOTHER!
UNCLE KAZU'S WORRIED ABOUT YOU TOO......
THAT'S ENOUGH! JUST GET OUTTA MY ROOM!!

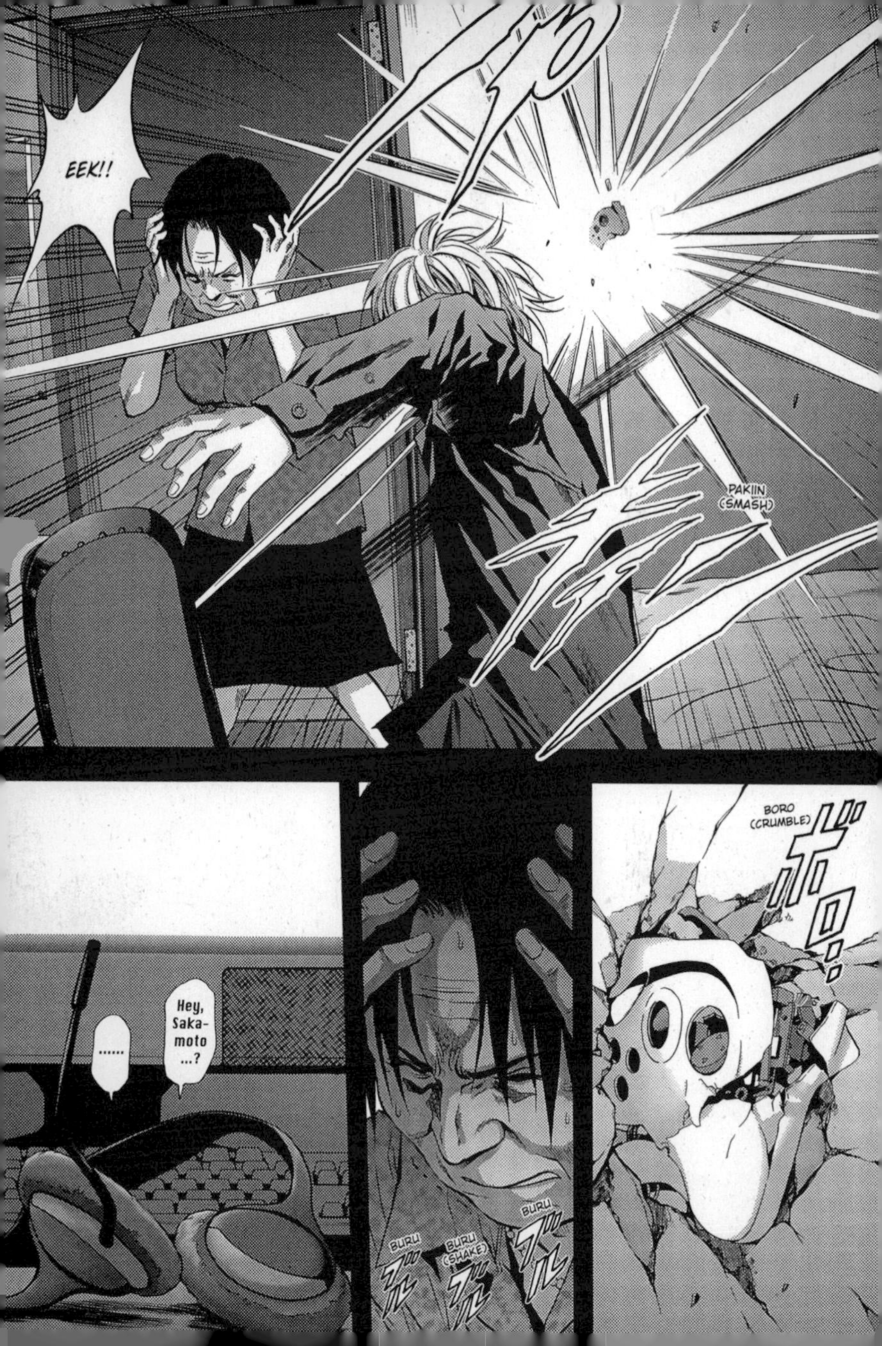
PAKIIN (SMASH)
EEK!!
BORO (CRUMBLE)
BURU
BURU (SHAKE)
BURU
Hey, Sakamoto ...?
......

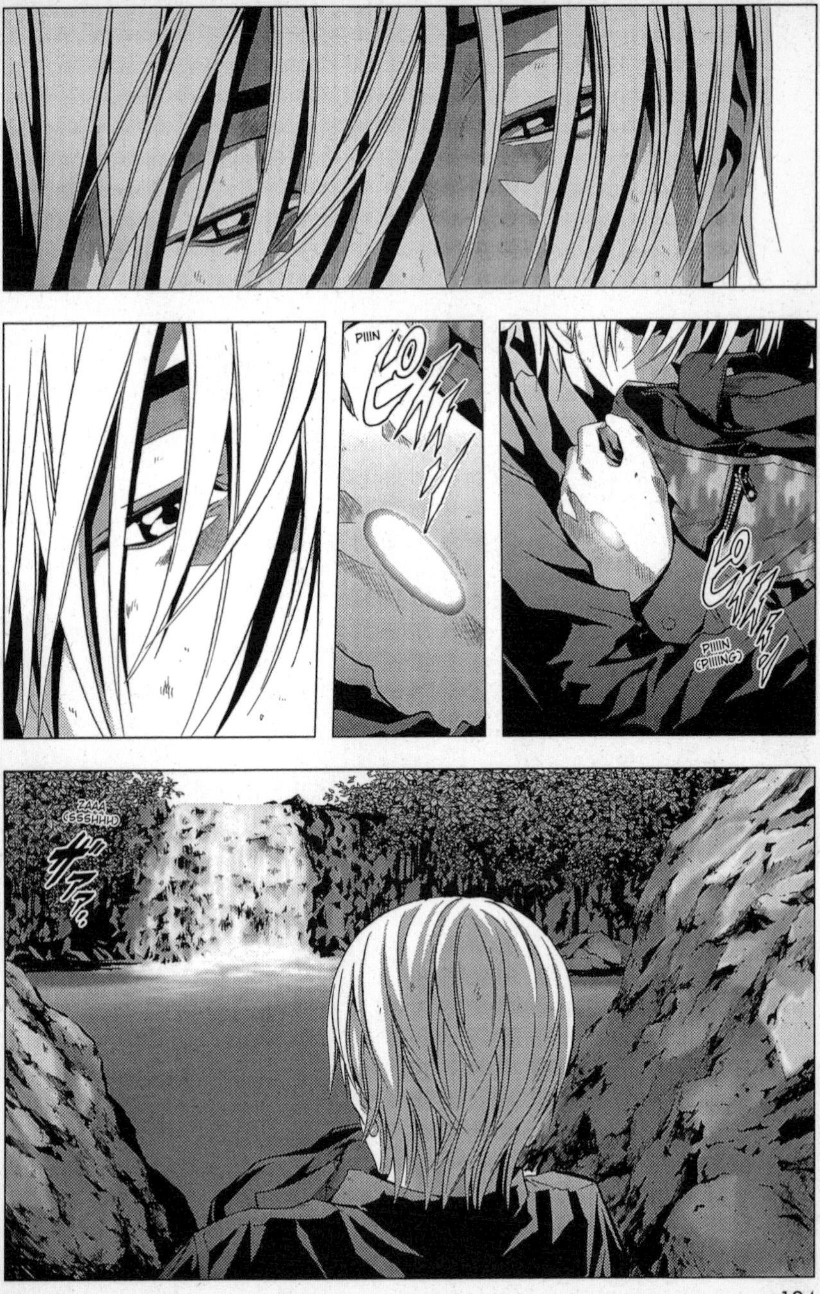
PIIIN (PIIING)
PIIIN
ZAAA (SSSHHH)

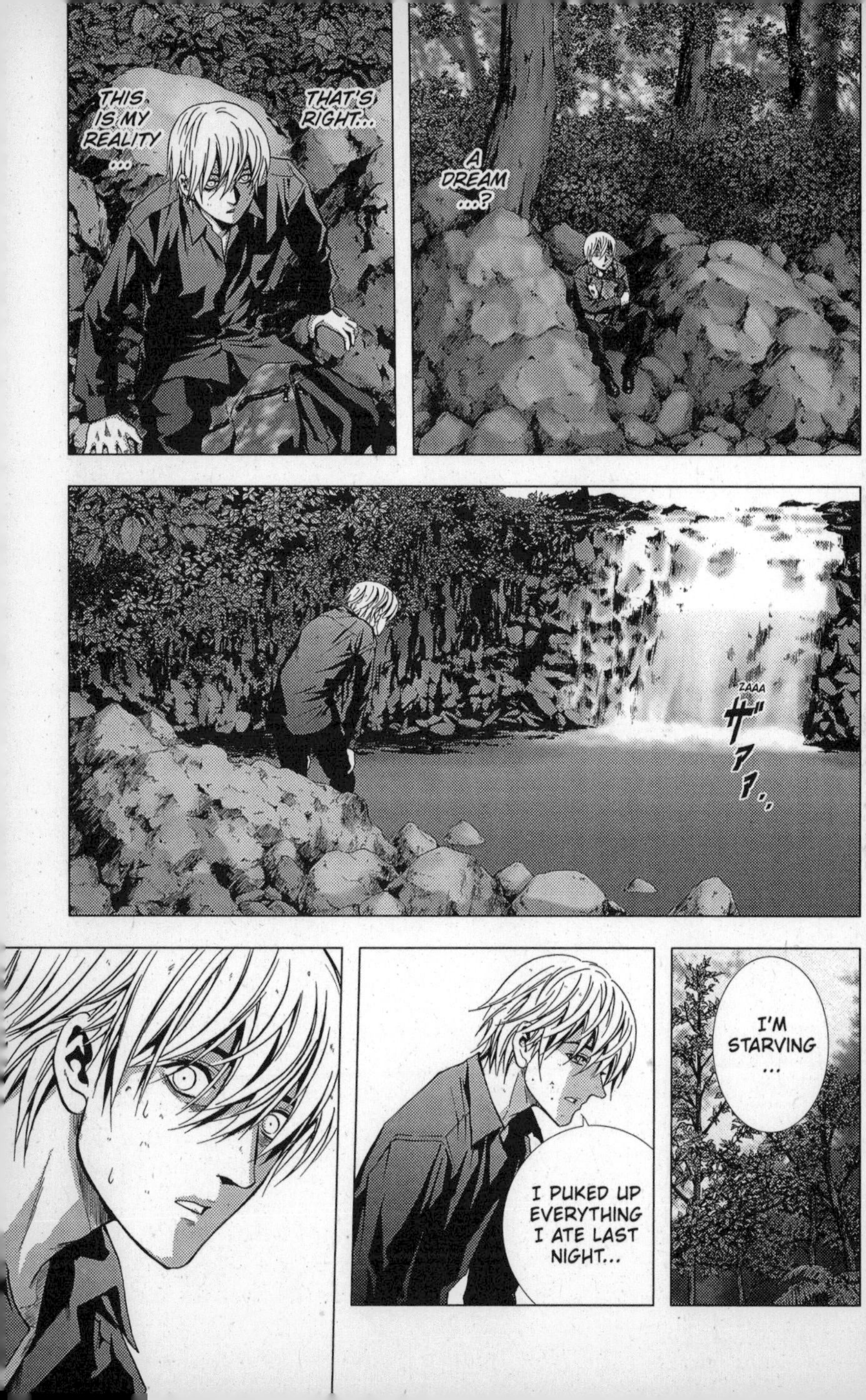
A DREAM ...?
THAT'S RIGHT...
THIS IS MY REALITY ...
ZAAA
ザァァ..
I'M STARVING ...
I PUKED UP EVERYTHING I ATE LAST NIGHT...

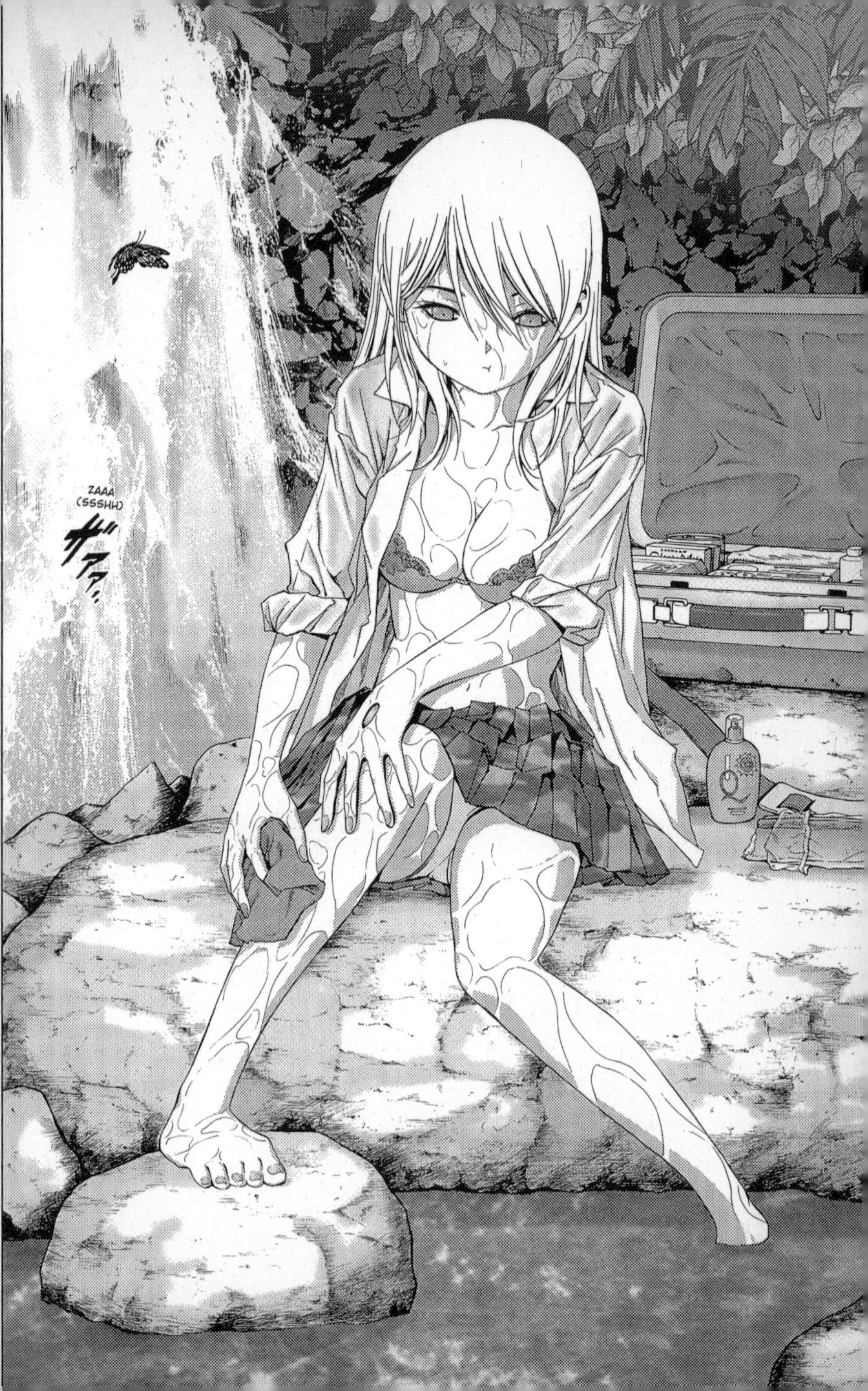
ZAAA
(SSSHH)
ザァァ…

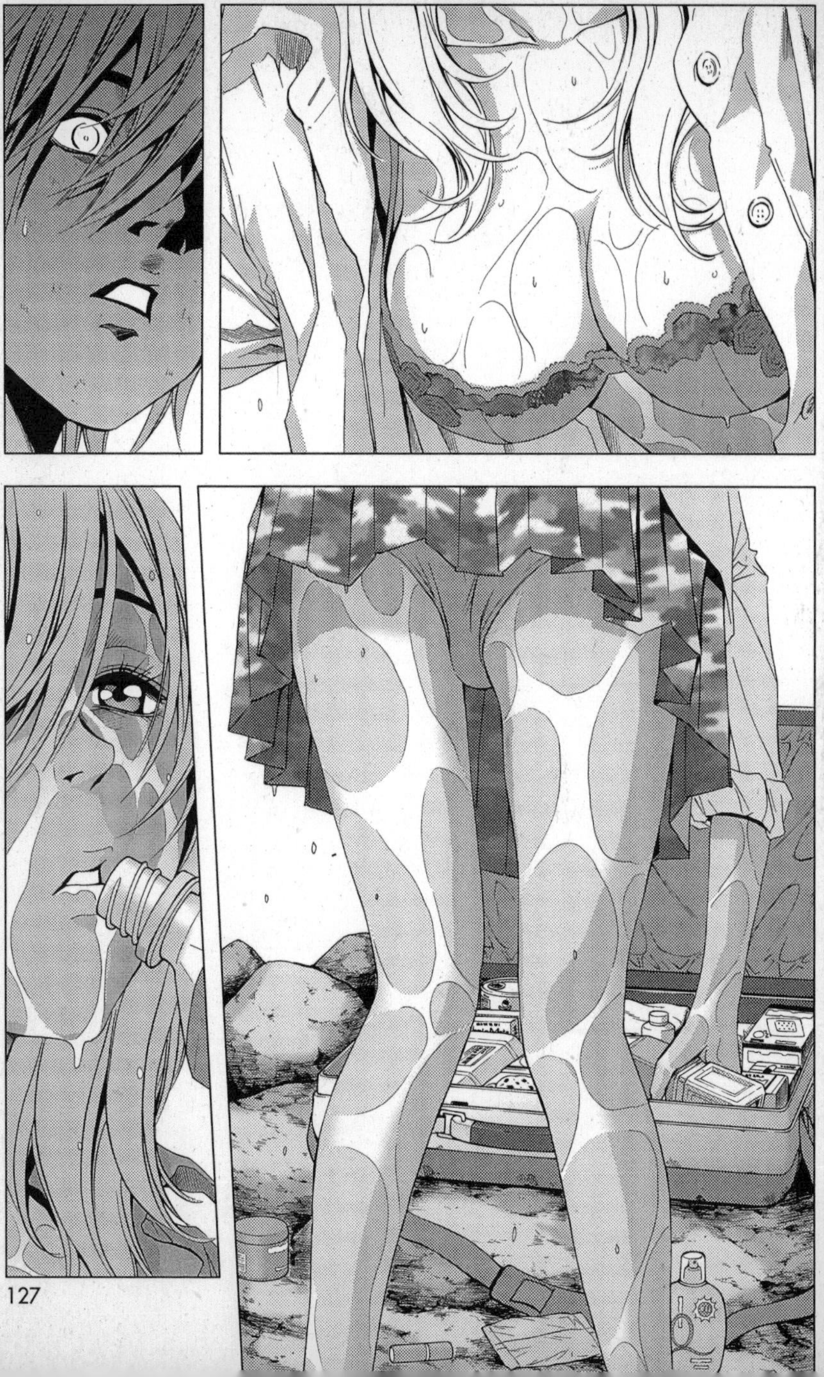

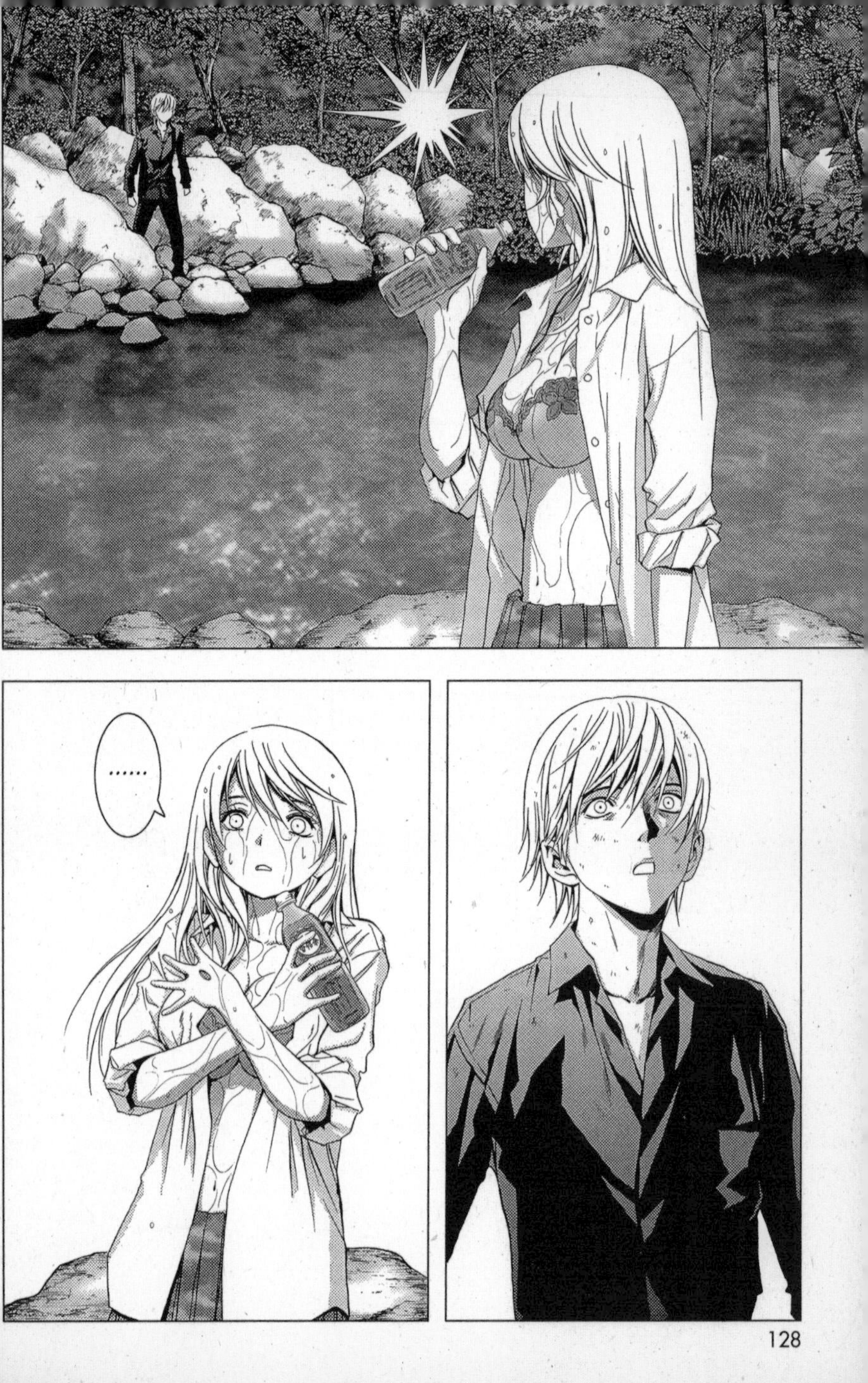
......

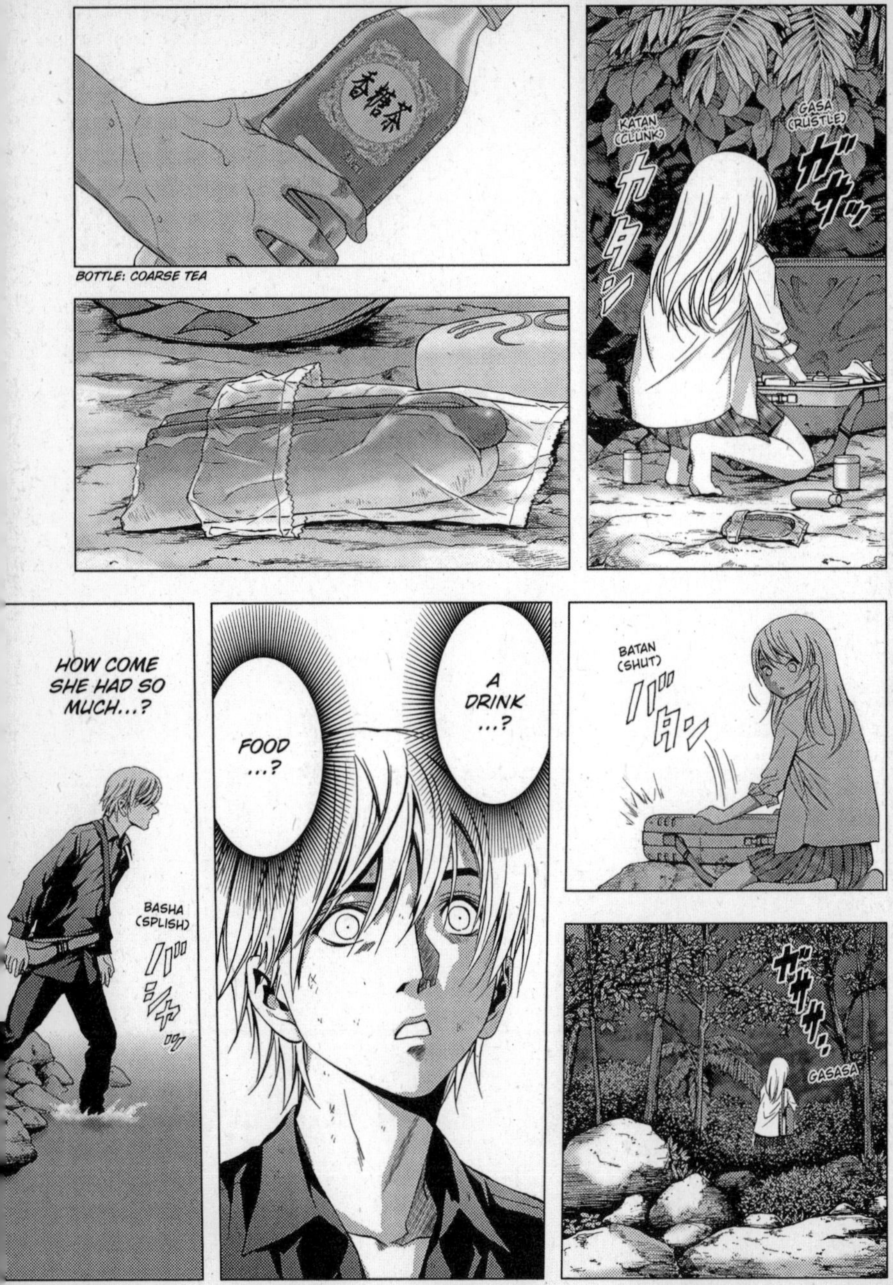
KATAN (CLUNK)
GASA (RUSTLE)
BOTTLE: COARSE TEA
BATAN (SHUT)
GASASA
A DRINK ...?
FOOD ...?
HOW COME SHE HAD SO MUCH...?
BASHA (SPLISH)

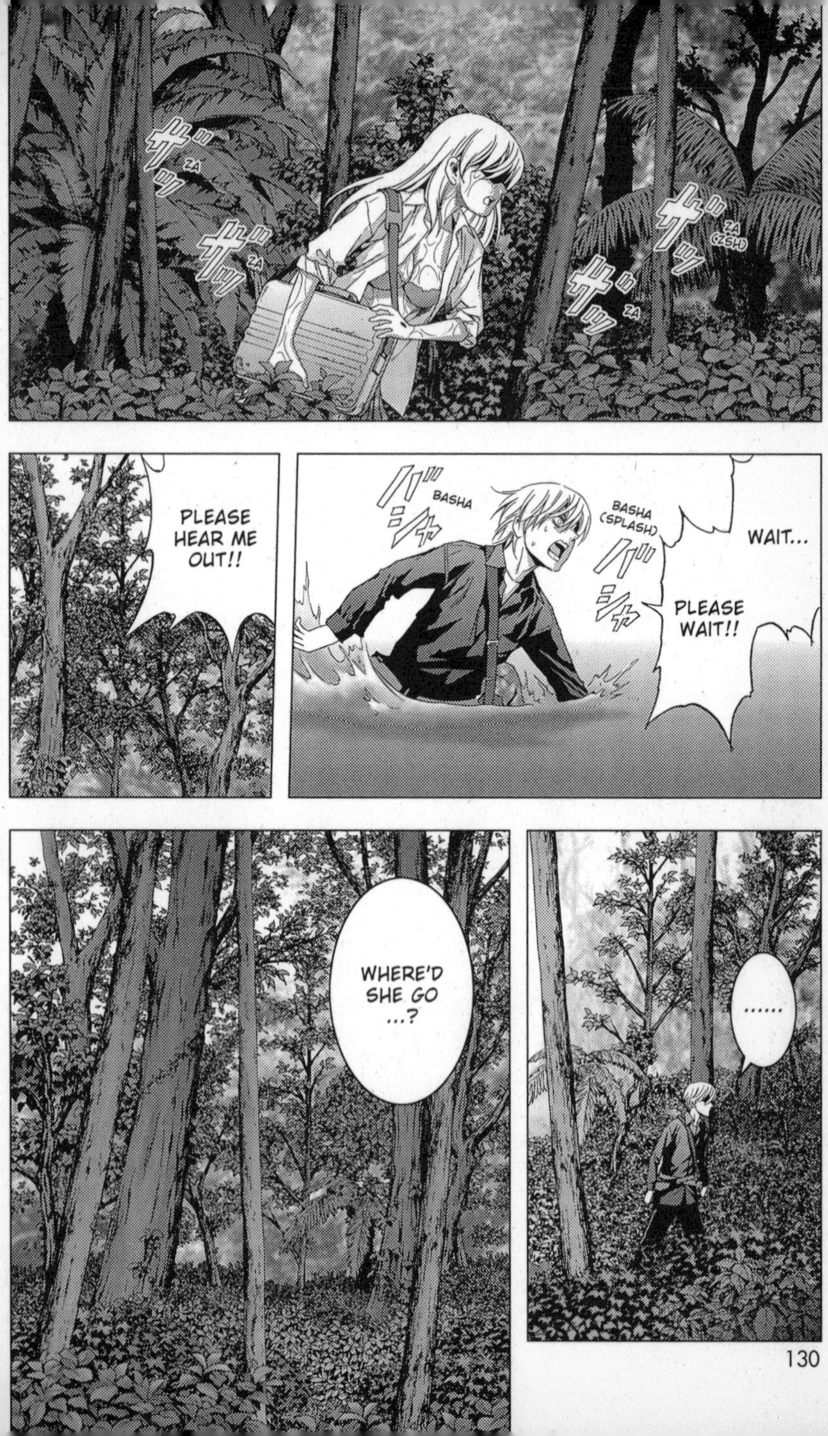
ZA (ZSH)
ZA
ZA
ZA
WAIT...
PLEASE WAIT!!
BASHA (SPLASH)
BASHA
PLEASE HEAR ME OUT!!
......
WHERE'D SHE GO ...?

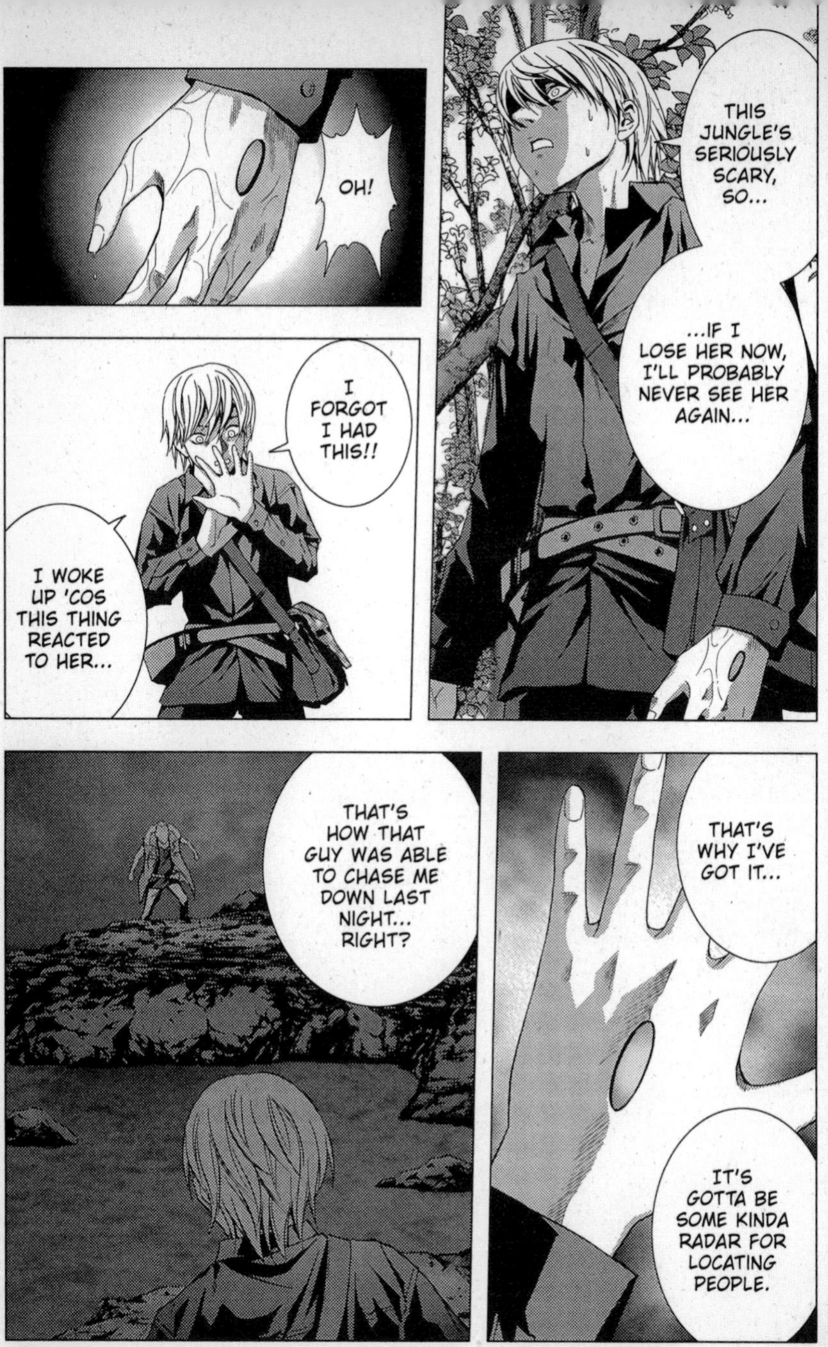
THIS JUNGLE'S SERIOUSLY SCARY, SO...
...IF I LOSE HER NOW, I'LL PROBABLY NEVER SEE HER AGAIN...
OH!
I FORGOT I HAD THIS!!
I WOKE UP 'COS THIS THING REACTED TO HER...
THAT'S WHY I'VE GOT IT...
IT'S GOTTA BE SOME KINDA RADAR FOR LOCATING PEOPLE.
THAT'S HOW THAT GUY WAS ABLE TO CHASE ME DOWN LAST NIGHT... RIGHT?

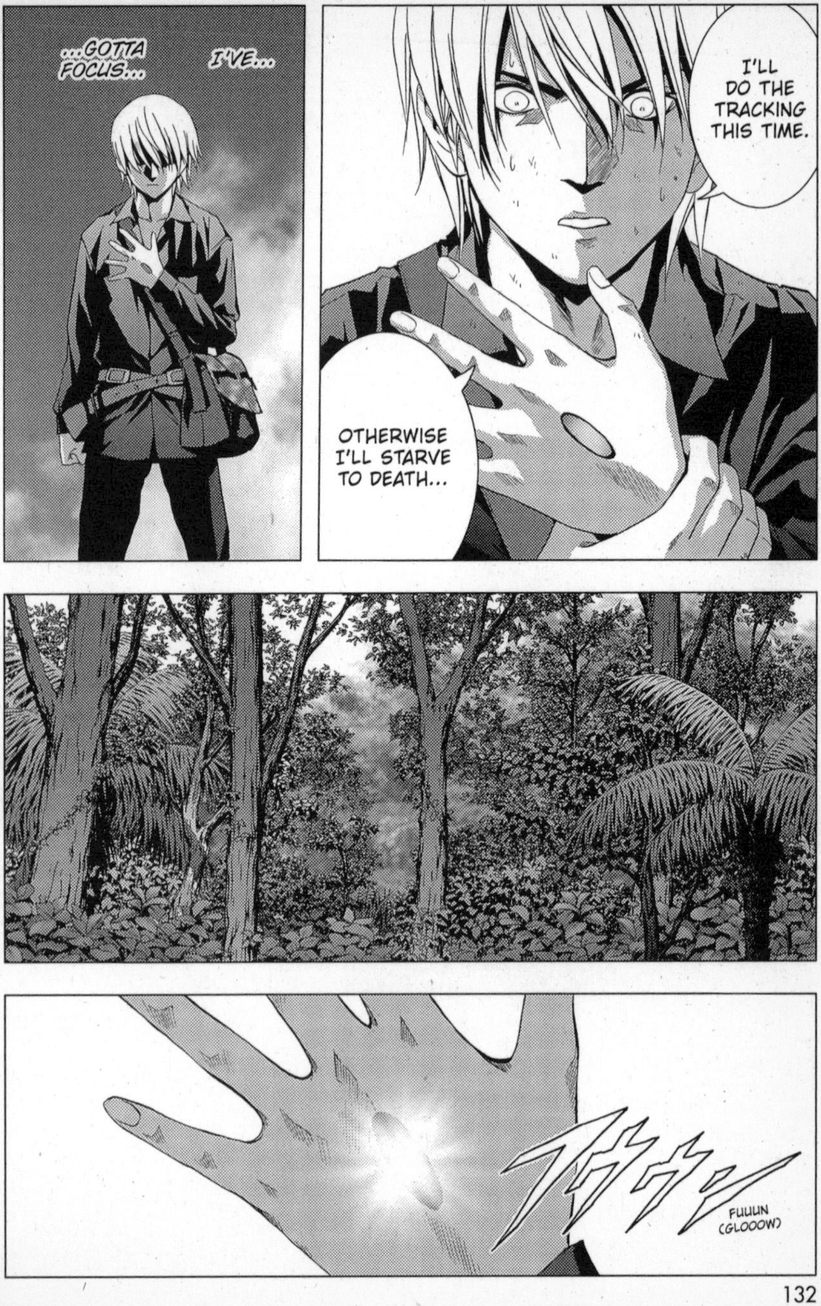
I'LL DO THE TRACKING THIS TIME.
OTHERWISE I'LL STARVE TO DEATH...
I'VE...
...GOTTA FOCUS...
FUUUN (GLOOOW)

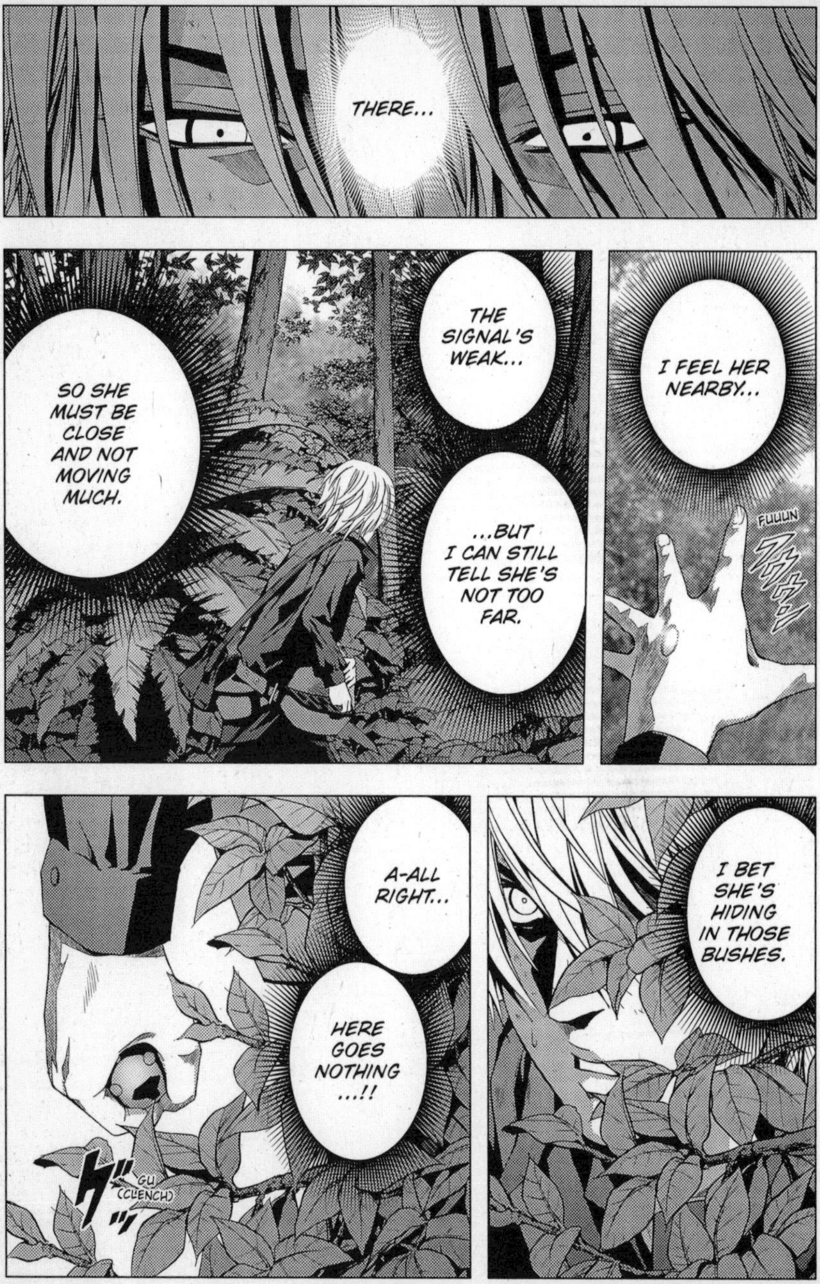
THERE...
I FEEL HER NEARBY...
FUUUN
THE SIGNAL'S WEAK...
...BUT I CAN STILL TELL SHE'S NOT TOO FAR.
SO SHE MUST BE CLOSE AND NOT MOVING MUCH.
I BET SHE'S HIDING IN THOSE BUSHES.
A-ALL RIGHT...
HERE GOES NOTHING ...!!
GU (CLENCH)

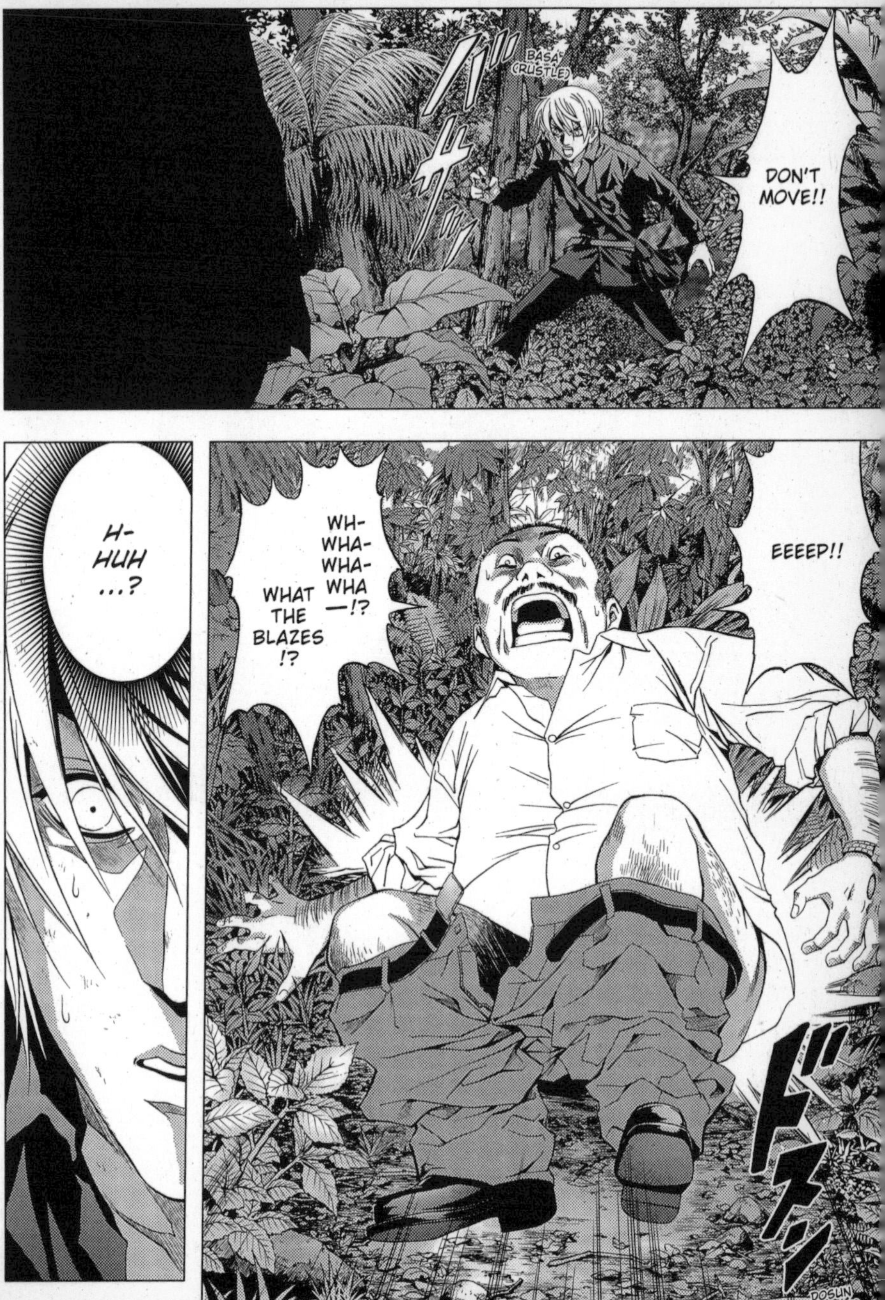
DON'T MOVE!!
BASA (RUSTLE)
EEEEP!!
WH-WHA-WHA-WHA—!?
WHAT THE BLAZES!?
DOSUN (WHUMP)
H-HUH ...?

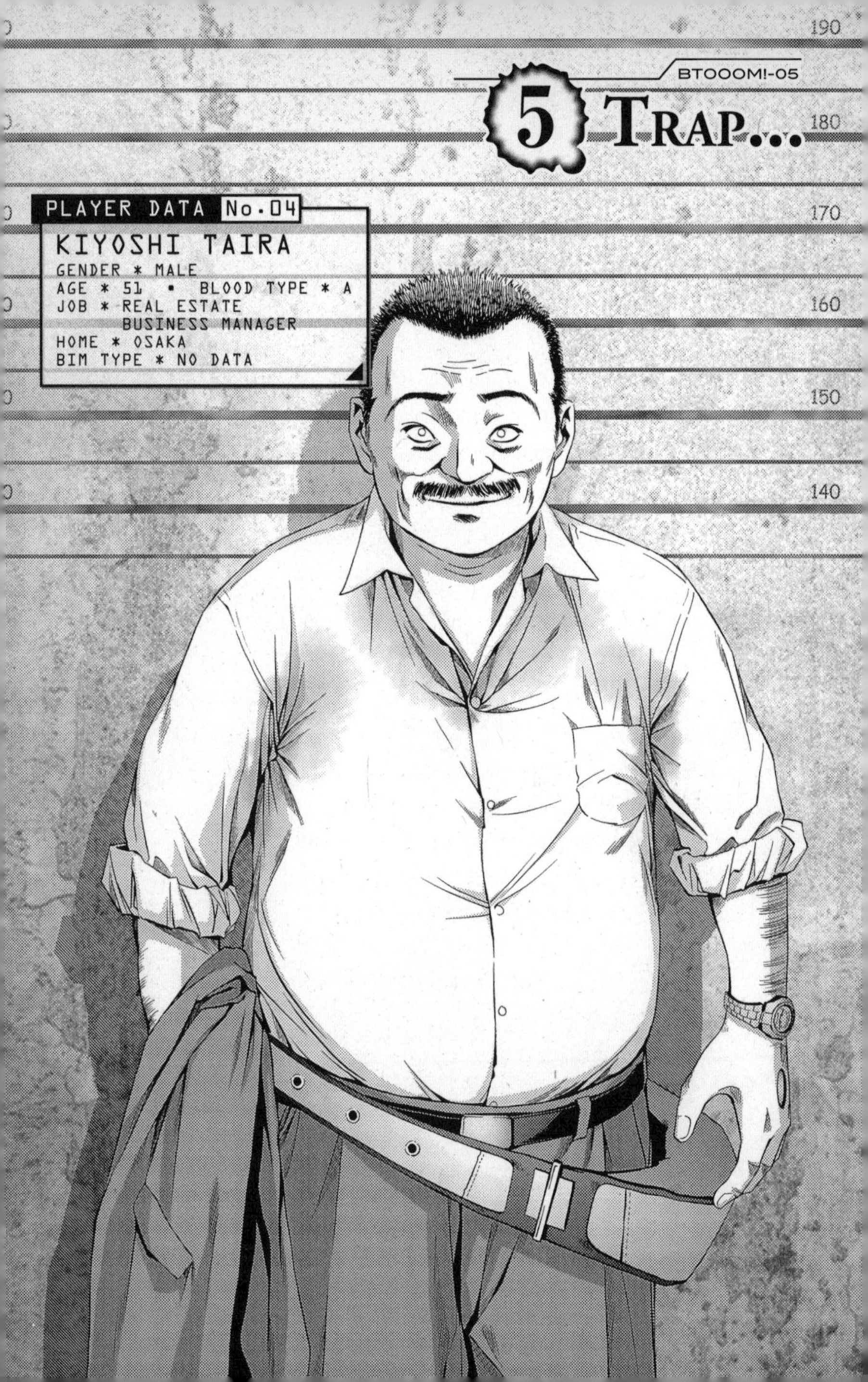
BTOOOM!-05
5 TRAP...
PLAYER DATA No.04
KIYOSHI TAIRA
GENDER * MALE
AGE * 51 • BLOOD TYPE * A
JOB * REAL ESTATE BUSINESS MANAGER
HOME * OSAKA
BIM TYPE * NO DATA
190
180
170
160
150
140

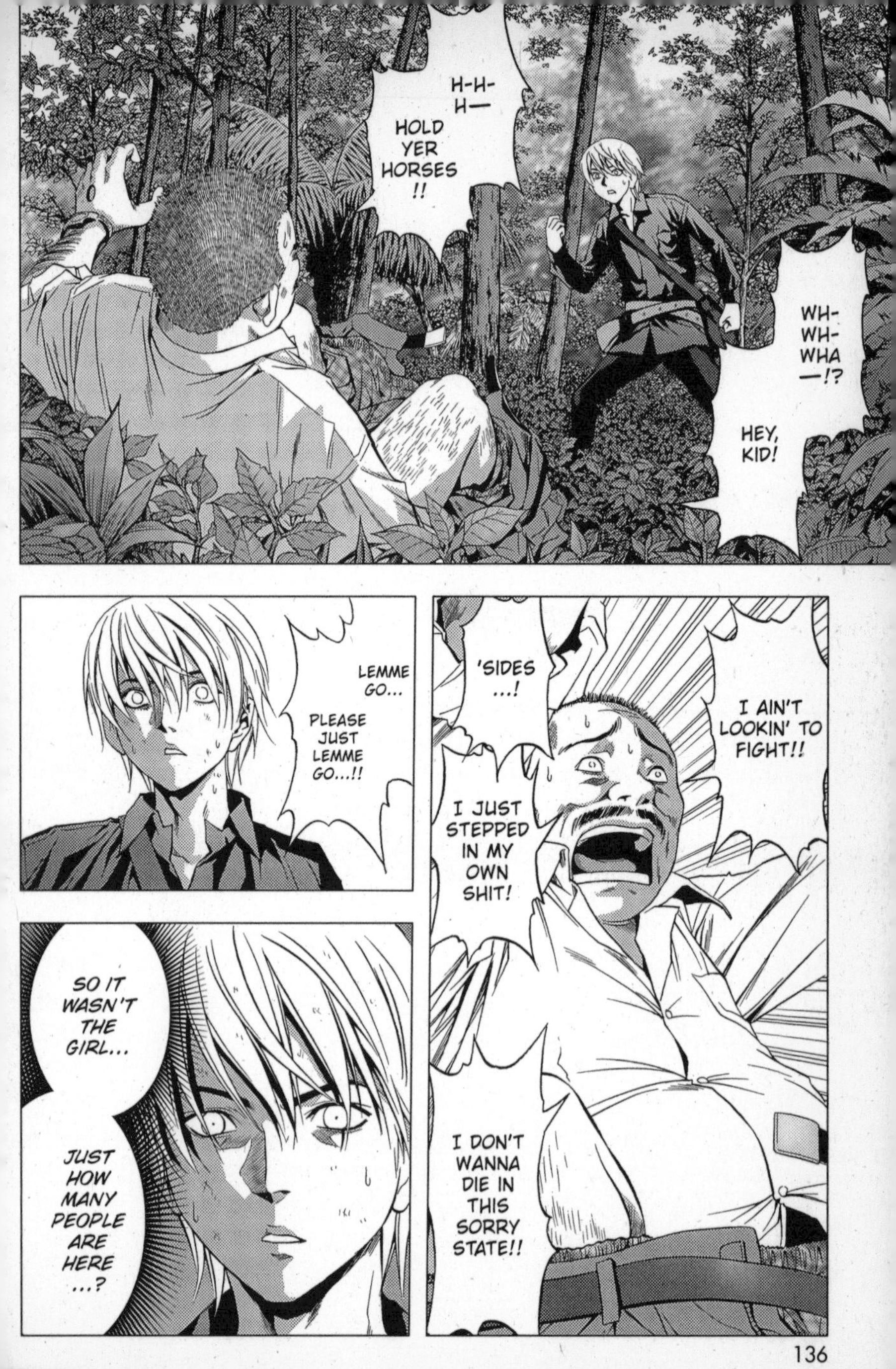
WH-WH-WHA—!?
HEY, KID!
H-H-H— HOLD YER HORSES!!
I AIN'T LOOKIN' TO FIGHT!!
'SIDES...!
I JUST STEPPED IN MY OWN SHIT!
I DON'T WANNA DIE IN THIS SORRY STATE!!
LEMME GO...
PLEASE JUST LEMME GO...!!
SO IT WASN'T THE GIRL...
JUST HOW MANY PEOPLE ARE HERE...?

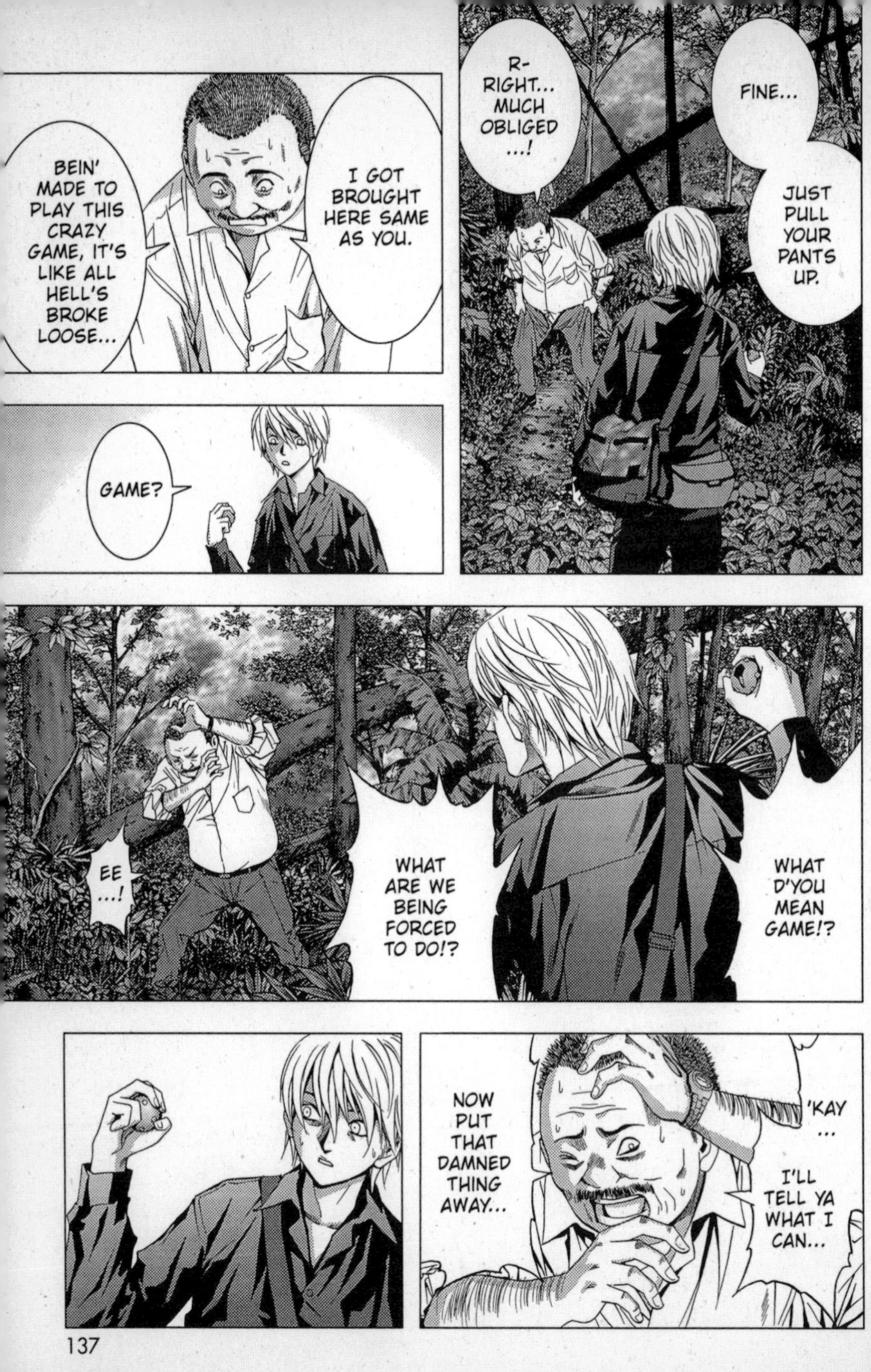
FINE...
JUST PULL YOUR PANTS UP.
R-RIGHT... MUCH OBLIGED...!
I GOT BROUGHT HERE SAME AS YOU.
BEIN' MADE TO PLAY THIS CRAZY GAME, IT'S LIKE ALL HELL'S BROKE LOOSE...
GAME?
WHAT D'YOU MEAN GAME!?
WHAT ARE WE BEING FORCED TO DO!?
EE...!
'KAY... I'LL TELL YA WHAT I CAN...
NOW PUT THAT DAMNED THING AWAY...

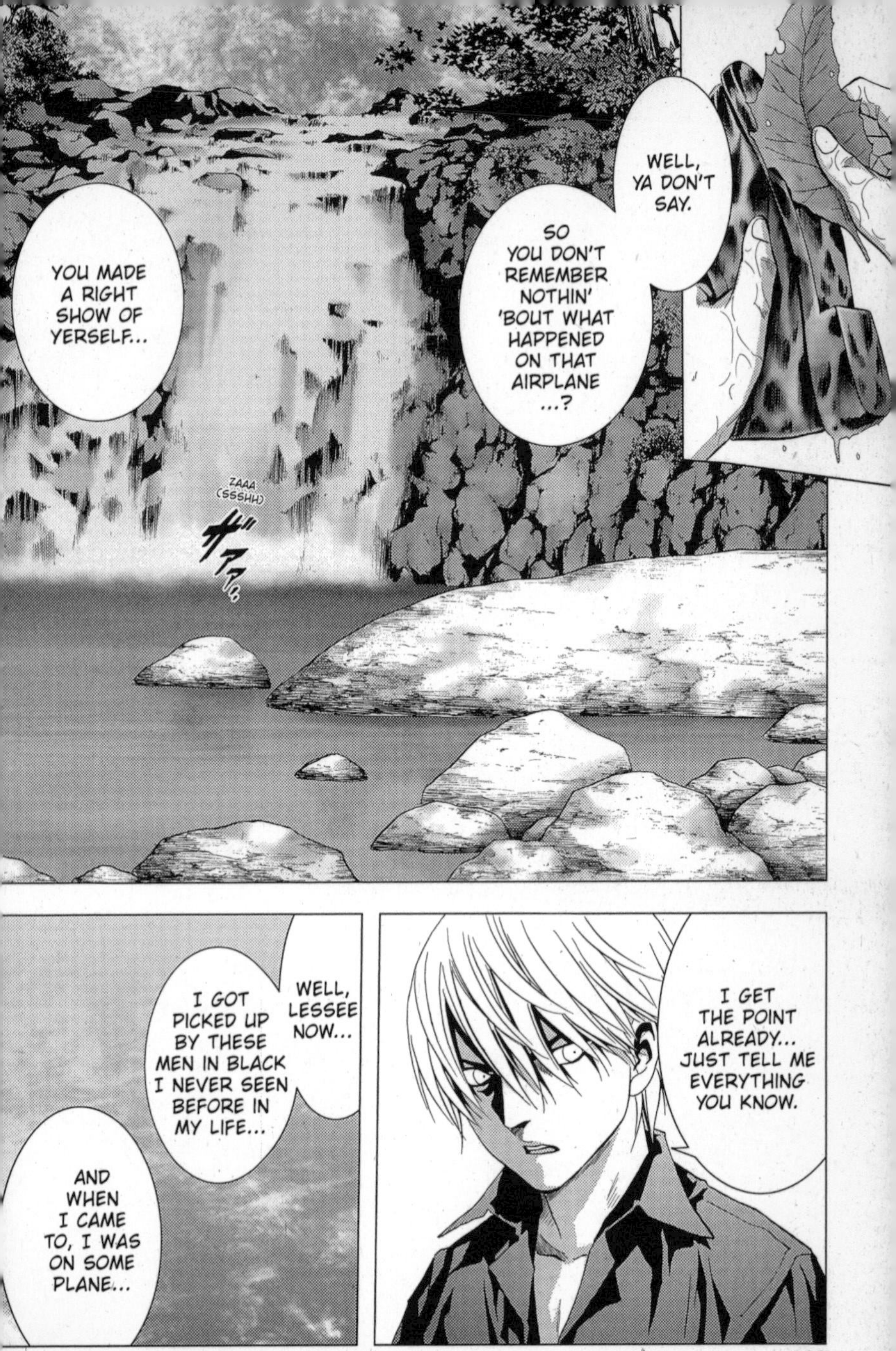

WELL, YA DON'T SAY.
SO YOU DON'T REMEMBER NOTHIN' 'BOUT WHAT HAPPENED ON THAT AIRPLANE ...?
YOU MADE A RIGHT SHOW OF YERSELF...
ZAAA (SSSHH)
ザアア。
I GET THE POINT ALREADY... JUST TELL ME EVERYTHING YOU KNOW.
WELL, LESSEE NOW...
I GOT PICKED UP BY THESE MEN IN BLACK I NEVER SEEN BEFORE IN MY LIFE...
AND WHEN I CAME TO, I WAS ON SOME PLANE...

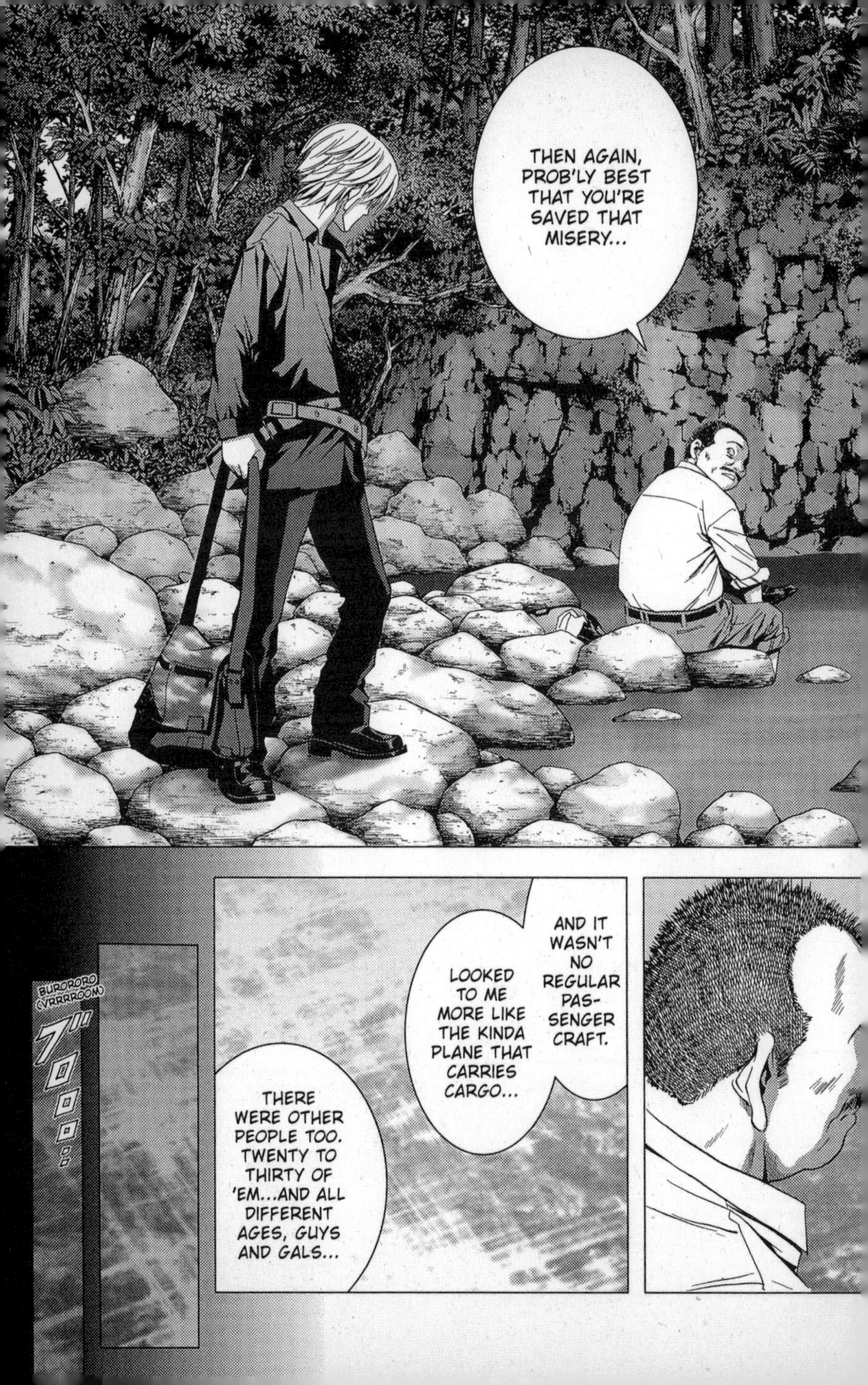
THEN AGAIN, PROB'LY BEST THAT YOU'RE SAVED THAT MISERY...
AND IT WASN'T NO REGULAR PAS-SENGER CRAFT.
LOOKED TO ME MORE LIKE THE KINDA PLANE THAT CARRIES CARGO...
THERE WERE OTHER PEOPLE TOO. TWENTY TO THIRTY OF 'EM...AND ALL DIFFERENT AGES, GUYS AND GALS...
BUROROROO (VRRRROOM)

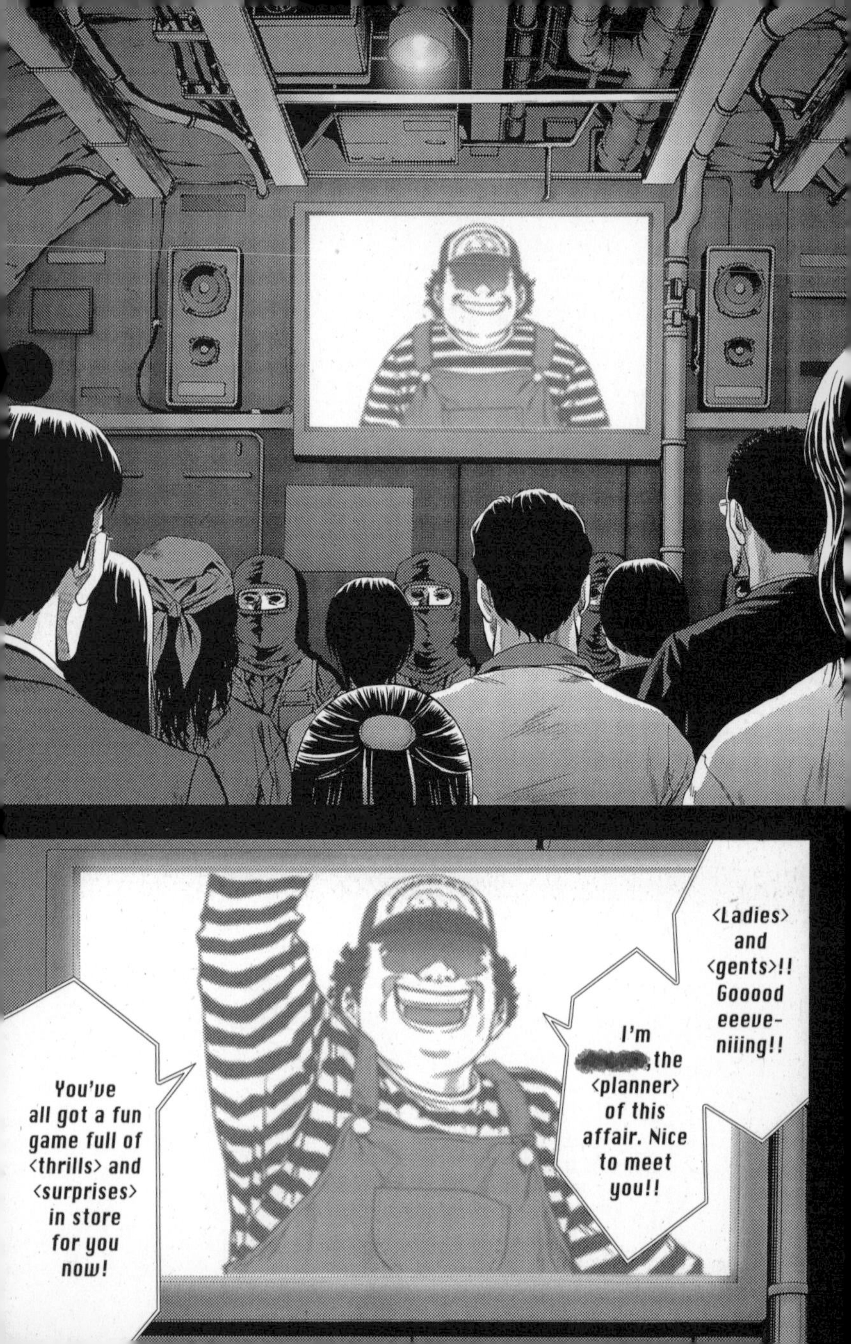
<Ladies> and <gents>!! Gooood eeeve-niiing!!
I'm [redacted], the <planner> of this affair. Nice to meet you!!
You've all got a fun game full of <thrills> and <surprises> in store for you now!

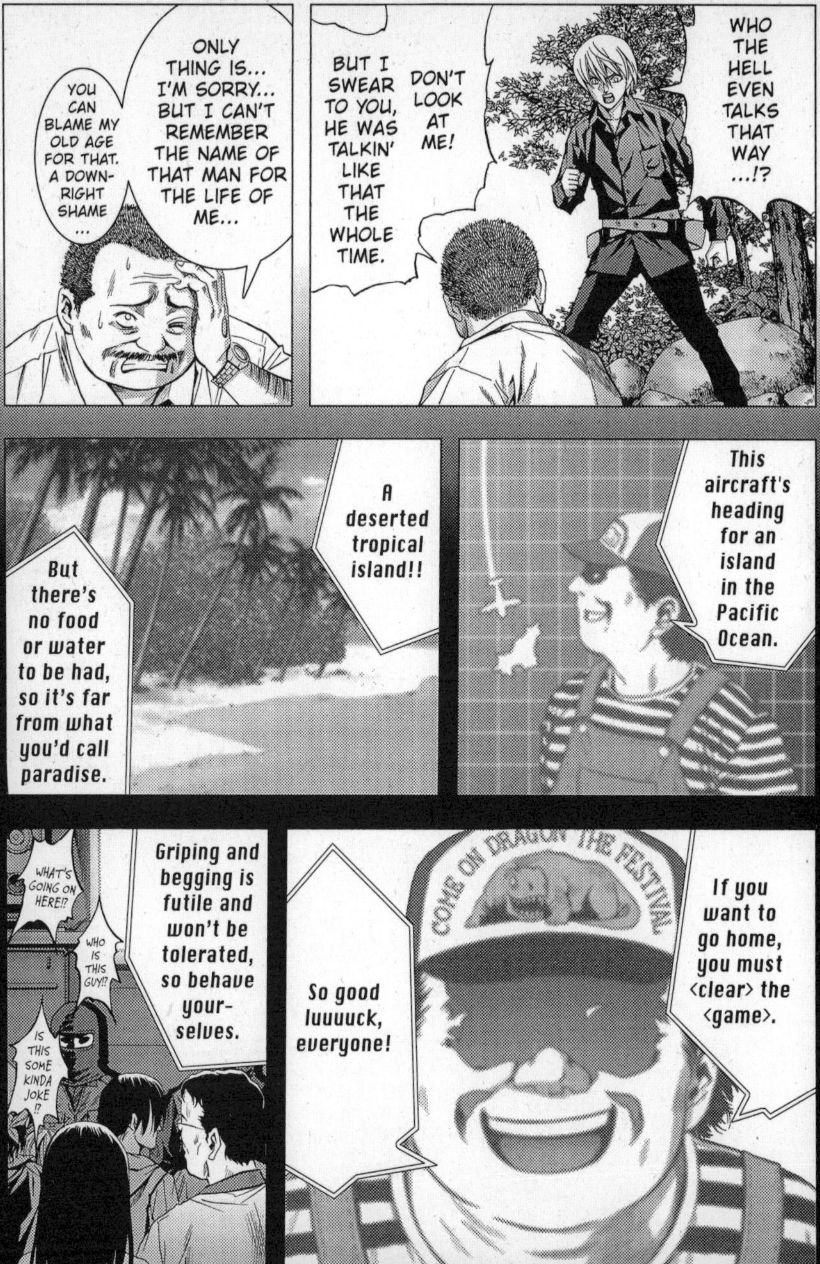
WHO THE HELL EVEN TALKS THAT WAY ...!?
DON'T LOOK AT ME!
BUT I SWEAR TO YOU, HE WAS TALKIN' LIKE THAT THE WHOLE TIME.
ONLY THING IS... I'M SORRY... BUT I CAN'T REMEMBER THE NAME OF THAT MAN FOR THE LIFE OF ME...
YOU CAN BLAME MY OLD AGE FOR THAT. A DOWN-RIGHT SHAME ...
This aircraft's heading for an island in the Pacific Ocean.
A deserted tropical island!!
But there's no food or water to be had, so it's far from what you'd call paradise.
COME ON DRAGON THE FESTIVAL
If you want to go home, you must <clear> the <game>.
So good luuuuck, everyone!
Griping and begging is futile and won't be tolerated, so behave your-selves.
WHAT'S GOING ON HERE!?
WHO IS THIS GUY!?
IS THIS SOME KINDA JOKE !?

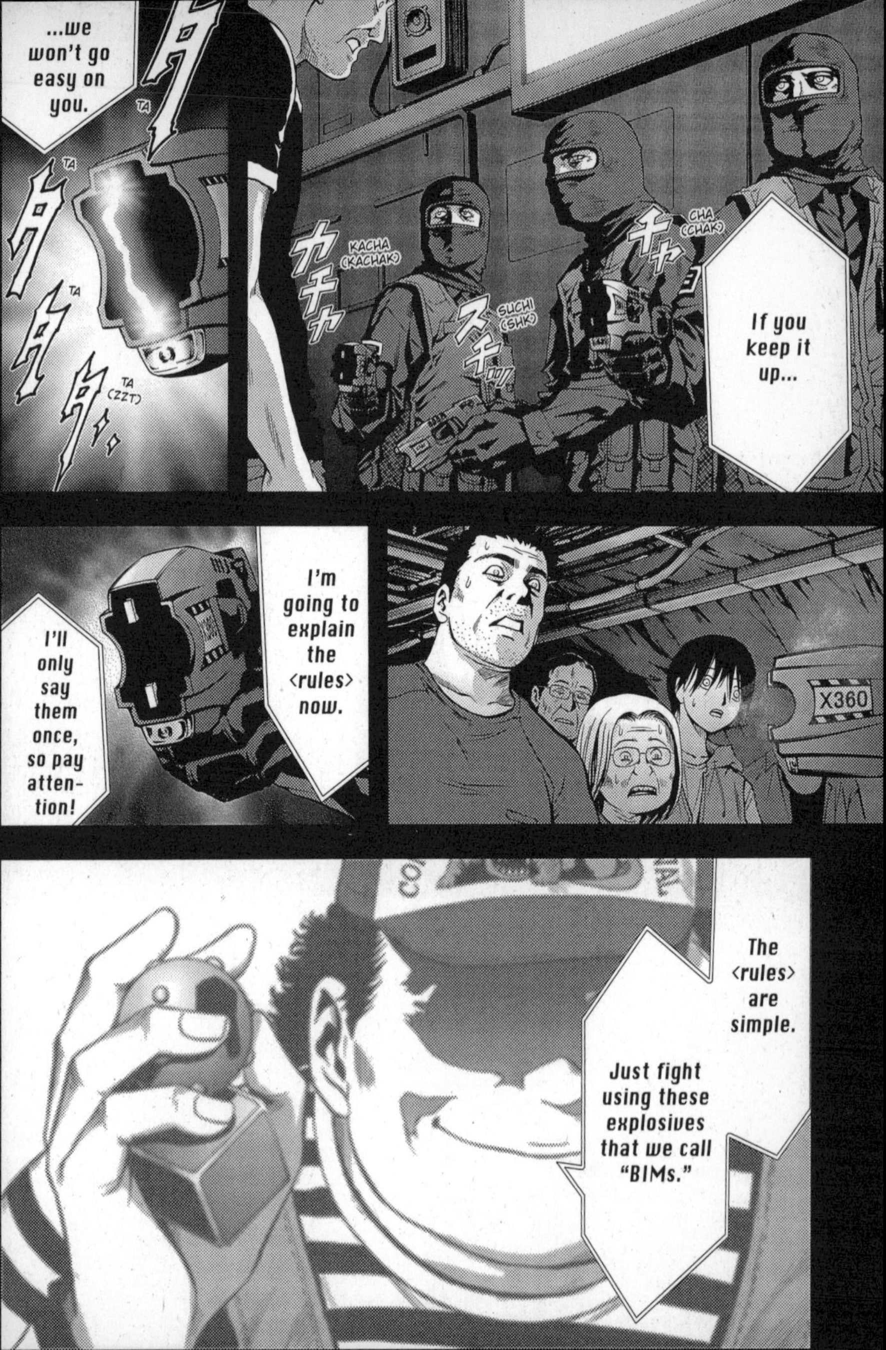
If you keep it up...
CHA (CHAK)
KACHA (KACHAK)
SUCHI (SHK)
...we won't go easy on you.
TA
TA
TA
TA (ZZT)
X360
I'm going to explain the <rules> now.
I'll only say them once, so pay atten- tion!
The <rules> are simple.
Just fight using these explosives that we call "BIMs."

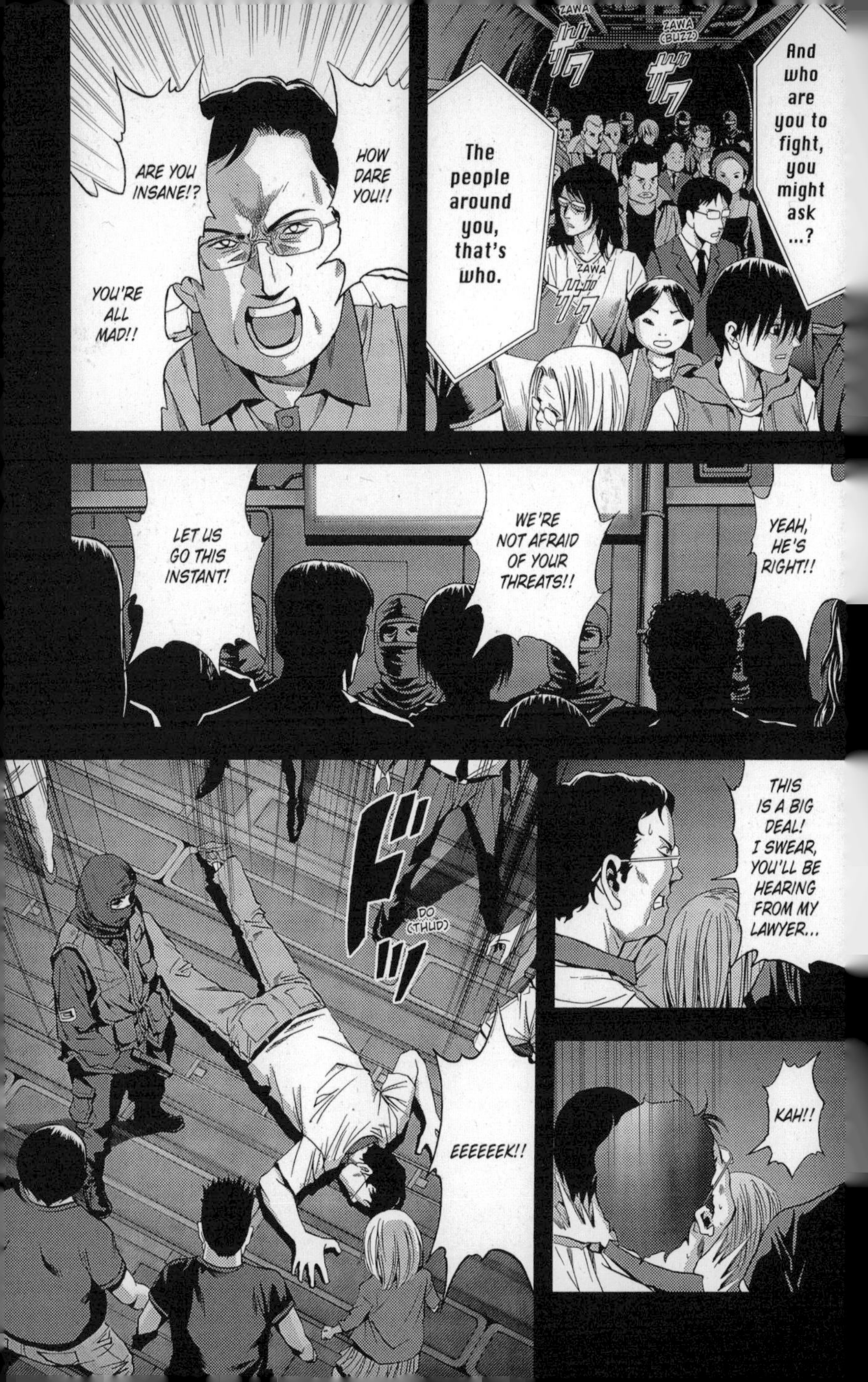
ZAWA
ZAWA (BUZZ)
And who are you to fight, you might ask ...?
The people around you, that's who.
ZAWA
HOW DARE YOU!!
ARE YOU INSANE!?
YOU'RE ALL MAD!!
YEAH, HE'S RIGHT!!
WE'RE NOT AFRAID OF YOUR THREATS!!
LET US GO THIS INSTANT!
THIS IS A BIG DEAL! I SWEAR, YOU'LL BE HEARING FROM MY LAWYER...
KAH!!
DO (THUD)
EEEEEEK!!

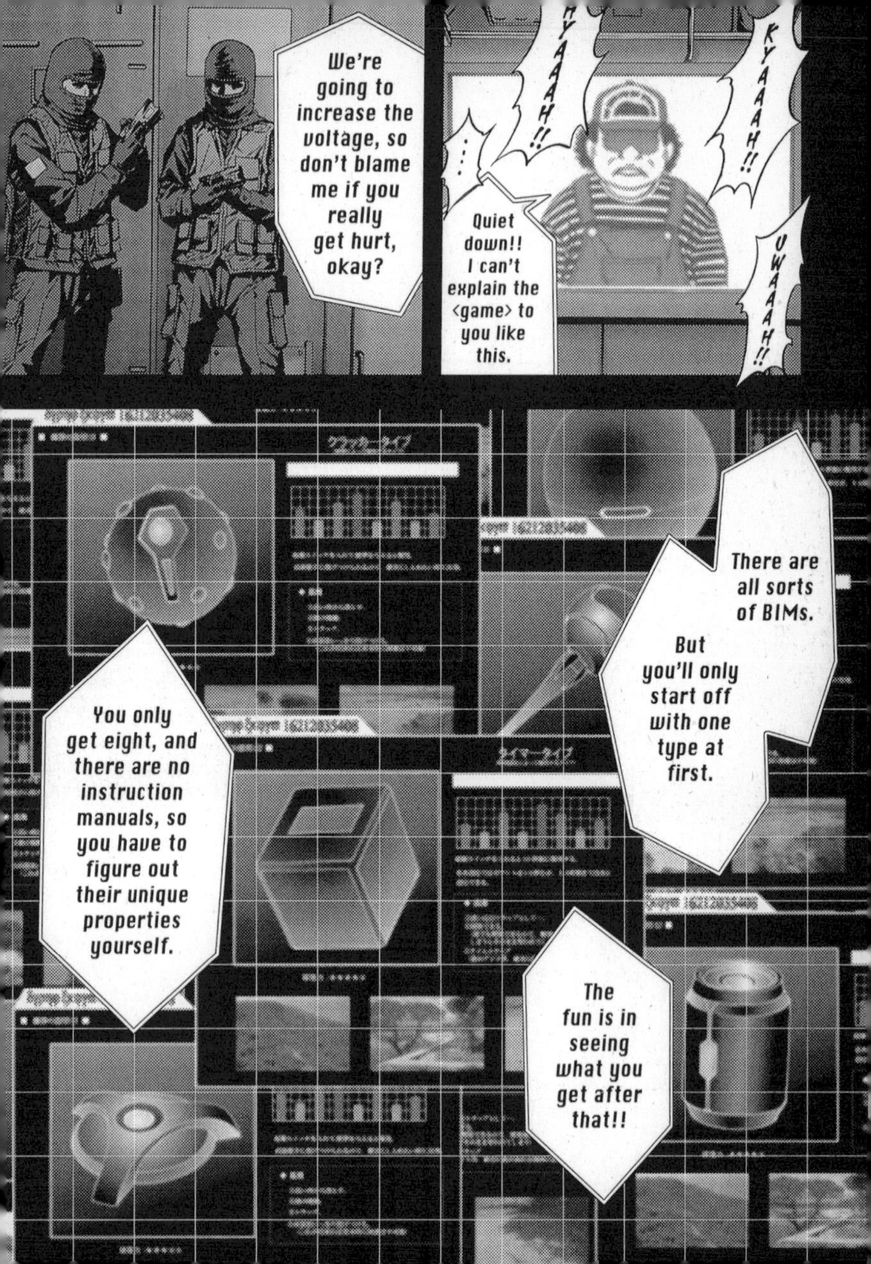
KYAAAAH!!
UWAAAAH!!
KYAAAAH!!
...
Quiet down!! I can't explain the <game> to you like this.
We're going to increase the voltage, so don't blame me if you really get hurt, okay?
There are all sorts of BIMs.
But you'll only start off with one type at first.
You only get eight, and there are no instruction manuals, so you have to figure out their unique properties yourself.
The fun is in seeing what you get after that!!

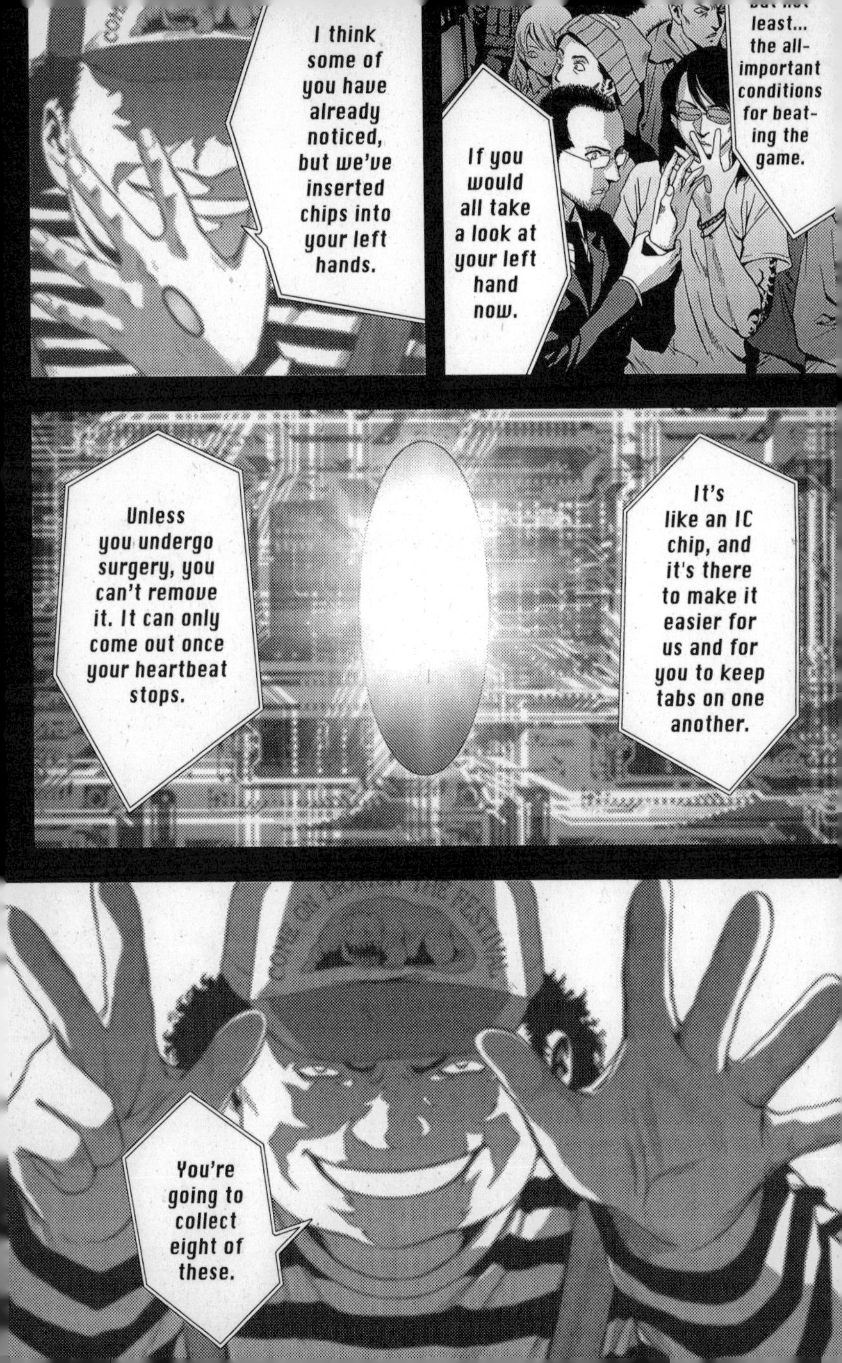
least... the all-important conditions for beating the game.
If you would all take a look at your left hand now.
I think some of you have already noticed, but we've inserted chips into your left hands.
It's like an IC chip, and it's there to make it easier for us and for you to keep tabs on one another.
Unless you undergo surgery, you can't remove it. It can only come out once your heartbeat stops.
You're going to collect eight of these.

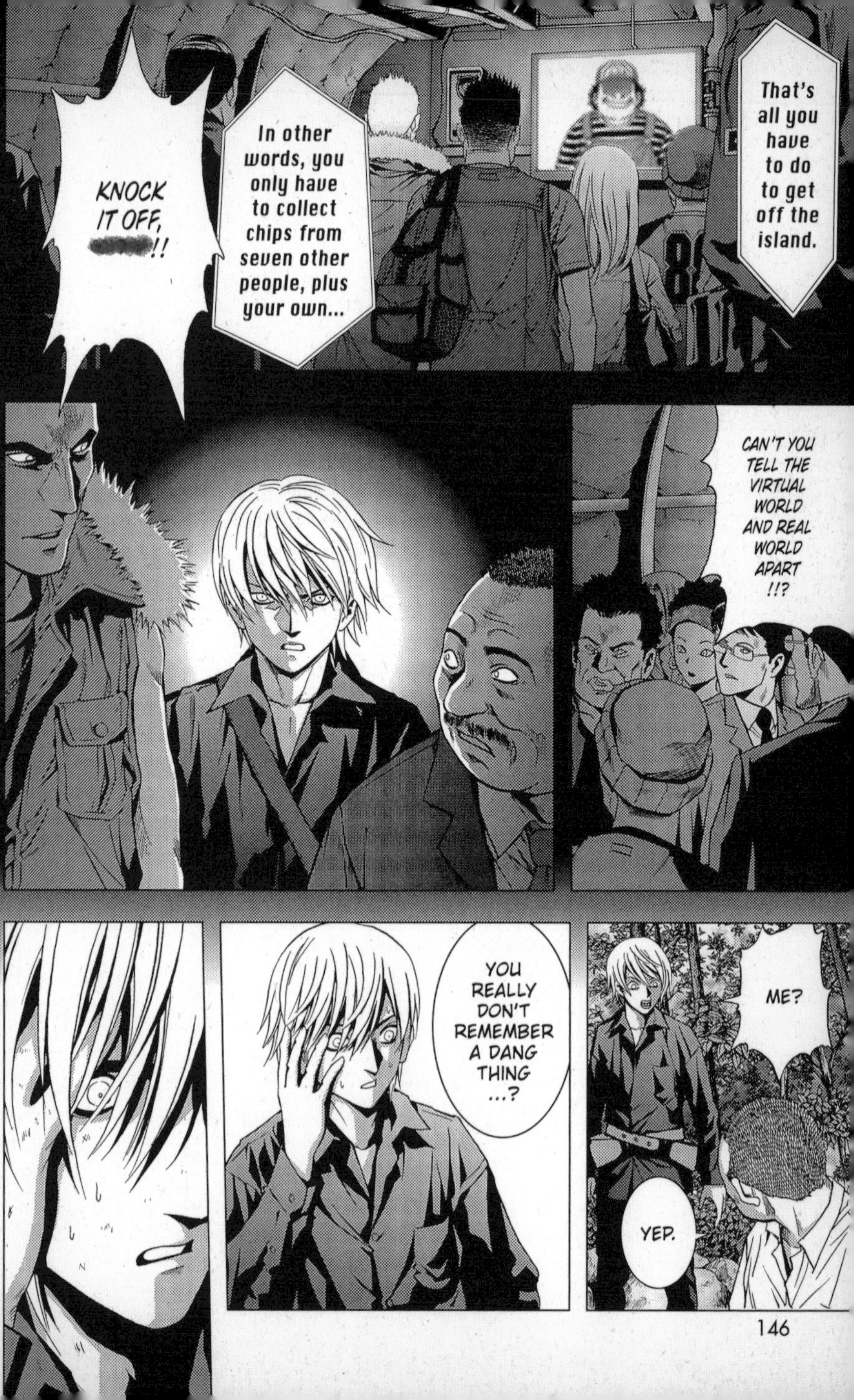
That's all you have to do to get off the island.
In other words, you only have to collect chips from seven other people, plus your own...
KNOCK IT OFF, [redacted]!!
CAN'T YOU TELL THE VIRTUAL WORLD AND REAL WORLD APART !!?
ME?
YEP.
YOU REALLY DON'T REMEMBER A DANG THING ...?

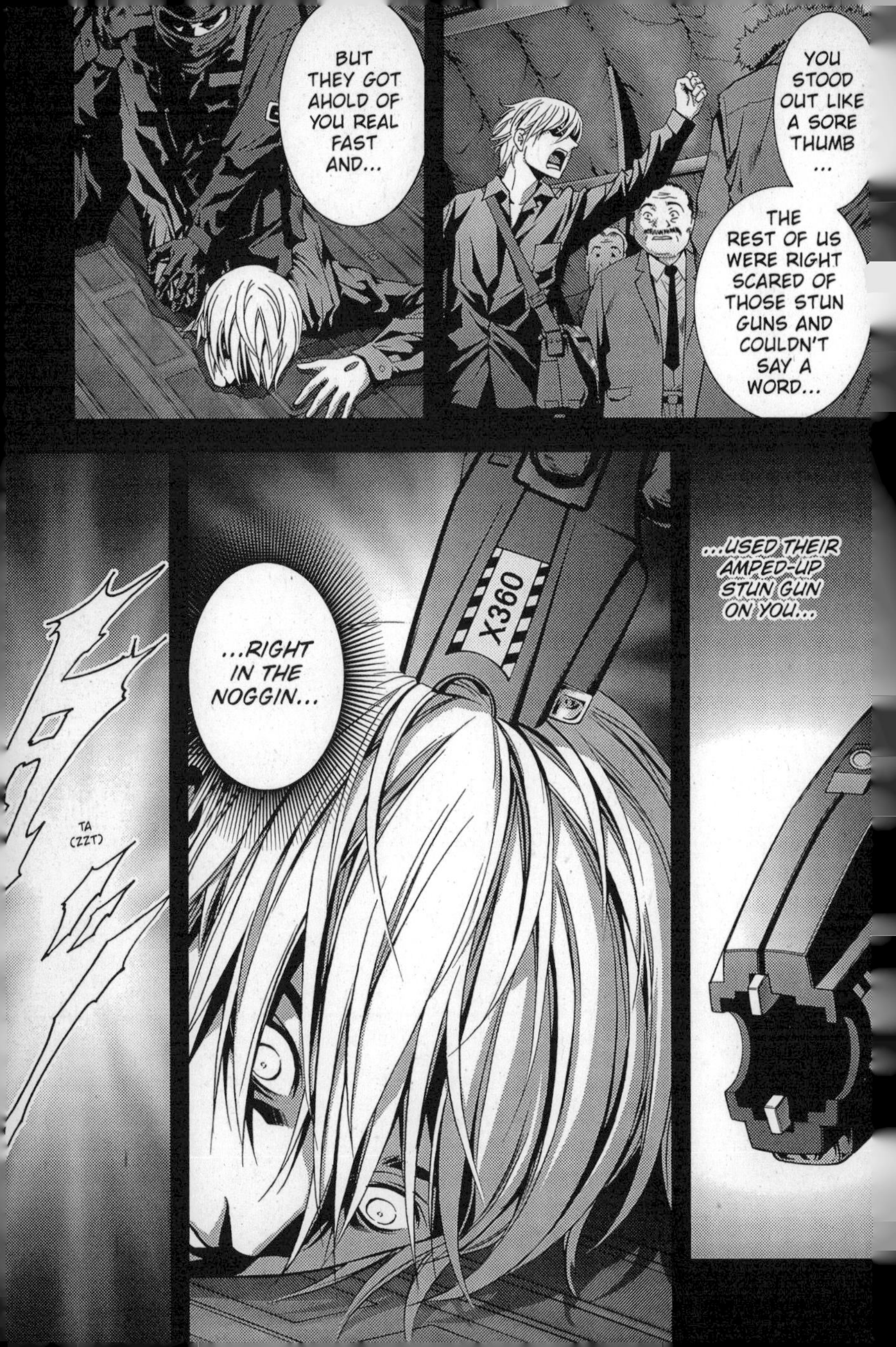
YOU STOOD OUT LIKE A SORE THUMB...
THE REST OF US WERE RIGHT SCARED OF THOSE STUN GUNS AND COULDN'T SAY A WORD...
BUT THEY GOT AHOLD OF YOU REAL FAST AND...
...USED THEIR AMPED-UP STUN GUN ON YOU...
X360
...RIGHT IN THE NOGGIN...
TA (ZZT)

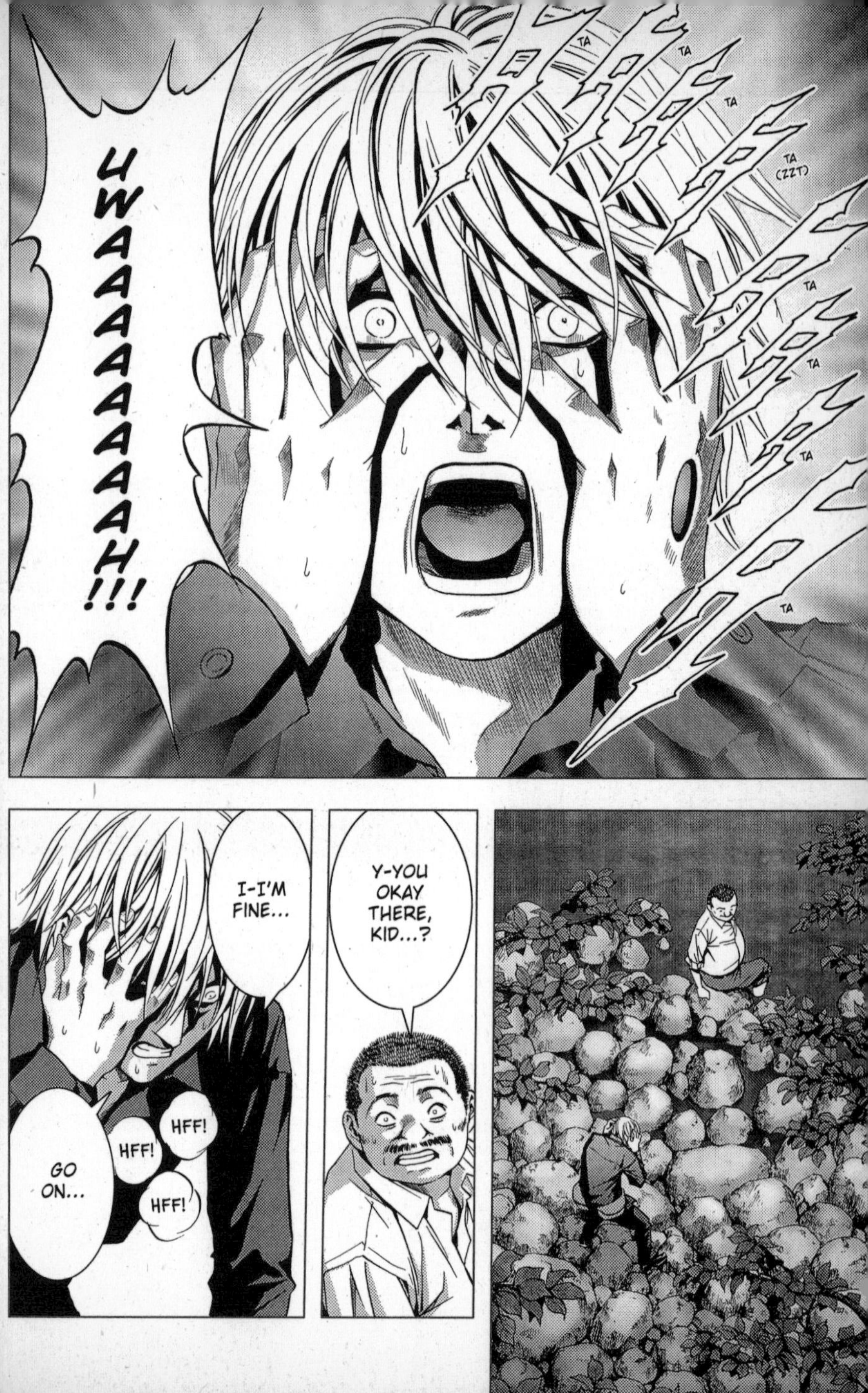
TA
TA
TA
TA
(ZZT)
TA
TA
TA
TA
UWAAAAAAAAH!!!
Y-YOU OKAY THERE, KID...?
I-I'M FINE...
HFF!
HFF!
HFF!
GO ON...

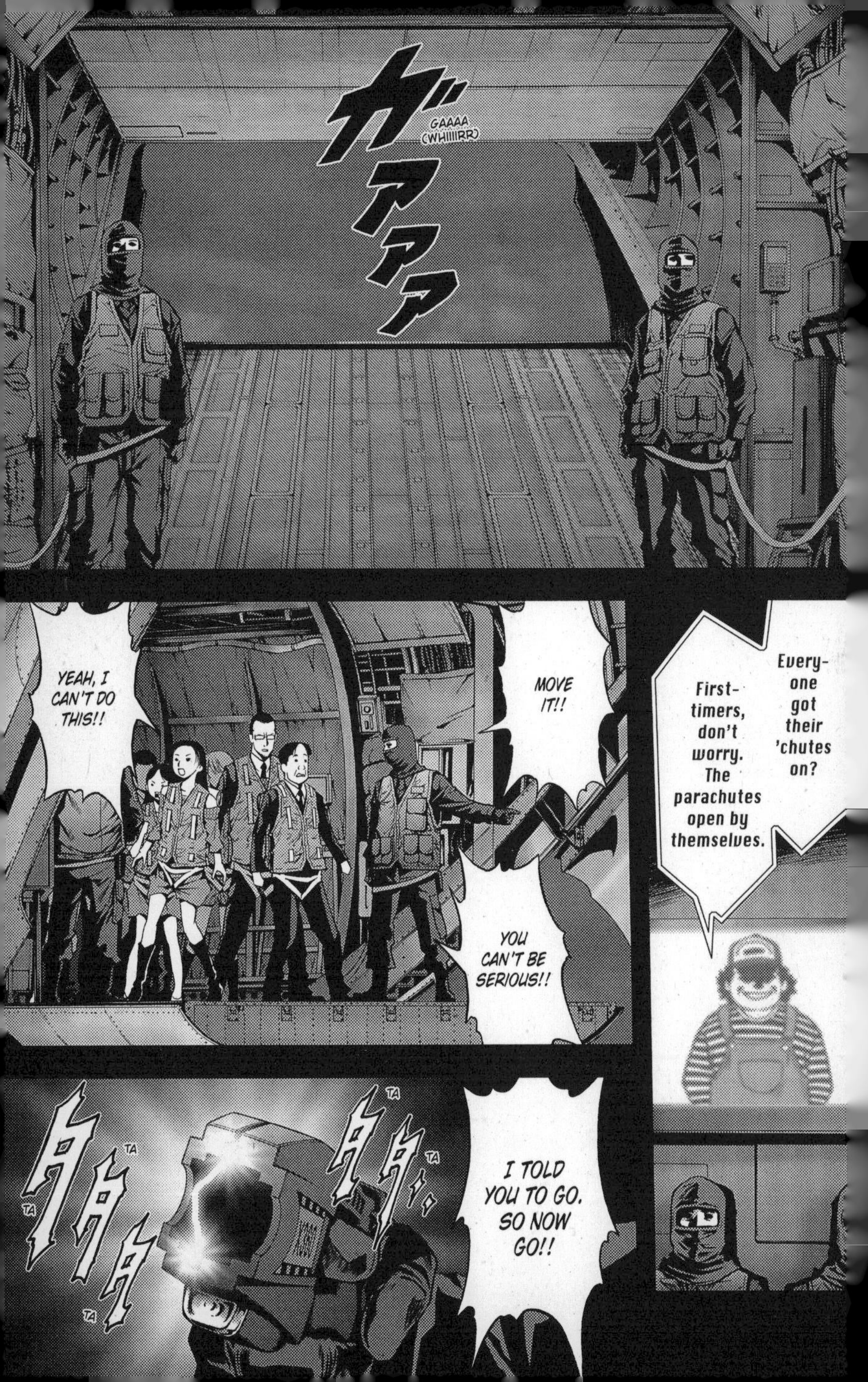
ガアアア
GAAAA (WHIIIIRR)
Every-one got their 'chutes on?
First-timers, don't worry. The parachutes open by themselves.
MOVE IT!!
YEAH, I CAN'T DO THIS!!
YOU CAN'T BE SERIOUS!!
I TOLD YOU TO GO. SO NOW GO!!
TA
TA
TA
TA

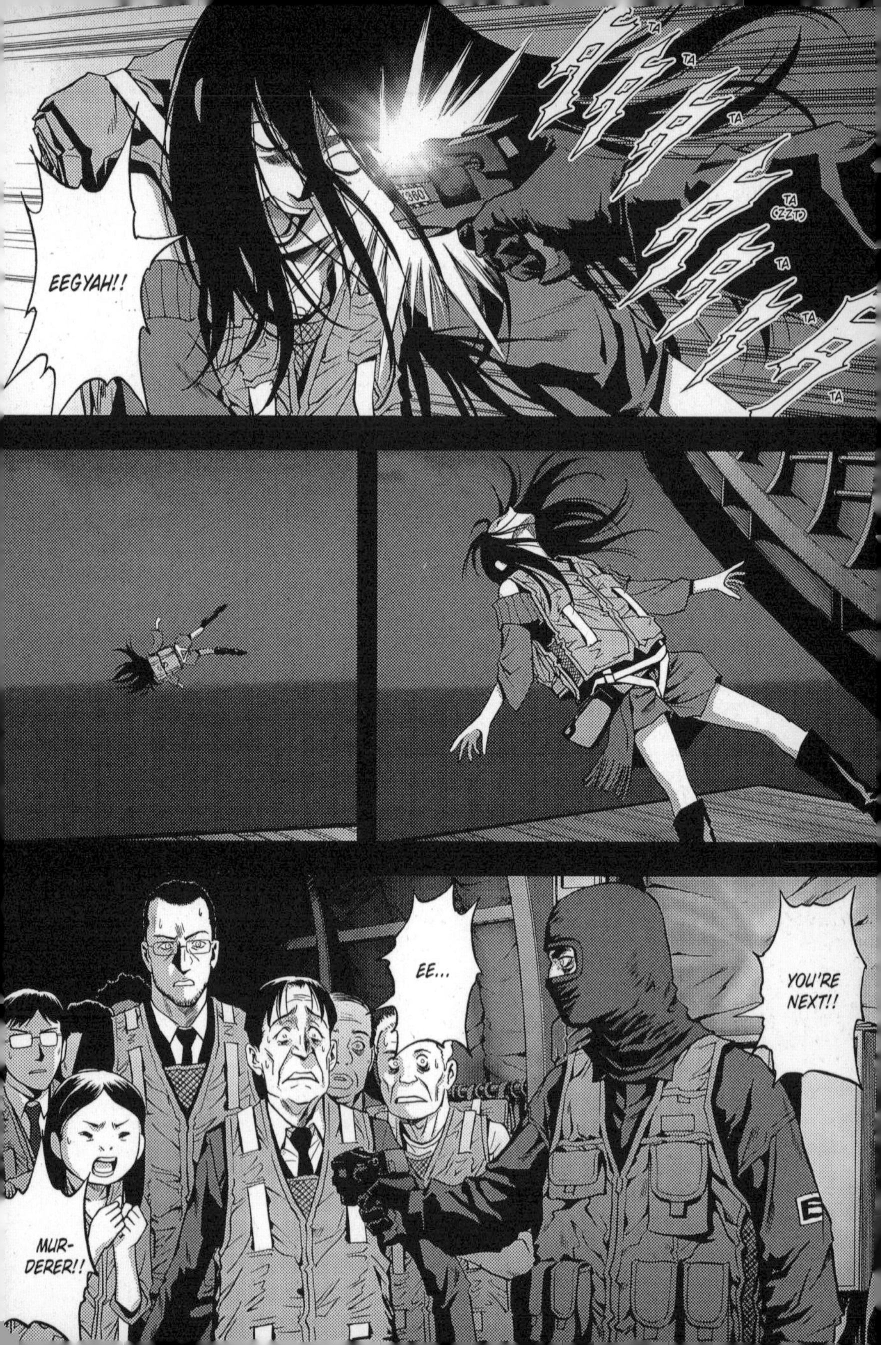
TA
TA
TA
TA
(ZZT)
TA
TA
TA
EEGYAH!!
YOU'RE NEXT!!
EE...
MUR-
DERER!!

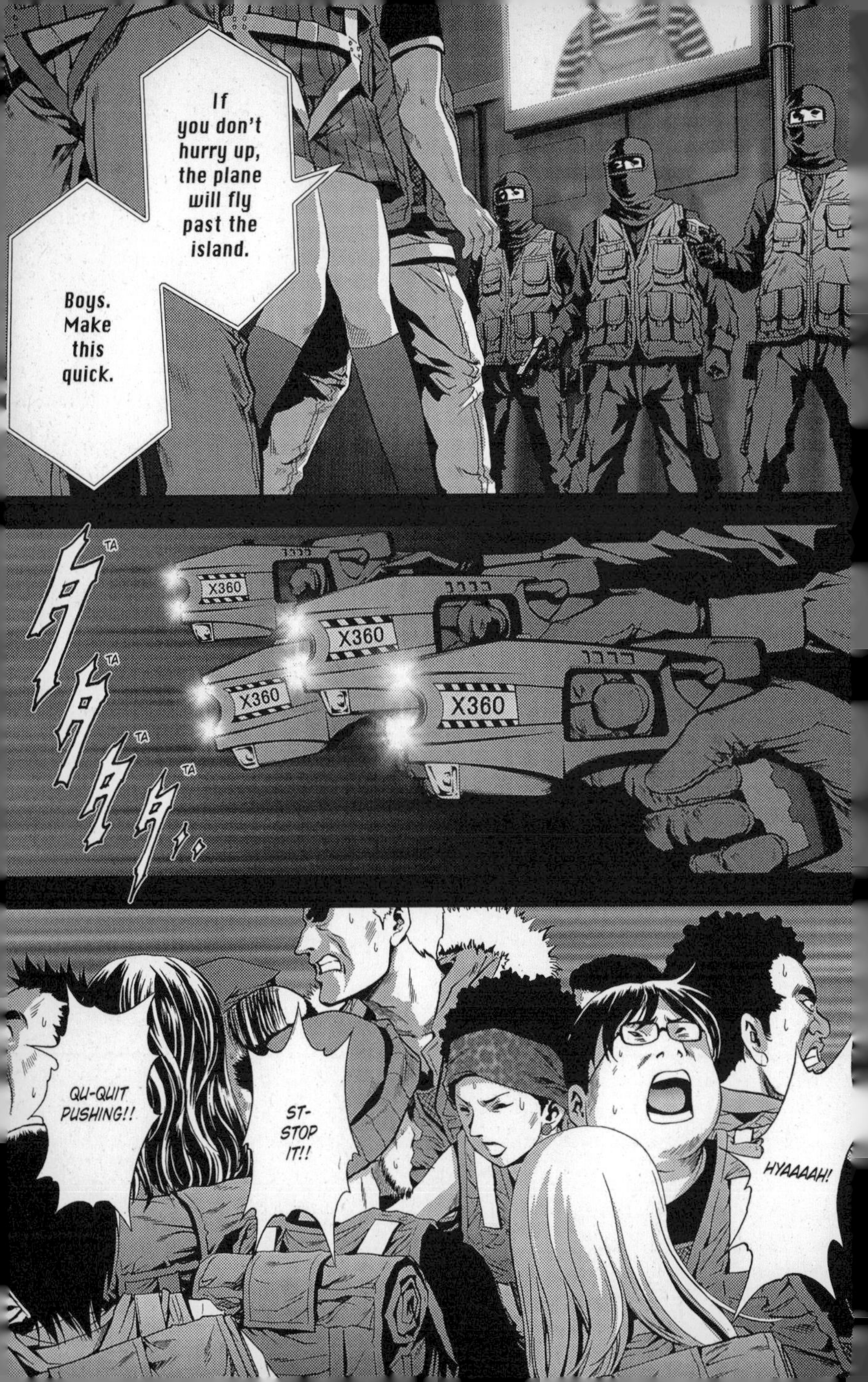
If you don't hurry up, the plane will fly past the island.
Boys. Make this quick.
TA
TA
TA
TA
HYAAAAH!
ST- STOP IT!!
QU-QUIT PUSHING!!

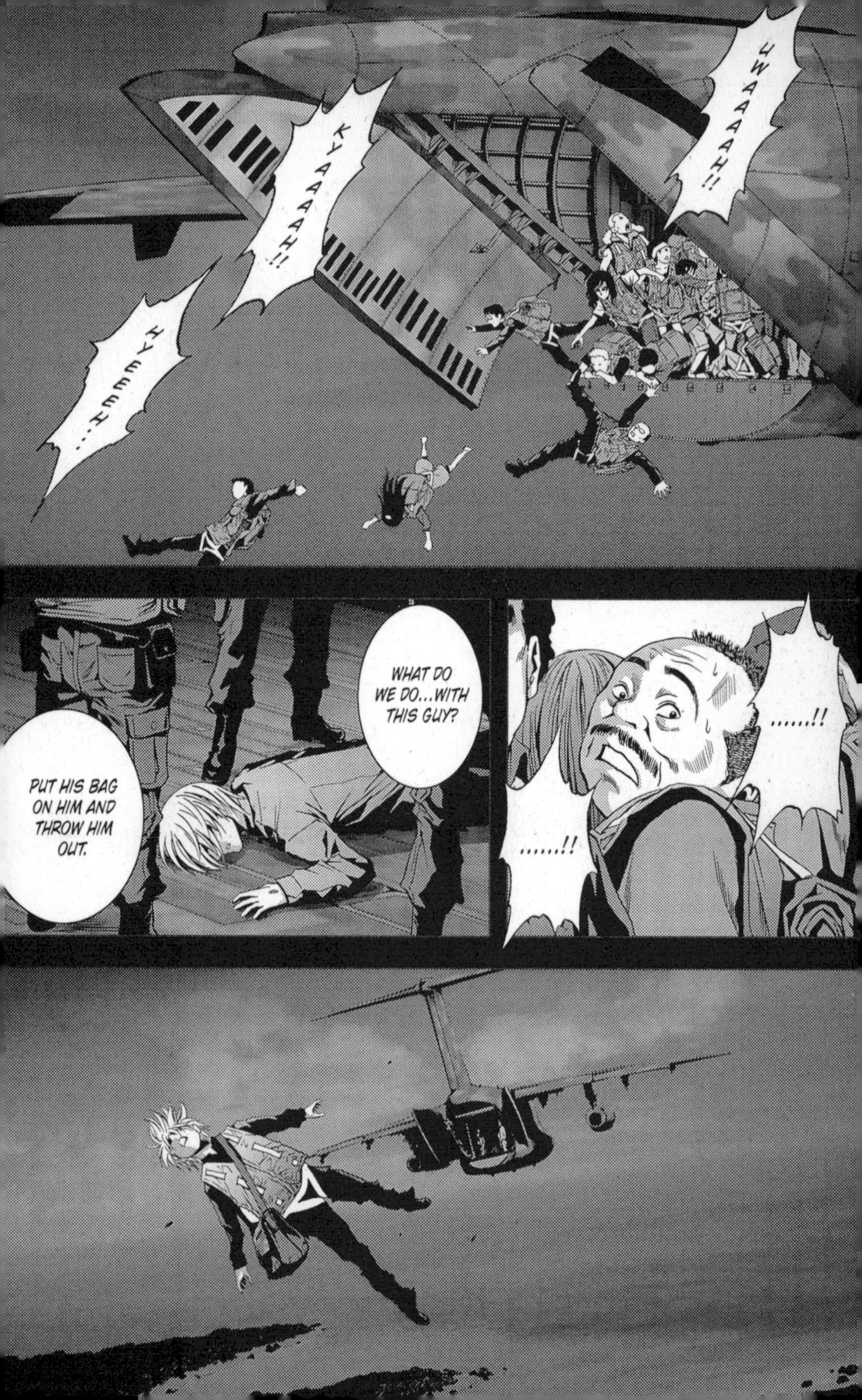
UWAAAAAH!!
KYAAAAAH!!
HYEEEEH...
......!!
......!!
WHAT DO WE DO...WITH THIS GUY?
PUT HIS BAG ON HIM AND THROW HIM OUT.

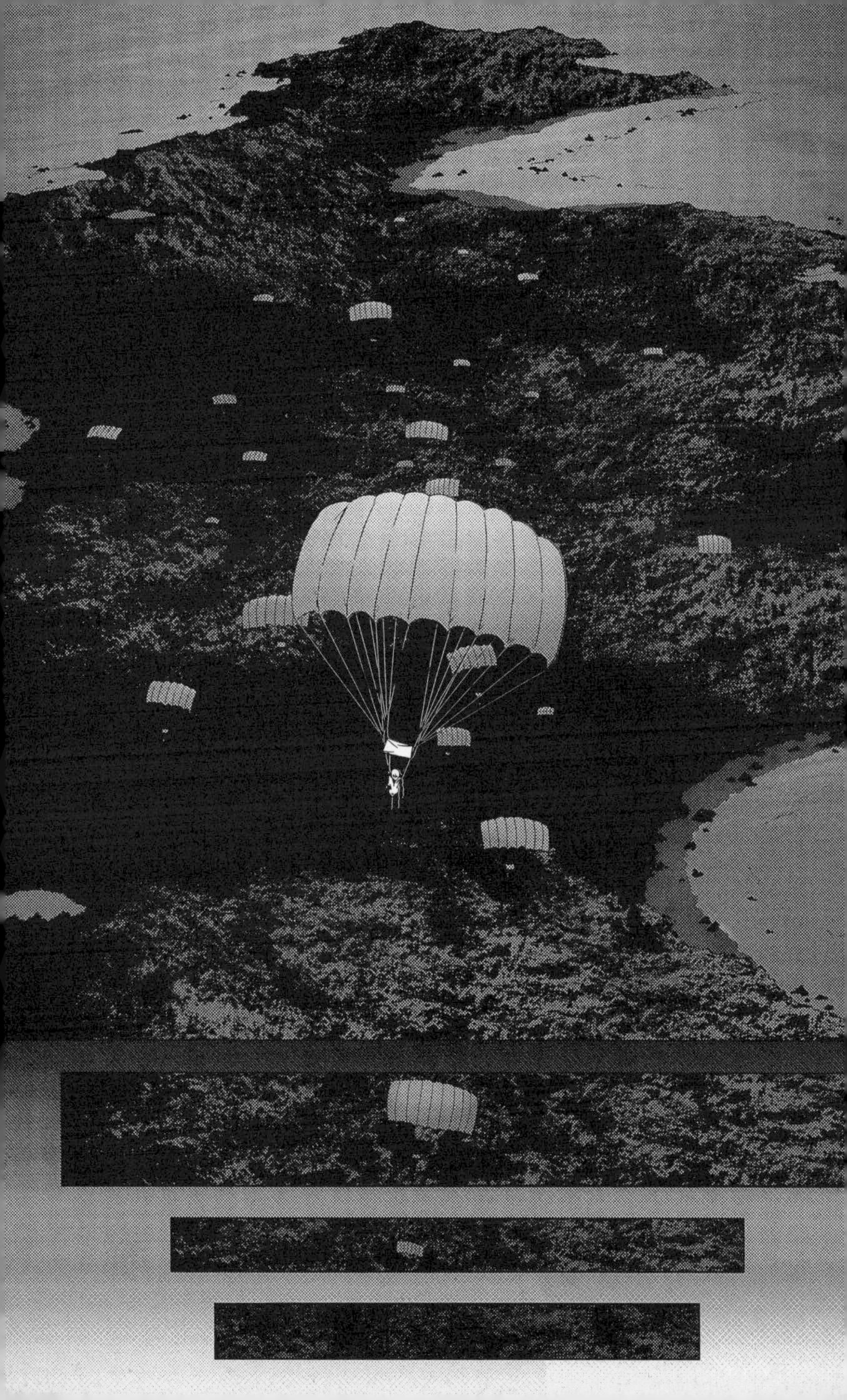

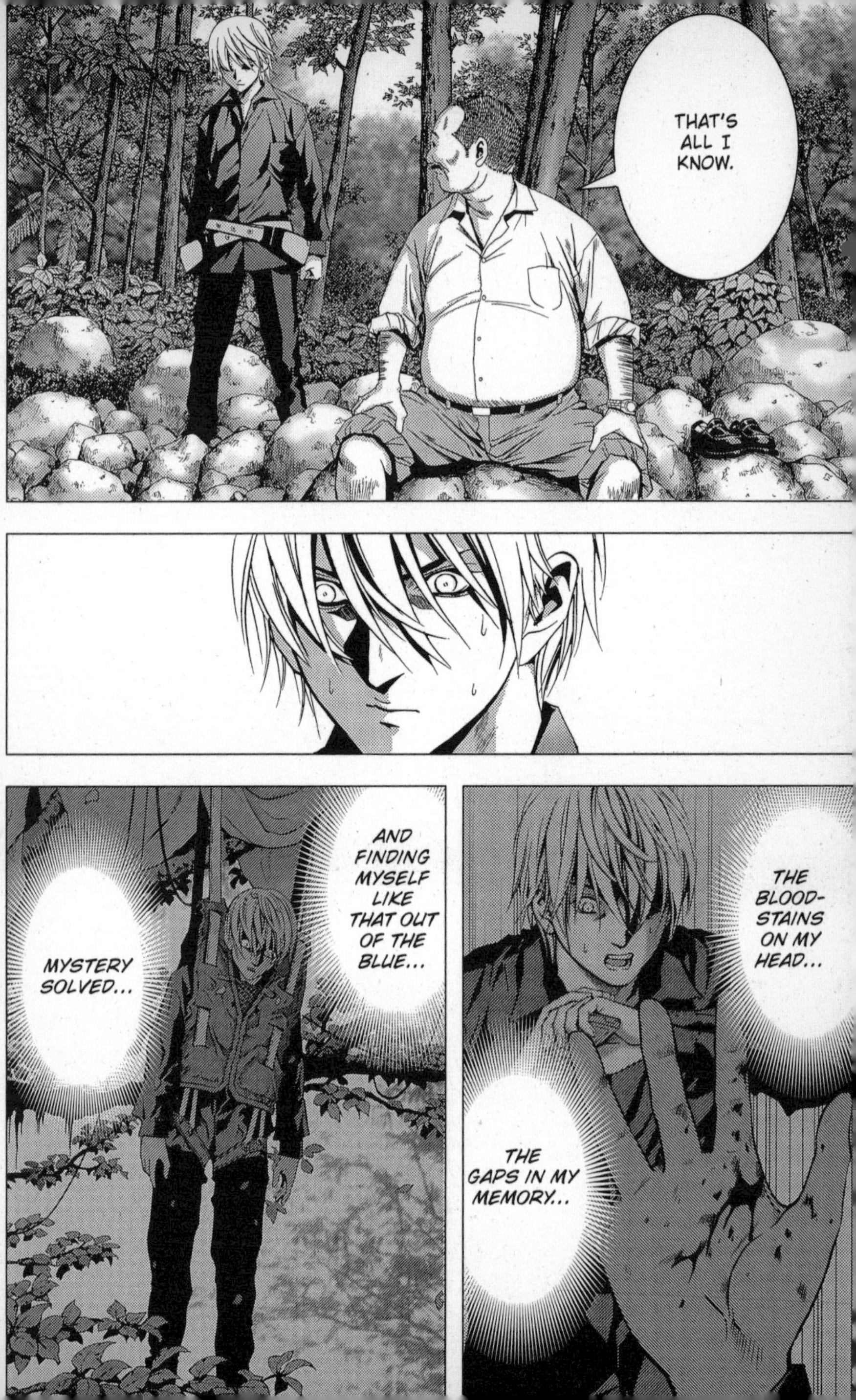
THAT'S ALL I KNOW.
THE BLOOD-STAINS ON MY HEAD...
THE GAPS IN MY MEMORY...
AND FINDING MYSELF LIKE THAT OUT OF THE BLUE...
MYSTERY SOLVED...

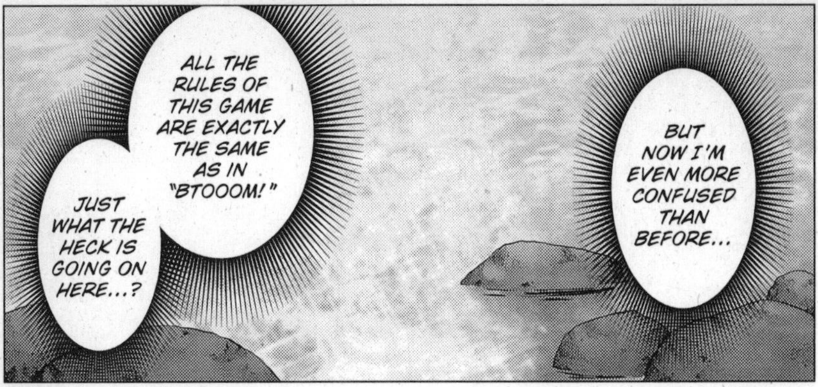
BUT NOW I'M EVEN MORE CONFUSED THAN BEFORE...
ALL THE RULES OF THIS GAME ARE EXACTLY THE SAME AS IN "BTOOOM!"
JUST WHAT THE HECK IS GOING ON HERE...?

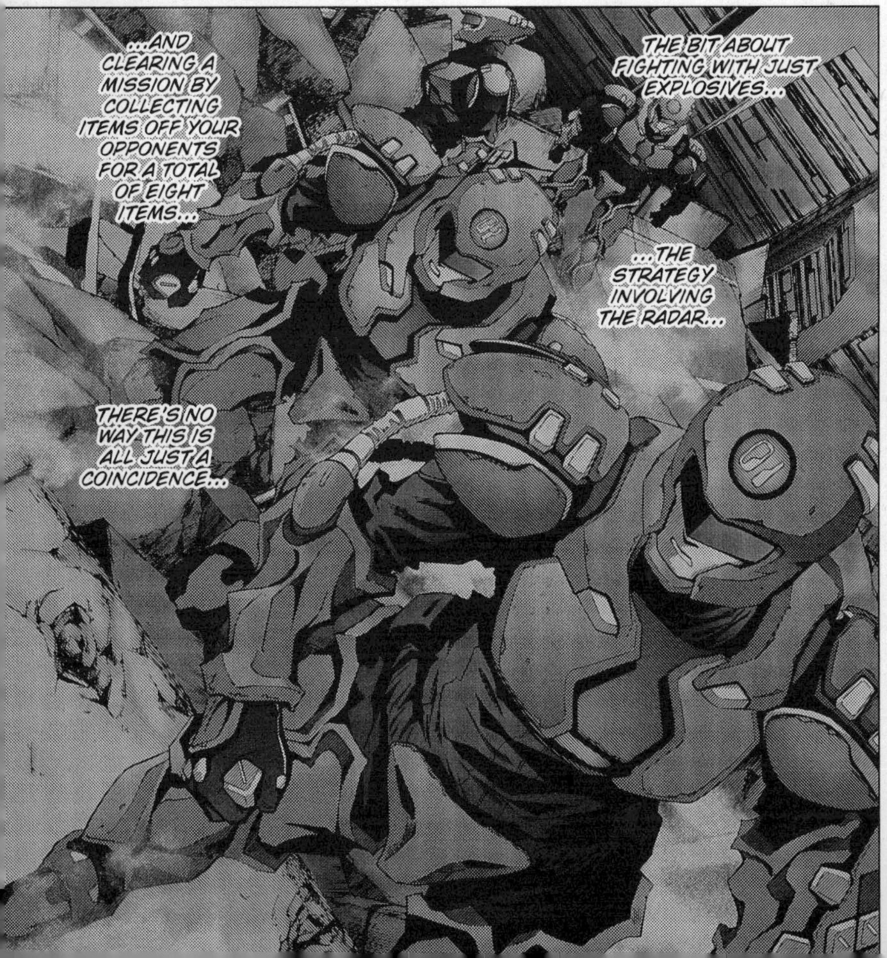
THE BIT ABOUT FIGHTING WITH JUST EXPLOSIVES...
...AND CLEARING A MISSION BY COLLECTING ITEMS OFF YOUR OPPONENTS FOR A TOTAL OF EIGHT ITEMS...
...THE STRATEGY INVOLVING THE RADAR...
THERE'S NO WAY THIS IS ALL JUST A COINCIDENCE...

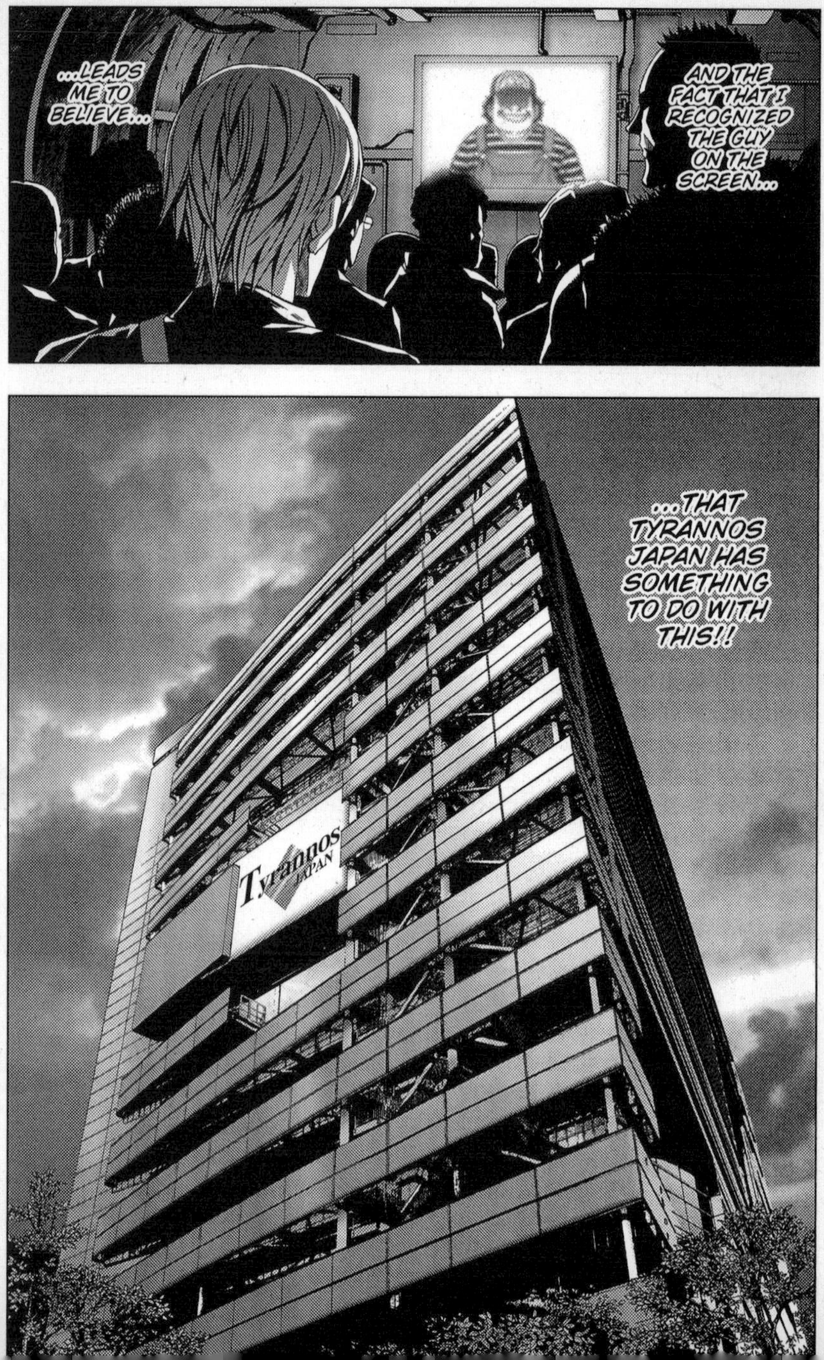
AND THE FACT THAT I RECOGNIZED THE GUY ON THE SCREEN...
...LEADS ME TO BELIEVE...
...THAT TYRANNOS JAPAN HAS SOMETHING TO DO WITH THIS!!
Tyrannos JAPAN

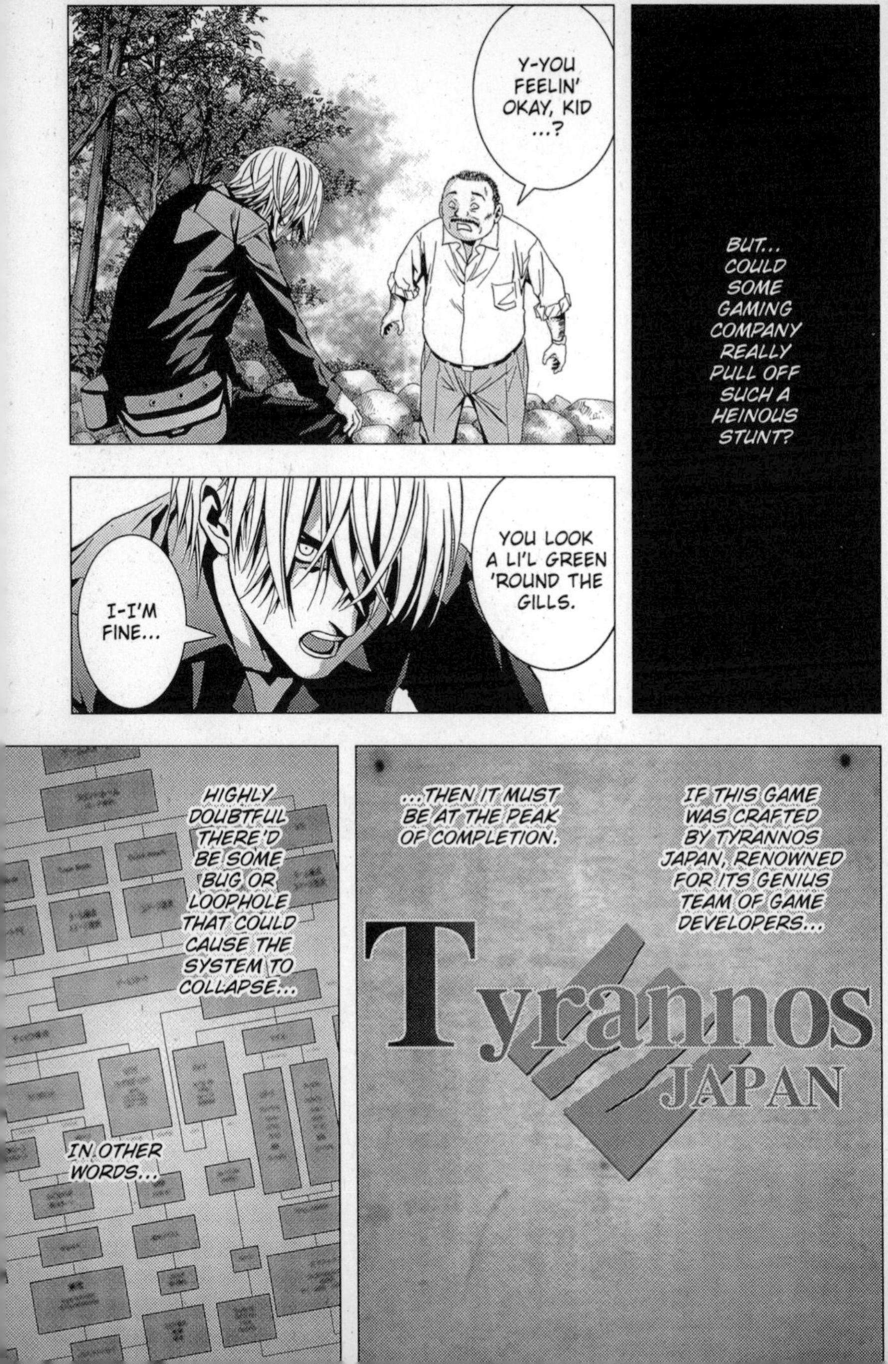
BUT... COULD SOME GAMING COMPANY REALLY PULL OFF SUCH A HEINOUS STUNT?
Y-YOU FEELIN' OKAY, KID ...?
YOU LOOK A LI'L GREEN 'ROUND THE GILLS.
I-I'M FINE...
IF THIS GAME WAS CRAFTED BY TYRANNOS JAPAN, RENOWNED FOR ITS GENIUS TEAM OF GAME DEVELOPERS...
...THEN IT MUST BE AT THE PEAK OF COMPLETION.
Tyrannos JAPAN
HIGHLY DOUBTFUL THERE'D BE SOME BUG OR LOOPHOLE THAT COULD CAUSE THE SYSTEM TO COLLAPSE...
IN OTHER WORDS...

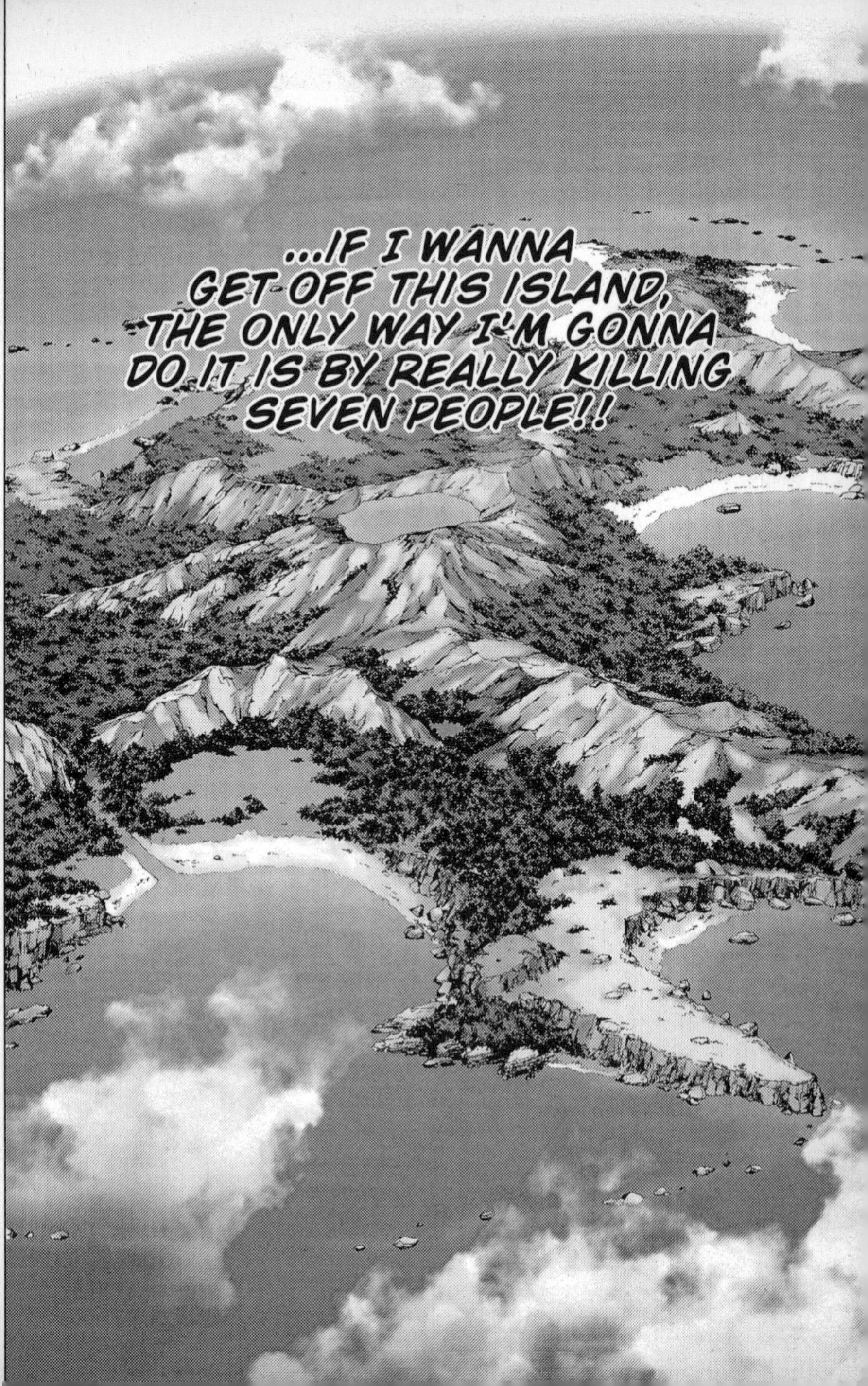
...IF I WANNA GET OFF THIS ISLAND, THE ONLY WAY I'M GONNA DO IT IS BY REALLY KILLING SEVEN PEOPLE!!

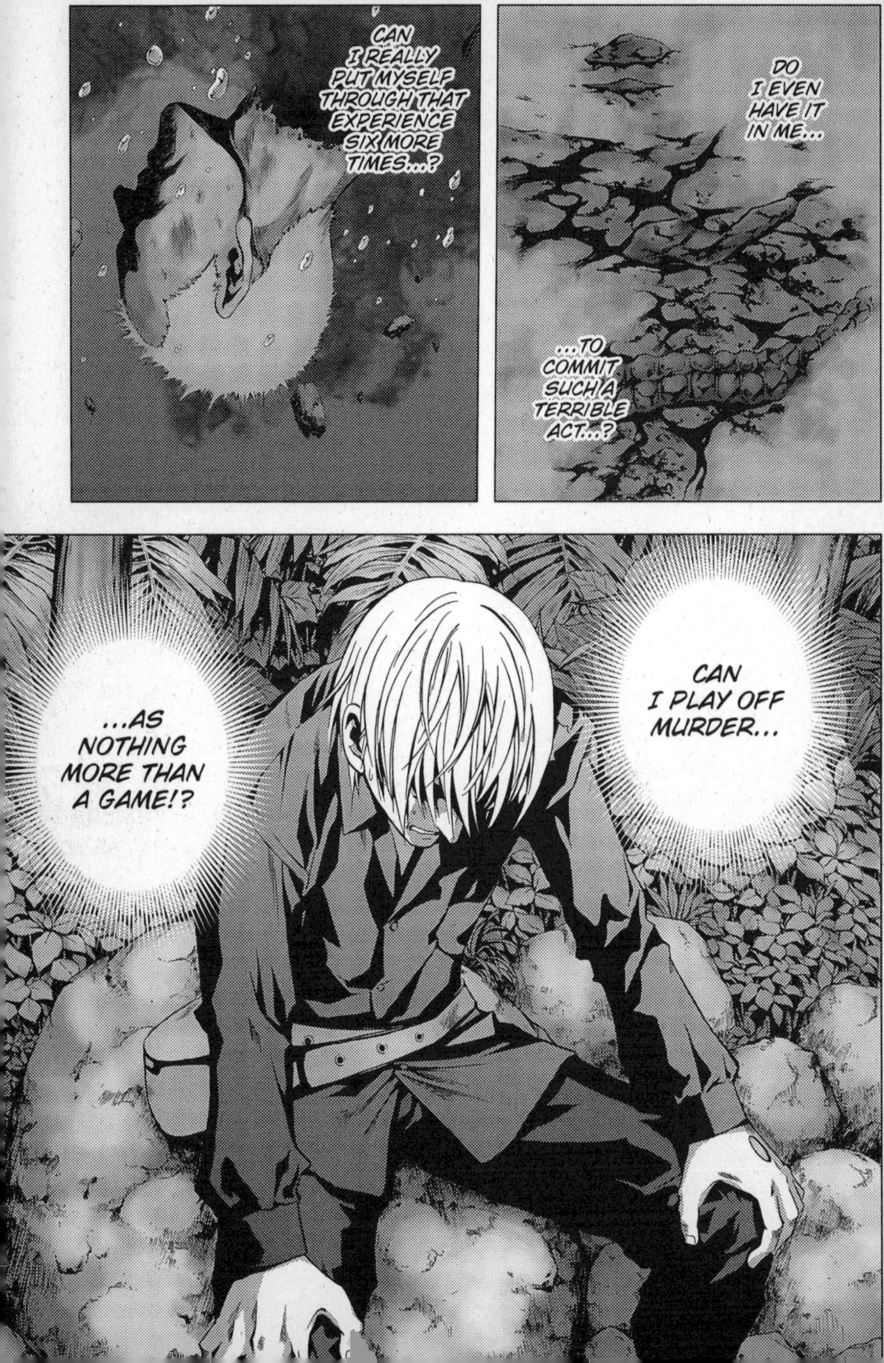
DO I EVEN HAVE IT IN ME...
...TO COMMIT SUCH A TERRIBLE ACT...?
CAN I REALLY PUT MYSELF THROUGH THAT EXPERIENCE SIX MORE TIMES...?
CAN I PLAY OFF MURDER...
...AS NOTHING MORE THAN A GAME!?

BIM DATA-01

CRACKER TYPE

■UPON PRESSING THE SWITCH, THE FUSE IS ACTIVATED, AND IT WILL EXPLODE ON IMPACT. THE MOST ORTHODOX STYLE OF BIM, IT IS MAINLY EMPLOYED IN COMBAT BY A DIRECT THROW. IT IS EASY TO USE, BUT RELATIVELY WEAK COMPARED TO OTHER BIMS. THE FACT THAT IT IS SO ORTHODOX IS THE REASON IT IS THE MOST UBIQUITOUS TYPE ON THE ISLAND.

DESTRUCTIVENESS ★★☆☆☆

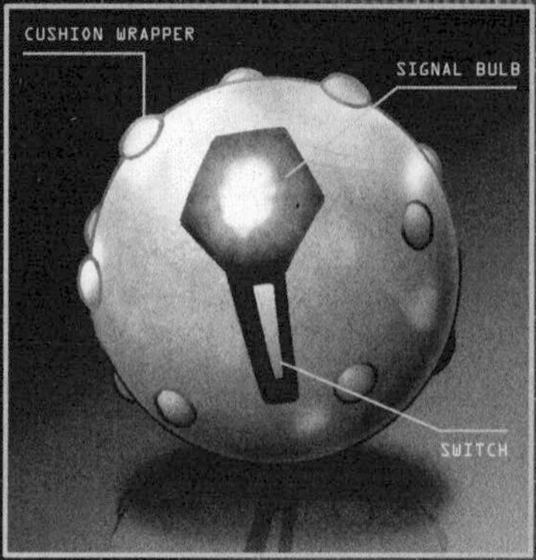
CUSHION WRAPPER
SIGNAL BULB
SWITCH

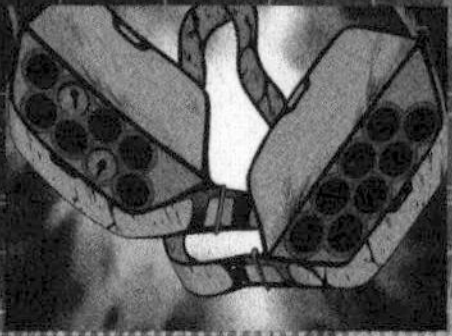

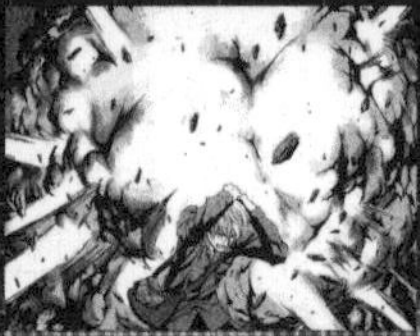

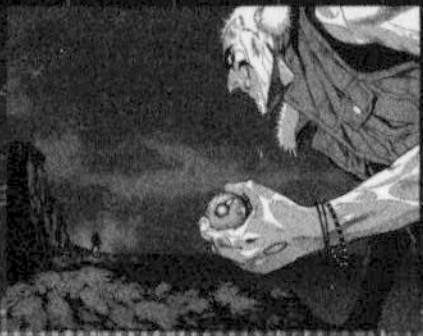

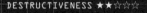

BIM DATA-02

TIMER TYPE

■PRESSING THE SWITCH WILL RESULT IN THE NUMBER "10" BEING DISPLAYED ON THE GLASS SCREEN. IT WILL THEN COUNT DOWN THE SECONDS UNTIL IT REACHES "00," AT WHICH POINT IT WILL DETONATE. IF YOU PRESS THE SWITCH AGAIN WHILE IN MIDCOUNT, THE TIMER CAN BE TEMPORARILY CANCELED.

■SUITED FOR STRATEGIC USE IN AMBUSH SCENARIOS AND TRAPS.

DESTRUCTIVENESS ★★★★☆

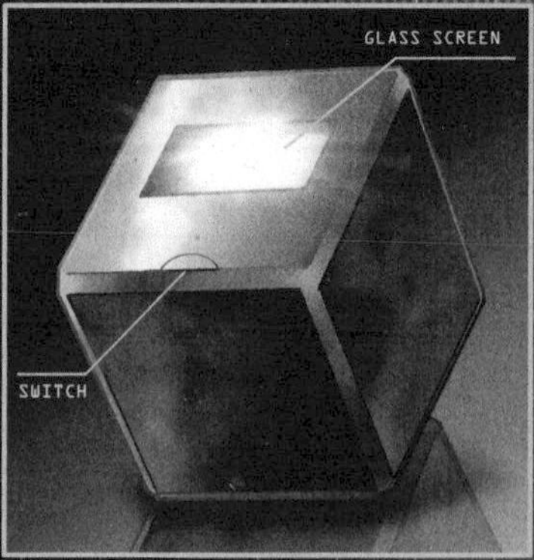
GLASS SCREEN
SWITCH

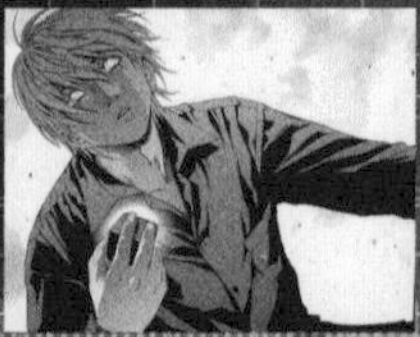

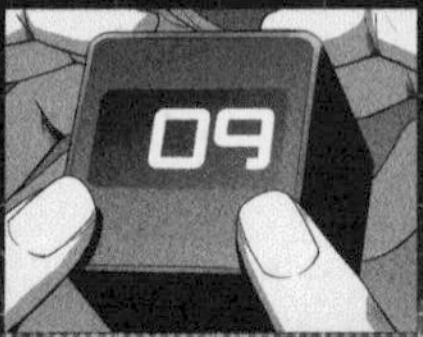
09

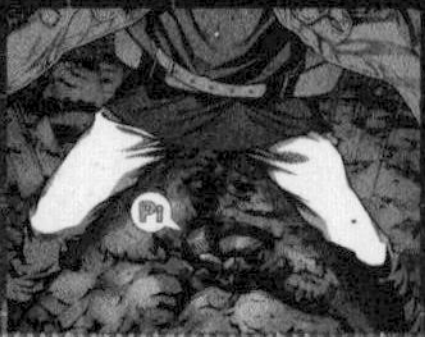

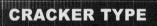

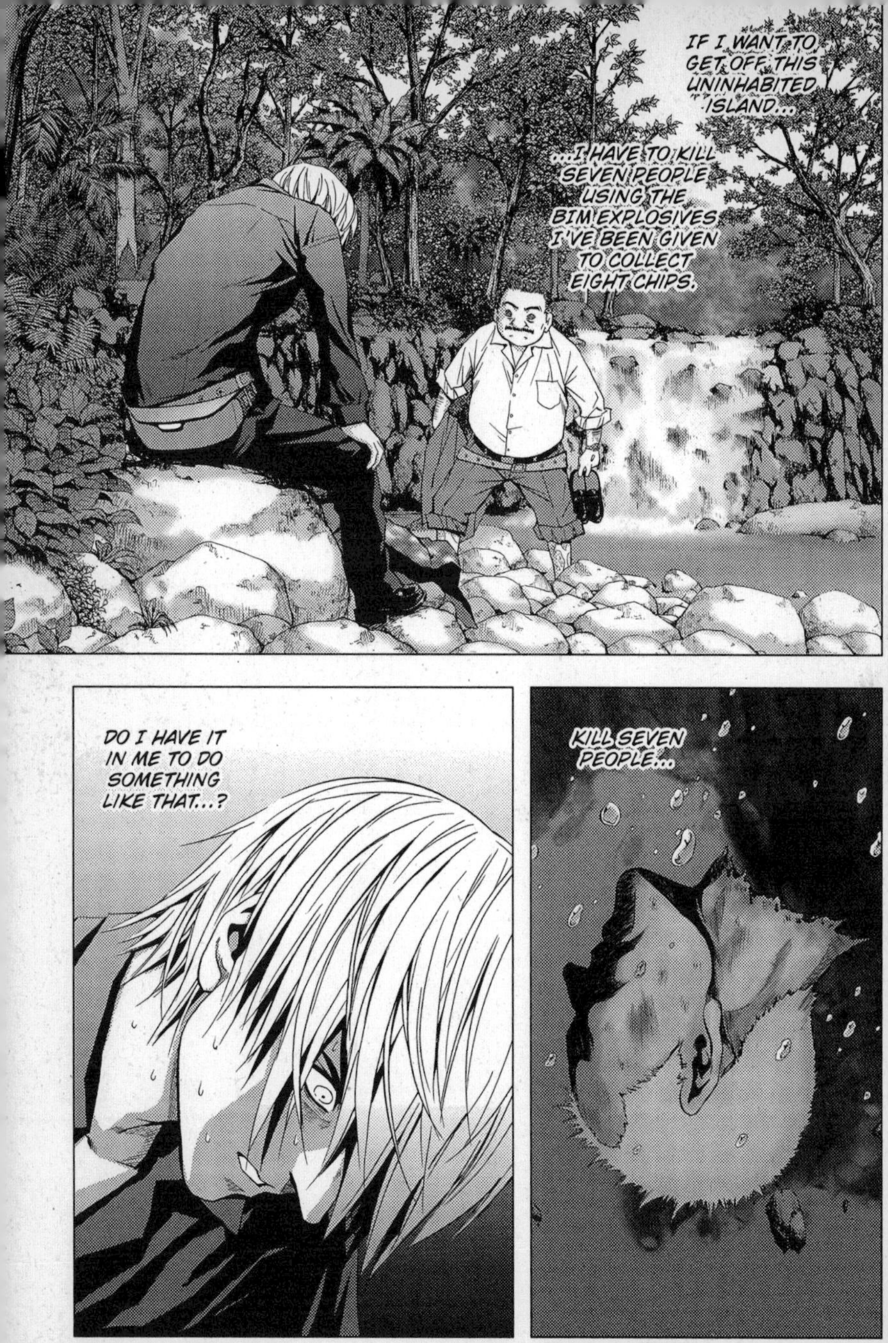
IF I WANT TO GET OFF THIS UNINHABITED ISLAND...
...I HAVE TO KILL SEVEN PEOPLE USING THE BIM EXPLOSIVES I'VE BEEN GIVEN TO COLLECT EIGHT CHIPS.
KILL SEVEN PEOPLE...
DO I HAVE IT IN ME TO DO SOMETHING LIKE THAT...?

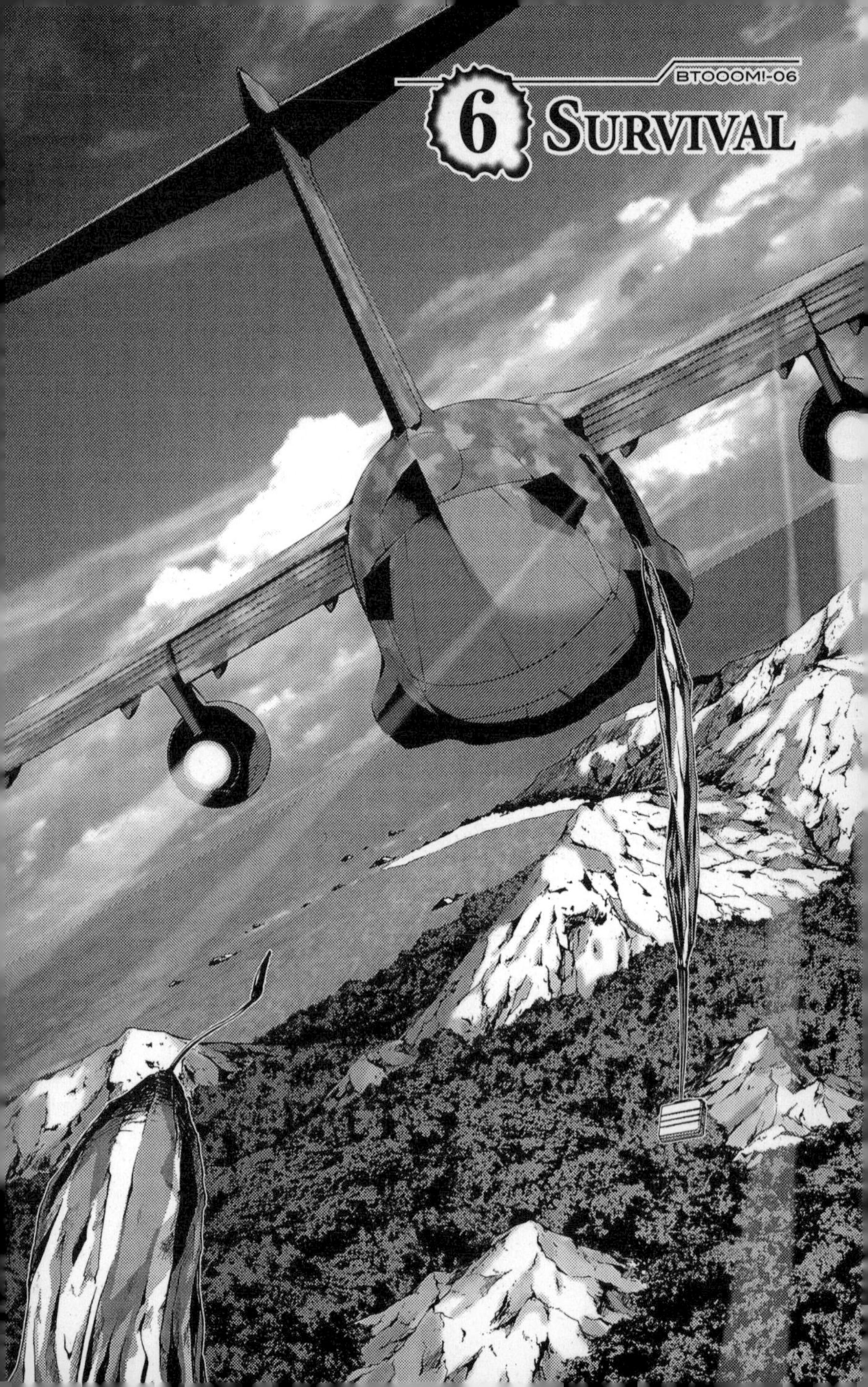
BTOOOM!-06
6 SURVIVAL

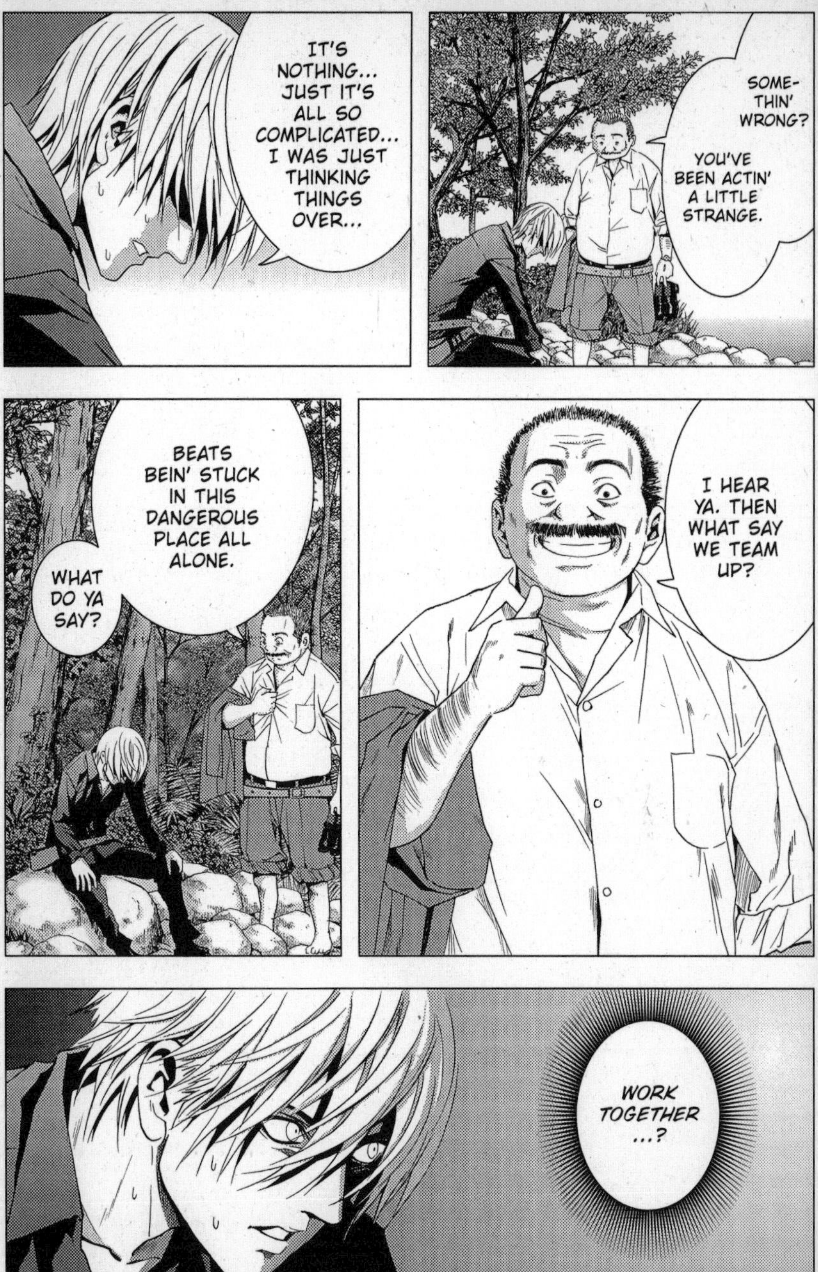
SOME-THIN' WRONG?
YOU'VE BEEN ACTIN' A LITTLE STRANGE.
IT'S NOTHING... JUST IT'S ALL SO COMPLICATED... I WAS JUST THINKING THINGS OVER...
I HEAR YA. THEN WHAT SAY WE TEAM UP?
BEATS BEIN' STUCK IN THIS DANGEROUS PLACE ALL ALONE.
WHAT DO YA SAY?
WORK TOGETHER ...?

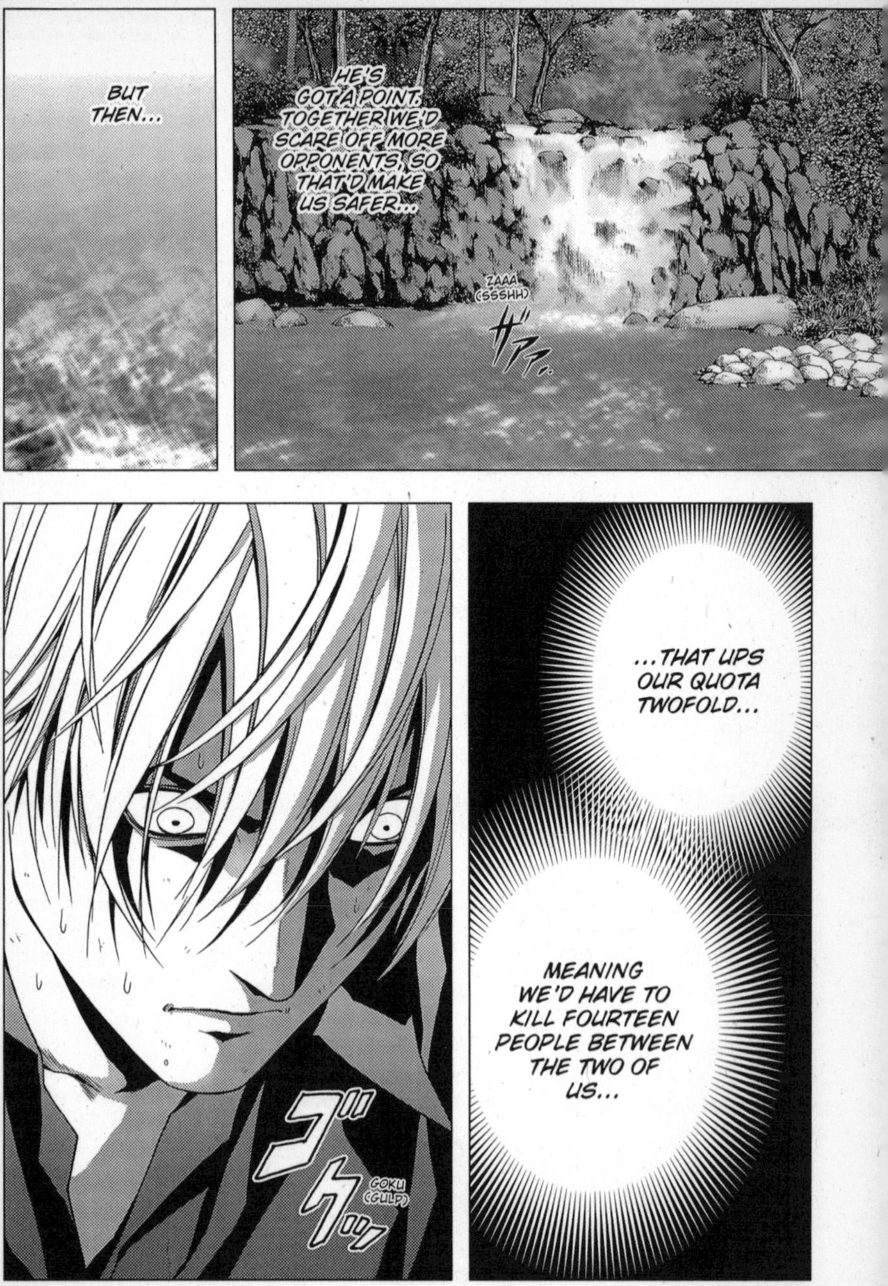
HE'S GOT A POINT. TOGETHER WE'D SCARE OFF MORE OPPONENTS, SO THAT'D MAKE US SAFER...
ZAAA (SSSHH)
BUT THEN...
...THAT UPS OUR QUOTA TWOFOLD...
MEANING WE'D HAVE TO KILL FOURTEEN PEOPLE BETWEEN THE TWO OF US...
GOKU (GULP)

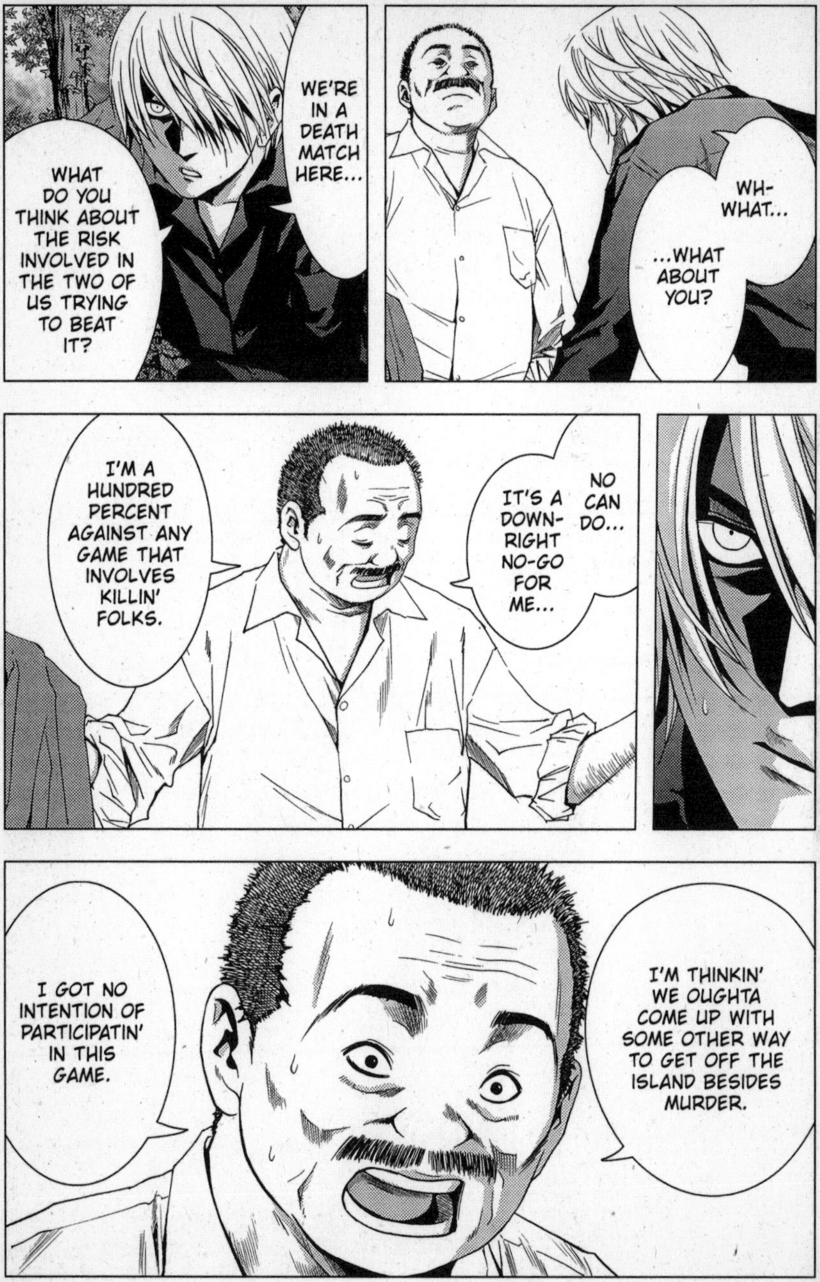
WH- WHAT...
...WHAT ABOUT YOU?
WE'RE IN A DEATH MATCH HERE...
WHAT DO YOU THINK ABOUT THE RISK INVOLVED IN THE TWO OF US TRYING TO BEAT IT?
NO CAN DO...
IT'S A DOWN-RIGHT NO-GO FOR ME...
I'M A HUNDRED PERCENT AGAINST ANY GAME THAT INVOLVES KILLIN' FOLKS.
I'M THINKIN' WE OUGHTA COME UP WITH SOME OTHER WAY TO GET OFF THE ISLAND BESIDES MURDER.
I GOT NO INTENTION OF PARTICIPATIN' IN THIS GAME.

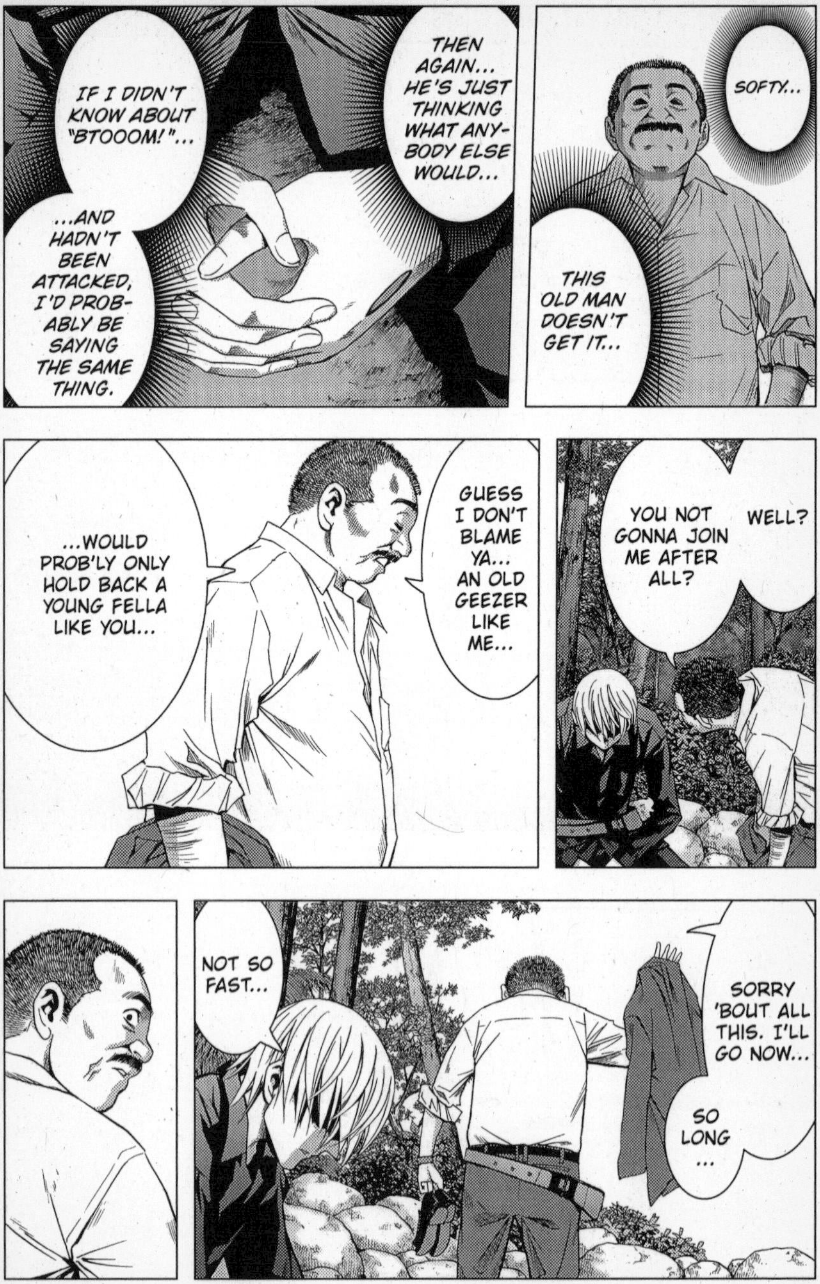
SOFTY...
THIS OLD MAN DOESN'T GET IT...
THEN AGAIN... HE'S JUST THINKING WHAT ANYBODY ELSE WOULD...
IF I DIDN'T KNOW ABOUT "BTOOOM!"...
...AND HADN'T BEEN ATTACKED, I'D PROBABLY BE SAYING THE SAME THING.
WELL?
YOU NOT GONNA JOIN ME AFTER ALL?
GUESS I DON'T BLAME YA... AN OLD GEEZER LIKE ME...
...WOULD PROB'LY ONLY HOLD BACK A YOUNG FELLA LIKE YOU...
SORRY 'BOUT ALL THIS. I'LL GO NOW...
SO LONG ...
NOT SO FAST...

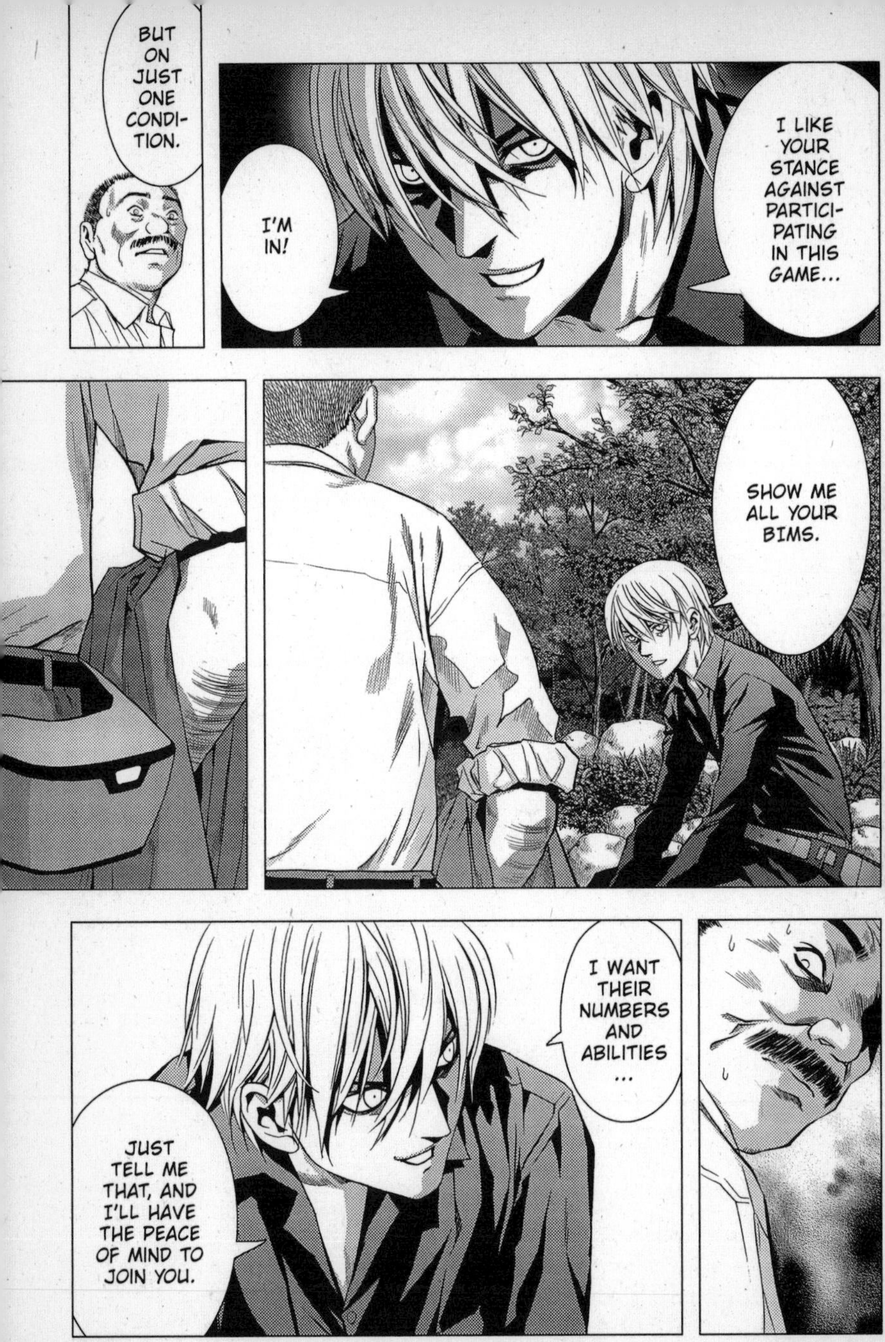
I LIKE YOUR STANCE AGAINST PARTICIPATING IN THIS GAME...
I'M IN!
BUT ON JUST ONE CONDITION.
SHOW ME ALL YOUR BIMS.
I WANT THEIR NUMBERS AND ABILITIES ...
JUST TELL ME THAT, AND I'LL HAVE THE PEACE OF MIND TO JOIN YOU.

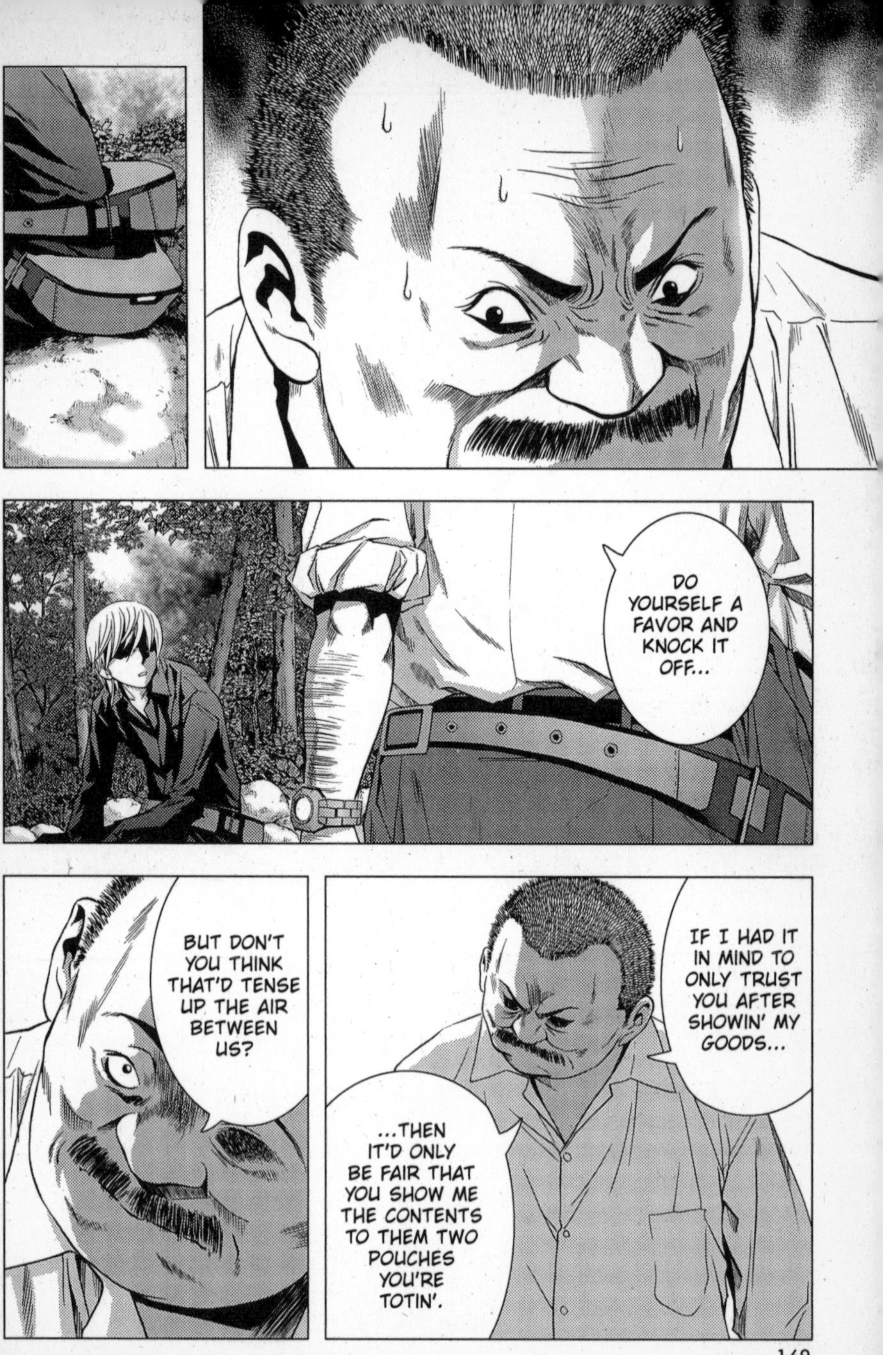
DO YOURSELF A FAVOR AND KNOCK IT OFF...
IF I HAD IT IN MIND TO ONLY TRUST YOU AFTER SHOWIN' MY GOODS...
...THEN IT'D ONLY BE FAIR THAT YOU SHOW ME THE CONTENTS TO THEM TWO POUCHES YOU'RE TOTIN'.
BUT DON'T YOU THINK THAT'D TENSE UP THE AIR BETWEEN US?

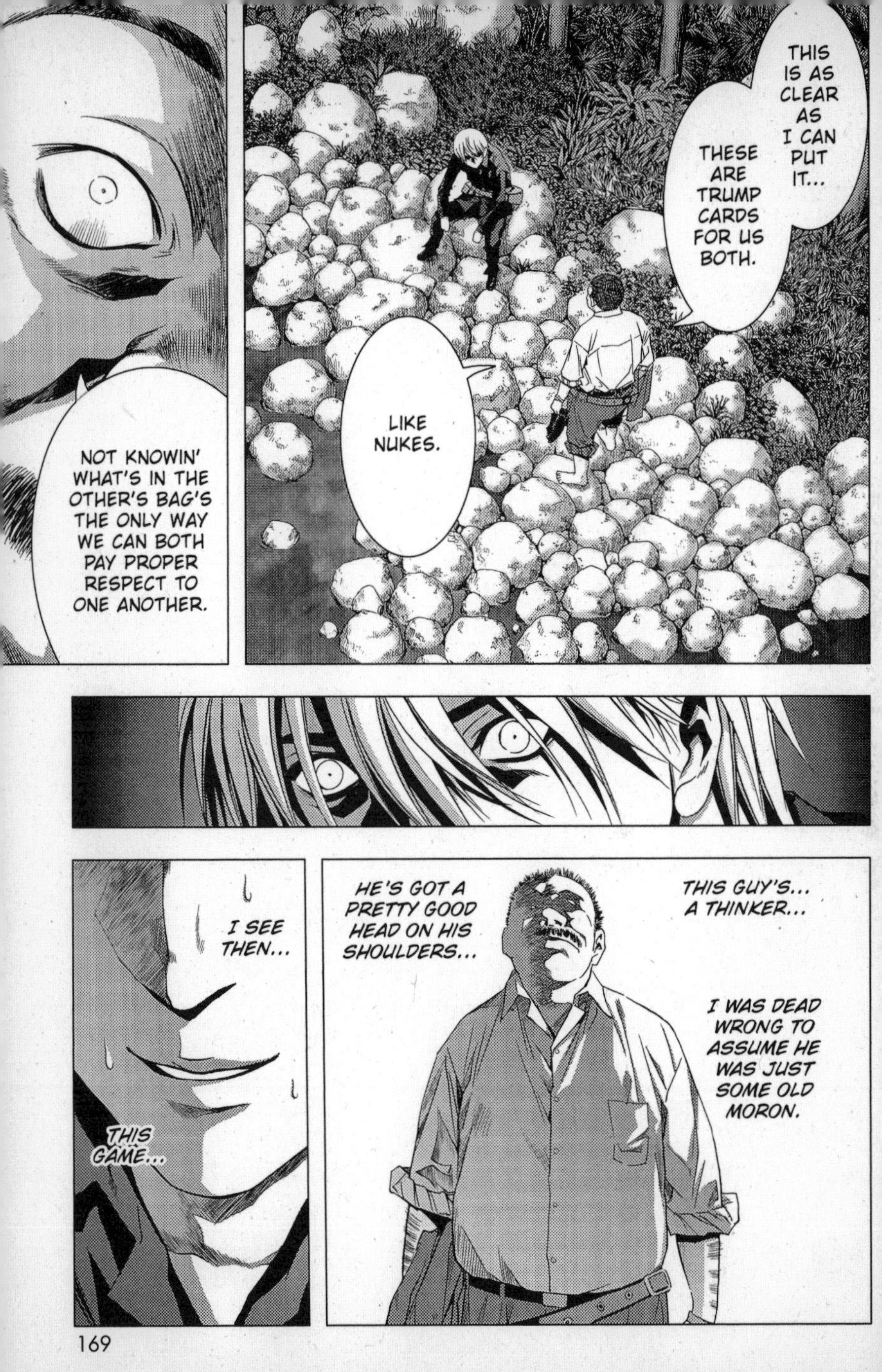
THIS IS AS CLEAR AS I CAN PUT IT...
THESE ARE TRUMP CARDS FOR US BOTH.
LIKE NUKES.
NOT KNOWIN' WHAT'S IN THE OTHER'S BAG'S THE ONLY WAY WE CAN BOTH PAY PROPER RESPECT TO ONE ANOTHER.
THIS GUY'S... A THINKER...
HE'S GOT A PRETTY GOOD HEAD ON HIS SHOULDERS...
I WAS DEAD WRONG TO ASSUME HE WAS JUST SOME OLD MORON.
I SEE THEN...
THIS GAME...

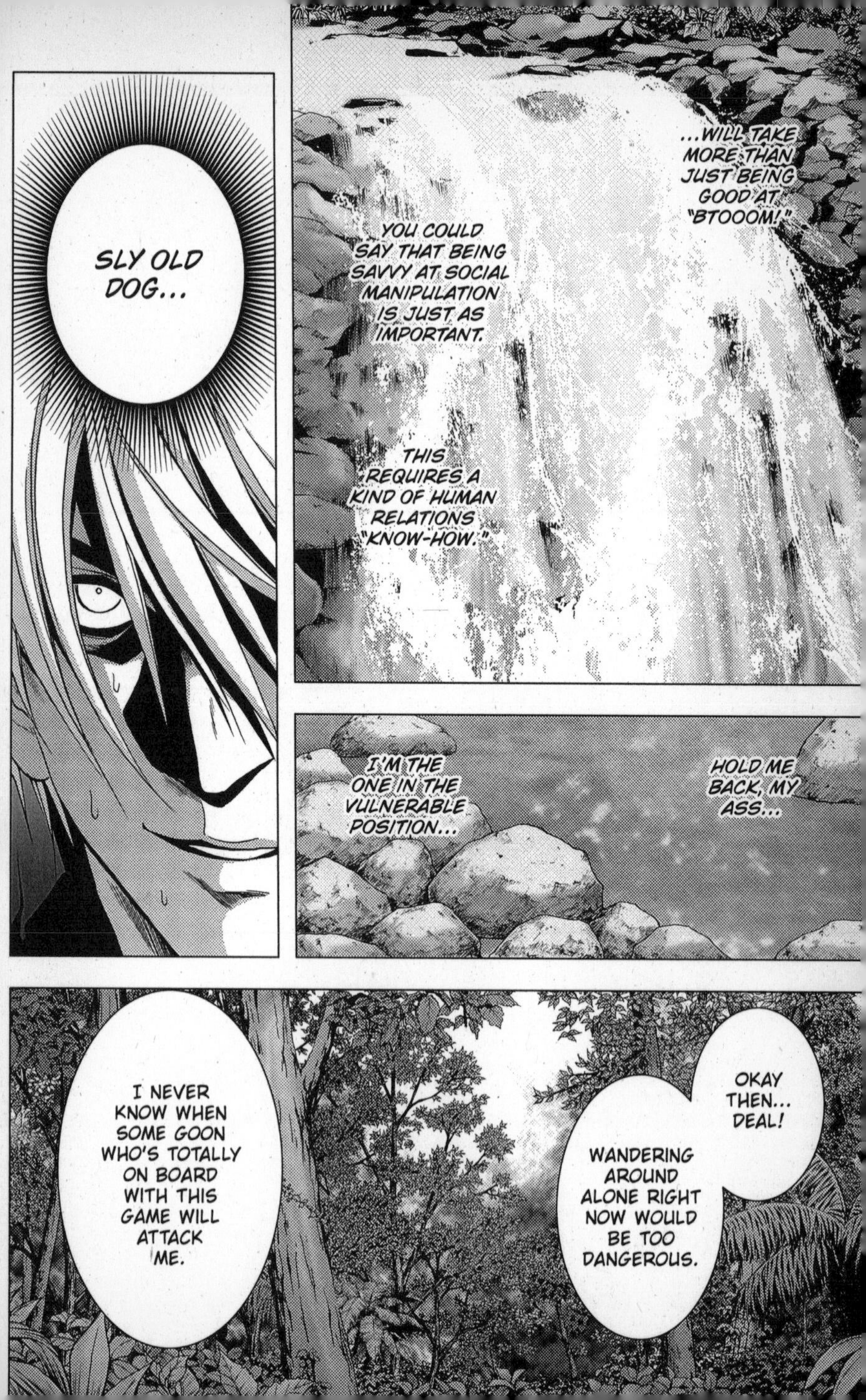
...WILL TAKE MORE THAN JUST BEING GOOD AT "BTOOOM!"
YOU COULD SAY THAT BEING SAVVY AT SOCIAL MANIPULATION IS JUST AS IMPORTANT.
THIS REQUIRES A KIND OF HUMAN RELATIONS "KNOW-HOW."
HOLD ME BACK, MY ASS...
I'M THE ONE IN THE VULNERABLE POSITION...
SLY OLD DOG...
OKAY THEN... DEAL!
WANDERING AROUND ALONE RIGHT NOW WOULD BE TOO DANGEROUS.
I NEVER KNOW WHEN SOME GOON WHO'S TOTALLY ON BOARD WITH THIS GAME WILL ATTACK ME.

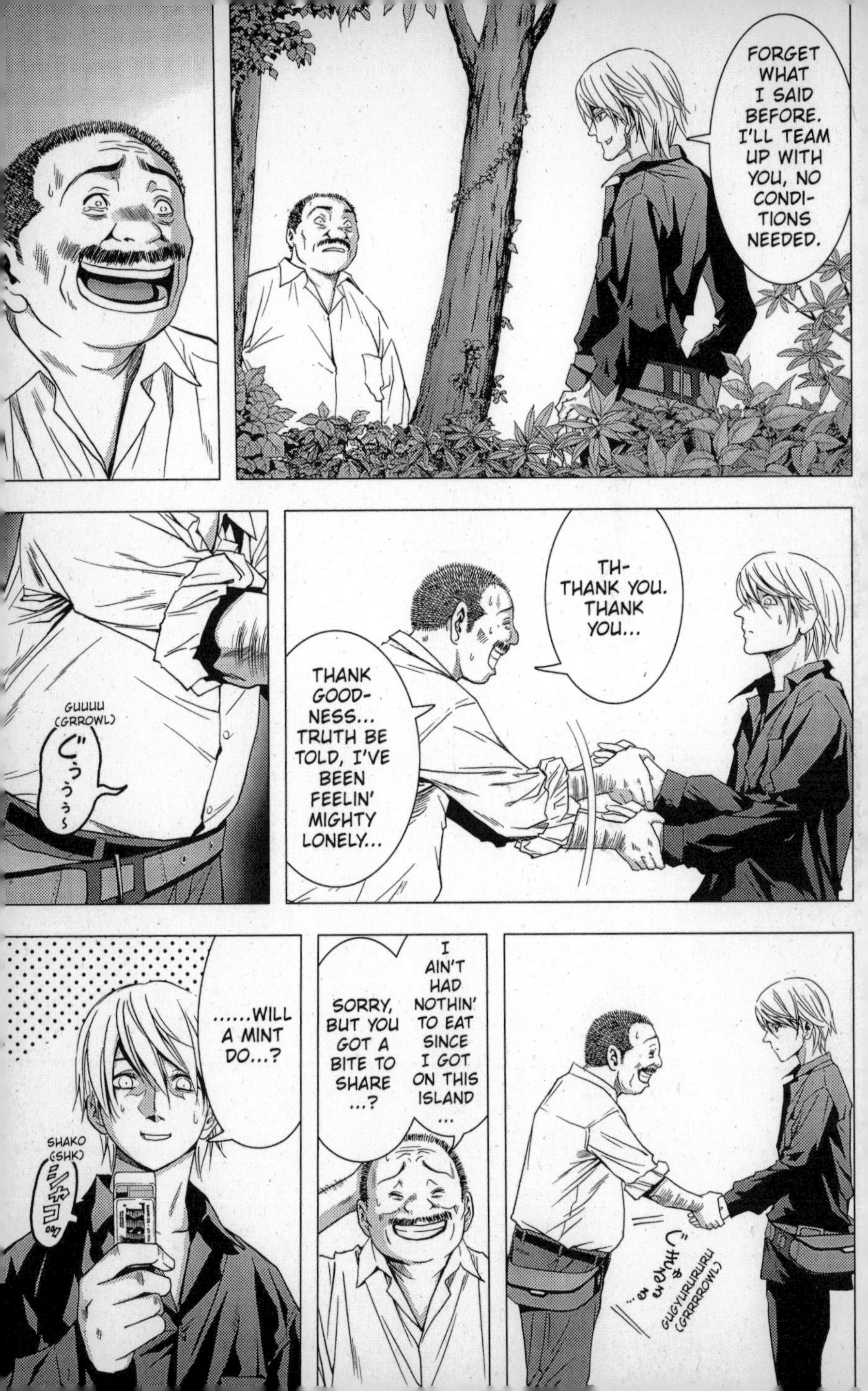
FORGET WHAT I SAID BEFORE. I'LL TEAM UP WITH YOU, NO CONDITIONS NEEDED.
TH- THANK YOU. THANK YOU...
THANK GOODNESS... TRUTH BE TOLD, I'VE BEEN FEELIN' MIGHTY LONELY...
GUUUU (GRROWL)
ぐうぅぅ～
GUGYURURURU (GRRRROWL)
I AIN'T HAD NOTHIN' TO EAT SINCE I GOT ON THIS ISLAND...
SORRY, BUT YOU GOT A BITE TO SHARE...?
......WILL A MINT DO...?
SHAKO (SHK)

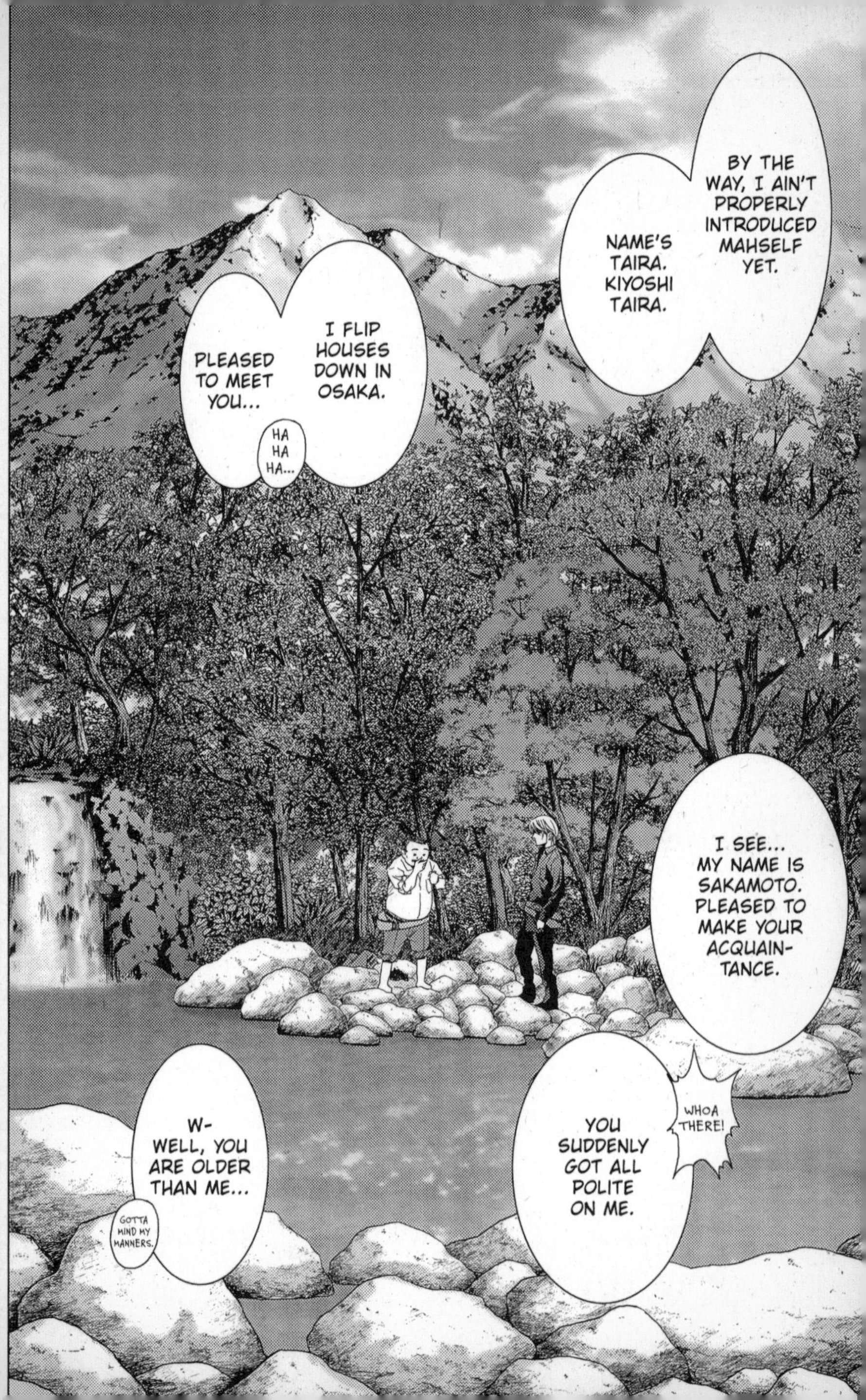
BY THE WAY, I AIN'T PROPERLY INTRODUCED MAHSELF YET.
NAME'S TAIRA. KIYOSHI TAIRA.
I FLIP HOUSES DOWN IN OSAKA.
PLEASED TO MEET YOU...
HA HA HA...
I SEE... MY NAME IS SAKAMOTO. PLEASED TO MAKE YOUR ACQUAIN-TANCE.
WHOA THERE!
YOU SUDDENLY GOT ALL POLITE ON ME.
W- WELL, YOU ARE OLDER THAN ME...
GOTTA MIND MY MANNERS.

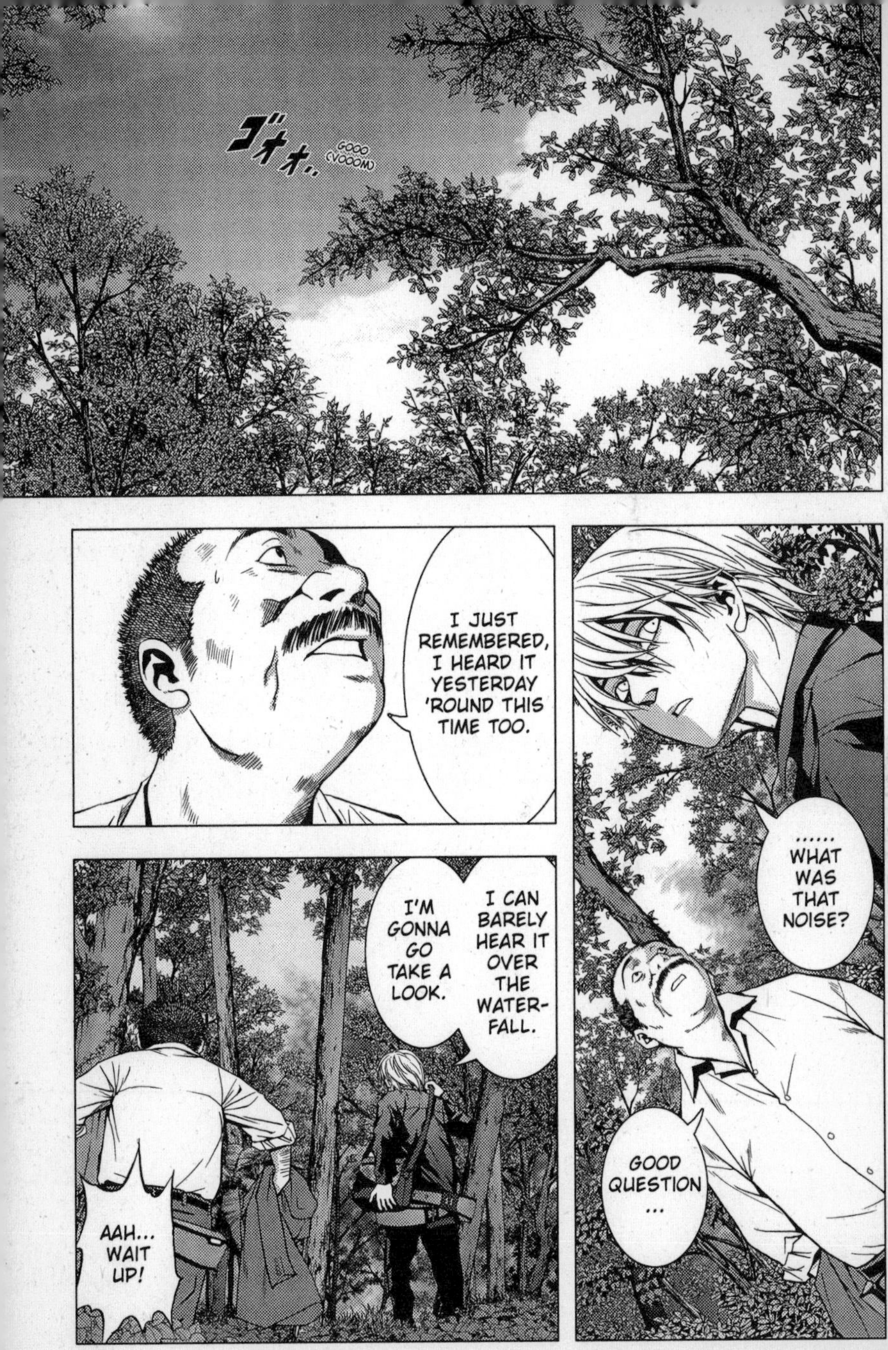
ゴォォ..
GOOO (VOOOM)
......WHAT WAS THAT NOISE?
GOOD QUESTION...
I JUST REMEMBERED, I HEARD IT YESTERDAY 'ROUND THIS TIME TOO.
I CAN BARELY HEAR IT OVER THE WATER-FALL.
I'M GONNA GO TAKE A LOOK.
AAH... WAIT UP!

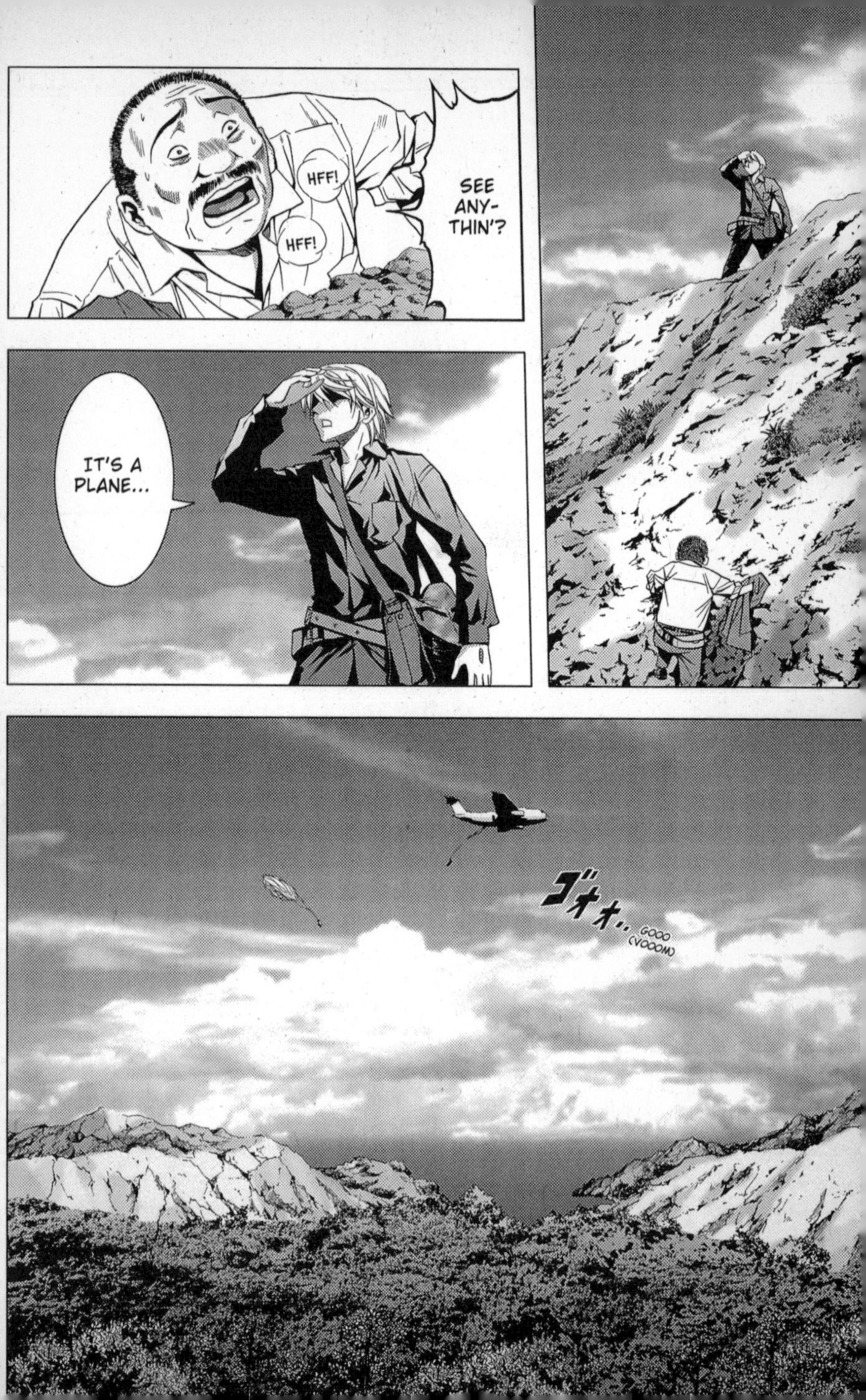
SEE ANYTHIN'?
HFF!
HFF!
IT'S A PLANE...
ゴオオ..
GOOO (VOOOM)

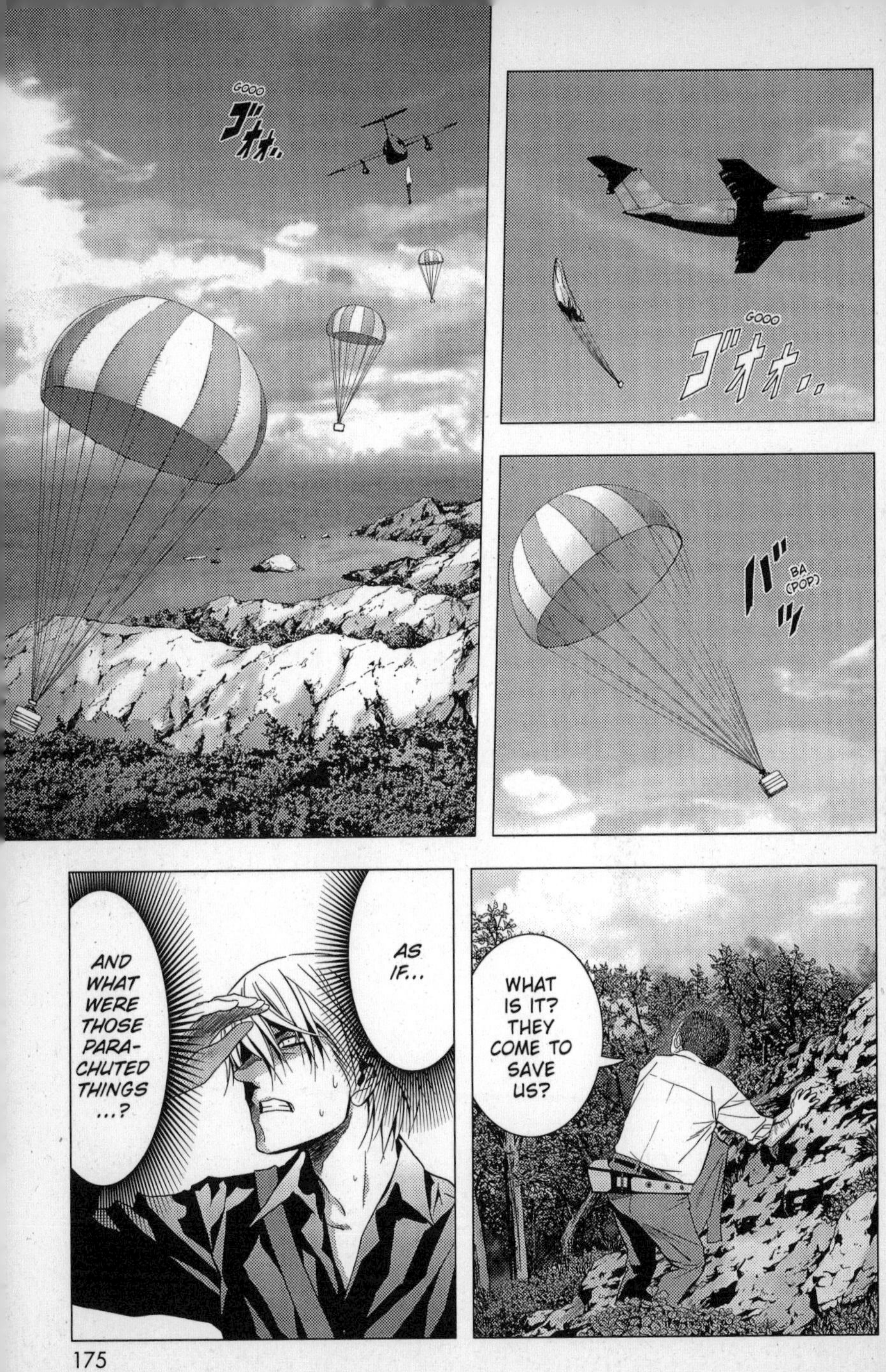
GOOO
ゴオオ。。
BA (POP)
バッ
GOOO
ゴオォ
WHAT IS IT? THEY COME TO SAVE US?
AS IF...
AND WHAT WERE THOSE PARA-CHUTED THINGS ...?

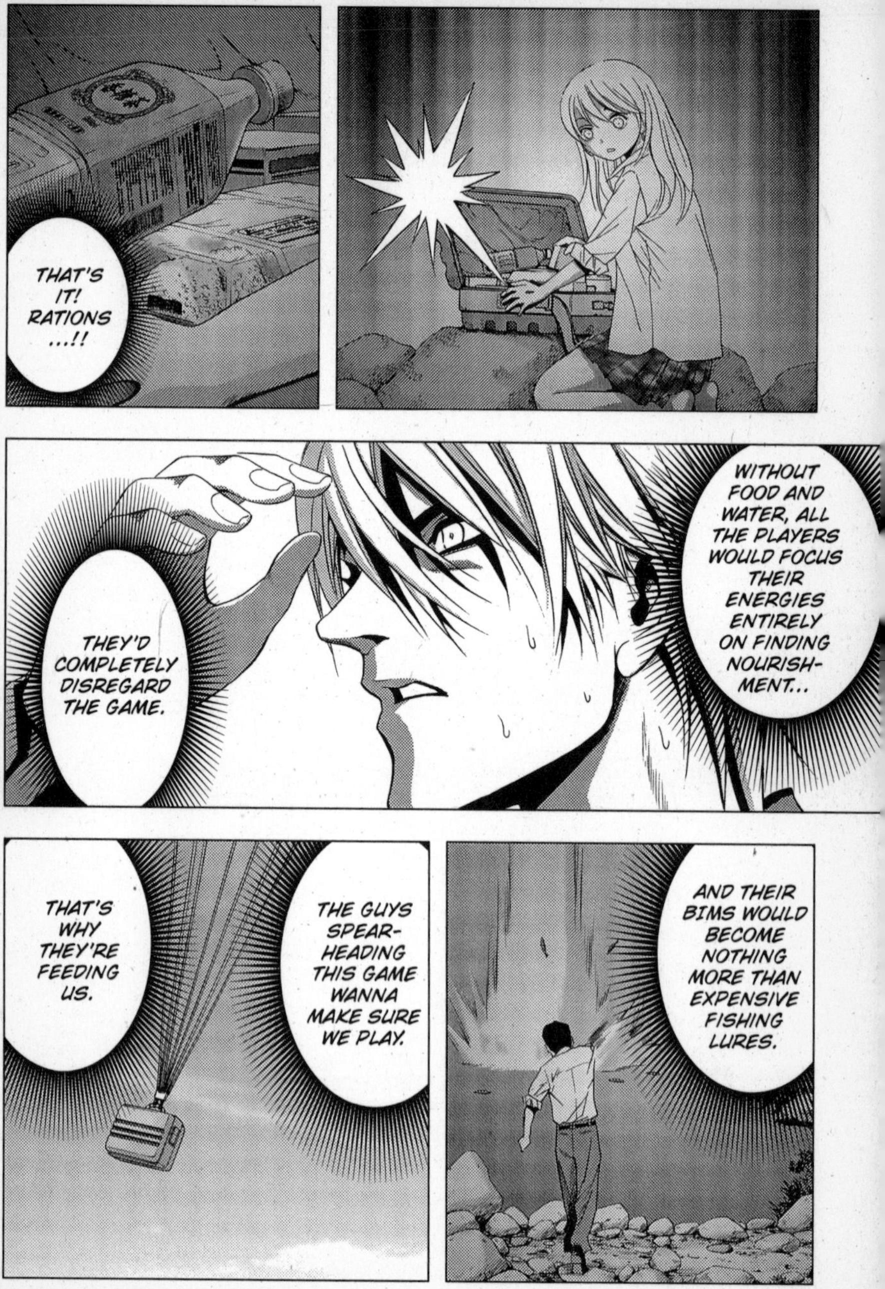
THAT'S IT! RATIONS ...!!
WITHOUT FOOD AND WATER, ALL THE PLAYERS WOULD FOCUS THEIR ENERGIES ENTIRELY ON FINDING NOURISH-MENT...
THEY'D COMPLETELY DISREGARD THE GAME.
AND THEIR BIMS WOULD BECOME NOTHING MORE THAN EXPENSIVE FISHING LURES.
THE GUYS SPEAR-HEADING THIS GAME WANNA MAKE SURE WE PLAY.
THAT'S WHY THEY'RE FEEDING US.

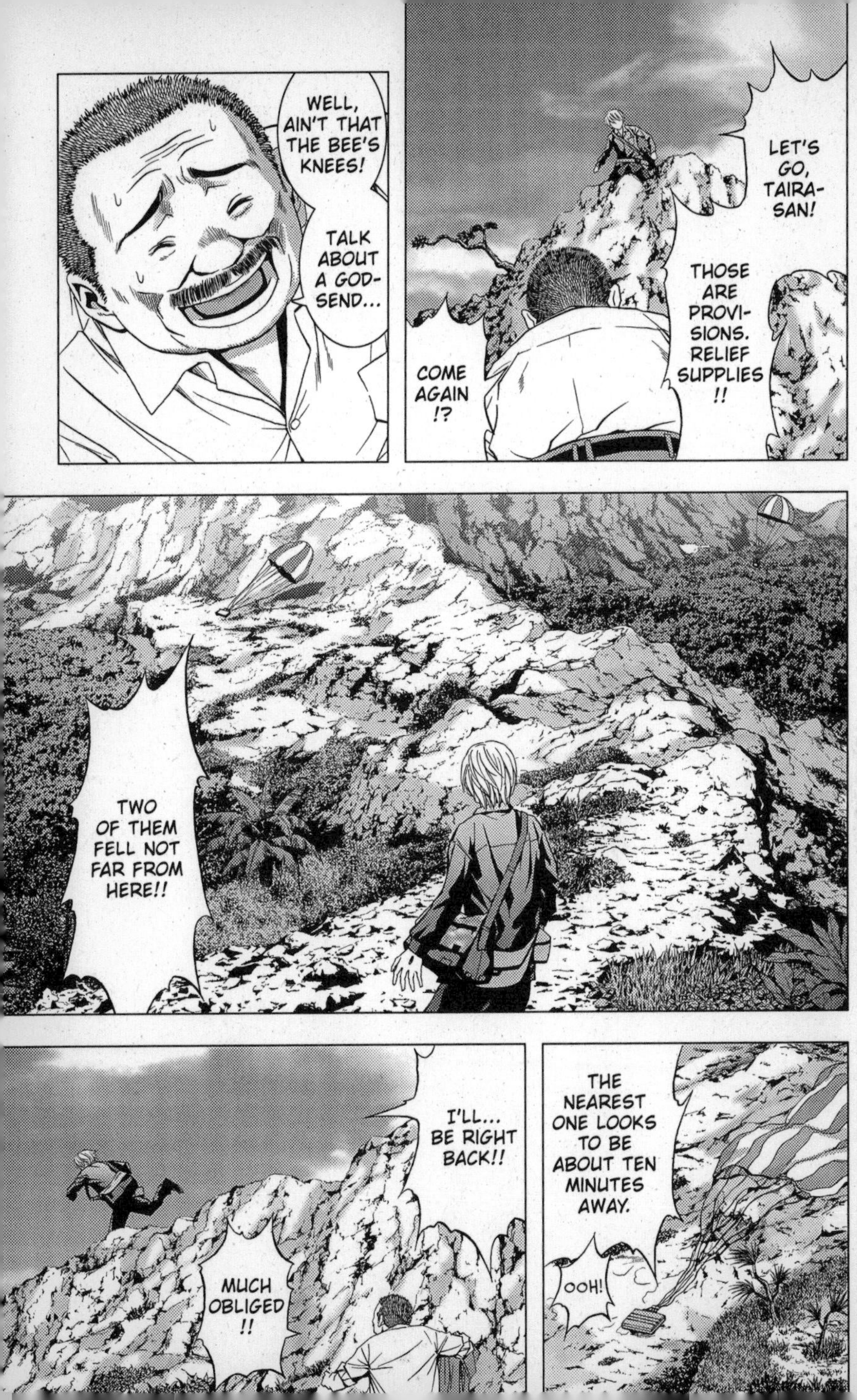
LET'S GO, TAIRA-SAN!
THOSE ARE PROVISIONS. RELIEF SUPPLIES!!
COME AGAIN!?
WELL, AIN'T THAT THE BEE'S KNEES!
TALK ABOUT A GODSEND...
TWO OF THEM FELL NOT FAR FROM HERE!!
THE NEAREST ONE LOOKS TO BE ABOUT TEN MINUTES AWAY.
OOH!
I'LL... BE RIGHT BACK!!
MUCH OBLIGED!!

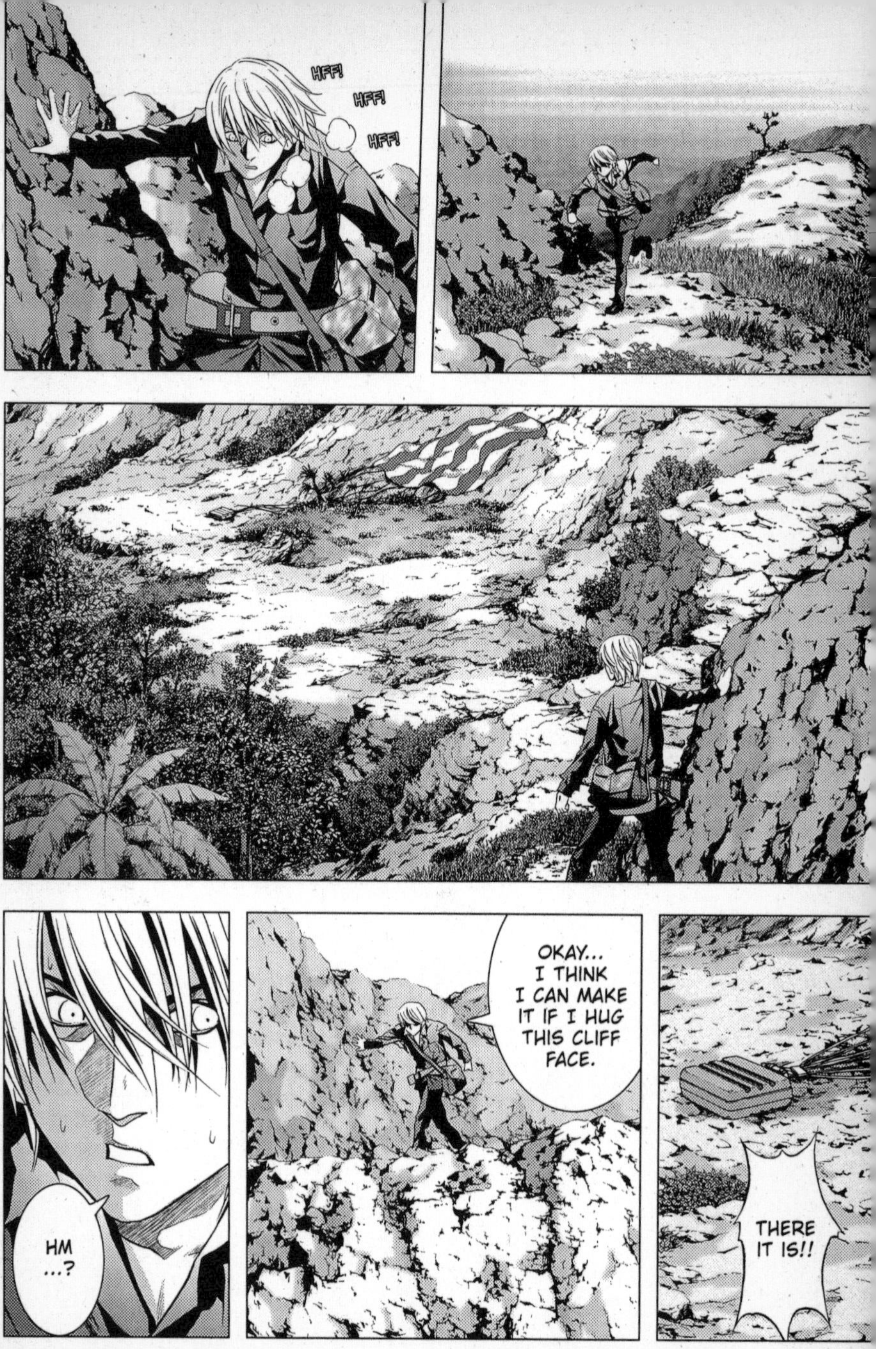
HFF!
HFF!
HFF!
THERE IT IS!!
OKAY... I THINK I CAN MAKE IT IF I HUG THIS CLIFF FACE.
HM ...?

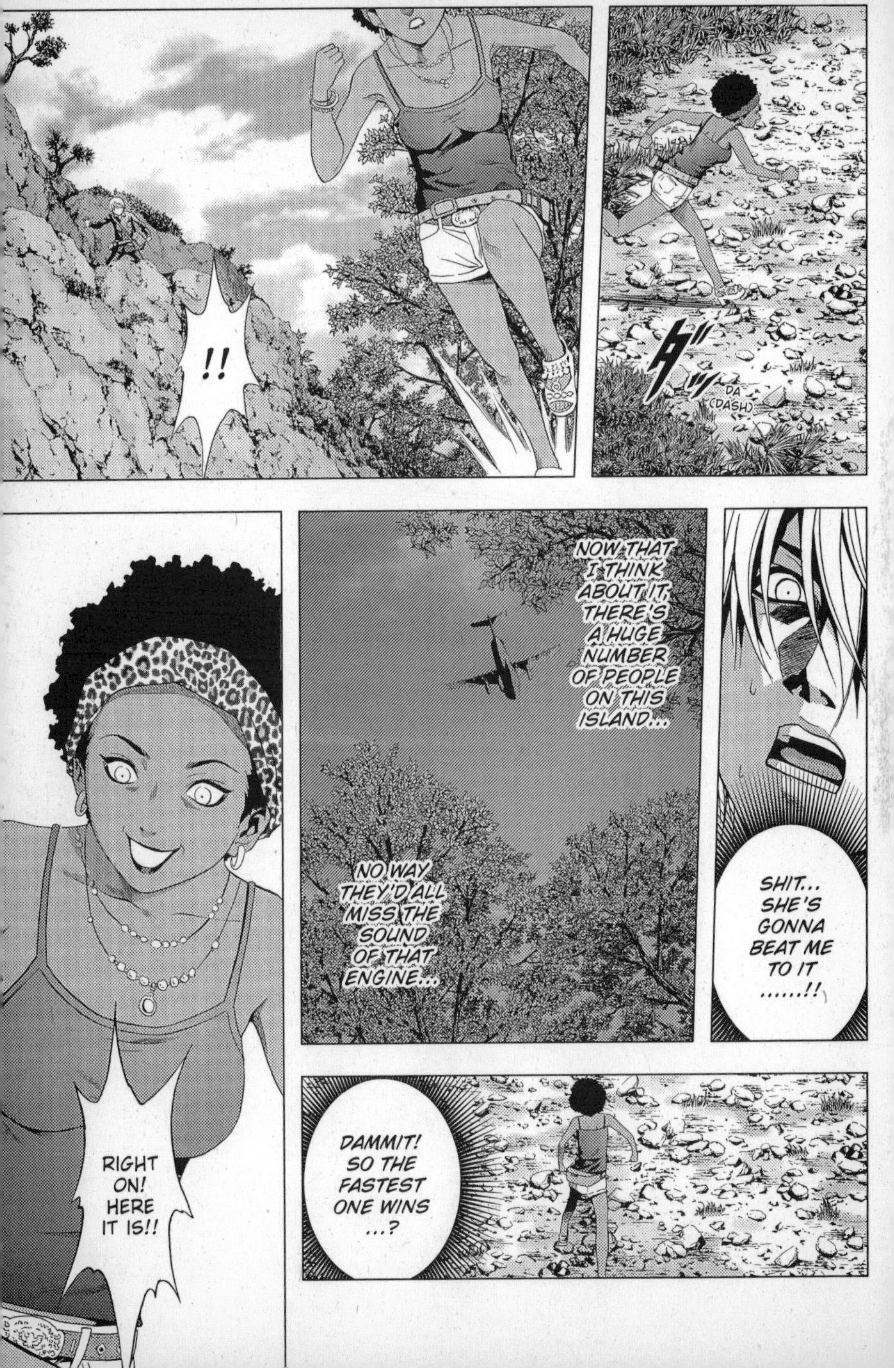
ダッ
DA (DASH)
!!
SHIT... SHE'S GONNA BEAT ME TO IT ......!!
NOW THAT I THINK ABOUT IT, THERE'S A HUGE NUMBER OF PEOPLE ON THIS ISLAND...
NO WAY THEY'D ALL MISS THE SOUND OF THAT ENGINE...
DAMMIT! SO THE FASTEST ONE WINS ...?
RIGHT ON! HERE IT IS!!

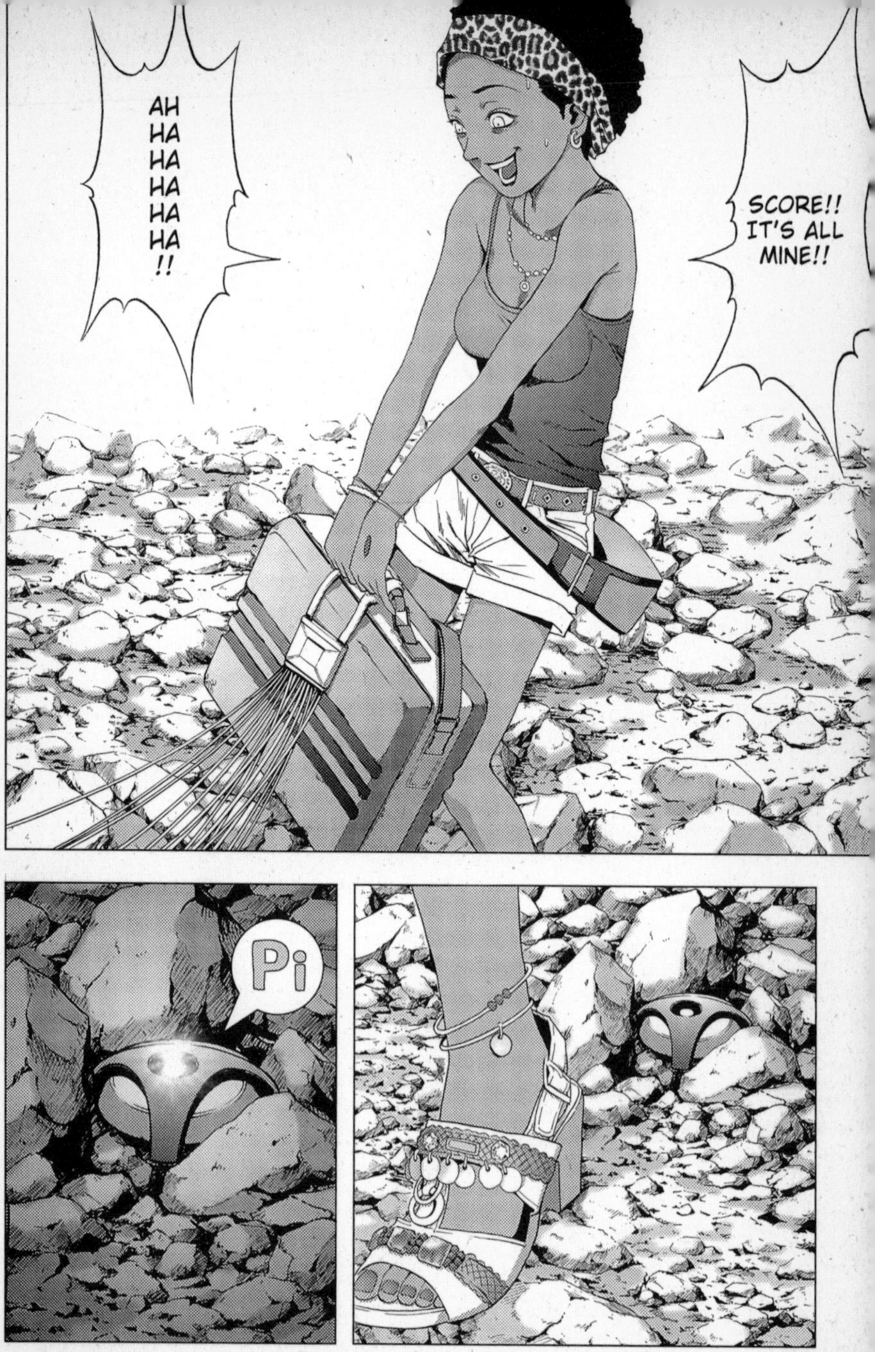
SCORE!! IT'S ALL MINE!!
AH HA HA HA HA HA!!
Pi

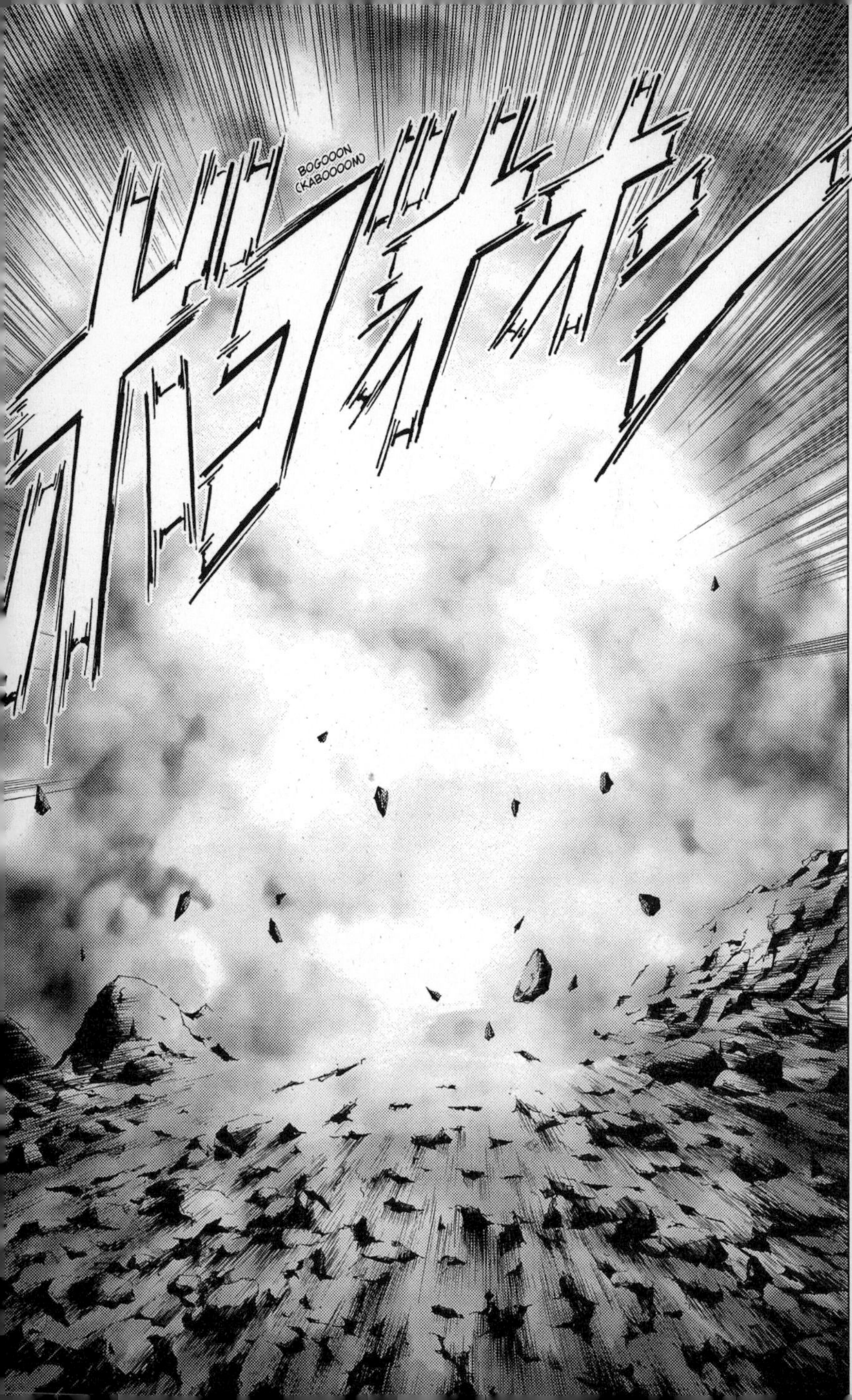
ドゴオォオ
BOGOOON
(KABOOOOM)

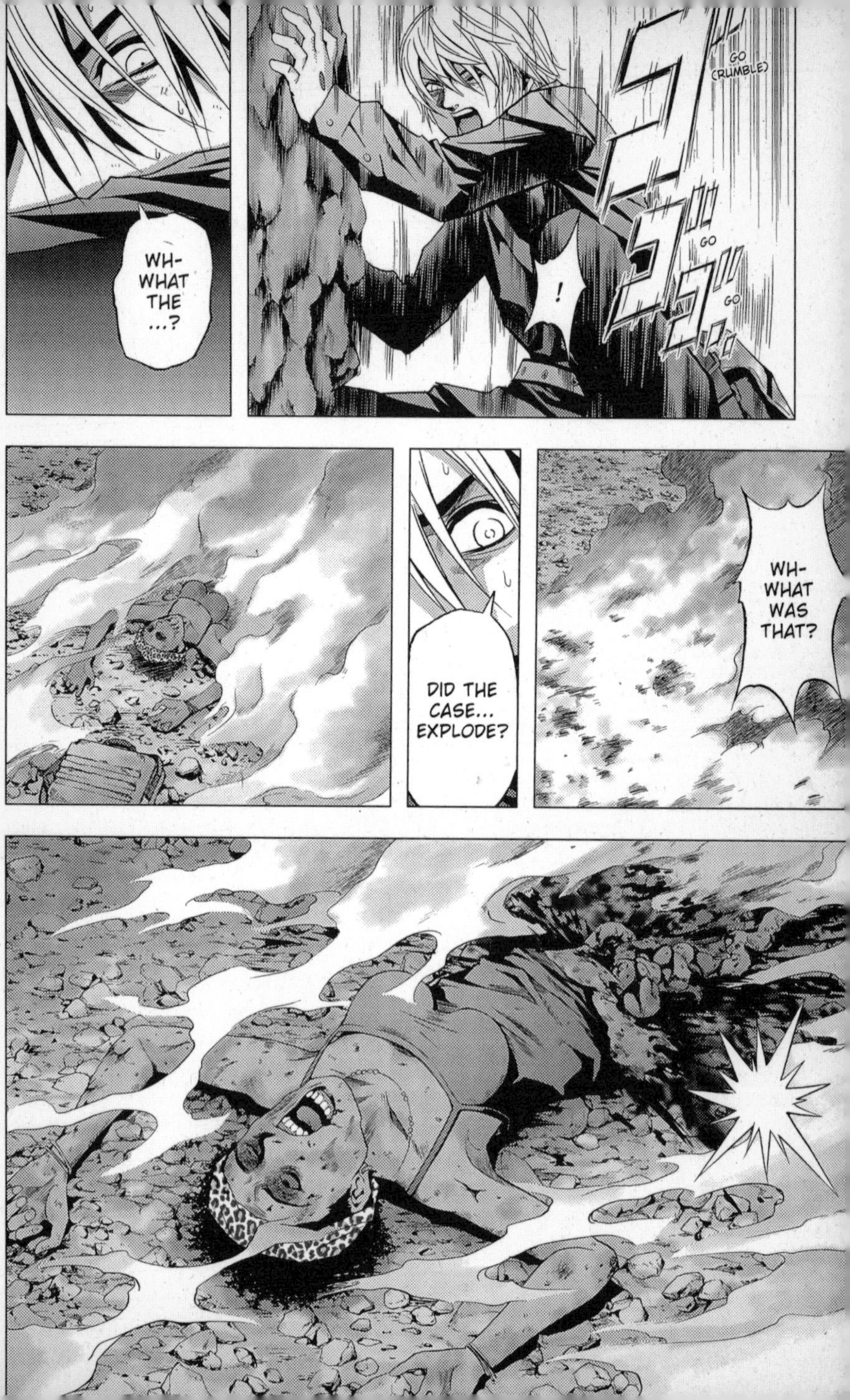
GO (RUMBLE)
GO
GO
!
WH- WHAT THE ...?
WH- WHAT WAS THAT?
DID THE CASE... EXPLODE?

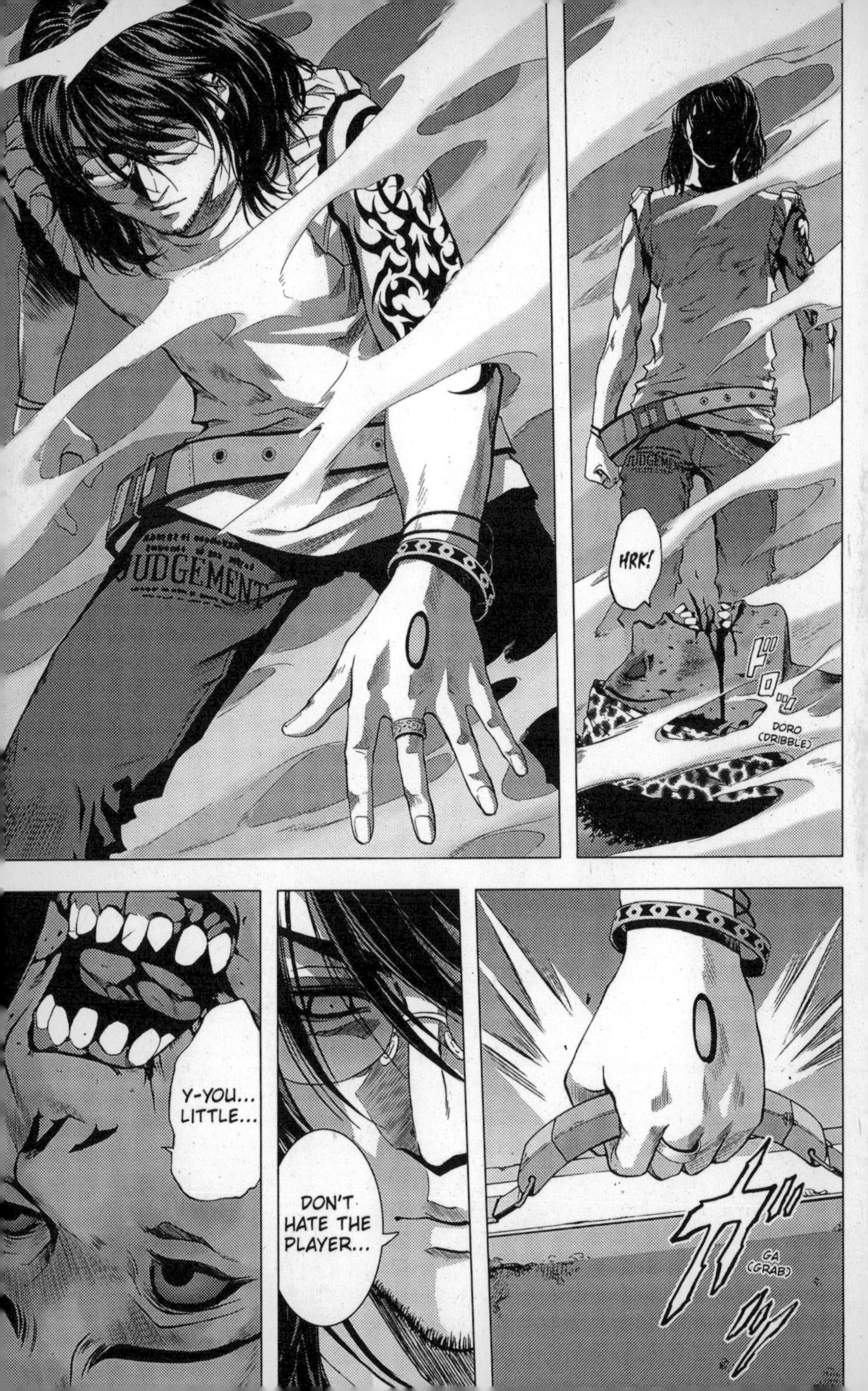
HRK!
DORO (DRIBBLE)
GA (GRAB)
DON'T HATE THE PLAYER...
Y-YOU... LITTLE...

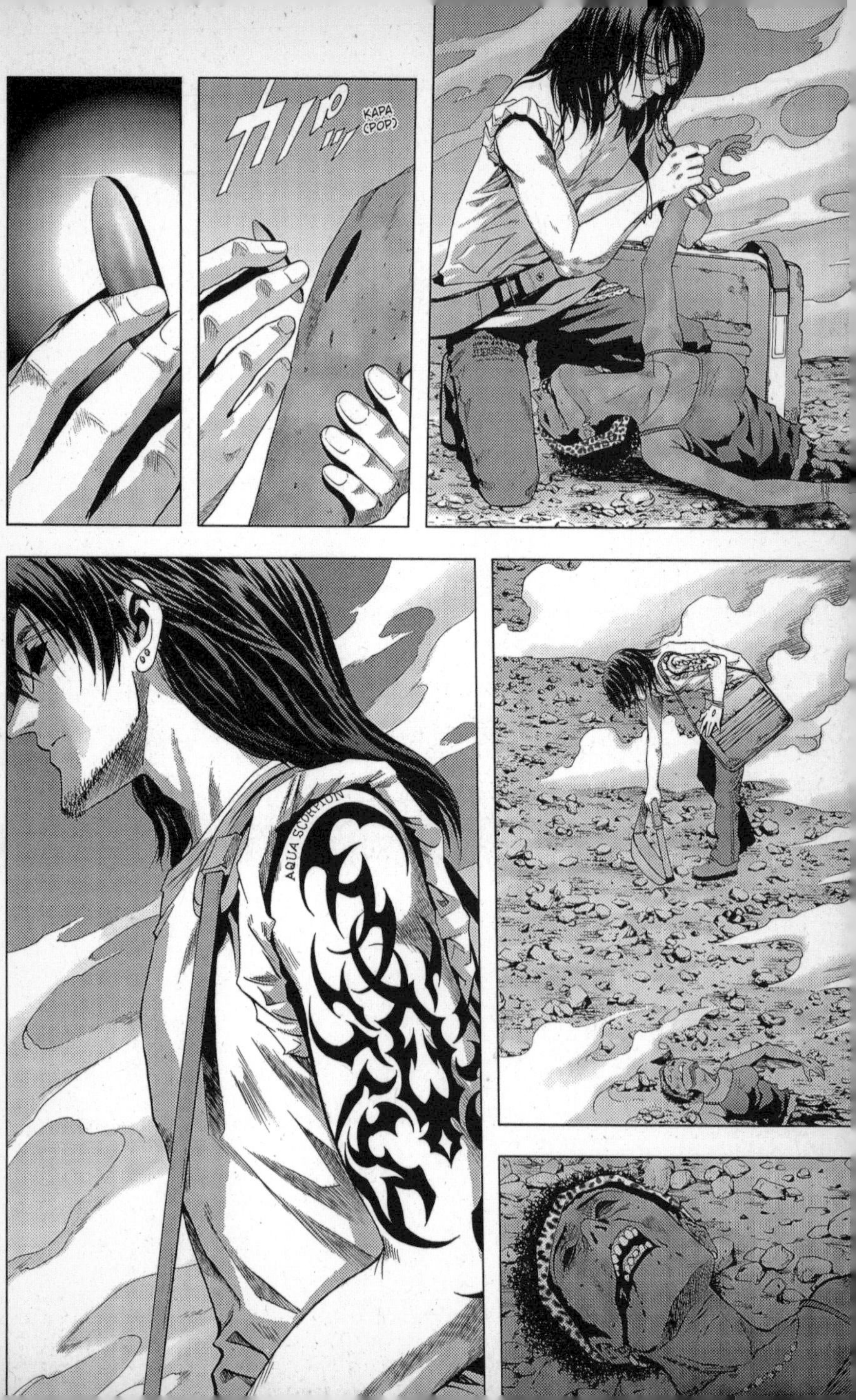
カパッ
KAPA (POP)
AQUA SCORPION

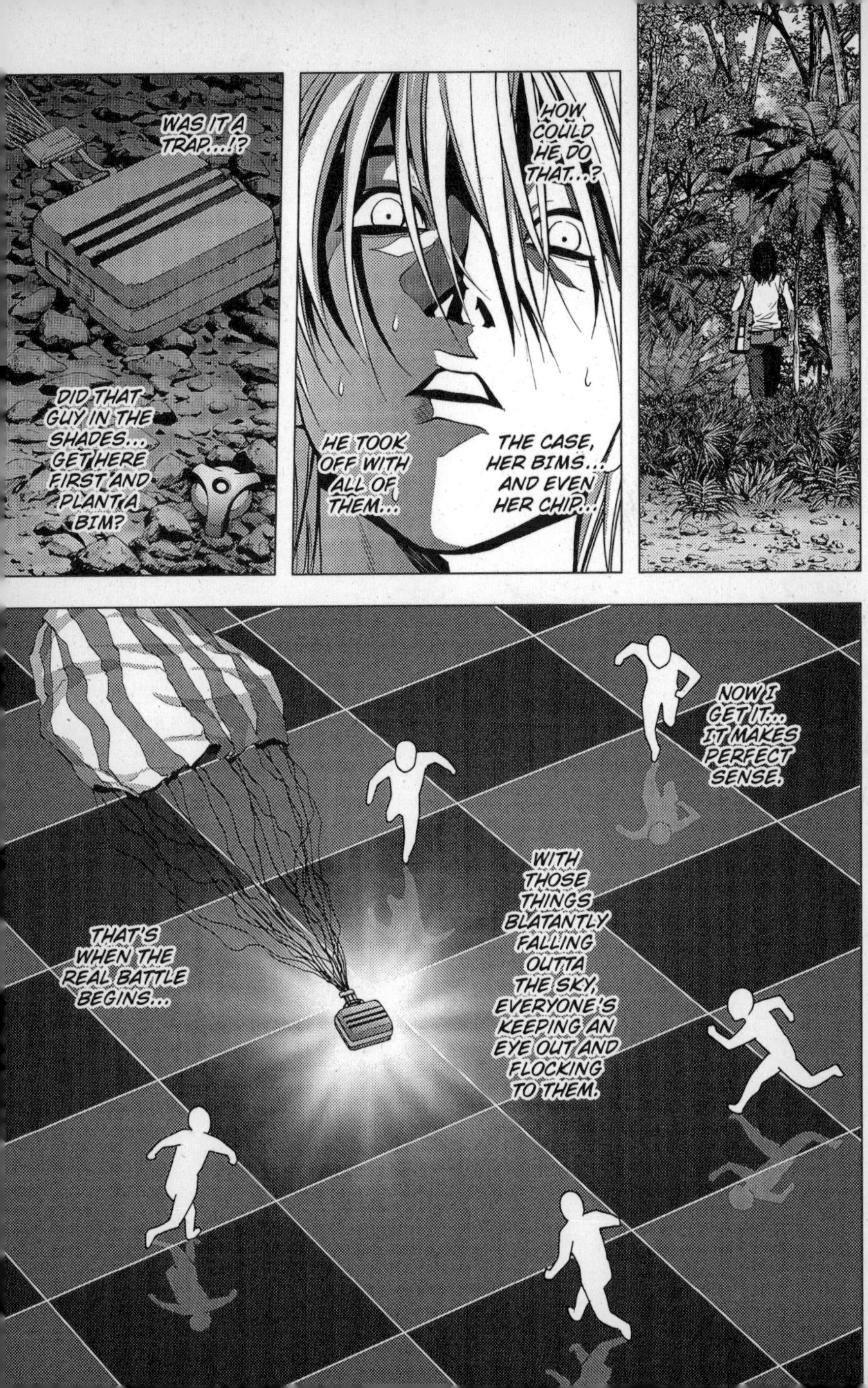
HOW COULD HE DO THAT...?
THE CASE, HER BIMS... AND EVEN HER CHIP...
HE TOOK OFF WITH ALL OF THEM...
WAS IT A TRAP...!?
DID THAT GUY IN THE SHADES... GET HERE FIRST AND PLANT A BIM?
NOW I GET IT... IT MAKES PERFECT SENSE.
WITH THOSE THINGS BLATANTLY FALLING OUTTA THE SKY, EVERYONE'S KEEPING AN EYE OUT AND FLOCKING TO THEM.
THAT'S WHEN THE REAL BATTLE BEGINS...

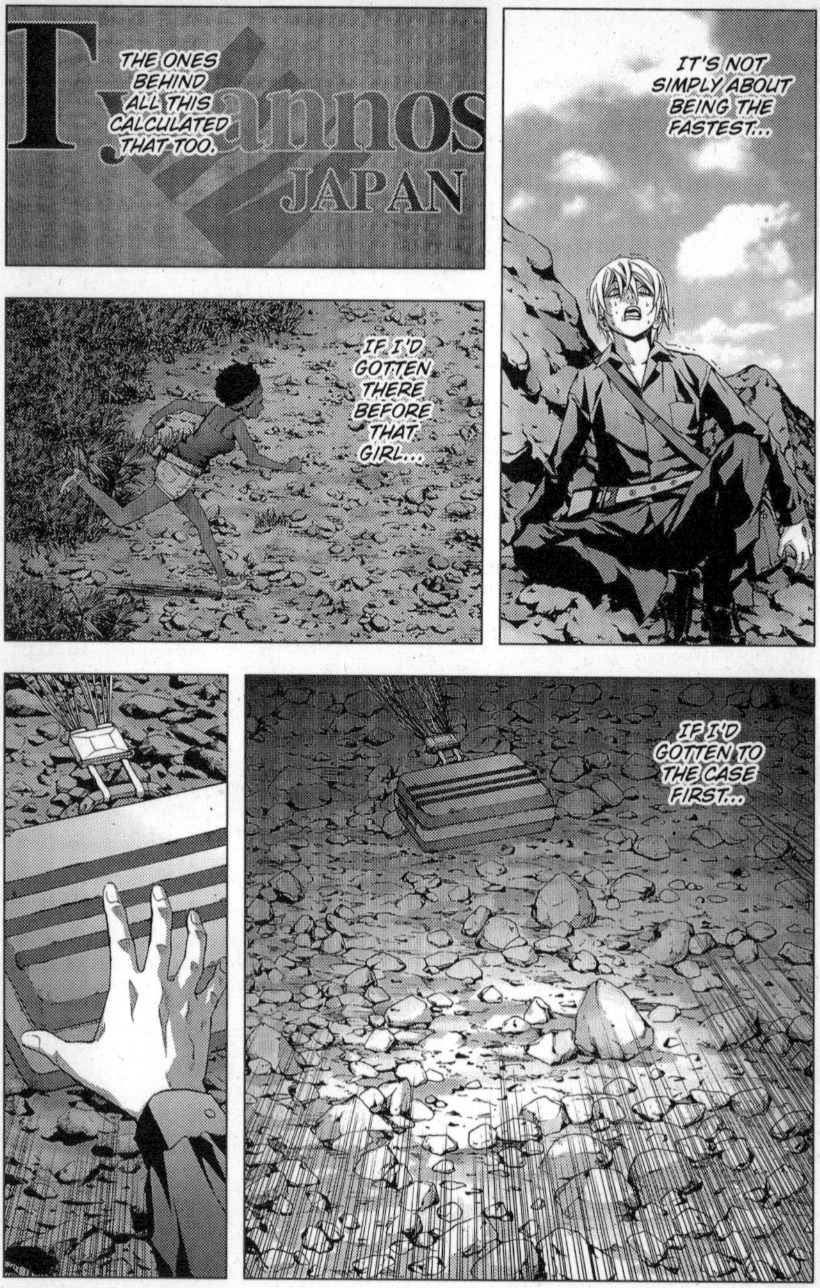
IT'S NOT SIMPLY ABOUT BEING THE FASTEST...
THE ONES BEHIND ALL THIS CALCULATED THAT TOO.
JAPAN
IF I'D GOTTEN THERE BEFORE THAT GIRL...
IF I'D GOTTEN TO THE CASE FIRST...

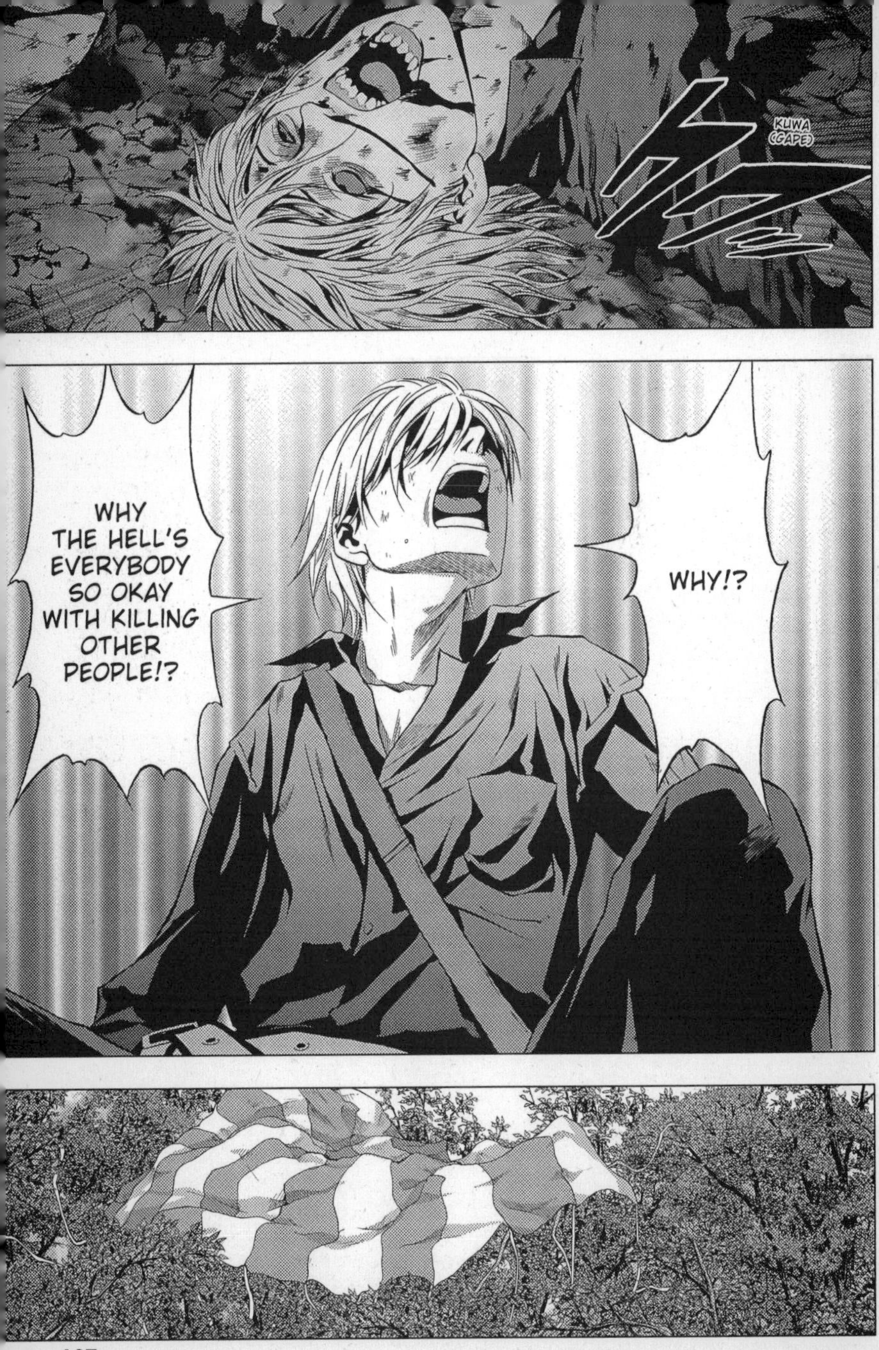
KUWA (GAPE)
WHY!?
WHY THE HELL'S EVERYBODY SO OKAY WITH KILLING OTHER PEOPLE!?

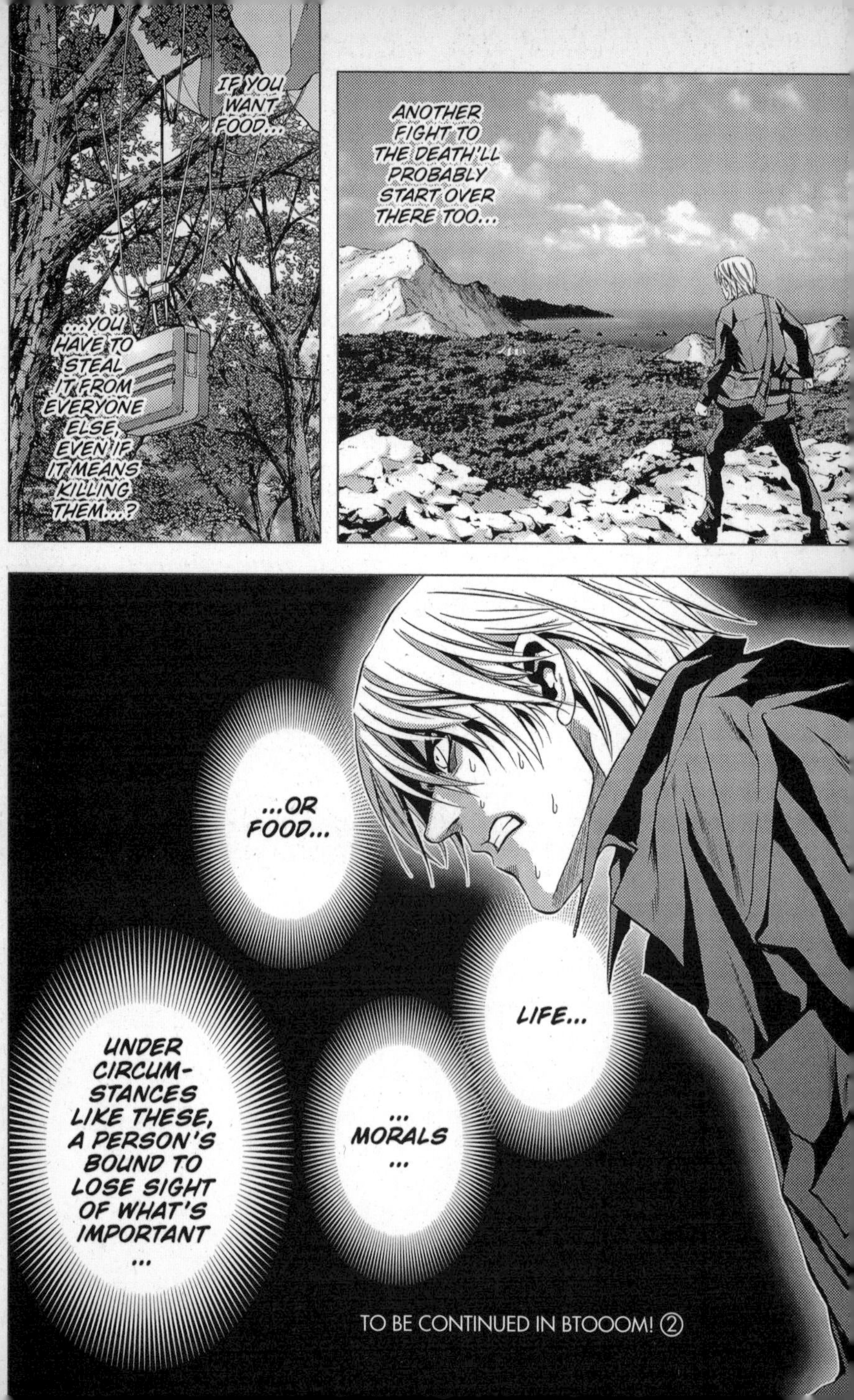
ANOTHER FIGHT TO THE DEATH'LL PROBABLY START OVER THERE TOO...
IF YOU WANT FOOD...
...YOU HAVE TO STEAL IT FROM EVERYONE ELSE, EVEN IF IT MEANS KILLING THEM...?
LIFE...
...MORALS...
...OR FOOD...
UNDER CIRCUM-STANCES LIKE THESE, A PERSON'S BOUND TO LOSE SIGHT OF WHAT'S IMPORTANT...
TO BE CONTINUED IN BTOOOM! ②

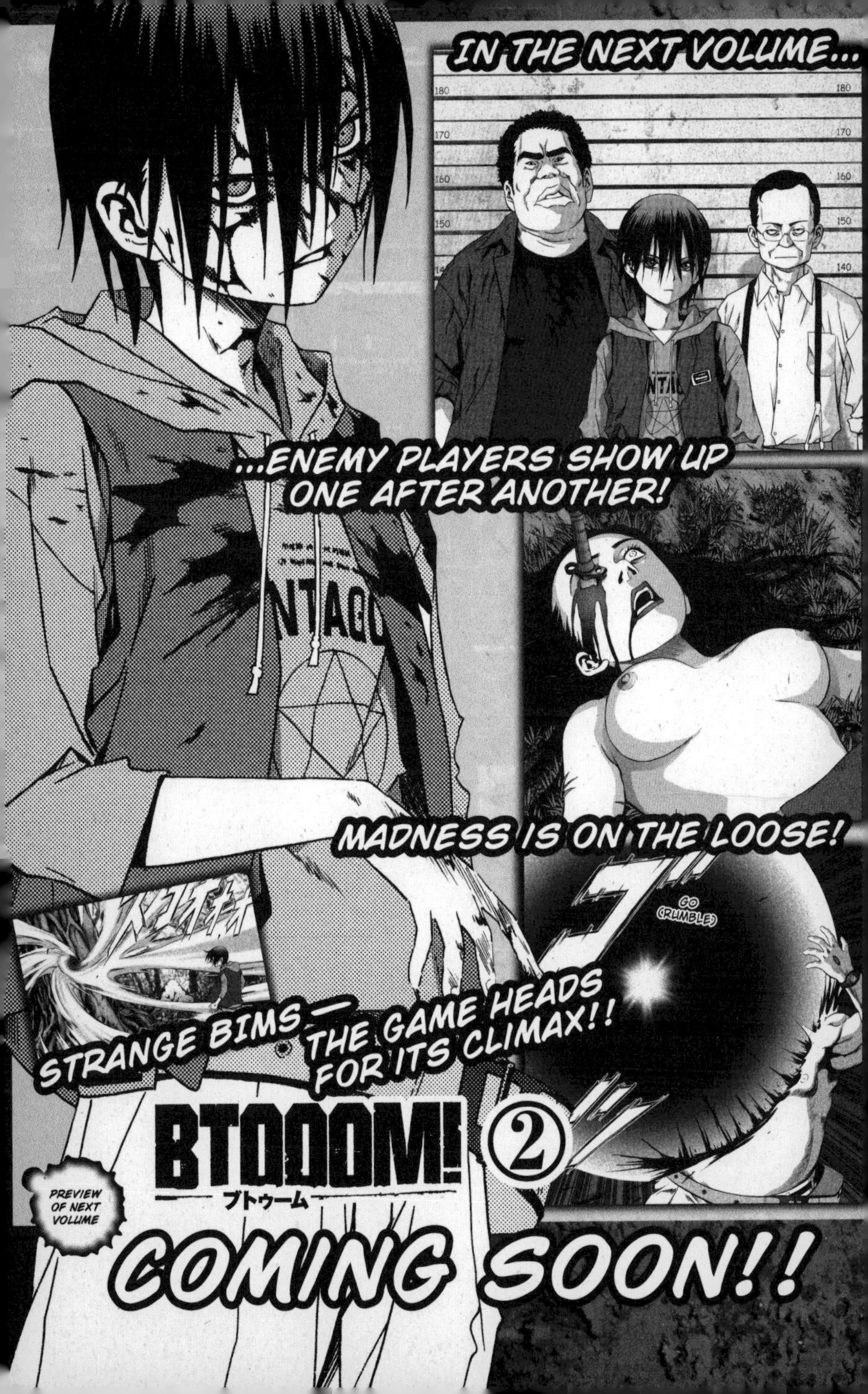
IN THE NEXT VOLUME...
...ENEMY PLAYERS SHOW UP ONE AFTER ANOTHER!
MADNESS IS ON THE LOOSE!
GO (RUMBLE)
STRANGE BIMS—
THE GAME HEADS FOR ITS CLIMAX!!
BTOOOM! ②
ブトゥーム
PREVIEW OF NEXT VOLUME
COMING SOON!!

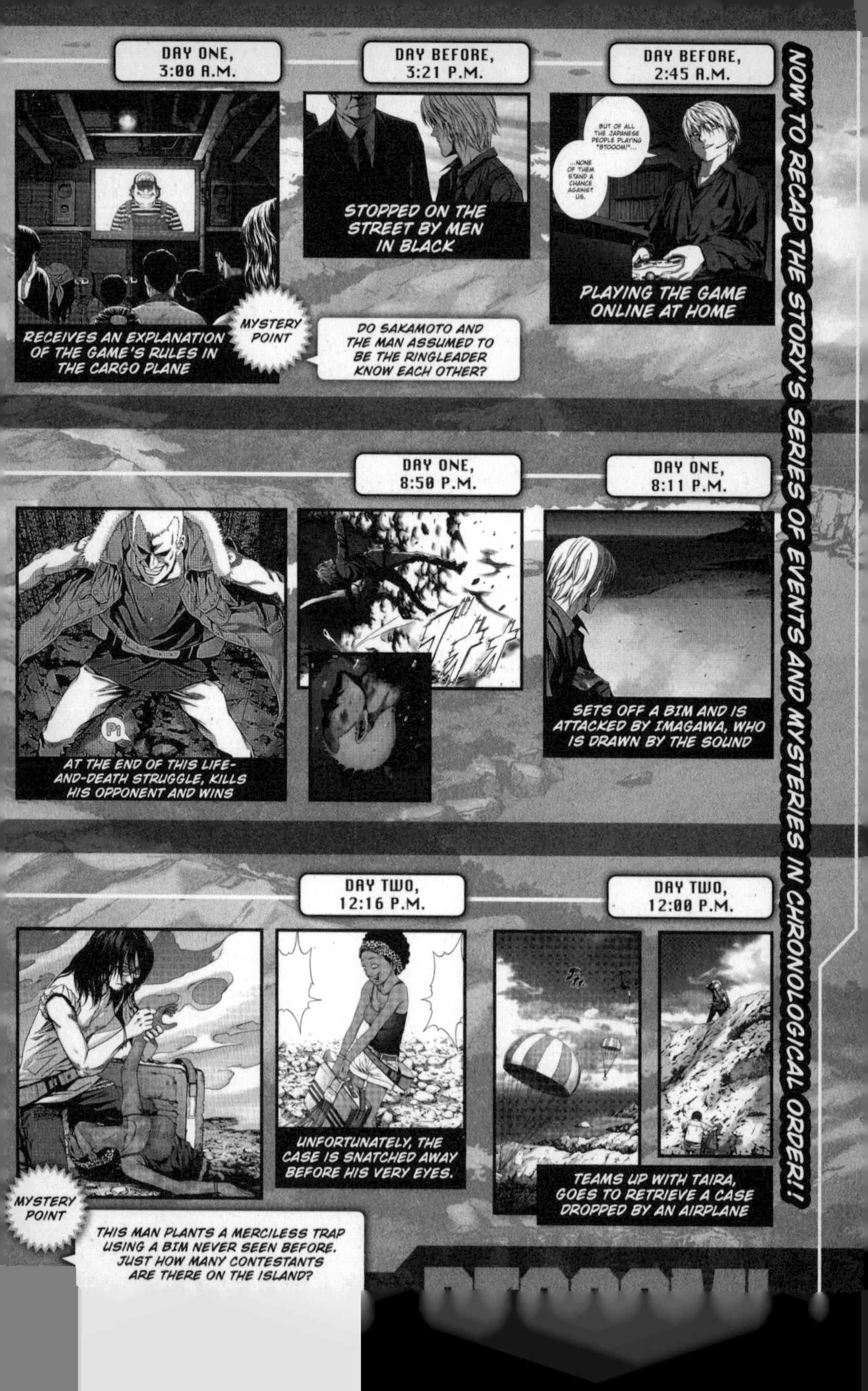
NOW TO RECAP THE STORY'S SERIES OF EVENTS AND MYSTERIES IN CHRONOLOGICAL ORDER!!
DAY BEFORE, 2:45 A.M.
BUT OF ALL THE JAPANESE PEOPLE PLAYING "BTOOOM!"...
...NONE OF THEM STAND A CHANCE AGAINST US.
PLAYING THE GAME ONLINE AT HOME
DAY BEFORE, 3:21 P.M.
STOPPED ON THE STREET BY MEN IN BLACK
DAY ONE, 3:00 A.M.
RECEIVES AN EXPLANATION OF THE GAME'S RULES IN THE CARGO PLANE
MYSTERY POINT
DO SAKAMOTO AND THE MAN ASSUMED TO BE THE RINGLEADER KNOW EACH OTHER?
DAY ONE, 8:11 P.M.
SETS OFF A BIM AND IS ATTACKED BY IMAGAWA, WHO IS DRAWN BY THE SOUND
DAY ONE, 8:50 P.M.
AT THE END OF THIS LIFE-AND-DEATH STRUGGLE, KILLS HIS OPPONENT AND WINS
DAY TWO, 12:00 P.M.
TEAMS UP WITH TAIRA, GOES TO RETRIEVE A CASE DROPPED BY AN AIRPLANE
DAY TWO, 12:16 P.M.
UNFORTUNATELY, THE CASE IS SNATCHED AWAY BEFORE HIS VERY EYES.
MYSTERY POINT
THIS MAN PLANTS A MERCILESS TRAP USING A BIM NEVER SEEN BEFORE. JUST HOW MANY CONTESTANTS ARE THERE ON THE ISLAND?

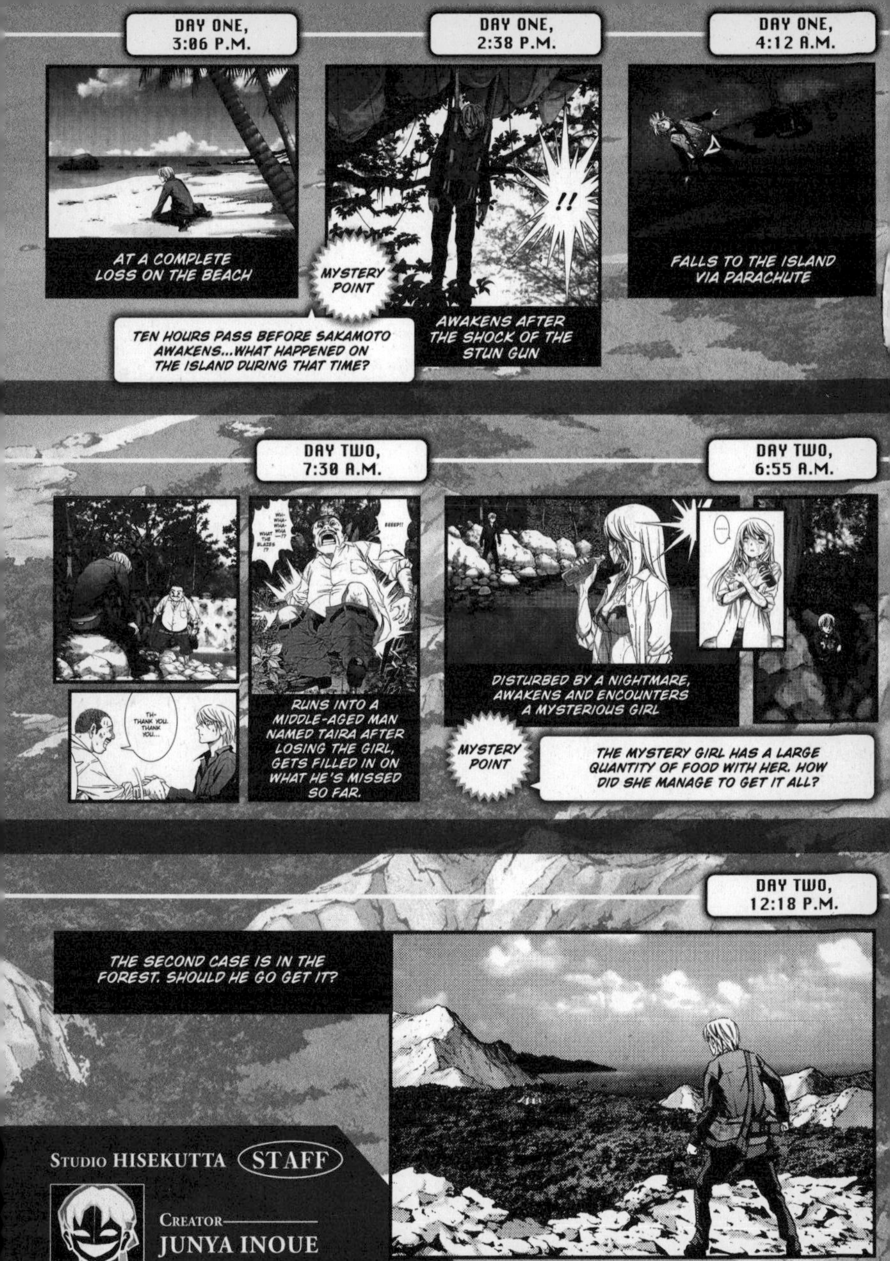
DAY ONE,
4:12 A.M.
FALLS TO THE ISLAND VIA PARACHUTE
DAY ONE,
2:38 P.M.
!!
AWAKENS AFTER THE SHOCK OF THE STUN GUN
MYSTERY POINT
TEN HOURS PASS BEFORE SAKAMOTO AWAKENS...WHAT HAPPENED ON THE ISLAND DURING THAT TIME?
DAY ONE,
3:06 P.M.
AT A COMPLETE LOSS ON THE BEACH
DAY TWO,
6:55 A.M.
......
DISTURBED BY A NIGHTMARE, AWAKENS AND ENCOUNTERS A MYSTERIOUS GIRL
MYSTERY POINT
THE MYSTERY GIRL HAS A LARGE QUANTITY OF FOOD WITH HER. HOW DID SHE MANAGE TO GET IT ALL?
DAY TWO,
7:30 A.M.
BEEEP!!
WH-WHA-WHA-WHA—!?
WHAT THE BLAZES !?
RUNS INTO A MIDDLE-AGED MAN NAMED TAIRA AFTER LOSING THE GIRL, GETS FILLED IN ON WHAT HE'S MISSED SO FAR.
TH-THANK YOU. THANK YOU...
DAY TWO,
12:18 P.M.
THE SECOND CASE IS IN THE FOREST. SHOULD HE GO GET IT?

STUDIO HISEKUTTA STAFF

CREATOR
JUNYA INOUE

BACKGROUNDS
TOM[illegible] ITOU, JUN KOBAYASHI, KAZUAKI SAIDA

FINISHING TOUCHES
SACHIKO KISAKI, SONOE FUKUSAWA, AYAKA ITOU

BTOOOM! 1

JUNYA INOUE

Translation: Christine Dashiell • Lettering: Terri Delgado

BTOOOM! © Junya INOUE 2009. All rights reserved. English translation rights arranged with SHINCHOSHA PUBLISHING CO. through Tuttle-Mori Agency, Inc., Tokyo.

English translation © 2013 by Hachette Book Group, Inc.

Yen Press
Hachette Book Group
237 Park Avenue, New York, NY 10017

www.HachetteBookGroup.com
www.YenPress.com

Yen Press is an imprint of Hachette Book Group, Inc. The Yen Press name and logo are trademarks of Hachette Book Group, Inc.

First Yen Press Edition: February 2013

ISBN: 978-0-316-23267-8

10 9 8 7 6 5 4 3 2 1

BVG

Printed in the United States of America